Cloud Native Architecture and Design

A Handbook for Modern Day
Architecture and Design
with Enterprise-Grade Examples

Shivakumar R Goniwada

Apress®

Cloud Native Architecture and Design: A Handbook for Modern Day Architecture and Design with Enterprise-Grade Examples

Shivakumar R Goniwada
Bangalore, India

ISBN-13 (pbk): 978-1-4842-7225-1 ISBN-13 (electronic): 978-1-4842-7226-8
https://doi.org/10.1007/978-1-4842-7226-8

Managing Director, Apress Media LLC: Welmoed Spahr
Acquisitions Editor: Celestin Suresh John
Development Editor: Mark Powers
Coordinating Editor: Shrikant Vishwakarma

Cover designed by eStudioCalamar

Cover image designed by Pexels

Distributed to the book trade worldwide by Springer Science+Business Media LLC, 1 New York Plaza, Suite 4600, New York, NY 10004. Phone 1-800-SPRINGER, fax (201) 348-4505, e-mail orders-ny@springer-sbm.com, or visit www.springeronline.com. Apress Media, LLC is a California LLC and the sole member (owner) is Springer Science + Business Media Finance Inc (SSBM Finance Inc). SSBM Finance Inc is a Delaware corporation.

For information on translations, please e-mail booktranslations@springernature.com; for reprint, paperback, or audio rights, please e-mail bookpermissions@springernature.com, or visit www.apress.com/rights-permissions.

Apress titles may be purchased in bulk for academic, corporate, or promotional use. eBook versions and licenses are also available for most titles. For more information, reference our Print and eBook Bulk Sales web page at www.apress.com/bulk-sales.

Any source code or other supplementary material referenced by the author in this book is available to readers on GitHub via the book's product page, located at www.apress.com/978-1-4842-7225-1. For more detailed information, please visit www.apress.com/source-code.

Printed on acid-free paper

This book is dedicated to all the unsung heroes and frontline workers continuously fighting the COVID-19 battle to save humanity and the world.

Table of Contents

About the Author

Shivakumar R. Goniwada is an enterprise architect, technology leader, and inventor with more than 23 years of experience in developing enterprise architecture with cloud native, event-driven systems. He currently works at Accenture and leads a team of highly experienced technology enterprise and cloud architects. In his 23 years of experience, he has led many highly complex projects across industries and geographic regions. He has ten software patents to his name in the areas of cloud, polyglot and polylithic architecture, software engineering, and IoT (a few yet to publish). He has been a speaker at multiple global and in-house conferences. He holds Master Technology Architecture Accenture, Google Professional, AWS, and data science certifications. His executive MBA is from the MIT Sloan School of Management. You can find him at https://www.linkedin.com/in/shivakumar-r-goniwada.

About the Technical Reviewer

Vishal Chaudhari is an IT professional with 18 years of extensive experience working with top IT organizations such as Wipro, Emerson, Sterlite, IBM, TechM Geometric, Saama technology, and Efkon. He holds a Master of Computer Applications degree and started his career as a Java developer, working more than a decade as an SOA integration architect, solution designer, project manager, enterprise architect, ethical hacker, SOC security analyst auditor, and IoT/RPA/bots engineer.

His experience in the IT industry includes digital transformations with cloud native architecture, microservice architecture, API-led connectivity, cloud migration, big data, streaming platforms, bare-metal hybrid cloud platforms, and service mesh and edge network security.

In his current role, he has adopted cloud native, digital architecture, cutting-edge approaches for next-generation applications. He has worked in various domains including telecom, finance, open banking, PSD2, insurance, payments, and more.

Vishal is an active mentor member of the Mulesoft community. When not working, he works on DIY projects. You can find him at https://www.linkedin.com/in/vishalkumarc/.

Acknowledgments

To my mother Jayamma S and late father Rudrappa G M, who taught me the value of hard work, and to my wife Nirmala and daughter Neeharika, without whom I wouldn't have been able to work long hours into the night every day of the week. Last, but not the least, I'd like to thank my friends, colleagues, and mentors at Accenture, Mphasis, and other corporations who guided me throughout my career.

Thank you to my colleagues Celestin Suresh John, Mathew Moodie, and Shrikant Vishwakarma for giving me an opportunity to work with you and Apress and all who have helped this book become a reality.

Introduction

The motivation to write this book goes back to the words of Swami Vivekananda: "Everything is easy when you are busy, but nothing is easy when you are lazy" and "In a day when you don't come across any problems, you can be sure that you are traveling on the wrong path."

Cloud computing has proven to be revolutionary in IT, and the need to adapt to the cloud across organizations has increased rapidly, especially after the COVID-19 pandemic. Cloud native architecture is part of the cloud revolution and gives you the benefit of more flexibility over legacy systems in your IT real estate. Cloud native architectures demonstrate seven essential components of designing, developing, and deploying modern present-day architecture: cloud, microservices, serverless, event-driven, containers, automation, and agility.

This book provides you with the end-to-end details of cloud native systems, from architecting to managing them. You will learn what a cloud adoption framework looks like and develop a cloud native architecture using microservices, serverless, and event-driven data, and you will learn how to adopt AI and ML in your end-to-end automation and engineering. You will not get cloud native benefits without modernizing your existing legacy systems, so you'll learn how to modernize your legacy systems and infrastructure to be cloud native.

You'll explore how to design for cloud native abilities and create fitness functions and learn ways to achieve operational excellence.

By the end of this book, you will have learned about the modern-day techniques and tools to design, develop, deploy, and operationalize cloud native architectures that meet your business requirements. You will also understand future cloud native trends across the industry.

This book will be helpful for people who want to learn and develop cloud native architecture. Whether it's design, development, deploy, or operation, the book will help you on a journey from beginning to end. By reading this book, you will get a full, clear picture of how the world of cloud native works, and you will be able to better manage your systems.

PART I

The Cloud Native Journey, Principles, and Patterns

CHAPTER 1

Introduction to Cloud Native Architecture

A comprehensive look at cloud native architecture must first begin with its definition. This chapter also details why cloud native plays a significant role in modern-day architecture.

It is important to understand the industries, stakeholders, compliances, and software producers who are affected by cloud native software architecture. This chapter will cover the benefits of cloud native architecture for an enterprise, the pivotal roles software architects need to play to embrace the cloud, and whether the cloud is right for all industries.

Specifically, in this chapter, we will cover the following topics:

- What is cloud native?

- What are the steps for a cloud native journey?

- How is cloud native architecture embraced across industries?

- Why is cloud native important?

- What is the software architect's role in cloud native?

© Shivakumar R Goniwada 2022
S. R. Goniwada, *Cloud Native Architecture and Design*, https://doi.org/10.1007/978-1-4842-7226-8_1

Introduction to Cloud Native

Today, enterprises of all sizes across industries and geographic regions are using software as a key disruptor and source of competitive advantage in their businesses. CxOs are looking at cloud computing as an enabler, especially during the COVID-19 pandemic, to create highly innovative products and services. During the pandemic, technology has proven to be the most important enabler of business continuity in a socially distanced market. The cloud sits right at the center of technology, powering significant industry transformation. To derive maximum value from the cloud, organizations must be planned much more than just virtualized infrastructure.

Many organizations are realizing that just simply lifting and shifting their existing monolithic enterprise legacy systems into the cloud does not sufficiently support modern-day business disruptions. Deploying an enterprise software application to the cloud does not make it cloud native; cloud native is about how the software is designed and implemented, not just where it is executed.

To address disruption in business, the cloud native approach and architecture need to be adopted as part of technology decisions. Cloud native is a lot more than just signing with various cloud providers and using them to run the existing enterprise applications. Cloud technologies and services can offer greater availability, elasticity, and security. Cloud native fundamentally changes the design, implementation, deployment, nonfunctional requirements, and operations of applications, and the cloud creates a new culture of technology services within industries, enabling them to become more agile and to operate faster.

Enterprises will benefit from infrastructure as a service (IaaS) as it is readily available, used on-demand, and scalable from 0 percent to 100 percent, and vice versa, depending on the load. The various industry practitioners such as Netflix, Amazon, telcos, Google, etc., have demonstrated the proven benefits of the cloud native approach to application development.

The adoption of cloud native architectures is helping many enterprise organizations to transform their IT landscape into a force of agility in the marketplace to support business disruption. This revolution in infrastructure services led to a new way of designing applications.

Cloud Adoption Across Industries

Despite the clear advantages that the cloud can offer and the potential for innovation, cost transformation, and greater agility, organizations across industries and geographies have yet to truly embrace the potential that the cloud offers. Recent research suggests that while public cloud consumption is increasing rapidly, there's also a level of disillusionment in the results being obtained. While 90 percent of enterprises have adopted the cloud in some form or another, only 37 percent of enterprises say they have fully achieved the benefits they expected from their cloud initiatives. Research organizations envision that tomorrow's industry leaders will be approximately 80 percent fully achieves the benefits from the cloud initiatives. The 37 percent of organizations, who have adopted the cloud-first approach are already seeing the benefit and return on investment (ROI).

Reducing Costs

A cloud-based deployment reduces the capital expenditure by eliminating the need to spend money on fixed assets such as servers, networks, real estate, software, etc. It also reduces operational expenditures by lowering costs such as IT support staff, electricity, security, etc.

Adopting the Cloud Native Mindset

Organizations within an enterprise chain together the various technologies, processes, and services of cloud native to produce an outcome that has actual business value. The cloud native approach is much more than just a programming model or a new way of writing code. Cloud native applications have been designed and developed from the bottom up to be deployed in the cloud. In other words, it changes the entire lifecycle of how requirements are collaboratively started, coded, tested, deployed, and maintained.

What Is Cloud Native?

According to the definition developed by the Cloud Native Computing Foundation, cloud native can "empower organizations to build and run scalable applications in modern, dynamic environments such as public, private, and hybrid clouds."

Cloud native refers to the architecture, design, delivery, and management of applications that truly exploit the unique characteristics of a native of the cloud, rather than just porting legacy monolithic applications to the cloud.

The objective of cloud native is to improve the speed and efficiency of service assembly, enabling the business to react faster to market change.

Cloud native is an approach to building and running an application that exploits the services of cloud computing. Cloud native is about around how your application is architected, developed, and deployed. The applications can be easily modifiable, is disposable without affecting the whole business use cases, and can react quickly to business changes. See Figure 1-1 and Figure 1-2.

Figure 1-1. *Monolithic legacy application*

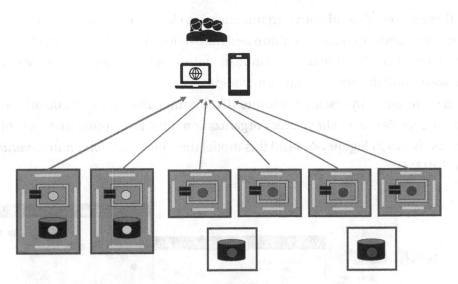

Figure 1-2. *Polylithic and polyglot cloud native application*

The enterprises that are embracing the cloud are already seeing the benefits from adopting microservices, containers, event-driven, serverless, and DevSecOps along with an agile development approach.

Cloud native architecture and design principles and patterns help to design, develop, and manage applications for their intended resilience and scale requirements and accelerate the software engineering process.

Cloud native provides enterprises with the capability to rapidly develop and deploy software applications that adapt to changing the business and operational condition automatically. Cloud native brings the greatest benefits when developing new applications or services that drive business disruption and enables the continuous deployment of software applications until moving to production in real time with the automation of infrastructure, which increases resiliency and business continuity for enterprise applications.

Cloud Native Maturity Model

Every book and blog mentions the maturity model of cloud native architecture; in reality, the model is entirely based on your organization's maturity. To gauge where your organization is, you need to conduct a maturity assessment. We will explain maturity assessment in Chapter 11.

The three waves of cloud native architecture are cloud enablement, cloud native transformation, and cloud native culture and innovation. Your maturity level is not an end; cloud native architecture will continue to mature as your organization progresses on these waves and through industry innovation.

Based on research by research institutes like Gartner, Forester, and consulting firms, and also my experience, I believe every organization must go through this cycle of maturity, as shown in Figure 1-3. I call this model the *cloud and cloud native maturity model* (CCNMM).

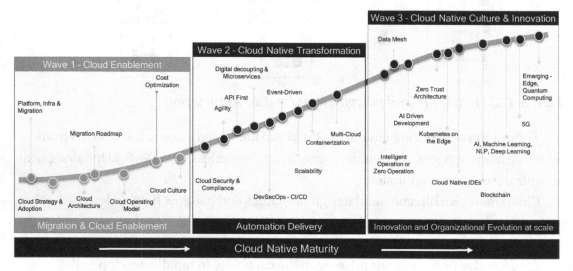

Figure 1-3. *Cloud and cloud native maturity model*

Cloud Enablement Wave

To understand where your enterprise and its landscape will fall on the CCNMM, it is important to assess which systems are ready for the cloud journey. In the cloud journey, being cloud native requires the adoption of cloud services. If your organization just started with the cloud, then you need to start the migration from your own data center to the cloud, such as migrating the VMs. During this period you need to prioritize the system for cloud migration and also create a cloud strategy across portfolios. Each cloud vendor will have its own set of services and cost models, with the most mature having an advanced set of features. In this wave, you need to recognize what cloud services you need to adopt, and in parallel, you need to embrace a cloud culture in your organization.

Regardless of which cloud provider you choose, the provider will have the basic building blocks of infrastructure, storage, networking, etc. To start on your cloud journey, you need to choose these services for your VM migration or lift-and-shift model. This model will move the on-premises systems to the cloud with no changes to the design, technology, etc. Therefore, these migrations only use the basic building blocks of the cloud.

The outcome of this wave that your organization will gain from this maturity stage is the basic premises of the cloud. For example, your organization will move its cost model from CAPEX to OPEX and be able to manage nonfunctional requirements such as scaling, high availability, etc. Besides learning how to analyze your landscape and cloud vendor, it's important to embrace a cloud culture across the organization. Even though the adoption of cloud in this wave is a relatively low level of maturity, it is critical for the organization to start the cloud journey.

Cloud Native Transformation Wave

Before the adoption of cloud native, the suggestion is to adopt a middle path between cloud enablement and cloud native; this is called *cloud optimization*. In cloud optimization, you need to optimize your migrated application that you already completed in the cloud enablement wave by using cloud native features without decoupling or redeveloping your cloud-enabled applications. Today, some organizations, especially after the pandemic, are moving to the cloud optimization world and experiencing the benefits of continuous delivery, autoscaling, redundancy, resilience, etc.

Once you have adopted the culture of the cloud in your organization after cloud enablement and cloud optimization, the next level of maturity is cloud native transformation. Cloud native maturity will begin with a culture of cloud principles and the team's understanding of cloud native implementation. In the whole cloud native transformation, the adoption of the cloud is one part of the design principle that is required to make a cloud native architecture. These are used in conjunction with other principles such as the culture of automation and culture of agility that is centered on microservice applications.

The cloud native transformation wave is about how the application is decoupled, designed, and architected. You need to adopt various principles and patterns to make your application truly cloud native. Adopting microservice principles in your application architecture is not cloud native, but you need to consider other elements of cloud native elements such as containerization, automation, etc. The 12-factor app is a methodology, as mentioned in Table 1-1, for building software-as-a-service applications (`http://12factor.net`). This 12-factor app methodology can be adapted to any programming techniques and database models. The objective of the 12-factor methodology is to consider 12 steps when designing an application for cloud native that minimizes cost and time.

Table 1-1. *Twelve-Factor App Steps*

Number	Step	Details
1	Codebase	One codebase tracked in revision control; many deploys
2	Dependencies	Explicitly declare and isolate dependencies
3	Config	Store config in the environment
4	Backing Services	Treat backing services as attached resources
5	Build, release, run	Strictly separate build and run stages
6	Processes	Execute the app as one or more stateless processes
7	Port binding	Export services via port binding
8	Concurrency	Scale out via the process model
9	Disposability	Maximize robustness with fast startup and graceful shutdown
10	Dev/prod parity	Keep developing, staging, and production as similar as possible
11	Logs	Treat logs as event streams
12	Admin process	Run admin/management tasks as one-off processes

In the cloud native transformation, you need to adopt microservice architecture principles for new developments and apply the digital decoupling method for the existing monolithic legacy applications. All the cloud native elements as mentioned in the next section will revolve around microservices development. You need to adopt DevSecOps for end-to-end automation, agility for software engineering, containerization, orchestration for deployment and elasticity, and so on.

Scalability and Flexibility Advantage

Taking advantage of cloud native architecture offers enterprises flexibility. The applications can scale up and down based on demand. Almost all cloud providers have a global scale. In addition, you can choose what kind of VM instances are required depending on the type of application such as if your application requires more CPU, your application is data-centric, or your application is an online gaming provider.

Cloud Native Culture and Innovation Wave

The third wave of the maturity model is to adopt a culture across the organization of innovation. Throughout this wave, the remaining maturity principles shown in Figure 1-3 need to be adopted. As your systems evolve and move further on the cloud native maturity model, they will rely more and more on applying intelligence into them. Similar to the cloud native transformation stage, a mature cloud native architecture is constantly evolving by adopting artificial intelligence, machine learning, and deep learning techniques to predict your architecture, failures, operations, event streams, integrated monitoring, etc.

In the cloud native journey, your organization might find a lot of use cases to adopt blockchain technology, digital twin, zero trust architecture, 5G, AI-driven development, cloud native IDEs, and quantum computing.

Blockchain as a Service

> *"Blockchain is a system of recording information in a way that makes it difficult or impossible to change, hack, or cheat the system. A blockchain is essentially a digital ledger of transactions that is duplicated and distributed across the entire network of computer systems of the blockchain."*
>
> —investopedia

The main characteristics of blockchain are decentralization, immutability, and public databases. The concept of blockchain is based on a peer-to-peer network architecture in which a transaction is not controlled by any single centralized entity. Cloud native architecture is best when stored data on the cloud is split into smaller chunks, which are stored on several different machines around the world. There are many options available like blockchain as a service (BaaS), which is a third-party cloud-based infrastructure and management of companies building and operating blockchain apps. These services are hosted on the web and run back-end operations for a blockchain-based platform.

Digital Twin

A digital twin platform is an effective means to reflect the physical status in virtual space. It breaks the barrier between the physical world and the digital world of manufacturing. The digital twin ideas were first evolved at NASA: full-scale mockups of early space capsules. Industry 4.0 is possible only with digital twins according to Dr. Michael Grieves.

A digital twin is a sensor-enabled digital model of a physical object that simulates the object in a live setting. All the major cloud providers have created a service for digital twins; for example, Azure Digital Twins provides services for users to create dynamic virtual replicas. The capabilities include flexible modeling that supports full graph technologies, a live execution environment, and easy integration with other Azure services. These cloud native platforms help to build digital twin capabilities, especially for manufacturing industries.

Zero Trust Architecture

The elements of cloud native and data continue to shift in enterprises, from monolithic to microservices, from centralized data lakes to data meshes, and from manual to automation delivery and deployment with the increasing proliferation of connected devices. The approach to securing enterprises' assets for the most part remains unchanged, with heavy reliance and trust in the network perimeter. Enterprises continue to innovate and adopt secured network configurations. Zero trust architecture (ZTA) is a paradigm shift in security architecture and an organization's strategy; it is built upon existing cloud native architecture and does not require you to replace existing architecture. The ZTA environment consists of a protected surface that contains a single Desktop as a Service (DaaS) element protected by a micro perimeter enforced by layer 7 and various tools available in the cloud. ZTA enforcing policies are code based on the least privilege, continuous monitoring, and automated mitigation threats using service meshes to enforce security control and implement binary attestation to verify the origin of binaries.

5G

5G is the fifth-generation technology standard for the broadband cellular network and delivers higher multi-Gbps peak data speeds, ultra-low latency, more reliability, massive network capacity, increased higher availability, and a more uniform user experience. The 5G technology comes with various features such as networking slicing, orthogonal frequency-division multiplexing (OFDM), and multiple input and multiple output (MIMO).

Your cloud native application needs to evolve and adopt a new way of responding to users to meet the speed of 5G; that is a latency of less than 1 millisecond. To support this speed and end-user experience, your existing cloud native application architecture needs to support changes that are nano and micro in nature with 2.0 code and built-in intelligence.

Quantum Computing

Quantum computing uses advanced physics to dramatically increase the computing power needed for complex calculations. Traditional computing relies on information that is translated, stored, represented, and processed in bits that can be only one of two discrete binary states. Quantum computing, in contrast, uses qubits that can exist either in the same discrete states as a traditional bit or in any number of superpositions in between. All cloud providers have come up with solutions for cloud-based quantum computing via *quantum as a service* (QaaS). QaaS allows enterprises to use and write algorithms and run them on quantum computers.

This is not the end of maturity; you need to keep innovate to adopt earlier than others, and you need to make sure your people are upskilled frequently to meet the maturity.

Elements of Cloud Native Computing

The traditional approach to architecture is no longer viable in the fast-paced digital economy where business decisions need to be made quickly, the cost of change is required to be low, and the cost of throwing away existing architecture needs to be affordable, if not negligible. These are the types of demands that are behind the drive toward cloud native architectures, a fundamentally new way to build software. This approach helps create a highly agile architecture that facilitates businesses to make changes quickly without impacting the rest of the enterprise systems.

In the cloud native technology era, the cloud is the execution platform; to the left are DevSecOps processes, which are driven by agility, all of which are the result of present-day polylithic and polyglot architecture, which are driven and invoked by business disruptions.

Figure 1-4 illustrates seven key elements of a cloud native architecture, which is used to develop cloud native applications.

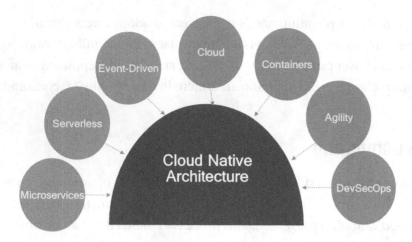

Figure 1-4. *Cloud native architecture elements*

Microservices Architecture

A microservice architecture approach allows you to build a system that is composed of many granular subsystems, whereby each system has its specialized architecture to meet specific business and technical needs. The principle features of a microservices architecture are as follows:

- *Exclusive infrastructure*: Each granular subsystem is deployed in its virtual or container hardware environment, isolating it from impacting other subsystems.

- *Exclusive ownership of data by each subsystem*: Access to subsystems is provided through a well-defined published interface.

- *Flexible system*: Each subsystem inherently supports multiple versions and backward compatibility and simplifies change management.

Serverless Architecture

A serverless architecture is an element of cloud native architecture. The challenges of on-premises data center management can be addressed by abstracting the infrastructure to the cloud. Management activities are automated as part of the platform, and near-zero downtime can be achieved through the modular independent images of the services. Operations of your application capability increase as your application can be scale up and down dynamically. With the technical aspects abstracted from the solution, the development team can focus on developing business user stories. The platform design allows for resiliency and service monitoring and logging. Leveraging a serverless architecture allows your enterprise to expand its IT strategy with new capabilities and offerings.

Serverless architectures dramatically simplify the development of microservices and event-driven architecture. The following are the characteristics of a serverless architecture:

- Asynchronous and concurrent

- Infrequent and irregular demand

- Stateless and ephemeral process

- Changing business requirements

Event-Driven Architecture

Event-driven architecture is a model for cloud native application design. It is a distributed, asynchronous software architecture that integrates applications and components through the production of handling events. In the event-driven architecture, events are triggered and communicate asynchronously between microservices. The event-driven architecture has three key components: event producer, event router, and event consumer. The following are the benefits of an event-driven architecture:

- Scale and fail independently

- Develop microservices with agility

- Audit your application with ease

Cloud Computing

Cloud computing is the use of computing resources that are delivered as a service over the Internet. Cloud computing has the potential to offer substantial opportunities in various IT scenarios. It is a flexible delivery platform. It can support many different architectural and development styles, from big, monolithic systems to large virtual machine deployments to nimble clusters of containers to data meshes and large farms of serverless functions. The cloud can host a variety of different software applications, including batch-style, back-end jobs; interactive, data-driven applications; and more. All the software is deployed and scaled out quickly through the rapid provisioning of VMs, containers, or bare metals.

The following are the main services of cloud offerings:

- Infrastructure as a service (IaaS)

- Platform as a service (PaaS)

- Software as a service (SaaS)

Containers

Cloud native applications are distributed in nature and utilize a cloud infrastructure. Numerous techniques and tools are used to implement cloud native applications, but from a computing perspective, mainly containers are used. Containerization became a de facto standard for cloud native. The container is a technology that allows you to incorporate and configure your binaries and their dependencies in a package called an *image*. This image can be used to spawn an instance of your services, called a *container*.

Agile Development

Agile management is about working smarter and generating more value. An iterative mindset that embraces failure and focuses on customer and business value is an essential building block of it. The agile process generally promotes a disciplined project management process that encourages frequent inspection, closer to business, and promotes the early release of use cases in terms of user stories. There are 12 agile principles are available to adapt to make your company truly agile. Agile embraces faster innovation with a focus on business value. These are the few benefits of truly agile:

- Predictable cost and schedule

- Focuses on business value

- Focuses on end users

- Stakeholder engagement and early feedback

- Faster time to market and early predictable delivery

- Reduced risk

DevSecOps

DevSecOps is the set of tools, practices, processes, and culture that enables development, operations, and security teams to work together during the entire lifecycle of a project or product. It focuses on speed and how quickly an artifact can get from the requirements to design stage to development and into production. It's largely about automation, i.e., eliminating the need for human involvement in the production process. Shift-left is the common usage in DevSecOps; the idea of bringing everything toward your left means starting early and detecting early instead of at the end. The following are a few benefits of automation:

- End-to-end automation with single touch deployment

- Cost reduction

- Speed of recovery

- Improved overall security

- Infrastructure as code

How Is Cloud Native Different Than Cloud-Enabled?

Cloud-enabled applications are developed by using a normal traditional software methodology but can deploy in the cloud without using many benefits of the cloud.

Cloud native applications are developed and deployed in the cloud or cloud-related environment by using cloud native software methodologies. This software delivers to a customer by using the benefits of the cloud such as autoscaling, infrastructure as code, etc.

Cloud Native Journey

Cloud migration is imperative, but that doesn't mean it's easy to implement. Anyone facing stumbling blocks on the cloud journey must understand that they are not alone. The road to the cloud transformational benefits is complex, involving multiple dimensions, including rethinking strategy, technology, skills development, business processes, as well as organizational design.

Although all enterprises are embracing cloud native, it is not always practical to change all the applications at once. Applications will exist in different stages of maturity, and there are multiple ways to achieve stages of maturity. We'll cover more details of the assessment to identify the maturity of your application in subsequent chapters.

The cloud native transformation starts by establishing a cloud native platform and then moving on to new application "greenfield" (development of an application from scratch) or the modernization of an existing application "brownfield" incrementally until enterprise-wide adoption.

The timeline shown in Figure 1-5 is dependent on the size of the enterprise. We'll explain more details about the timeline and risks in subsequent chapters.

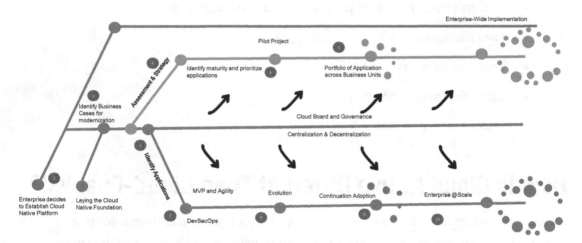

Figure 1-5. *Journey to the cloud*

Start with Lift and Shift

The agility and speed offered by cloud native environments can be transformative for an enterprise. To make everything cloud native, you need to adopt a culture, process, and way of working. But your organization cannot become cloud native from day one, so every organization has to start on a cloud journey. How and where to start? For most organizations, start with the lift and shift of existing monolithic applications to an IaaS cloud environment. Lift and shift means lifting monolithic applications from your data center and shifting them to the cloud environment without much modification. This is also called *migrating* into VMs.

Shifting VMs from your data center to the cloud, that is, using the cloud as a commodity data center, offers a few advantages. Some of the advantages are as follows:

- Fewer resources are required because the VMs are owned by the cloud, so you have less maintenance.

- Reduced capital expenditure on facilities.

- Fewer data centers.

In the new usage model, you provision servers as and when required.

Re-engineer Migration

Enterprises that are truly moving to be cloud native organizations will follow the re-engineering approach for their legacy applications so they can take advantage of scale, agility, and innovation. The applications that are migrating to the cloud get the benefits of being cloud native, but decoupling in the process might take a longer time. These types of applications do not lift and shift; they are designed to follow cloud native principles as much as possible.

Benefits of Cloud Native

For many industries, the cloud represents a part of digital transformation. Some industries might have started their cloud journey for several reasons, including scalability, improved customer experience, greater agility, cost savings, and access to innovation. However, to take full advantage of the value of cloud computing, enterprises must adopt new methodologies and processes. As mentioned, a cloud native development is an approach to building and running applications that uses a service-based architecture, microservices, containers, and APIs. Here are a few benefits when enterprises adopt a cloud native approach as part of their cloud strategy:

> *Agility*: By splitting the development process into time windows and providing a continuous feedback loop, agile enables rapid, more effective development—and the creation of nimble organizations that can innovate quickly.

Speed: Cloud native applications can gain development speed and improve automation by migrating an application to a container-based platform, decreasing the time it takes to deliver new products and business services to market.

DevSecOps culture: To adopt a cloud native approach, portfolios within IT and the business need to collaborate. The development team must align with IT operations and the lines of business to deliver needed business functionality. The applications are the realization of DevSecOps as they automate operational processes such as integrated monitoring, scaling, resilience, etc.

Efficient resource consumption: Containers allow applications to be rapidly deployed in servers with greater density than VMs and destroyed easily and recreate with same configuration.

On-demand infrastructure: The cloud native development model promotes on-demand provisioning that allows developers throughout the organization to access the infrastructure they need when they need it.

Reusability: Cloud native applications take advantage of a ready-to-use infrastructure that allows developers to access and reuse existing components such as caching, APIs, rules, data virtualization, etc.

Portability: Cloud native applications are container friendly and abstract away dependencies on their external environment and are more easily deployed across different environments.

Scalability: Cloud native applications can automate scaling applications based on various parameters such as CPU, load, etc.

Cloud Native Organization and Culture

The transition to cloud native is not just a technical change; it carries with it changes to large parts of cloud usage. Infrastructure as a service (IaaS) means that IT can reduce its expenditures on data centers, and by taking advantage of business continuity and disaster recovery (BC and DR) capabilities in the cloud, as well as other capabilities, it can further reduce expenses and redirect spending to more profitable users. Moreover, by taking advantage of more modern cloud architectures such as containers, orchestration, serverless technologies, automation, etc., enterprises should find that development and updates can be greatly accelerated, improving time to market and responsiveness to business needs.

In the cloud, you can spin up services quickly, try them, and terminate them when no longer needed. This stands in stark contrast to the traditional old way. Many enterprises use hackathons to determine the value of new technology for a given problem. In such events, the development team comes together and learns new technology quickly. If the experiment fails, little has been lost. If it succeeds, your teams have gotten a real head start.

The IT finance organization has changed the way the model was approached compared to the earlier traditional approach, which was based on capital expanse and deprecation. Facilities, servers, and software were purchased and typically depreciated over time, after which the refresh cycle started. Cloud services are subscription-based. With the cloud, the IT department and finance organization within an enterprise can gain more control and insight into their IT spend.

Consider the following when you start your journey to the cloud:

- Monitor cloud spend.

- Verify that computing resources are used efficiently.

- Look at the CPU utilization.

- Drive accountability to the business where possible.

You need to involve the information security and risk management teams as soon as you can when planning to move to the cloud. There are many technological and environmental aspects of security in cloud native. You need to make sure to consider the following questions:

- Do you have a data classification schema?

- Do you have a common authentication mechanism?

- What new regulations apply once in the cloud?

- Do you consider countries' compliances and regulations?

The development and operations groups will experience a significant change in the way they are working depending on the extent to which they embrace the cloud native paradigm. In the traditional approach, a team usually follows the waterfall process. In today's world, many projects and teams follow an agile methodology with full implementation of automation, a shift-left approach, etc.

As more and more of your organization's focus is on cloud enablement, your team requires upskilling into cloud technologies. HR organizations should be prepared to help train or retain individuals to gain the new cloud skills they are expected to need. Many enterprises started upskilling on cloud technologies by enabling cloud certifications, cloud advisory roles, etc.

Finally, organizations should put controls and standards in place to verify that their cloud journey proceeds thoughtfully. Many enterprises have created cloud steering committees (CSCs), central bodies that facilitate departments and the adoption and use of the cloud. The CSC comprises individuals from enterprise architecture, finance, information security, HR, the business team, etc. The objectives of the CSC are to do the following:

- Determine the order and priority of the enterprise applications to migrate to the cloud.

- Create a culture of automation.

- Analyze and contract with cloud vendors.

- Keep track of emerging technologies, etc.

How Is Cloud Native Architecture Embraced Across Industries?

Many enterprises have made a start on their cloud journey but have yet to fully commit. A few enterprises have advanced a bit further, and now their challenge is how to move deeper to the cloud and take greater advantage of cloud native capabilities.

Amid the pandemic, organizations are responding to this changing landscape with a mix of business strategies. These strategies aim to disrupt the future with more relevant services. They're seeking to harness digital to drive greater efficiency and become more agile in the face of volatile market conditions and to compete with the new disruptive competition.

Regardless of your approach and priorities, making progress requires leadership that is commitment to targeted business outcomes and the right focus on creating a cloud native culture, not to mention creating an environment in which the team can thrive. It is also essential for industries such as banking and insurance to engage with regulators and county-specific compliances as they plan for their journey.

Industries should pick the right migration path depending on their priorities and the current degree of cloud maturity. You need to categorize these journeys into migrate, accelerate, and scale and innovate in the cloud, and you can choose whichever path you want depending on your strategy.

Migrate

Cloud migration is about much more than lift-and-shift; a successful migration requires a common language, common understanding, and organizational ability to align technology solutions to meet business needs.

For a range of reasons—technology, security, complexity, legacy, data sovereignty—many industries' systems remain in the data center. Unless you migrate most of your systems to the cloud, you will be unable to realize the full business value from these systems, whether that's making the business more resilient, efficient, or customer-focused. This stage is essential to get systems to the cloud rapidly, securely, and with confidence by selecting the right infrastructure for your business.

The following are the steps you need to consider for your migration:

1. Conduct an assessment of applications, data repositories, and infrastructure for either retirement, leave-as-is, rehost, refactor, or rewrite.

2. Determine the design, cost, and timeline for migration activities.

3. Perform a software engineering lifecycle for migrated applications.

4. Perform the post-migration retirement of applications, data repositories, and infrastructure in the source data center and cloud.

Accelerate

Just getting to the cloud doesn't mean your enterprises have become a cloud native enterprise. To do that, you need to modernize. That means building applications and services specifically for a cloud environment and changing the operating model to drive new business agility. The accelerated stage is where banks can ramp up their organizational speed and agility by restructuring architectures, applications, and data for the cloud. The COVID-19 crisis has accelerated an industry need for the cloud:

- Run an agile business and respond to changing events, for example, regulatory impacts.

- Focus on new revenue streams enabled through digital and disruptive technologies.

- Reduce infrastructure costs and transition to proportional technology costs.

- Improve operating efficiencies for change and run activity.

- Provide enhanced dynamic risk management and security capabilities.

- Monetize APIs in open banking.

- Monetize the data as a service across enterprises.

Scale and Innovate

With the scale and speed provided by the cloud when working with cloud providers, enterprises can free up people and funds to focus on adopting systems to what the business and its customer will need next. The scale and innovate stage is where your enterprises can use the cloud as a digital transformation level, creating a foundation for rapid experimentation, innovation, and new business model.

What Is a Software Architect's Role in Cloud Native?

A software architect in a cloud native architecture is expected to have skills and knowledge of a variety of topics including cloud and noncloud. This book focuses on many of those topics. They include technical and nontechnical duties such as the following:

- Understanding cloud environments, microservices, automation, and agility

- Understanding nonfunctional requirements such as scalability, elasticity, resilience, etc.

- Providing leadership

- Understanding architecture principles and patterns for cloud native architecture

- Knowing how to manage client stakeholders' concerns

- Ability to create architecture blueprint

- Ability to create runtime, development, integration, and operation architecture details

- Understanding the business domain

- Participating in gathering and analyzing requirements

- Communicating with various technical and nontechnical stakeholders

- Creating as is progress for various stakeholders

- Helping teams to design and implementation of the design

- Helping teams to choose tools and platforms

- Having the vision for future tools and a platform roadmap

- Effective verbal and written communication skills

- Able to estimate changes

- Being able to design software architecture that adapts to change and evolve over time

- Mentoring team members

Summary

In this chapter, we defined what cloud native architecture is. We also discussed the current adoption of cloud native across industries and what area of focus you require to develop a cloud native architecture. We identified a cloud maturity model that has three waves required for mature cloud native architectures. The three waves are cloud enablement wave, cloud native transformation, and cloud native culture and innovation. These three waves help you to gauge your current organization's maturity and the steps to consider. Finally, we covered what a cloud native journey for enterprises is and what culture and skills need to be adopted for a cloud native journey. In a nutshell, this chapter introduced cloud native and how to start the journey, as well as what organizational skills are required for cloud native.

The next chapter covers the evolution of services, especially cloud services, and the elements of cloud native architecture.

CHAPTER 2

Cloud Native Services

In the previous chapter, I discussed cloud native architecture and its importance in the IT industry. In this chapter, I will explore that topic further, but in the context of supporting cloud services.

Cloud services were developed to support a cloud native architecture. Many organizations start their journey by adopting various cloud services; as a result, the organization's business goals, objectives, and processes greatly affect how they will provision resources and develop cloud native applications.

This chapter focuses on various cloud services and the evolution of each service. We will look at services in detail and how to adopt these services.

In this chapter, we will cover the following topics:

- Evolution of infrastructure as a service (IaaS)

- IT infrastructure laws

- Evolution of server technology

- What is containerization?

- What is IaaS?

- What is platform as a service (PaaS)?

- What is software as a service (SaaS)?

Evolution of Infrastructure Services

An IT infrastructure service is the shared technology resources that provide the services to the applications. Infrastructure services include the hardware, software, operating system (OS), networking services, telecommunication services, Internet services, etc.

© Shivakumar R Goniwada 2022
S. R. Goniwada, *Cloud Native Architecture and Design*, https://doi.org/10.1007/978-1-4842-7226-8_2

Infrastructure services are a result of five decades of evolution in computing. To reach the present-day container technology level, the infrastructure has undergone six stages of evolution, each representing different subservices. Figure 2-1 shows the six stages.

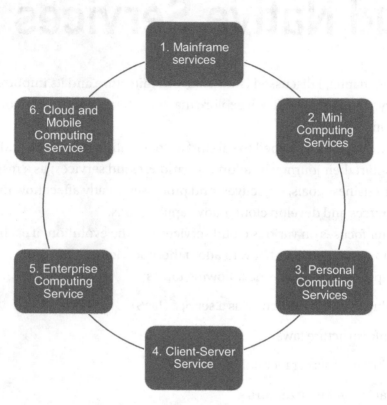

Figure 2-1. *Six stages of infrastructure services*

Technologies that are used in one stage may also be used in another stage for other business services. For example, a lot of financial- and insurance-sector business processes are using mainframe services, and these mainframe services are consumed by container-based microservice use cases. The mainframe shared model demonstrates a stage 1 evolution used by a stage 6 evolution in many enterprises as shown in above figure.

Figure 2-2 shows the stages of IT infrastructure.

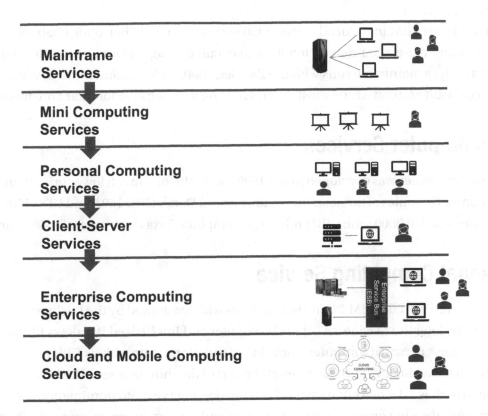

Figure 2-2. *Stages in IT evolution*

Mainframe Services

The first general-purpose automatic digital computer was built by IBM around 1944. It was an electromechanical machine developed in conjunction with Harvard University. In 1952, IBM announced its first fully electronic data processing system, the IBM 701; in the next few years, the IBM 650 was created. In 1959, IBM introduced two of its most important computers. These were the 1401 Data Processing System, widely used for business applications, and the 1620 Data Processing System, a small scientific and engineering computer used for such diverse applications as automatic typesetting, highway design, etc.

The IBM introduced the large-scale 7000 series, the 1410, and Stretch (IBM 7030), the most powerful scientific computer ever designed. In the 1960s, IBM announced

System/360, which was the first system where companies integrated all of their data processing systems.

In the 1990s, IBM introduced System/390 with high-speed fiber-optic channels, ESCON architecture, ultra-dense circuits, and circuit packaging for higher performance.

Currently, a mainframe runs with the Z series, z900, which includes the newly designed 64-bit z/architecture; most enterprises use a mainframe for their core business.

Minicomputer Services

The small computer was developed in the 1960s and sold for a much lower price than mainframes. Examples of minicomputers are Control Data's CDC 160A and CDC 1700, HP 3000 series and HP 2000 series, IBM midrange computer, Texas Instrument T1-990, etc.

Personal Computing Service

The PC started with the IBM PC in 1981 and was widely adopted by the business community; later the Macintosh (Apple) computer and Intel-based Windows PCs came on the scene. A personal computer works in a stand-alone state with its CPU and is used by an individual. Worldwide sales at the end of the third quarter of 2020 were $71.4 million, which is a 3.6 percent increase from the previous year. Predominantly PCs are used by end users to connect various ancillaries and servers. In recent years, the PC has become more and more difficult to pin down. A PC can be any personal device with a microprocessor.

Client-Server Service

Client-server architecture is a computing model in which the server hosts and manages most of the services to be consumed by the client. This type of architecture has one or more client computers connected to a central server (the central server can be Linux, Solaris, AIX, or Windows) over a local or wide area network or the Internet. Currently we are calling this *legacy software*; these legacy software packages are based on a client-server architecture. The server is a single monolithic application and provides services to a thick client hosted on a PC, and the data is exchanged between the client and server over the network by using RPC.

Enterprise Computing Service

Enterprise computing was among the most important developments in information technology in the 1990s. Nearly every top company has implemented some form of enterprise system. Enterprise computing involves the use of computers in networks, such as LANs and WANs, or a series of interconnected networks encompassing a variety of different operating systems, protocols, and network architectures.

The enterprises turned to network standards and software tools that could integrate disparate networks and applications within and across business units (BUs) over the TCP/IP protocol. The commonly used tools in enterprise computing include enterprise resource planning (ERP), customer relationship manager (CRM), reporting, order systems, etc. All these systems are in a monolithic single unit and running on a single CPU in memory.

Cloud and Mobile Computing Services

Cloud computing as a term has been around since the 2000s, but the concept of computing as a service has been around for much longer, since the 1960s, when IBM allowed companies to rent time on a mainframe, rather than have to buy one themselves.

The growing bandwidth power of the Internet and disruption in business and technology pushed the client-server model to the cloud computing model. Cloud computing is the result of the evolution and adoption of existing technologies and paradigms. The goal of cloud computing is to allow users to get the benefits of all the services without the need for deep knowledge about or expertise in each one of them.

According to Wikipedia, cloud computing is the on-demand availability of computer system resources, especially cloud storage and computing power, typically over the Internet and on a pay-as-you-go basis.

Rather than each enterprise owning its infrastructure or data centers, companies can rent services from cloud providers. This helps enterprises to outsource servers, space, resources, etc., with the most security possible.

Cloud computing services provide a vast range of options starting with infrastructure, software, storage, platform, networking, natural language process, and artificial intelligence, and also provide traditional software like ERP, CRM, etc.

Today, cloud computing is becoming the de facto standard for all enterprises, and some software providers are discontinuing on-prem licenses and provide only cloud service licenses.

Enterprises can use single cloud provider services or a combination of multicloud provider services or hybrid services or private cloud services. Cloud providers are now in competition, so each provider provides free tools and solutions to port from one cloud provider to another provider seamlessly.

In the future, the cloud will become the de facto standard for all computing. Especially after the COVID-19 pandemic, most enterprises (even financial enterprises) are moving toward the cloud. Various research institutes predict that half of all global enterprises use the cloud now.

According to Gartner, global spending on cloud services will reach $350 billion by 2021 and will reach $500 billion by 2023.

IT Infrastructure Laws and Prediction

As the stages progress as shown in Figure 2-1, infrastructure services are becoming cheaper, with exponentially increased computing power. The following are the theories that predict the IT infrastructure changes in the years to come.

Moore's Law

Moore's law is a prediction made by American engineer Gordon Moore in 1965 that the number of transistors per silicon chip will double every year. He observed that the number of transistors on a computer chip was doubling about every 18–24 months. This is an observation and projection based on historical trends, rather than a law of physics.

There are three interpretations of Moore's law.

- The power of microprocessors doubles every 18 months.

- Computing power doubles every 18 months.

- The price of computing falls by half every 18 months.

For example, Moore's law means we get ever-more powerful personal computers for less and less money. A computer chip that contained 2,000 transistors and cost $1,000 in 1970, $500 in 1972, $250 in 1974, $0.97 in 1990, and less than $0.02 to manufacture today.

The Laws of Mass Digital Storage

The amount of information is roughly doubling every year, and the cost of storing digital information is falling at an exponential rate. Currently, the compound annual growth rate is roughly around 60 percent, with an exponential decrease in the cost of storing data.

Metcalfe's Law

Metcalfe's law states that the effect of a telecommunication network is proportional to the square of the number of connected users of the system. The law shows that a network's value to participants grows exponentially as the network takes on more members. The increasing scale of that network grows exponentially as more and more people join the network, as shown in Figure 2-3. As the number of members in a network grows linearly, the value of the entire system grows exponentially and continues to grow as members increase.

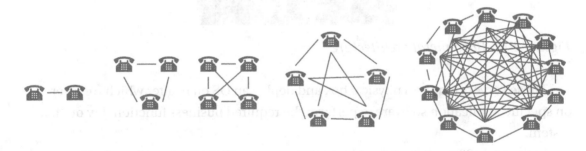

Figure 2-3. *Network increases linearly*

Communication Cost and Internet

There has been a rapid decline of the cost of communication and an exponential growth in the size of the Internet. Estimated Internet access is around 4.12 billion, which means more than 50 percent of the global population is connected to the Internet. As communication costs fall, the utilization of communication and computing facilities grows.

Evolution of Servers

The servers used have evolved from bare-metal physical servers to virtual servers to cloud servers and containers to serverless.

Bare-Metal Servers

We began with a bare-metal server/physical server, as shown in Figure 2-4. Each server offered for rental is a distinct physical piece of hardware that is a functional server on its own; in other words, each physical box hosts one piece of hardware.

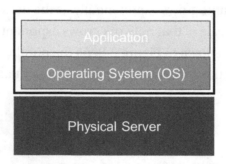

Figure 2-4. *Bare-metal architecture*

These servers require a physical box and deploy an OS on it, after which we layer on specific application software to perform the required business functionality on that system.

In the early 2000s, it became evident that enterprises were not getting appropriate value for their server dollar. The CEOs of enterprises questioned why so many expensive servers were running such low utilization rates.

Virtual Machine Revolution

Virtualization uses the same physical hardware, but rather than installing a single OS and running a single workload on that physical box, install a hypervisor OS and set it up to support multiple virtual machines or virtualized servers that can run many different business applications all at the same time on one physical server.

The VMs are hosted with their CPU, memory, network interface, and storage on physical hardware, as shown in Figure 2-5. The hypervisor separates the single physical server resources from the hardware and provisions them appropriately so they can be used by the VM. The VMs that use physical server resources are guest machines, guest computers, and guest OSs. The hypervisor treats compute resources such as CPU, memory, and storage as a pool of resources.

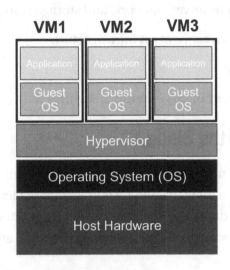

Figure 2-5. *Virtual machine architecture*

Virtualization technology allows you to share resources with many virtual environments. The hypervisor manages the hardware and separates the physical resources from the virtual environments. Resources are partitioned as needed from the physical environment to the VMs. When the VM is running and a user or program issues an instruction that requires additional resources from the physical environment, the hypervisor schedules the request to the physical system's resources so that the VM's OS and applications can access the shared pool.

Each VMs is isolated from the rest of the VMs and can be co-located on a single piece of hardware, and VMs can allow multiple OSs to run simultaneously on a single computer, such as a Linux distro on a macOS laptop or a Linux distro on a Windows OS laptop.

Adoption of Virtual Machines

Organizations soon recognized that they could get much more value by virtualizing applications. Virtualization provides a significant improvement in enterprise computing and realizes benefits from managing servers and the applicable costs, as mentioned here:

- Better utilization of server, network, and storage resources

- Better return on investment on infrastructure

- Better portability

- Better management of server setup, network, etc.

Virtual Machines in the Cloud

The introduction of virtual machine technology into the organization's own data center was hardly a cure-all, from a financial and resource point of view. The organization still faced the high costs of data center real estate, electricity, and environmental conditioning, of computer storage and networking hardware, and of managing the software and platforms.

To alleviate some of these issues in the data center and managing platforms, enterprises turned to co-location, third-parties, and a service model; this means renting data center space from a third party and outsourcing the server management to the third party in their data center. This strategy relieved enterprises of the cost of maintaining real estate and facilities, but companies directly or indirectly own the servers and other accessories.

With the availability of the public cloud, a new cost model—renting capacity— emerged, which allowed companies to think of computing as an on-demand resource. A few enterprises started to migrate a few systems from their own data centers to VMs in the cloud; this process is called *lift and shift*. This type of model started with AWS in 2006 and followed by others like Google's GCP and Microsoft's Azure. These infrastructure as a service solutions provided a way to run your VMs on their cloud. Thus, this was the beginning of the cloud revolution.

Let's discuss a few benefits and drawbacks of VM migration to the cloud.

Here are the benefits:

- Less management required because VMs in the cloud are developed and maintained like VMs on-premises

- Vastly reduced the real-estate expenditure

- New cost model based on a rental approach to computing instead of a capital expense

- New usage model for scaling up and down depending on the demand

Here are the drawbacks:

- Costs can increase with VMs if care is not taken in the planning stage.

- Without changes, some applications are not an ideal fit for the cloud.

- It is a better, but still suboptimal, use of server resources.

Container Revolution

Many organizations first experienced the cloud by migrating virtual machines from the data center to the cloud and then facing costs that were higher than expected or business value that was less than anticipated. Over the last few years, a new form of virtualization has arisen, called *containers*.

The concept of containers has been around for a while; for example, IBM supported the notion of web application containers. However, these early approaches suffered from an increasing scope, compounding rather than alleviating the issue of idle capacity on servers.

The philosophy of a container is to put in what you need to make it whole, and nothing more. Easy-to-use and compact container technology supporting a higher degree of isolation has been mainstream only since mid-2014, when Docker introduced version 1.0. Since then, containers have become widely popular.

A container is a standard unit of software that packages the application code and all its dependencies, so the application runs quickly and reliably and is abstracted from the environment in which it runs. It is a lightweight, standalone, executable package of software that includes everything needed to run an application. This decoupling allows container-based applications to be deployed easily and consistently, regardless of whether the target environment is a private data center, the public cloud, or even a PC.

The container uses the same physical hardware and OS but in an isolated, lightweight silo for running an application on the host OS. Each container can host a single service or multiple services depending on the nature of services.

As mentioned in Figure 2-6, in VMs, the guest OS such as Linux or Windows runs on top of the host OS with virtualized access to the underlying host hardware. Like VMs, the containers allow you to package your application together with libraries and dependencies, providing isolated environments for running software services.

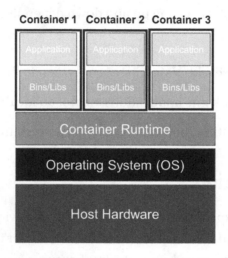

Figure 2-6. *Container environment architecture*

The virtual machines are virtualized on the hardware stack, and containers virtualize at the OS kernel, start much faster, and use a fraction of the memory compared to booting an entire OS. A virtual machine virtualizes CPU, memory, storage, and network resources at the OS level.

Containers can run virtually anywhere: on Linux, Windows, and macOS; on VMs or on bare metal. All cloud native applications will use a container to host business use cases. There are many companies that provide container images other than Docker such as Mesos, Open VZ, CoreOS rkt, and more.

Figure 2-7 shows a high-level comparison between virtual machines and containers.

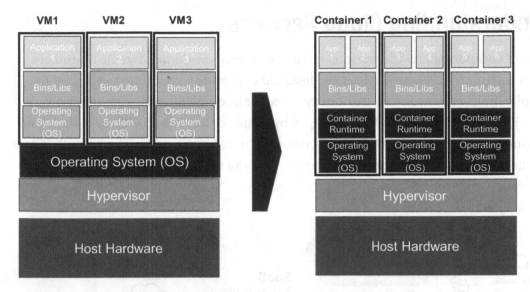

Figure 2-7. *Virtual machine and container comparison*

Since their introduction, containers have become wildly popular for several reasons, including the following:

- *Server density*: There is only one copy of the OS; you can often create many container images on a given VM server.

- *Startup time*: You do not need any initialization required like the OS; startup time is much faster.

- *Portability*: Containers can run in a variety of environments including public, private, hybrid, or on-prem.

- *Scalability*: They can scale up and down in few seconds without any human intervention.

- *Wide support*: All the cloud providers support containers, and wide community support is available.

VMs have a few limitations. Since there is only a copy of the operating system, you can't run an application written in a different OS on the same server. For example, if your application is running on Windows, Red Hat, or Ubuntu, then all applications in a container run this as a full VM.

Understanding Cloud Services

Cloud computing provides various services delivered on-demand to the customers over the Internet. These services are designed to provide easy, affordable access to applications and resources, without the need for internal infrastructure or hardware.

The cloud services are fully managed by cloud computing providers, as shown in Figure 2-8; they're made available to customers or enterprises from the provider's data center, so there's no need for a company to host the application on its on-premises servers.

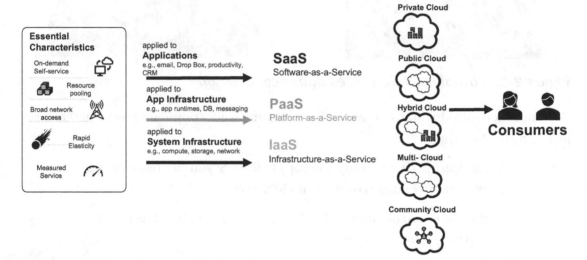

Figure 2-8. *Cloud services*

The benefits of cloud services are the ability to scale, increased flexibility, lowered cost, etc.

The following are the types of services offered by various cloud providers.

Infrastructure as a Service

IaaS is a form of cloud computing that delivers fundamental compute, network, and storage resources to consumers on-demand over the Internet and on a pay-as-you-go basis. IaaS enables consumers to scale and shrink resources on an as-needed basis. This service reduces an enterprise's need for high, up-front capital expenditure or unnecessary procured infrastructure.

IaaS consists of a collection of physical and virtualized resources, as shown in Figure 2-9, that provide consumers with the building blocks needed to run business applications.

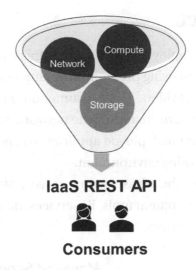

Figure 2-9. *IaaS*

IaaS providers manage large data centers across geographies that contain the physical and virtual machines and create a layer on top of these servers over the web. The end users do not interact directly with the physical infrastructure in the data center but are provided as REST services to them with parameters.

IaaS is typically a virtualized environment; IaaS providers manage the hypervisors, and end consumers can provision them through program and REST APIs with the desired amount of compute and memory for different types of use cases.

Networking in a cloud environment is defined by the software, and the consumer can access the required networking resources such as routers and switches through REST APIs. A consumer can create a virtual private cloud (VPC) on a single DC or multi-DC.

IaaS offers three types of storage options, listed here:

- *Block storage*: Block storage is used to store data files on a storage area network (SAN).

- *File storage*: File storage is a hierarchical storage methodology like the file or folder organization on your PC. The file storage can be organized on hardware or a network-attached storage (NAS) device.

- *Object storage*: This type of storage stores large amounts of unstructured data such as images, documents, etc. This data is organized in a folder called a *bucket*.

Platform as a Service

With PaaS, the consumer can deploy onto the cloud infrastructure consumer-created or acquired applications written using programming languages, libraries, services, and tools supported by the cloud providers. The consumer does not manage or control the underlying cloud infrastructure, including the network, servers, operating system, or storage, but has control over the deployed applications and possibly configuration settings for the application-hosting environment.

Like IaaS, the PaaS includes the infrastructure: servers, storage, and networking. The middleware services, development tools, BI services, data services, etc., as shown in Figure 2-10, will be used IaaS services.

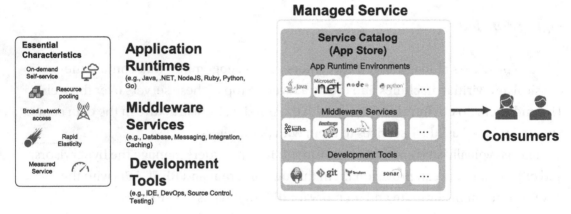

***Figure 2-10.** Platform as a service*

PaaS Taxonomy

As of 2020, Gartner has identified 21 categories of xPaaS offerings, as shown in Figure 2-11, which refer to a particular type of application infrastructure functionality. aPaaS and xPaaS can be used together or independently.

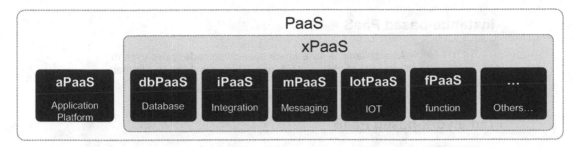

Figure 2-11. *PaaS taxonomy*

The application platform as a service (aPaaS) platform consists of the following:

- Automated deployment of code (IaC)

- Multitenant platform

- Service catalog

- Provisioning middleware services

- Provisioning development tools

- Tenant management

- Role-based access

- DevOps tools

PaaS Architecture Styles

The PaaS architecture style is a family of architectures that share certain characteristics. The architecture styles don't require the use of particular technologies, but some technologies or services are well suited for certain styles. The architecture styles in Figure 2-12 are not related to any xPaaS and can be used across xPaaS services.

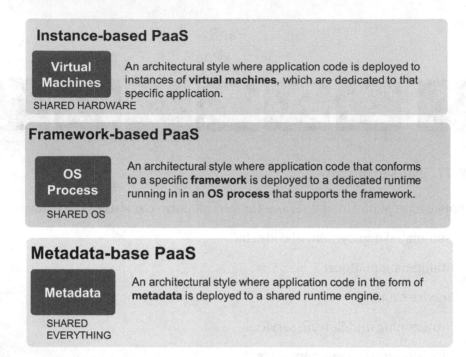

Figure 2-12. *PaaS architecture styles*

PaaS Deployment Model

The PaaS model can be deployed in three ways, as shown in Figure 2-13.

> *Public cloud model*: The PaaS capability provisioned for use by the general public over the Internet. The characteristics of the public cloud model are elasticity, utility pricing, and leverage of expertise, and a public cloud can be shared with all tenants with limited customization.

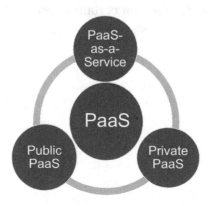

Figure 2-13. *PaaS deployment model*

Private PaaS model: The PaaS capability provisioned for exclusive use by a single organization. It offers the same characteristics of the public cloud, such as elasticity and resource utilization but with total control and regulation flexibility. This type of model can run in the cloud or on-premises.

PaaS-as-a-service model: The PaaS capability is provisioned for exclusive use by a single organization and managed by a third party. It offers the same characteristics of both public and private PaaS but is managed privately by a single organization.

The following are some PaaS limitations and concerns:

- *Data security*: The enterprises can run their developed apps and APIs using PaaS platforms. The data will reside on the vendor platform. The vendor-controlled cloud servers pose a concern. Every enterprise needs to do a thorough security review with the vendor before using services.

- *Vendor lock-in*: The enterprises make decisions based on certain requirements that drive them to use certain PaaS solutions; these decisions may not apply in the future due to business and technology disruption. Enterprises need to review the migration policies when moving to another vendor.

Software as a Service

SaaS is essentially on-demand software that is provided to the client over the Internet. SaaS has found more traction from small and midsize enterprises primarily due to its low capital and operational overhead.

According to Wikipedia, "SaaS is a software licensing and delivery model in which software is licensed on a subscription basis and is centrally hosted. It is sometimes referred to as on-demand software and was formerly referred to as software plus services by Microsoft. SaaS applications are also known as web-based software, on-demand software, and hosted software."

Figure 2-14 shows a high-level view of the SaaS architecture. SaaS utilizes the Internet to provide services that are managed by third-party vendors. Most SaaS applications run directly through your web browser via an API.

> *Client apps*: Application modules/features that a client subscribed to as a service, provided by SaaS.

> *SaaS layer*: Provides common and cross-product functional and technical services and abstracts the SaaS services.

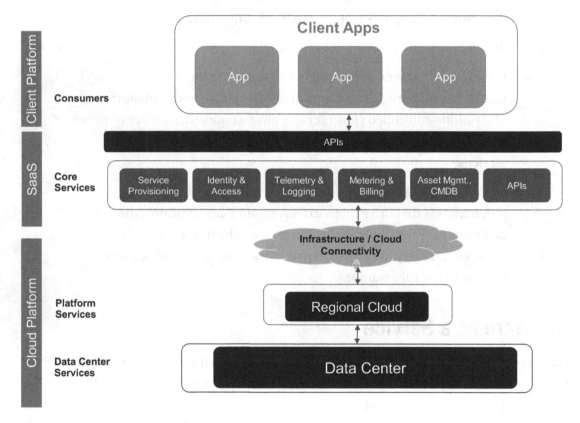

Figure 2-14. *SaaS architecture*

> *Platform layer*: Provides virtualized computing power, storage, networking, and cloud availability zones.

> *Data center services*: Provides the physical facility, network services, etc.

SaaS provides numerous advantages to enterprises by reducing operational activity such as installing and managing applications.

Common software offered vi a SaaS model includes sales software, CRM solutions, tax software, etc.

SaaS Limitations

The following are the limitations of SaaS:

- *Vendor lock-in*: It is easy to join SaaS services but difficult to leave. Most SaaS providers are not flexible on portability and compatibility, so it takes a huge amount of time to port from one vendor application to another.

- *Interoperability*: It is not easy to integrate SaaS applications with an existing legacy application. You need to modify existing applications to the vendor's SaaS APIs. Sometimes you may require a separate integration layer for consumer SaaS services.

- *Data security*: SaaS software holds most of your business data. Security at rest and security in transit are concerns, even though all the APIs are security enabled and data is stored with encryption.

Architectural Considerations: How to Decide on a Custom vs. SaaS Platform

You can compare a custom platform to a SaaS platform solution, as shown in Figure 2-15. Identify the key contrasting dimensions and compare the architect's involvement in those dimensions across the two platforms.

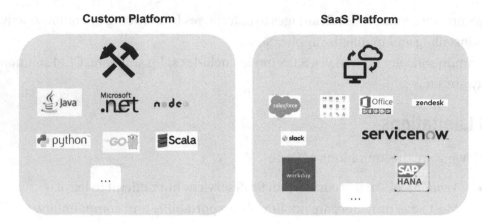

Figure 2-15. *Custom and SaaS platforms*

Table 2-1 shows the key factors to use when comparing custom and SaaS platforms.

Table 2-1. *Custom vs. SaaS Platform*

Factors	Custom Platform	SaaS Platform
Customization	By definition is fully customized to your needs.	Meets most needs based on your requirements but does not necessarily meet them 100 percent.
Continuously evolving for business disruption	A custom platform can keep up-to-date with the business requirements and optimization and standards. However, every enhancement must undergo development, which has its pros and cons.	A SaaS platform keeps close watch on business disruption and continuously improves its product features.
Integration	You can design your custom-built software to integrate with any software and with any protocols.	Open APIs allow most SaaS solutions to integrate with a wide range of third-party software.

(continued)

Table 2-1. (*continued*)

Factors	Custom Platform	SaaS Platform
Cost impact	It is expensive due to team setup and must go through the entire SDLC process.	It is cheap and based on the subscription cost model. This eliminates up-front cost, and SaaS providers indirectly distribute the development costs across all subscribers.
Delivery and deploy maturity	Custom platforms have a mature DevOps process with the presence of continuous integration and continuous delivery. Implementation takes its own time.	May not have high DevOps maturity; a SaaS platform allows custom language and platform code storage. The DevOps process is dependent on the built-in tooling of the SaaS provider. Implementation is quick.
Platform upgrades	Upgrades can be seamless based on requirements.	The upgrades are vendor driven, and sometimes certain vendors are required for upgrades.
Data	You are owning your data.	You leave your data with the vendor you are subscribed to.

The chart in Table 2-2 indicates the extent of various indicators on both the custom and SaaS platforms.

Table 2-2. *Custom vs. SaaS Platform Indicators*

	Customization	Functional Evolvement	Integration	Cost Impact	Delivery & Deploy	Platform Upgrades	Data
Custom Platform	●	●	●	●	●	●	●
SaaS Platform	●	●	●	●	●	●	●

Both custom and SaaS are good solutions, but you need to evaluate which one is best for you based on your business requirements and other needs. In some cases, SaaS is good. As mentioned, you do not have any operational and management headaches compared to custom, and in some cases customization is good for custom software. It is important to evaluate alternatives on both sides of the development spectrum and choose the option that is best for your business requirements. SaaS services like Gmail, Office 365, etc., are difficult to customize, but it is better to use these SaaS services instead of reinventing the wheel.

Cloud Computing Deployment Models

As cloud computing adoption has increased, several different deployment strategies have emerged to help you to meet the specific needs of your enterprise. Each type of cloud service and deployment method provides you with different levels of control, flexibility, and management. Various models can be utilized to deploy the application in production. Understanding different deployment models, as shown in Figure 2-16, will help you to decide what set of services is right for your needs.

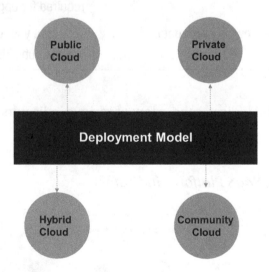

Figure 2-16. *Cloud deployment model*

A cloud deployment model is defined according to where the infrastructure for the deployment resides and who has control over the infrastructure.

Deciding which deployment model you will choose is one of the important organization strategies. Each cloud deployment model satisfies different organizational needs, so it is important to choose a model that meets your strategy. One of the main strategies is based on the value proposition and cost associated with it.

Public Cloud

In public cloud computing, the use of computing resources and software is based on the subscription model. The resources are provisioned for open use by the public and various organizations. The architecture of the public cloud is a multitenant type. This kind of architecture allows you to share resources across organizations and applications, but data is isolated from each other, and there will be a stricter security firewall between tenants. A multitenant is like houses on one floor of an apartment, with each apartment separated by walls, but with the common area being shared by all apartments on that floor.

The flexibility, reliability, scalability, and cost are advantages of the public cloud.

Private Cloud or On-Premises Cloud

In private cloud computing, the infrastructure is used by a single organization. Such an infrastructure is managed within an organization or dedicated infrastructure in the cloud. Technically, there is no difference between the public and private clouds. We often think that a private cloud is only on-premises, but that assumption is not true; you can deploy your application entirely on a private cloud at various cloud providers and provision exclusive use by a single organization comprising multiple portfolios within an organization.

The private cloud offers some benefits and features the public cloud, but there is no compromise of security on both the public and private clouds. A private cloud may be necessary due to various compliances and regulations like HIPAA, PCI DSS, etc.

The benefits of the private cloud are flexibility in the deployment and customization of infrastructure based on your requirements, but all these come with a cost, so the price of this model is higher than the public cloud.

Community Cloud

In community cloud computing, multiple organizations share computing resources that are part of a community. The community must have a shared concern, for example, shared policies, SLAs, shared security requirements, etc. The concern may be owned by one organization or a third-party provider, and it may exist on or off-premises.

Hybrid

A hybrid model is a combination or composition of two or more distinct cloud infrastructures, such as private, public, or community. It is a way to connect infrastructure and applications between cloud-based resources and existing enterprise resources that reside in your data center. This model is most adopted across organizations. A hybrid cloud architecture helps organizations to integrate their on-premises and cloud operations to support various use cases using a set of cloud service tools and APIs on-premises and across cloud environments.

Cloud Services

Table 2-3 lists the main feature services of three cloud providers: AWS, Azure, and Google.

Table 2-3. *Main Services of Top Three Cloud Providers*

Product Type	AWS	Azure	GCP
Compute	EC2	Azure VM	Compute Engine
Serverless	Lambda	Azure Functions	App Engine Cloud Function
Containers	Elastic Container Service (ECS) Elastic Kubernetes Service (EKS)	Container Instances Azure Kubernetes Service (AKS)	Google Kubernetes Engine (GKE)

(continued)

Table 2-3. (*continued*)

Product Type	AWS	Azure	GCP
RDBMS	Aurora	Azure SQL	Cloud Spanner
NoSQL	DynamoDB	Cosmos DB	Cloud BigTable
Object storage	S3	Blob	Cloud Storage
Caching	ElastiCache	Azure Redis	Memorystore
Managed database (MySQL/PostgreSQL)	RDS	Azure Database	Cloud SQL
Event-driven	SQS, MQ, SNS	Event Hubs	Pub/Sub
Streaming	Kinesis, Kafka		Kafka
Data warehouse	Redshift, EMR		Bigquery
Developer tools	AWS DevOps		GCP Developer Tools
Monitoring and OpsWorks	CloudWatch, CloudTrail, OpsWork		Cloud Monitoring, Cloud Trace, logging
Security	Identity and access Cognito CloudHSM WAF		Cloud key management, workloads
API integration	Gateway	API management	Cloud endpoints

Cloud service providers offer all types of services to develop and deploy cloud native applications. Depending on the maturity of the organization and the skills of its employees, starting the cloud native journey might mean leveraging basic services such as the ones mentioned in the table. Adopting these services is a bare-minimum step to developing cloud native applications. You can use a combination of various cloud services to develop a cloud native application. For example, you can use containers, NoSQL, event-driven architecture, monitoring, and API integration to develop a microservices application; all these combinations depend on the use cases and resources within your organization. Along with the major cloud providers, there are various vendors such as Alibaba, IBM, OpenShift, and VMware Tanzu. Lots of financial clients and other industries are embracing OpenShift and Tanzu. Recently I used OpenShift for payment infrastructure.

Summary

This chapter covered how infrastructure has evolved from mainframes to the present-day containers. We also looked at some principles behind this evolution that helped you to reduce the infrastructure costs.

To illustrate the evolution of servers, we covered bare-metal servers, VMs, and containers, and we provided the scenarios for which you would adopt them.

We explained types of cloud services such as IaaS, PaaS, and SaaS, and when to use SaaS over custom services, etc. We talked about their usage and provided the details of the featured cloud services of major cloud providers.

We explained the different cloud deployment options like the public cloud, private cloud, community cloud, and hybrid cloud.

The next chapter provides more about the principles of cloud native architecture.

CHAPTER 3

Cloud Native Architecture Principles

Cloud native principles define the underlying general rules and guidelines for the use and architecture of your system. They reflect a level of consensus for the various elements of your system and enterprise and offer a basis for making future decisions. The principles are typically created at the same time as the architecture is defined.

Without architecture principles, your enterprises has no compass to guide its journey from its current state to its future cloud native state and no standard way to measure its progress.

In this chapter, we will cover the following principles; some have existed for three to four decades, but they are still very much relevant in modern cloud native architecture and design.

- Orthogonal architecture principles such as coupling and cohesion

- Principles such as KISS, DRY, isolate, encapsulate, group-related function, use layering

- The SOLID design principles such as single responsibility, open-close principle, Liskov substitution, interface segregation, etc.

- Modern architecture principles such as automated deployment, no single point of failure, polylithic and polyglot, API first, event-driven, choreography, etc.

- Cloud native architecture principles such as infrastructure independent, location independent, resilient to latency, etc.

- Development principles such as shift-left testing, shift-left security, containerization, infrastructure as code, agile, etc.

© Shivakumar R Goniwada 2022
S. R. Goniwada, *Cloud Native Architecture and Design*, https://doi.org/10.1007/978-1-4842-7226-8_3

What Are Architecture Principles?

A principle is a law or rule that is usually followed when making key architecture decisions. It's important to note that principles are not commandments; exceptions are acceptable when necessary.

Architecture and design principles play a critical role in guiding the software architecture work that includes defining an enterprise's future direction and the transitions it needs to reach the future state of architecture. The principles are usually created at the beginning of the architecture definition and are reviewed and ratified by the architecture board. While defining principles, you need to align with the existing enterprise's principles.

Architecture and design principles define the fundamental assumptions of the IT organization when creating and maintaining the IT capabilities. Without principles, IT projects have no compass to guide their journey. Without a common set of principles, the executives in an IT organization will be left on their own to determine which projects will be funded, which assets will be leveraged, which cloud model will be used, etc.

It is useful to understand the definition of various architecture and design principles. In addition, you need to understand the associated rationale and implications of these principles. The most important step is to promote these principles across all the stakeholders and development teams so that the adoption of the principles will achieve the desired result.

Architecture and design principles are usually developed by architects and designers, in conjunction with various key stakeholders, and all the defined principles must be clearly traceable and clearly articulated to guide the decision-making.

According to TOGAF,

> *"A good set of principles will be founded in the beliefs and values of the organization and expressed in language that the business understands and uses. Principles should be few in number, future-oriented, and endorsed and championed by senior management. They provide a firm foundation for making architecture and planning decisions, framing policies, procedures, and standards, and supporting the resolution of contradictory situations. A poor set of principles will quickly become discussed, and the resultant architectures, policies, and standards will appear arbitrary or self-serving, and thus lack credibility. Essentially, principles of driver behavior."*

These are six criteria to distinguish a good set of principles:

- *Understandable*: The principles should be written in plain language that is easy to understand.

- *Robust*: The principles should enable good-quality decisions about the architecture and plans.

- *Complete*: The statements must be accurate and complete.

- *Consistent*: All the principles must be consistent and work together.

- *Stable*: The principles should be enduring and accommodate change when required.

- *Resilience*: Failure is unavoidable in systems; these principles enable companies to self-heal quickly from difficulties.

Cloud Native Design Principles

The following sections cover cloud native design principles.

API First Principle

Using an application programming interface (API) is not a new approach in IT, as APIs have been used in IT for more than 20 years. But APIs were limited to specific internal applications.

The *API first principle* is the de facto principle of modern architecture. Every application is designed and developed with the API first principle. This principle allows all implementation details to be exposed through APIs to the consumers and encourages the application design and development teams to have resources accessible through REST HTTP interfaces.

The API first approach means designing an API so that it has consistency, as well as adaptability, regardless of the type of projects. The API first principle is as follows:

- The API is the first user interface of an application.

- The API comes first and then the implementation.

- The API is described.

- The API is contracted between the provider and the consumer.

For example, let's say client 1 and client 2 are two client-facing applications, as shown in Figure 3-1, and interact with various users by consuming its implementation in services A, B, and C through APIs via API management. The APIs are contracts between clients 1 and 2 with services A, B, and C.

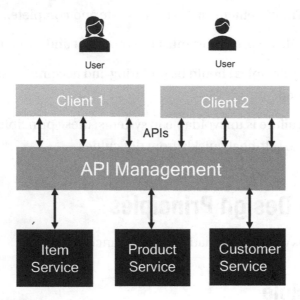

Figure 3-1. *API management*

These are the benefits of the API first principle:

- *Development teams can work in parallel*: API first involves establishing the contract. Creating a contract between services that are followed by the team across enterprises allows those teams to work on multiple APIs at the same time.

- *Reduces the cost of developing an application*: The reusability of the API first approach allows code to be recycled from project to project so that development teams always have a baseline architecture with which they can work.

- *Increases speed to market*: Automated discoverable APIs have the ability to be discovered quickly and automate development with readily available tools like Swagger.

- *Improved developer experience*: The consumers of APIs are most often the development team. API first ensures the developers have a positive experience using APIs.

- *Reduce the risk of failure*: The possibility of error is greatly reduced due to the inherent reliability and consistency of the design and implementation.

Monolithic Architecture Principle

The *monolithic architecture principle* (MAP) is building the architecture as a single unit with a single codebase. Most applications in an enterprise are based on this principle because enterprises have been using this approach for ages. Sometimes these applications are called multitiered applications and use the Model-View-Controller (MVC) pattern. The monolithic architecture can expose APIs to the client applications and also focus on desktop/laptop devices with a web browser as a client, as shown in Figure 3-2.

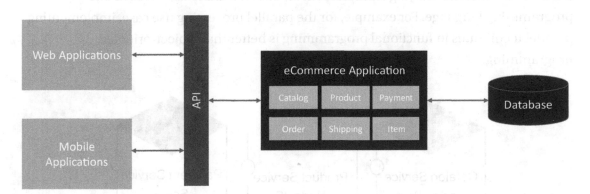

Figure 3-2. *Monolithic application*

The following are the drawbacks of monolithic applications:

- Scaling a monolithic application is a challenge.

- It is difficult to embrace agility.

- Monolithic applications require more infrastructure due to scaling the entire application irrespective of load.

- Monolithic applications are not business friendly, do not support business disruption, and are slow to market.

Polylithic Architecture Principle

The polylithic architecture principle (PAP) provides a different variant of microservices. Each microservice provides domain functionality. These separated modules are consolidated through several programming techniques. This principle refers to a technology-agnostic approach of building systems as a composition of multiple mini/microarchitectures for the granular subsystem.

The PAP simplifies your back-end services and tools by enabling you to construct them as modular monoliths using composable components.

In the polylithic principle, you create a domain-based service by using a domain-driven design methodology. Most communication within the polylithic system is done using industry-standard communication protocols.

Applying the Polylithic Principle in Architecture

An e-commerce platform, as shown in Figure 3-3, will deal with many types of business functionality instead of trying to implement all these business use cases in one programming language. For example, for the parallel processing use case, implementing parallel techniques in functional programming is better than object-oriented programming.

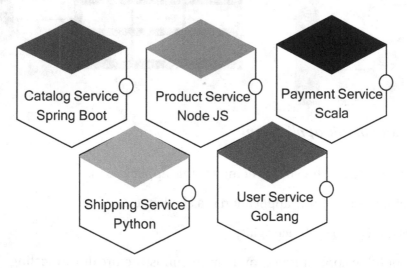

Figure 3-3. *Microservices with polylihic programming languages*

Properties of Polylithic Principles

The simplicity of a domain-based service makes for good building blocks of code. But the architecture approach will be incomplete without a discussion about the essential properties that enable, deliver, and sustain operations.

- *Encapsulation*: Services hide their implementation and expose only their signature.

- *Simplicity*: Services have a single responsibility.

- *Stateless*: Services are just code; they don't contain state or instances.

- *Purity*: Services can be pure, which makes them easy to understand, reuse, test, and parallelize.

The polylithic principle refers to an approach of a building system as a composition of multiple granular subsystems, each of which has its specialized architectures selected to suit specific needs on a best-fit basis.

- Each granular subsystem will be housed in its container environment and isolated from other subsystems.

- Each subsystem will take exclusive ownership of data and provide access through a well-defined published interface.

To support change management, polylithic principle will also make backward compatibility and interface versions aware of first-class architectural concerns, which means that each subsystem will support the coexistence of multiple versions of the same service.

Polyglot Persistence Principle

Neal Ford coined the term *polyglot* in 2006 to express the idea that applications should be written in a mix of languages to take advantage of the fact that different languages are suitable for different problems. The polyglot persistence principle is about is choosing the way data is stored based on the way data is being used by individual applications. In short, you need to pick the right storage for the right kind of data.

Applying the Polyglot Persistence Principle in Architecture

Let's take the example of Martin Fowler's ecommerce application, as shown in Figure 3-4 (Amazon, Flipkart, JioMart, etc.), that can be broken down into many microservices such as catalog, user, audit, inventory, etc. Storing all this data in one single monolithic database would be a nightmare. Instead, use the appropriate database technologies for the respective use cases.

Figure 3-4. *Polyglot persistence*

Modeled with Business Domain Principle

The *modeled with business domain principle* (MBDP) is about using domain-driven design (DDD), which will be explained in Chapter 10.

DDD is an approach for developing software for complex needs by deeply connecting the implementation to an evolving model of the core business concept.

DDD is needed to decouple the existing system that you do not have any knowledge of or a large enterprise with a complex map of departments and systems, for which you are asked to implement a solution that is coherent and works seamlessly.

When you are applying this principle, follow the nine steps shown in Figure 3-5 of event storming to identify the microservices.

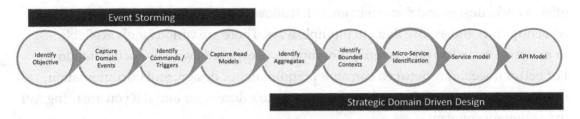

Figure 3-5. DDD with event storming

When you are identifying microservices by using this principle, some designers try to separate the parts by business domain and domain entities, users, and individual requests from the UI, but this leads to your design becoming data-oriented and technical-centric and doesn't help you to design your microservices across business capabilities. Always think of each request or service as a collection of capabilities.

Consumer First Principle

The *consumer first principle* (CFP) is about designing your API services to the consumers, before starting any design activity. The first thing is that you need to analyze what a consumer wants. It is not about consumer rights advocacy, but it's about recognizing that when we create all these services for the consumer, the services need to be called by all types of consumers.

Before the start any services design, you need to ask questions like, do you know who your consumers are? Do you know where they are in an organization? Do you have any collaboration with which you can interact? In nutshell, you need to have the full request details before initiating a design.

Every design starts with the basics, meaning consumer-driven contracts, as those contracts define for your consumers the process in your microservices.

Next, you need to decide on standards and consistency across all APIs. In the consumer-first approach, each person or design team defines their APIs differently. Some teams define them with nouns, some teams define with verbs, and some teams handle user search, error handling, and pagination in different ways. To address this, you need to define an organizational standard for API design that will be useful for API governance and operations.

You need to make sure you define the documentation for APIs. For anyone in a client organization who wants to consume an API, knowing what the API does is important. There are many ways to create a document, but nowadays developers use Swagger effectively to design and document an API. It allows you to define metadata about API endpoints and expose them in multiple ways. There are various tools available to annotate metadata on your endpoints and have exposed Swagger documentation. For better traceability between consumer requirements, design, and documentation, integrate Confluence, JIRA, and Swagger or create a developer portal if you are using API management software.

Decentralize Everything Principle

The *decentralize everything principle* (DEP) is about providing self-direction, self-sufficiency, and self-reliance to cloud native development, deployment, and governance; this provides much freedom to the development community to think, develop, and deploy each service.

When you're thinking about decentralization, you need to provide autonomy to solve the problem without necessarily having to coordinate with lots of other people, but coordination is required but not at the extent of snatching freedom from the core problem-solving team. Teams building microservices prefer a different approach to standards too, rather than using a set of the standard defined by a centralized team. Netflix is a good example of an organization that follows this philosophy.

In software development, the decentralization to be adopted is as follows; note that not every problem is a nail, and not every solution a hammer:

- Decentralize microservices that are isolated from other microservices to help the team to achieve concerns such as testability, extensibility, scalability, etc. Apply domain-driven design and bounded context to decentralize domain-based microservices.

- Deploy microservices independently on any environment without affecting other services, use containers, and use Kubernetes technology by using infrastructure as code.

- Decentralize governance, popularized by Amazon. This promotes innovation and speed to market.

- Decentralize DevOps, and let each team have its pipeline with the various self-service tools. Centralizing the tools doesn't help.

- Decentralize data management, and use the polyglot principle to decentralize data for each microservice. But be cautious about licenses, data dependency, transactions, etc.

In the end, you need to know that decentralizing everything doesn't ease your problem. Sometimes it can get out of control. To mitigate this, you need to audit each team regularly.

Culture of Automation Principle

The *culture of automation principle* (CAP) states that it's imperative for organizations to first create a foundation that is conducive for automation. Automation must be threaded into the company culture and fully embraced across the business at all levels.

Apparently, 75 percent of an IT professional's time is spent "keeping the lights on," with the remaining 25 percent focused on innovation that moves their business forward. Everyone wants to flip those percentages.

Look at how Netflix, Amazon, Google, etc., are embracing cloud native, and the time it took them to get up to speed moving from a few hundred services to thousands of services into production: all of that work was centered around the culture of automation, tooling, and discipline. A few teams in your organization are probably pretty good at automating their everyday work, but the challenge is to apply a culture of automation across the entire enterprise so that the organization can drive toward the common goal of developing applications faster and more efficiently.

The most important thing in automation is developer mindset and quality; when developers check in the code in SCM tools, they should be confident that the code can go into production. Modeling the process from check-in through production, I get my release candidate, move my code through my pipeline, and think it's good enough for the build; if it fails a test, I move the next version through, and hopefully, I can move it into the production environment. This sort of automation and visibility of the quality of the software is key in enterprises because we want to move software as quickly as possible without human intervention. Once base automation available, you can leverage the AI-driven development principle to take it further and develop a foundation for streamlining processes, accelerating application production and deployment, and allowing everyone to learn from each other.

The following best practices should be helpful to adopt a culture of automation:

- Change the mindset.

- Create an automation community of practice.

- Have a common repository for automation code.

- Create a product mindset, not a project mindset.

- Treat automation as a product, not a project.

- Embrace AI in your automation process.

Always Be Architecting Principle

One of the core objectives of cloud native applications is the *always be architecting principle* (AbAP), which means always keep evolving. You should always use this principle when you are architecting the system as your application seeks to refine, simplify, and improve the architecture to support business disruption, organization change, system change, and technology disruption. Dead, rigid IT systems bring the organization to a standstill and are unable to support business disruption.

Cloud native architecture does not replace traditional architecture, but it is better adapted to the very different environment of the cloud.

Interoperability Principle

The interoperability principle is an enterprise architecture principle that states that software and hardware should conform to defined standards that promote interoperability for data, applications, and technology platforms.

Enterprise architecture frameworks state the principle as follows:

- The ability of a system to use the parts of another system

- The ability of a business entity to use functionality or information provided by another business entity

Interoperability improvement across applications and business can be realized through the following objectives:

- Design your application based on open industry best practices; this helps your application interoperate across any public, private, or hybrid cloud infrastructure.

- Design your application with industry best practices and standards; therefore, the information and services are shared across various other applications in an enterprise.

Here's how to manage the interoperability across various architecture segments:

- At the architecture level, you need to specify and/or define how you exchange or share information across various modules or systems.

- At the data level, you need to specify and/or define information exchange model details and the content of the information exchange.

Here's how to apply interoperability in architecture:

- *User experience integration*: A common look-and-feel approach is used to access the underlying functionality of the applications.

- *Information integration*: A commonly accepted corporate ontology is followed for seamlessly sharing information across applications.

- *Application integration*: Use choreography or the orchestration principle to seamlessly link functionality to avoid duplication.

- *Technical integration*: Use common methods to share data across application platforms and communication infrastructure domains.

Digital Decoupling Principle

The *digital decoupling principle* (DDP) was coined by Accenture and is as follows

> *"A process of using new technologies, development methodologies and migration methods to build systems that execute strategy on top of legacy systems. The organization can decouple the rapid execution of their business strategy from the lengthy and gradual transformation of the enterprises."*

> —Accenture

When applied to the enterprise landscape, digital decoupling leads to exponential IT, a scalable, flexible, and resilient architecture that gives companies the agility to innovate.

A few examples of DDP include data meshes, APIs, agile, DevSecOps, journey to cloud, microservices, RPA, and automation, as shown in Figure 3-6. Using these approaches, enterprises can gradually decouple their core systems, migrating critical customer-facing functionality and data to new service-based platforms.

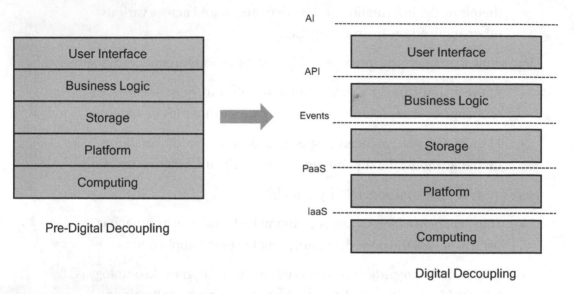

Figure 3-6. *Digital decoupling*

Here are some tips to achieve digital decoupling in your enterprise:

- Automate using RPA.

- Utilize cloud native to quickly build microservices.

- Use a data lake or data mesh with real-time eventing capabilities.

- Adopt API first and consumer first principles.

- Use interactions that react in real time to use behavior.

- Use systems of intelligence to enable smart interactions.

- Remove conflicts of interest and increase agility and enable future replacement.

- Do not use batches; the systems go straight through with minimal human interaction.

- Leverage cloud capabilities to isolate the infrastructure and platform.

By adopting DDP, enterprises can focus on continuous modernization without the pain of wholesale migration of legacy systems. The more systems are decoupled, the more enterprises can evolve toward an even greater service-based exponential IT architecture that maximizes agility. This approach helps manage costs, diminishes the accumulation of technical debt, and significantly reduces legacy transformation risk.

Single Source of Truth Principle

The *single source of truth principle* (SSOTP) is not a tool but a practice of aggregating the data from many sources in an enterprise to a single location. In an enterprise, data exists everywhere, and this data exists in silos and does not help a business to make data-driven decisions. Without a single source, how can an organization improve the efficiency and effectiveness of its operational environment, its transparency, and its future growth?

If the company does not have any single authentic source of information, it often spends far too much time debating the accuracy of numbers, and this hinders the decision-making ability and loses competition to their peers.

Use various tools and techniques to aggregate data from across systems in an enterprise to a single location in near real time so the team can run business intelligence tools to generate the required information.

Evolutionary Design Principle

The main idea of the *evolutionary design principle* (EDP) is that design elements are changeable later. When you build in an evolutionary change in your architecture, changes will become cheaper and easy.

Traditionally, software architecture and design phases have been considered as an initial discovery phase. In this approach, the architecture and design decisions were considered valid for the entire life of the system.

In a modern system architecture and design, you need to assume that you don't have all the required details up front. As a result, having a detailed design phase at the beginning of the project is impractical. The domain services must evolve through iteration, and services mature as they progress. This evolution is necessary for modern-day architecture, which necessitates a different set of approaches in the direction of continuous planning, continuous integration, integrated monitoring, and tools thus providing guiderails for the system to evolve.

As a result of this principle, the team can build a minimum viable product (MVP) with a set of features and rollout to the users. The development team doesn't need to cover all the design features to roll out features; instead, the development team can focus on the needed pieces and evolve the design as customer feedback comes in. You can freeze initial feedback, refactor, and complete the service.

The following software design patterns (more details in Chapter 4) can be used to achieve evolutionary design:

- Sidecar extends and enhances the main service.

- Ambassador creates helper services that send network requests on behalf of the consumer service or application.

- The chain provides a defined order of starting and stopping containers.

- The proxy provides surrogates or placeholder.

- An iterator is a way to access the elements of aggregate objects.

Infrastructure as code provides additional automation for container images and deploys automatically in any place at any given point of time.

Cloud Native Runtime Principles

These are the cloud native runtime principles.

Isolate Failure Principle (IFP)

Embracing a cloud native architecture doesn't automatically make your system more stable. Designing to isolate failure in your microservices can ensure that your microservices don't become fragile. Microservices are not reliable by default; therefore, you can't assume that your microservices become more resilient or scalable by default.

For example, say you have five microservices in one system, as shown in Figure 3-7. For this system to work, all five services have to be up and running. If any service is down, it may impact the whole process; therefore, all five must be available at any given point of time or the system stops processing all requests. In other words, if one service goes down, it takes them all down.

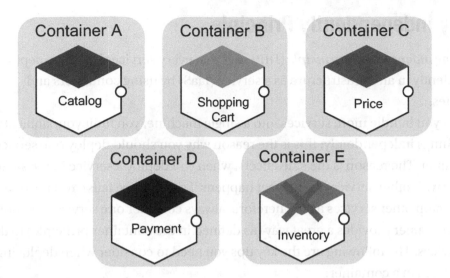

Figure 3-7. *Microservice failure*

If any one of the services fails, the system stops working; if any one of the networks between services stops, it fails, and your services stop working. Therefore, your services are less reliable.

You must consider the failure of microservices so you can avoid the single point of failure. Ask yourself, what happens if one of your services fails? Can your system keep running? Do you even know what happens when your users talk to your services? For example, the user clicks Catalogs, and your application invokes the catalog microservice, and the catalog microservice depends on the inventory microservice for an inventory, but your catalog microservice cannot invoke the inventory services to show the catalog because the inventory microservice is in a failed status. In this case, do you want to stop the whole system, or do you want to allow users to buy a product without availability in the inventory?

A particularly subtle sort of failure that can happen in a distributed system is the cascading failure, where all the way down the chain fails (service A calls service B and service B calls service E); this ripples all the way down the whole system.

A cascading failure can hurt a whole system, and you need to design your system to protect against this. You need to isolate the failure in every part of your system.

Deploy Independently Principle

The *deploy independently principle* (DIP) says that every service should be deployed independently in an infrastructure as a service (IaaS) by using containers and Kubernetes.

When you bundle more services into a single machine, you limit your ability to change things independently; this is the reason why you should deploy one service per container. The reason is the side effects; when you deploy a service in the same container with other services on it, what happens if one service fails? You need to forcefully stop other services also. Therefore, always consider one service per container.

The container provides a great way (as defined in the container principle) to deploy microservices. The following are the key tips you need to consider when deploying microservices in a container:

- Bundle the microservices into a container image.

- Deploy each service instance as a container.

- Deploy state and storage outside of the container.

Be Smart with State Principle

The *be smart with state principle* (BSSP) states when and how you store state in your design. Storing the state is the hardest aspect of architecting a distributed, cloud native architecture. Therefore, architect your system as stateless wherever it is possible.

Stateless means that any state must be stored outside of a container, and this external state can be stored in various storage. By storing data externally, you remove data from the container itself, meaning that the container can be cleanly shut down and destroyed at any time without fear of data loss. If a new container is created to replace the old one, you just connect the new container to the same datastore or bind it to the same disk.

Stateless components are as follows:

- *Easy to destroy and easy to create*: The stateless components have no dependency on the state to carry; therefore, the application in a container can be destroyed and created easily with no hassle.

- *Easy to repair*: If you want to repair failed instances in your deployment, simply terminate gracefully and spin up a replacement.

- *Auto scale/horizontal scale*: To scale more instances, just add more copies; the orchestrator can manage the scale-up and down. This scale can be managed automatically based on load or CPU usage.

- *Rollback*: If you have a wrong deployment, the stateless containers are much easier to replace with new ones without any human intervention.

Load balancing across services is much easier since any instances can serve any request from the requestor. If you have a state for an instance, you need to send a request to the same instance, and this can be managed with sticky sessions.

Location-Independent Principle

The *location-independent principle* (LIP) is about abstracting the physical location of the data from the logical representation that an application on a server uses to access data. In the cloud native application, the location of your deployment does not matter to the end customer or user, but they both should be able to access services ubiquitously and responsively regardless of location.

In a cloud native application, your services do not require you to define where you want to deploy a service, and one service doesn't need to know another service as both services are loosely coupled in nature if the services are required to communicate, though only in terms of API and events, as shown in Figure 3-8.

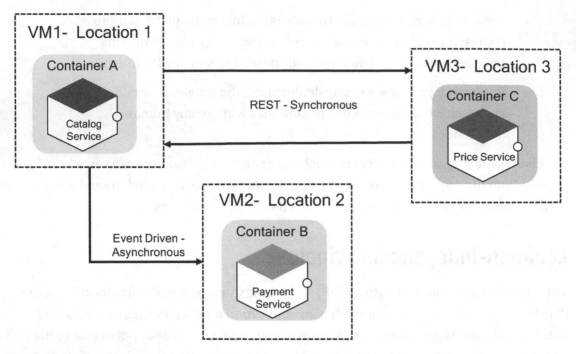

Figure 3-8. *Microservice deployments*

Follow these best practices when implementing location independence:

- Design your services based on a domain model and bounded context, which helps to avoid intercommunication.

- A distributed cloud provides public cloud options to a different physical locations, which helps latency and data privacy and regulations that require certain data to remain in a specific geographic location.

- Use the automation principle to deploy your services on any location.

Design for Failure Principle

The *design for failure principle* (DFFP) states that applications need to be designed so that they can tolerate the failure of services. Since services can fail at any time, it is important to be able to detect the failures quickly and, if possible, automate to restore quickly. Designing a failure means testing the design and watching services cope with deteriorating conditions. Design of failure yields a self-healing application and infrastructure.

Any call to microservices could fail due to the unavailability of the service; the client code must respond to the user as gracefully as possible. This emphasizes the real-time integrated monitoring of the application. Semantic monitoring can provide an early warning system of something going wrong that triggers stakeholders to follow up and investigate.

Designing for failure will help your services have greater availability and customer confidence on your application. Here are the key factors from the 12-factor app pattern methodology (more details in the "Architecture and Design of microservice Chapter 5") that provide best practices when designing for failure:

- *Disposability*: Maximize robustness with fast startup and graceful shutdown. Use lean container images and strive for processes that can start and stop in a matter of seconds.

- *Logs*: Treat logs as event streams. If a system fails, ensure you have collected all the integrated logs to troubleshoot.

- *Dev/prod parity*: Keep development, staging, and production as similar as possible.

Implement the failure as a service model to test all your services; for example, Netflix uses Simian Army or Chaos Monkey to test the failure of services. Amazon's use of a microservices architecture for its application means that the application never goes down, but there could be a problem in individual services. Amazon has built a user interface to gracefully degrade in the face of service failures.

Security Principles

These are security principles.

Defense in Depth Principle

The *defense in depth principle* (DiDP) provides a series of security mechanisms, and controls are layered throughout a computer network to protect the confidentiality, integrity, and availability of services.

Services in a cloud native architecture deploy and process requests for Internet applications, and there will always be a threat from external and internal attacks. Always use an authentication mechanism between services, that increases the trust between those services, whether it is an internal or external service.

You will apply this principle not just for authenticating the services to avoid rate limiting or script injection, but also you should protect your services from any threat. This makes your architecture more resilient and easier to deploy and creates more trust for your services. The DiDP principle ensures network security is redundant, preventing any single point of failure.

An effective DiDP strategy may include the following security best practices, tools, and policies:

- Strong credentials management

- Firewalls

- Intrusion prevention or detection system

- Endpoint detection and response

- Network segmentation

- Patch management

- APIs authentication

- Auditing and accounting

Security by Design Principle

The *security by design principle* (SBDP) means that the product has been designed from the ground up to be secure. The alternate security patterns are researched, and the best are selected and enforced by the architecture design.

Most attacks of any Internet-facing services either in a private or public cloud are performed because of software vulnerabilities. Software vulnerabilities are often found in the design and development lifecycle, so if you ignore any findings, you leave your service exposed to the hands of cybercriminals.

As I mentioned in Chapter 2, cloud applications are made up of IaaS, PaaS, and SaaS. In IaaS, a cloud vendor provides the physical or virtual infrastructure; you are responsible for the administering of network and system infrastructure, applications, and data. With the PaaS model, the cloud provider manages the infrastructure and managed components such as databases, middleware, etc., and you are responsible for the application and data security. In a SaaS model, the cloud provider provides everything from the infrastructure to the application, and you are responsible for access and data.

In a cloud native application, you are responsible for most of your application and data security; therefore, you need to provide utmost importance for security. There are various techniques and best practices available to secure your application.

The following practices help when designing and developing an application:

- *Minimize attack surface area*: This restricts the services that a user can access.

- *Establish secure defaults*: Implement strong security rules for how users are registered to access your services.

- *The principle of least privilege*: The user should have the minimum set of privileges required to perform a special task.

- *The principle of defense in depth*: Add multiple layers of security validations.

- *Fail securely*: Failure is unavoidable; therefore, fail in a secure way.

- *Don't trust services*: Don't trust third-party services without implementing a security mechanism.

- *Separation of duties*: Prevent individuals from acting fraudulently.

- *Avoid security by obscurity*: There should be sufficient security controls in place to keep your application safe without hiding core functionality or source code.

- *Keep security simple*: Avoid the use of very sophisticated architecture when developing security controls.

- *Fix security issues correctly*: Developers should carefully identify all affected systems.

- *Implement shift-left security*: Implement security from the developer box.

The Open Web Application Security Project (OWASP) provides security design techniques and best practices that designers should adopt while designing services. The OWASP updates the list of vulnerabilities often and rates them based on the security reports. You need to well aware of the implementation and adherence of the security risks. The following are the few implementation of OWASP security risks.

SQL Injection

SQL injection is a security risk where a SQL query is input to your query. If an attacker can exploit your SQL query and can read sensitive data from your databases and even modify the data, the consequences are confidentiality, authentication, authorization, and integrity.

- *Standard SQL syntax*: `select id, firstname, lastname from customer;`

- *With query string*: `select id, firstname, lastname from customer where firstname='Peter's' and lastname ='john'`

The database tries to run this example but provides incorrect syntax.

Figure 3-9 shows the correct implementation.

```
String url;
Connection connection = DriverManager.getConnection(url);
String firstname = request.getParameter("firstname");
String lastname = request.getParameter("lastname");
// FIXME: do your own validation to detect attacks
String query = "SELECT id, firstname, lastname FROM customer WHERE firstname = ? and lastname = ?";
PreparedStatement pstmt = connection.prepareStatement( query );
pstmt.setString( 1, firstname );
pstmt.setString( 2, lastname );
try
{
    ResultSet results = pstmt.execute( );
}
```

Figure 3-9. *SQL injection implementation*

Cross-Site Scripting (XSS)

XSS attacks are type of injection like SQL injection; here the attacker injects malicious scripts into a web application. Flaws in your user experience code like Angular, JavaScript, etc., allow these attacks to succeed. XSS attacks occur when:

- Data enters a web application through an untrusted source.

- The data included in the dynamic content is sent to a web user without any proper validation for request.

Implement the following best practices to avoid XSS in your web application:

- Use the OWASP XSS prevention sheet from the OWASP community (`https://cheatsheetseries.owasp.org/cheatsheets`).

- Turn off HTTP trace, or an attacker can steal cookie data.

- Use the proper syntax in your code, don't hard-code, and use variables and parameters.

Here I have provided a few examples. You can find more details and implementation best practices on the OWASP.org community website.

Software Engineering Principle

These are software engineering principles.

Products Not Projects Principle

Amazon states that the core benefit of treating software as a product is an improved end-user experience. When an enterprise treats its software as an always improving product rather than a one-off project, like with the *products not projects principle* (PNPP), it will produce code that is better architected for future work.

Traditionally, enterprises and service organizations delivered software as a project with a set of resources and start and end dates with a list of predefined features. A product-centric development lives for an indefinite period and evolves and has no fixed predefined features.

In the project-centric approach, there will be a little room for iteration and improvement as the software spends a small amount of time in the hands of end users before the budget is exhausted. But in the product-centric approach, you will adopt the MVP approach, where the smallest increment is delivered to real users as soon as possible, so the team can get early feedback that sets the future direction.

The core benefits of treating software as a product are the following:

- Improved end-user experience

- Matured architecture

- Automation and innovation culture

- MVP approach

- Easier to extend, maintain, and test

- More visibility into how their software is performing in real-world scenarios

- Accelerates feedback loop

The following concepts are crucial for adopting a product approach:

- *Automated provisioning with cloud-enabled*: Use the infrastructure automation principle.

- *Self-service, self-healing*: Configure own dependencies and better configuration management by adopting the separation of concerns principle.

- *DevSecOps pipeline with infrastructure as code*: Adopt automation culture.

Shift-Left Principle

The *shift-left principle* (SLP) refers to a practice in software engineering development in which scrum teams can focus on quality, work on problem anticipation instead of detection, and begin testing from the developer system.

This principle in DevOps is a set of a process aimed at the following:

- Finding and preventing defects early in the software delivery lifecycle

- Beginning testing, security, and performance earlier than ever before

- Focusing on quality

The idea of this principle is to improve quality by moving tasks to the left as early in the lifecycle as possible, thus reducing the technical debt and cycle time.

Shift-Left Security

SLP will be applicable to functional, security, and performance testing and related processes, techniques, and tools to be integrated as part of the DevSecOps and developer integrated development environment (IDE).

The shifting left of the security review process requires a new way of developing the application compared to the traditional approach; these changes are not a significant deviation. You need to follow these tips for shift-left security:

- Involve an information security expert early in the lifecycle of the project.

- Use security tools.

- Integrate security tools as part of the continuous integration and as part of the developer IDE.

Shift-Left Performance

Shifting performance testing means enabling developers and testers to conduct performance testing in the early stages of the development lifecycle. Performance means not just a request or stress; actual performance starts with the code and therefore involves practices at the developer level to prevent performance-related issues. To implement the shift-left approach, implement best practices, tools, and techniques as part of the continuous integration pipeline and as part of the developer environment. The following are the best practices to be adopted for shift left:

- Implement performance testing with or in parallel to development activities.

- Include performance testing along with the unit, system, and integration test lifecycles.

- Create performance attributes.

- Integrate tools as part of DevSecOps.

Container Principles

The following are the container principles.

Single Concern Principle

In many ways, the *single concern principle* (SCP) is like the single responsibility principle from SOLID, which says that a module or class must have only one responsibility.

In a cloud native architecture, SCP highlights higher level of single of responsibility. The single responsibility enables you to define a clear boundary for every microservices.

The main motivation for the single responsibility principle is to have a single reason for a change; the main objective of the SCP is for container image reuse and replaceability. You can create a container that addresses a single responsibility with the common feature, and then you can reuse the same container image in different applications without modification and testing.

The SCP principle objective is that every container must address a single resposibility with a microservices architecture style. Always use a single responsibility in the container even though your microservice provides multiple resposnibility. If you have microservices with multiple resposibility, use sidecar and init-containers patterns as explained in Chapter 4 to combine multiple containers into a single deployment unit (pod), where each container still holds single responsibility, as shown in Figure 3-10. You can swap a container that addresses the same responsibility. For example, replace service A container with service C by using infrastructure as code.

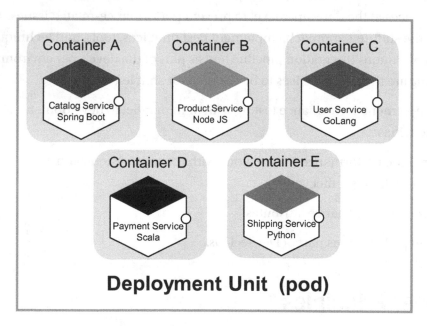

Figure 3-10. *Microservices deployed in separate containers*

High Observability Principle

Observability is a measure of how well internal states of microservices can be derived from external outputs. The concept of observability was introduced by Rudolf E. Kalman for linear dynamic systems.

The observability principle states that an application is said to be observable if one can determine the behavior of the entire application from the application output.

Logs, metrics, traces, liveness, readiness, and process health are known as the pillars of observability, as shown in Figure 3-11, in a cloud native architecture. While having access to these pillars doesn't make your application more observable, you need to create interfaces to access these pillars for further analysis.

Containers provide a unified way of packaging and running microservices by treating the application as a black box. You need to configure containers with APIs to access runtime environments to observe the container health and act accordingly. These are the prerequisite for automating container updates and lifecycles in a unified way, which in turn improves the system's resilience and user experience.

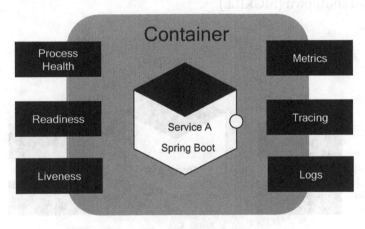

Figure 3-11. *Observability in cloud native application*

You need to design your container and application with APIs for the different kinds of health checks. The microservices should log events into the standard error (STDERR) and standard output (STDOUT) for log aggregation by using tools such as FluentD, Logstash, Nagios, etc., and should integrate with tracing and metrics-gathering libraries such as Zipkin, open tracing, etc.

At runtime, your application is a black box to you; implement the necessary APIs to help the platform observe and manage your application in the best way possible.

Lifecycle Conformance Principle

The *lifecycle conformance principle* (LCP) states that a container should have a way to read the events coming from the platform and conform by reacting to those events.

All kinds of events are available for managing platforms that are intended to help you to manage the lifecycle of the container and microservices, based on all types of available events; it is up to you to decide which events to handle and whether to react to those events or not.

By looking into all sorts of events, you need to pick important events, as shown in Figure 3-12, for example.

- Graceful shutdown process

- Terminate message (SIGTERM)

- Forceful shutdown (SIGKILL)

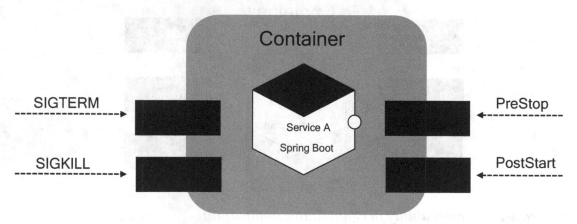

Figure 3-12. *Container lifecycle*

When you issue a `docker stop` command, Docker will wait for 10 seconds to stop the process; if there no action in 10 seconds, then it will forcibly kill the process.

Command to stop process:

$$\$ \ docker \ stop \ Container \ A$$

The docker stop command attempts to stop running the container by sending a SIGTERM signal to the root process in the container; if the process hasn't exited within the timeout period, a SIGKILL signal will be sent.

Command to kill process:

$ docker kill Container A

There are other events such as PreStop and PostStart, which might be significant in your application lifecycle management. For example, some applications need to warm up before a service request, and some need to release resources before shutting down clearly, as shown in Figure 3-13.

```
apiVersion: v1.0
kind: Pod
metadata:
  name: lifecycle-cloudnative
spec:
  containers:
  - name: containerA
    image: nginx
    lifecycle:
      postStart:
        exec:
        command: ["/bin/sh", "-c", "Event from ServiceA >
/usr/share/message"]
      preStop:
        exec:
        command: ["/bin/sh","-c","nginx -s quit; while killall -0 nginx; do sleep
1; done"]
```

Figure 3-13. Configuration file

In this configuration file, you can see how to use the PostStart and PreStop command to write a message file to the container's /usr/share directory. The presto command shuts down Nginx gracefully

Image Immutability Principle

The *image immutability principle* (IIP) states an image is unchangeable once it is built and requires creating a new image if changes need to be made. Container applications like microservices are meant to be immutable. Once you have developed applications, they aren't expected to change between different environments except for runtime data like environment configuration and variables such as listening port, runtime options, etc. You need to store configurations and variables external to the container. For each image change, you need to build a new image and reuse it across various environments in your development lifecycle.

Immutability makes deployments safer and more repeatable. If you need to roll back, you simply redeploy the old image. This approach allows you to deploy the same container image in all your environments. Containers are usually configured with environment variables or configuration files mounted on a specific path. You can use secrets and config maps to inject configurations in containers as environment variables or files of Kubernetes. If you need to update a configuration, deploy a new container (based on the same image) with the updated configuration, as shown in Figure 3-14.

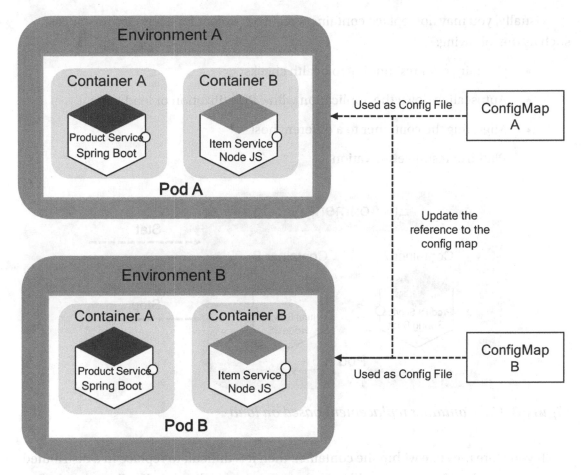

Figure 3-14. *Immutable container images across all environments*

Immutability is one of the best qualities of container-based infrastructure. Immutability along with statelessness allows you to automate deployments and increase their frequency and reliability.

Process Disposability Principle (PDP)

The *process disposability principle* (PDP) is a container runtime principle and states applications must be ephemeral as possible and ready to be replaced with container instances at any point of time by using infrastructure as code, as shown in Figure 3-15.

Usually, you may not replace containers regularly except for a few circumstances such as the following:

- Container not responding to health checks

- Autoscaling down the application with CPU utilization or load

- Migrating the container to a different host

- Platform resource starvation

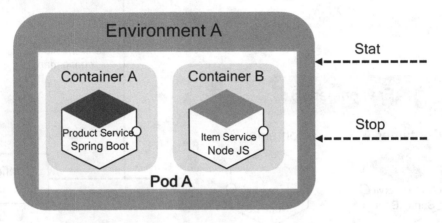

Figure 3-15. *Container replacement based on load*

If you store the state within the container, then it is difficult to replace in a distributed environment; therefore, you should keep their state externalized or distributed and redundant.

Figure 3-16 illustrates how the PDP principle is applied.

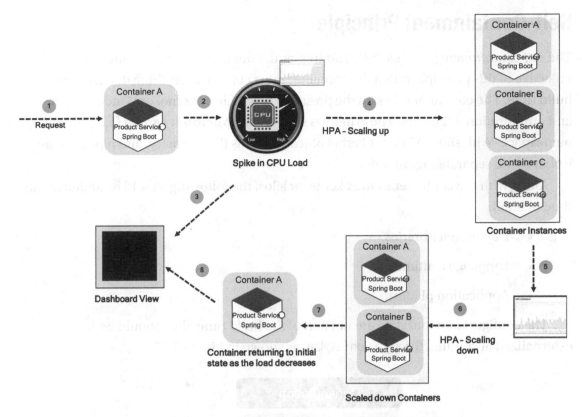

Figure 3-16. *Container scale-up and down based on Spile in CPU*

At the beginning of your day, service A has only one container instance, but as the day progresses and the load increases, the containers autoscale to three instances to meet the demand. The container instances dispose gradually as and when the load decreases, and finally it reaches the original state. This can be achieved by using the PDP.

You need to follow best practices for the size of containers and functionality of microservices. For example, it is better to create small containers, which leads to quicker start and stops because, before the spin of the new container, the containers need to be physically copied to the host system.

Self-Containment Principle

The *self-containment principle* (SCP) addresses the build time concern, and the objective of this principle is that the container must contain everything that it needs at build time. The container relies on the presence of the Linux kernel or Windows silos and any additional libraries. The Windows silos are the Microsoft variant for the Linux namespace. With silos, Windows kernel objects such as files, registry, and pipes can be isolated into separate logical units.

Along with the container's Linux kernel or silos, the following should be added at the time of build:

- Dependent libraries

- Language runtime

- Application platform

The configuration and state are not part of the build time; they should be externalized at runtime through `ConfigMap`, as shown in Figure 3-17.

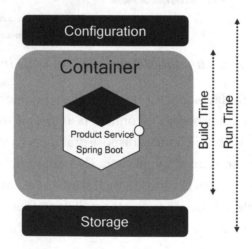

Figure 3-17. *Containers with build and runtime environments*

Some of your applications require multiple container components. For example, your containerized microservices may also require a database container. This principle does not suggest merging both containers; instead, this principle suggests each container requires a dependent configuration to run respective containers.

Runtime Confinement Principle

The *runtime confinement principle* (RCP) states that every container should declare its resource requirements and pass that information to the hosted platform.

The SCP addresses the build-time perspective, and RCP addresses the runtime perspective. The container is not just a single black box, but it has multiple dimensions as follows:

- CPU usage dimension

- Memory usage dimension

- Resource consumption dimension

- Control groups dimension

The container, as shown in Figure 3-18, shares the resource profile of a container to a hosted platform in terms of CPU, memory, networking, and disk influence to specify how the platform performs scheduling, autoscaling, capacity management, and SLAs of the container.

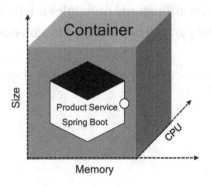

Figure 3-18. *Container runtime characteristics*

In addition to passing the resource requirements to the host platform, it is important that the application stay confined to the indicated resource requirements. If the application stays confined, the platform is less likely to consider it for termination and migration when resource starvation occurs.

Principles of Orthogonal

In mathematics, orthogonality describes the property of two vectors. As shown in Figure 3-19, they are perpendicular, or 90°, to each other. Each vector will advance indefinitely into space, never to intersect.

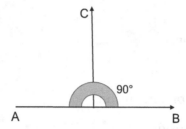

Figure 3-19. *Orthogonal*

Well-architected software is orthogonal, and each of its components or modules can be modified without affecting another. By considering agility in both business and technology, the software applications undergo many changes to support business disruption. The cost of applying orthogonal principles is a little high, but by considering the cost at the end, the overall cost will be managed by considering changeability, testability, extensibility, etc.

The orthogonal design is based on two principles, as shown in Figure 3-20.

- Cohesion

- Coupling

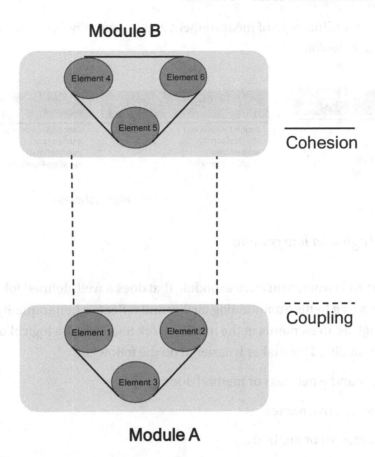

Figure 3-20. *Orthogonal principle*

Cohesion

Cohesion is the degree to which the elements inside a module belong together. It is the strength of the relationship of elements within the module. It is the internal glue that keeps the module together.

It is a measurer that defines the degree of intradependability within elements of a module. The greater the cohesion, the better the program design. It is a natural extension of the information hiding concept.

A cohesive module performs a single task within a software procedure, requiring little interaction with procedures being performed in other parts of a program. We always strive for high cohesion, but sometimes the middle path of the spectrum is always acceptable, as shown in Figure 3-21.

Cohesion is an ordinal type of measurement and is generally described as *high cohesion* and *low cohesion*.

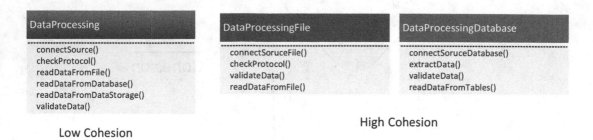

Figure 3-21. *High and low cohesion*

High cohesion is where you have a module that does a well-defined job with similar elements; it gives us a better-maintaining facility and reflects a better quality of a design. Reusability is high as all elements in the module work together as a logical unit of work with clear functionality. This makes it easier to do the following:

- Understand what class or method does

- Use descriptive names

- Reuse classes or methods

Low cohesion is where you have a module that does a lot of unrelated jobs and results in a monolithic module that is difficult to maintain, extend, and test. The extra complexity in modules with low cohesion makes it more likely that defects may be introduced and leads to high technical debt. Reusability is reduced for modules as it performs diverse functionality.

Types of Cohesion

Cohesion is a qualitative measure; the cohesion is measured based on the level of cohesion in a module, as shown in Figure 3-22. Let's examine the type of cohesion.

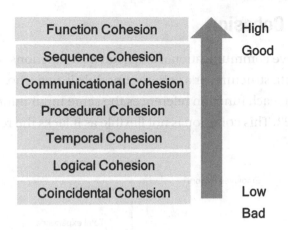

Figure 3-22. *Types of cohesion*

Function Cohesion

This is the highest degree of cohesion. Every essential element for a single computation is contained in the component because they all contributed to a single well-defined function. It can also be reused. Modules with functional cohesion perform exactly one action.

Here are some examples:

- Lexical analysis of XML. Converting a sequence of characters or elements in XML into a sequence of tokens. The group of elements is grouped together to analyze XML.

- Assign a seat to train passengers.

- Calculate the interest rate; calculate the sales commission.

Sequence Cohesion

Sequential cohesion is like a sequential operation. The elements of a module are grouped because of the output from one element and input to another element. This type of cohesion you can see in streaming data or file or ETL jobs.

Here are some examples:

- In an ETL application, the extract, transfer, and load functions are grouped into one module for each data element.

- In streaming, it is the continuous transmission, validation, storage, and display of audio or video of data files.

Communication Cohesion

A module is said to have communicational cohesion if all functions of the module refer to or update the same data structure, or a cohesive module is one whose elements perform different functions, but each function references the same input information or output, as shown in Figure 3-23. This cohesion is not flexible as it lacks the reusability principle.

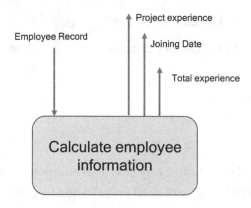

Figure 3-23. *Communication cohesion example*

Procedural Cohesion

Procedural cohesion is when elements of a module are grouped as they always follow a certain sequence of execution and are commonly found at the top of the hierarchy such as the main program. It is like sequential cohesion, as shown in Figure 3-24, except for the elements in the sequence are unrelated in procedural cohesion.

The weakness of procedural cohesion is that actions in a sequence are weakly connected and modules are unlikely reusable.

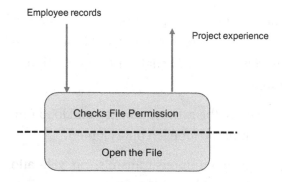

Figure 3-24. *Procedural cohesion example*

These two separate elements in a module are cut along the dotted line. We could do separate activities in each element. Checking the file permission operation can be used for another file also, and we can open the file if no checks are available.

Temporal Cohesion

The elements in this cohesion are related to the time; all the tasks must be executed in the same period.

The actions of this module are weakly related to one another but strongly related to actions in other modules. The elements are not reusable in this cohesion.

For example, consider a module in a digital twin that invokes the factory tasks that are not functionally similar or logically related, but all tasks are needed to happen at the moment when the failure occurs. The module might do the following:

- Cancel all outstanding requests for services.

- Cut power to all assembly line machines.

- Notify the operator console.

- Make an entry in the database.

- Invoke an alarm if a catastrophic failure occurs.

Logical Cohesion

Logical cohesion is when elements of a module are grouped because they are logically categorized to do the same thing, even if they are different by nature.

The following are the drawbacks of logical cohesion:

- The interface is difficult to understand.

- Code for more than one action may be intertwined.

- Reusability is lessened.

The actions of this module are all logically read as input content.

The type of input, as shown in Figure 3-25, tells the module what part of its internal logic to apply to the particular transaction data coming in for each specific invocation.

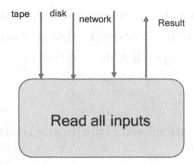

Figure 3-25. Logical cohesion example

Coincidental Cohesion

Coincidental cohesion is when elements of a module are grouped; the only relationship between the parts is that they have been grouped.

- Elements contribute to activities with no meaningful relationship to one another.

The drawbacks of this cohesion are degraded overall application maintainability and that modules are not reusable in nature.

Helper or utility classes in your application, usually utility classes, contain many functions that are unrelated and accessible from various other classes or modules. Changes in one function in the utility class affect the utility class and also the calling class.

Applying High Cohesion to Software Design

Design your application by keeping high cohesion in mind. Each module should have a single well-defined functionality. The elements within the module must be related and perform on the same set of data.

There are ancillary elements in the module that are not directly related, and they work on a different set of variables; consider moving nonrelated functionality into other related modules that have the same purpose.

Coupling

Coupling is the degree of interdependence between software modules or microservices; a coupling measures how closely connected two modules or microservices are and the strength of the relationship between modules or microservices. Coupling tells at what level the modules interface and interact with each other, as shown in Figure 3-26, Figure 3-27, and Figure 3-28. The coupling can be low or weak and high or strong or tight. The degree of the coupling between modules reflects the quality of the design.

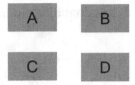

Figure 3-26. *No dependencies*

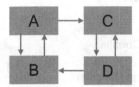

Figure 3-27. *Loosely coupled with some dependencies*

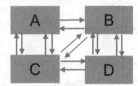

Figure 3-28. *Highly coupled with many dependencies*

Coupling is the measure of the interdependence of one module to another. Modules should have low coupling; low coupling minimizes the ripple effect where changes in one module cause an error in the other module.

Software modules that are *tightly coupled* are more complex; it is the degree to which one module is connected to another module. If a module is tightly coupled, then you are bound to use/edit the rest of the connected modules where editing only one module could have served the purpose. This impacts the principle of maintainability, extensibility, and testability. You need to carry out the full suite on the entire connected modules irrespective of modification, which increases the cost and effort.

The *loose coupling* design is to reduce the dependency that a change made within one module or microservice will create unanticipated changes within other elements. Individual modules can be altered or extended without the need to consider a lot of information from other modules. Errors of data flow can be pointed out easily. The loose coupling supports the principle of maintainability, extensibility, and testability.

Types of Coupling

There are different types of coupling, as shown in Figure 3-29. This section covers the details of these types in order from lowest to highest coupling. The coupling between the modules can be more than one way.

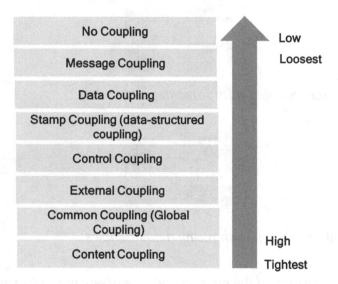

Figure 3-29. *Types of coupling*

No Coupling

In this coupling, the modules are isolated and do not communicate with each other.

Message Coupling

This is the loosest type of coupling. Modules are not dependent on each other; instead, one module calls a method or interface on another and does not pass any parameters. They are coupling only on the name of method or interface.

Example: Dependency injection and observable. Figure 3-30 depicts how message coupling helps to interact between two modules.

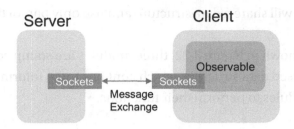

Figure 3-30. *Message coupling*

In this example, the server and clients are loosely coupled and exchange details over the socket.

Data Coupling

When data of one module is shared with another module, this condition is said to be data coupling.

Data coupling occurs when methods share data regularly through parameters. The two modules, Module1 and Module2, exhibit data coupling if Module1 calls Module2 directly, and they communicate using parameters. Each parameter is an elementary piece, and the parameter is the only data shared between Module1 and Module2.

Example: As shown in Figure 3-31, the two modules Calculate EMI and Calculate Total Loan are data coupled as they communicate by passing the parameters.

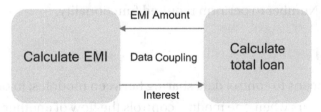

Figure 3-31. *Data coupling*

Stamp Coupling (Data-Structured Coupling)

Stamp coupling occurs when modules share a composite data structure. If the module interacts by sharing or passing a data structure that contains more information than the information required to perform their actions, then these modules are said to be stamp coupled.

Two modules, module A and module B, exhibit stamp coupling if module A passes directly to module B a composite piece of data such as record, array, tree, or list.

101

Modules A and B will share a data structure and use only part of the whole data structure.

For example, ss shown in Figure 3-32, three modules are stamp coupled if they communicate via passed data structure, which contains more information than necessary for the modules to perform their functions.

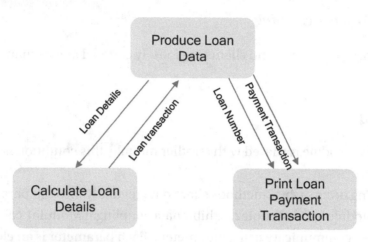

Figure 3-32. *Stamp coupling*

Here we assume Loan Number contains the loan number, date, address, etc. We are sending more information than what it requires. In this scenario, Calculate Loan Details requires only Loan Number to perform required functionality.

Control Coupling

Control coupling means to control data sharing between modules; in other words, control coupling occurs when one module controls the flow of another module by passing control information.

Two modules exhibit control coupling if module A passes to module B, a part of the information that is intended to control the internal logic of module B.

For example, as shown in Figure 3-33, the two modules Error Module and Notification Module are control coupled if they communicate using at least one control flag, denoted as Notification Flag.

Figure 3-33. *Control coupling*

When an error occurs in an application, the error module captures the error and sends the notification flag to the notification module to send a notification to the stakeholders. Here the error module controls the notification module with the notification flag as a control flag.

External Coupling

External coupling occurs when two modules share an externally imposed data format, communication protocol, or device interface. This coupling is related to the communication to external tools and devices such as printers, IoT devices, etc.

For example, module A and module B exhibit external coupling if both modules share direct access to the same I/O devices or are tied to the same external IoT devices in some other way.

Common Coupling (Global Coupling)

Common coupling occurs when two or more modules share global data. Any changes to them have a ripple effect on all the modules; in other words, changing the shared resources implies changing all the modules using them.

For example, as shown in Figure 3-34, three modules are commonly coupled if they both share the same global data area.

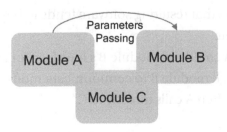

Figure 3-34. *Common coupling*

One of the design principles we have been using for many years is this: don't use global data; it impacts security.

Content Coupling (Pathological Coupling)

When a module can directly access or modify or refer to the content of another module, it is called content-level coupling. Changing the inner workings will lead to the need of changing the dependent module. Module A refers to or changes the module B internal data or statement directly. This type of coupling is very high or tight in nature.

Module A and module B are content coupled if:

- Module A changes a statement in module B

- Module A references or alters data contained inside module B

- Module A branches into module B

For example, the search method that adds an object that is not found in the internal structure of the data structure is used to hold information.

Law of Demeter (LoD) or Principle of Least Knowledge

Introducing coupling increases the instability of a system. The law of Demeter is the important principle to reduce the coupling between modules. This law is a specific case of loose coupling. This law says:

- Each module or microservice has knowledge about only other modules or microservices closely related to the current module or microservices.

- Each module or microservices should talk only to its immediate friends; don't talk to strangers.

The advantage of LoD is that resulting software tends to be more testable, maintainable, extensible, etc.

For example, module A could call module B's interface for any intercommunication, but module A should not call module B to communicate module C. If module A needs to intercommunicate with C, then A calls directly to C.

Applying Loose Coupling to Software Design

Coupling is unavoidable; we need to have coupled. Otherwise, each class in a module or microservices would be its module. However, achieving a low coupling should be one of the primary objectives in system design, such that individual module or microservices can be studied and altered without the need of taking into account a lot of information from other module or microservices and applying domain design concepts while designing a module or microservices.

Loose coupling leads to high cohesion and together leads to a highly maintainable, extensible, and testable system.

Software Quality Principles

"A good architecture is important; otherwise it becomes slower and more expensive to add new capabilities in the future. Good architecture is something that supports its evolution."

—Martin Fowler

As architects, designers, or programmers, we spend a lot of time analyzing, designing, and developing code, but we spend even more time maintaining that developed code. How often do we go back and find that the application has become a tangled mess? Sometimes we park that system as a legacy application.

The purpose of quality principles is to reduce complexity in a manageable way. Complexity can never be eliminated; however, architects and designers can reduce it by using quality principles.

Several problems lead to a highly complex and unmanageable system.

- The architect team does not analyze the business problems properly.

- The architect team does not have a clear view of what the end user wants from our application.

- The architect team does not have full visibility of the enterprise or business unit applications.

- The architect team may not get sufficient time to analyze the architecture.

- The architecture team is to embrace business and technology disruption.

- There are too many software programming languages and platforms with diverse features.

These complexities lead to several problems in software while creating an architecture.

- May cause the software to behave in an unanticipated state

- May create security vulnerabilities that could raise the management of application to an enterprises

- May lead to big operation team and end up with more cost

- May lead to a schedule overrun

Minimizing the complexity and improving the quality of software helps to eliminate or manage the difficulties. Some of the principles related to improving the quality and reducing the complexity are covered next.

KISS Principle

The *keep it short and simple* (KISS) principle was created by the late Kelly Johnson, who was the lead engineer at Lockheed Skunk Works. Kelly's version of the phrase was "Keep it simple, stupid." This phrase was embraced by Lockheed designers. There are many variants of KISS: "Keep it simple and straightforward," "Keep it super simple," etc.

We are using the phrase "short and simple" in this book of cloud native architecture. The objective of this principle is to deliver the simplest possible outcome.

Some of the famous quotes related to KISS are:

> *"Among competing hypotheses, the one with the fewest assumption should be selected"* —Occam's Razor

> *"Make everything as simple as possible but not simpler"* —Albert Einstein

This principle has been key for many years, typically when an architect or developer is breaking down an application into smaller pieces to address the business problems and then they think they understood the business problem and try to design and develop a particular problem but end up with complexity. Based on my experience. it is a complex process on how and where to break complex into simple.

Applying KISS to Software Design

Simplicity is a highly desirable quality in software applications. Making software more complicated than it needs to be lowers the overall quality of software. The maintainability, testability, and supporting the business disruption are reduced when complexity increases.

Here are some ways to follow the KISS principle in your day-to-day work:

- Focus on a simple solution that meets the requirements.

- Avoid the "Rolls Royce" solution when you need a low-end car.

- Break down your problems into many small problems. Each problem should be able to be solved.

- Apply design methodologies to solve the problem and then code it.

- Design the problem as easy to develop and easy to throw away; sometimes throwing away and re-creating is simpler and cheaper than maintaining it.

- Make it easier for the developer to visualize the various aspects of the application, mentally mapping the possible effects of any change. This involves knowing the dependencies and state of the application.

- Avoid abstraction and dependencies.

- Avoid flaunting. Most architects and designers flaunt their skills and knowledge, which makes design unnecessarily complicated.

Try to keep it as simple as possible. This is the hardest behavior pattern to apply, but once you have it, you'll look back and will say " I can't imagine how I was doing work before."

Don't oversimplify a design. Stop breaking things down when you reach a point that negatively affects the design of the application.

Don't Repeat Yourself

The *don't repeat yourself* (DRY) principle aims to reduce repetition in the software application. It says that every piece of knowledge must have a single, unambiguous, authoritative representation within a system."

This principle applies at the code level and architecture level. When code is duplicated across many packages in the application, it makes maintainability harder, and this leads to a bigger codebase that is difficult to modify. Finally, it becomes a technical debt. In an architecture decision, you don't need to build everything; use the packages or software already available on the market instead of building on your own.

Duplication Is Waste

Every line of code that goes into the system must be organized and maintained or it will be a potential source of future bugs. Duplication needlessly bloats the codebase, resulting in more opportunities for bugs and adding accidental complexity into the system. The maintainability of the code becomes a nightmare. It can lead to technical debt, and enterprises need to spend effort and time on refactoring the codebase.

The DRY Principle in Polylithic and Polyglot Architecture

When designing microservices, the DRY rule applies here also, as Sam Newman said in his book *Building Microservices*: "Don't repeat yourself inside microservices. The dilemma is about reusing across microservices. The basic principle of microservices is to "avoid dependencies between microservices." Even though there is a dependency, but it should be very minimal. As part of the microservices design, we need to reuse some utility or generalized functionality across microservices, but the challenge is how to find the right balance to apply the DRY principle.

As shown in Figure 3-35, one of the well-known approaches is to create a package as a library for reusing code and maintain the package separately outside of the microservices code, and then use well-structured build pipeline to include relevant libraries into the microservice package.

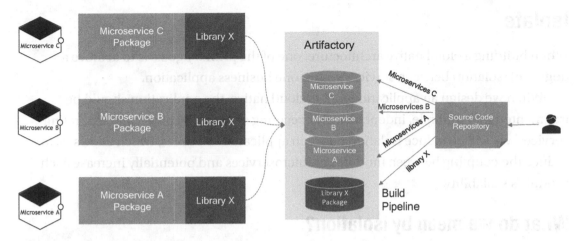

Figure 3-35. *DRY principle in microservices*

Let's examine several considerations when you are applying the DRY principle in the context of microservices.

- Use semantic versioning from the beginning of the project.

- Limit the code and functionality in libraries by design.

- Design a package such a way that the functionality of the code doesn't change often.

- Standardize on a naming convention so that other microservices teams can discover these packages.

- You need to set up proper governance to manage these packages

How does the DRY principle reduce maintenance costs?

If the code is duplicated and needs to be changed, you need to find all the places where it is duplicated and apply changes to all of them. This is more difficult than modifying in one place, and this leads to more errors and technical debt. You can think of it like you accidentally apply it differently in one location than another location, or you can modify code that happens to be the same. Duplicate code tends to obscure the structure and intent of your code, making it harder to understand and modify.

In some places, the DRY principle is good to follow, but some places need to maintain duplication due to unavoidable situations, but in that duplication, make sure you follow proper packaging such as using a library and governance to manage such code.

Isolate

When building a cloud native architecture, one of the primary goals is to achieve a degree of isolation between services within one business application.

When we design an application that is cloud native, the application should be fragmented into multiple, independently executing services. By physically separating services, we will introduce isolation between application modules, which allows us to reduce the coupling between modules or microservices and potentially increase each module's scalability.

What do we mean by isolation?

The concept of isolation means that changes to one module of the architecture generally don't impact or affect elements of another module. The change is isolated to the elements within the module, which does not have any knowledge of the inner workings of another module.

Isolation in Cloud Native Applications

When working with cloud native architecture, we focus on three dimensions of isolation: state, space, and failure.

One of the primary characters of a cloud native application is the state. The individual module or microservices are wholly responsible for maintaining the state; any access to this state from other modules is through REST APIs.

Space refers to the location in which modules are deployed. The deployment strategy changes radically for cloud native applications. In a cloud native architecture, the modules are deployed independently and execute with the separate process in containers. This allows each service to be managed independently. The ability to manage application elements independently allows remediating defects and new features to be deployed automatically with infrastructure as code.

Failure refers to how the application modules isolate the failure between modules. Each module in a cloud native architecture executes independently; the failure will no longer crash the entire application. During application design, avoid propagation of failure and try to use the Bulkhead pattern to both isolate and mitigate failure; the patterns are explained in Chapter 4.

Applying Isolation to Software Design

Software architects should design modules by following isolation principles. These best practices will help you while designing an application:

- Limit or restrict unneeded interactions or dependencies.

- Protect system integrity by preventing one process from interfering with another.

- Provide boundaries so individual failures do not compromise the whole system.

- Limit exposure to a particular area of the system.

Separation of Concern

Separation of concern (SoC) is a design principle that manages the quality and complexities of an application by decoupling the software system so that each isolated module is responsible for a separate concern, minimizing the dependency as much as possible. At a low level, this principle is closely related to the single responsibility principle.

The SoC involves decoupling larger problems into smaller manageable problems. It improves the quality of software by reducing complexity.

The term *separation of concern* was probably coined by Edsger W. Dijkstra in his 1974 paper "On the role of scientific thought."

In 1989, Chris Reade in his book *Elements of Functional Programming* describes SoC. The programmer has to do several things at the same time, namely, the following:

- Describe what is to be computed.

- Organize the computation sequencing into small steps.

- Organize memory management during the computation.

Applying SoC to Software Design

SoC is achieved by establishing boundaries. A boundary is any logical or physical constraint that delineates a given set of responsibilities. Some examples of boundaries include the use of modules, methods, layers, and services.

At the design level, the application can follow an SoC by separating different elements such as user interfaces, APIs, database, business logic, etc. An example of a pattern is the Model-View-Controller pattern.

Use Layering

The most common principle is the use layering principle. This pattern was the de facto standard principle for all the web applications since the MVC pattern and has been in use for quite some time. In today's world, this principle is still relevant in cloud native architecture.

Elements within a layered architecture are organized into horizontal and vertical layers, and each layer within an application performs specific functionality. Although this principle does not specify the number and types of layers that exist, it all depends on what type of application you are developing.

Layering in Traditional Application

As shown in Figure 3-36, traditional software architecture consists of four standard layers: presentation, business, persistence, and database. A smaller application may have only three layers, and a large and complex application may have four to five layers.

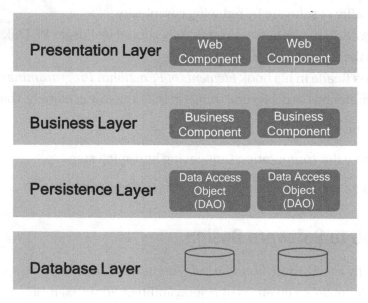

Figure 3-36. *Traditional architecture layering approach*

The presentation layer is responsible for handling all user interfaces, whereas the business layer is responsible for executing specific business functionality, the persistence layer is responsible for connecting and managing database access, and the database layer is responsible for storing information.

Layering in Cloud Native Application

A cloud native application is composed of various logical layers, as shown in Figure 3-37, and grouped according to responsibility and deployment. Each layer in a cloud native application runs specific tasks, and each task can be a separate microservice.

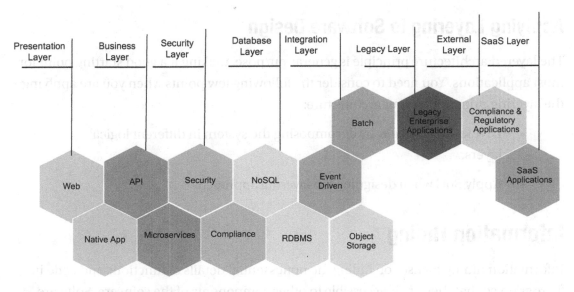

Figure 3-37. *Cloud native architecture layering approach*

The presentation layer provides a user experience through the web application and mobile native application.

The business layer runs stateless services that expose the API; this layer can dynamically expand and shrink depending on the usage at runtime by using the autoscaling option of the cloud.

The security layer provides security as a service to the entire application including access, security at rest, and security at transit.

The database layer has stateful services that are backed by polyglot persistence. Stateful services rely on traditional RDBMS, NoSQL, object storage, graph storage, etc.

The integration layer has an event-driven architecture and batch jobs; the event-driven architecture can use a variety of services in the cloud that connects various internal legacy and external third-party applications. The interconnection may be synchronous or asynchronous or batch.

Cloud native applications interoperate with the existing enterprise applications at the legacy layer; these legacy applications may host in the cloud or on-premises.

Cloud native applications interoperate with various third-party applications such as payment, regulatory systems, etc.

Some cloud native applications can interoperate with third-party SaaS providers; these SaaS applications may host in the same cloud or multicloud environment.

Applying Layering to Software Design

The layered architecture principle is general-purpose, making it a good starting point for most applications. You need to consider the following few points when you are applying the layering principle in your architecture:

- Divide and conquer by decomposing the system in different logical layers.

- Apply SoC when designing the layering approach.

Information Hiding

Information hiding focuses on hiding the nonessential details of functions and code in a program so that they are inaccessible to other components of the software. Software designers and developers apply information hiding in software design and coding to hide unnecessary details from the rest of the modules. The objective of the information hiding is to minimize complexities among different modules of the application.

The information hiding principle suggests the architecture be designed as modules or microservices in such a way that they hide implementation details from the consumers.

D.L. Parnas introduced the term *information hiding* in 1972 in "On the Criteria to be Used in Decomposing Systems into Modules." The idea was that each module should hide some design decisions from the rest of the system, especially decisions that would have cross-cutting effects if changed.

114

A well-designed system means that it needs to be well-organized. We presented various principles to achieve. You do not need everything in your system to know about everything else. So, how do you limit the information the various modules can have access to? Information hiding allows elements of the module to give accessors the minimum amount of information needed to use them correctly and hide everything else. Information hiding is often associated with encapsulation.

Why Information Hiding?

Information hiding is relevant in all levels of application; exposing only the details that are required improves the quality of the software and reduces the complexity. Most importantly, it improves maintainability and security. Hiding implementation reduces potential coupling and dependent modules, which will reduce the effect of the change on your implementation.

Applying Information Hiding to Software Design

Information hiding can be useful in designing your module and APIs. The gap between theory and practice in module design is wide, and among many designers, the decision about what to put into an API amounts to deciding what interface would be easiest to write internal code to, which results in exposing as much of the elements in the APIs as possible. I have seen that most programmers would rather expose all the elements and write extra lines of excess code to keep module secrets intact.

Asking about what needs to be hidden supports good design decisions at all levels. It promotes the use of named constants instead of literals at the implementation level. Get into the habit of asking "What does a consumer want?" or "What should I hide?" You'll be surprised at how many decisions vanish before you.

You Aren't Gonna Need It

You Aren't Gonna Need It YAGNI is an acronym that stands for "You Aren't Gonna Need It" or "You Ain't Gonna Need It." It is a principle from the Extreme Programming methodology. YAGNI states that you should prioritize the functionality in a backlog until it is completed.

Idea of YAGNI

The idea of YAGNI is that you should only implement features that are required and not just because you think you may require them sometime later. Ron Jeffries, the author and cofounder of XP, said this:

> *"Always implement things when you need them, never when you just foresee that you need them."*

Even if you are sure that you will need a feature or piece of code later, do not implement it now. Implement it when the feature required. Most likely, you will not need it after all, or what you need is quite different from what you foresaw needing earlier.

The reason you may consider building presumptive features is that you think it will be cheaper to build it now rather than build it later. Before making a decision, the cost and time comparison must be made against the cost of delay. Spending time and money on a feature you don't need now takes away time and money that are required for other immediate features. This doesn't mean you should avoid building flexibility into your application. It means you shouldn't overengineer something based on what you think you might need later.

The idea of YAGNI is that you save time because you avoid writing code that you do not need; our code is better because you avoid polluting it with guesses or assumptions that turn out be wrong and end up with technical debt and require refactoring.

How to Decide What You Need

Martin Fowler wrote in his blog, "YAGNI only applies to capabilities built into the software to support a presumptive feature; it does not apply to effort to make the software easier to modify." YAGNI is a viable strategy only if the code is easy to change, so expending effort on refactoring isn't a violation of YAGNI because refactoring makes the code more malleable.

In cloud native architecture, we are building loosely coupled independently deployable software with the principle of ease of maintenance, ease of test, and ease of extension. By considering this, the YAGNI principle is very relevant now. It means you can add any feature at any time without affecting the existing implementation. What you need is to manage backlog smartly so that the features can be mapped to the particular microservices features, this helps the team to pick easily for development.

SOLID Design Principles

SOLID principles are an object-oriented approach that is applied to software design and coding. It was conceptualized by Robert C. Martin in 2000, and the acronym was coined by Michael Feathers. These five principles are the de facto standard for OO programming.

The idea of the SOLID principle is to reduce dependencies so that developers can change one area of software without impacting others. These principles are intended to make designs easier to understand, maintain, and extend. Ultimately, using these principles makes it easier for software development to avoid issues and to build adaptive, effective, and cloud native software.

These principles have become important in cloud native applications. When followed correctly, you can achieve maintainability, extensibility, and testability of software design.

The SOLID principle is a framework consisting of complementary principles that are generic and open for interpretation but still give enough direction for creating a good object-oriented design. The SOLID is a mnemonic acronym for five design principles intended to make software designs more understandable, flexible, and maintainable.

SOLID stands for the following:

- Single responsibility principle

- Open-closed principle

- Liskov substitution principle

- Interface segregation principle

- Dependency inversion principle

Single Responsibility Principle

The single responsibility principle is one of the most tried and tested in software design. Every module or microservices should do one thing.

This principle states that each module should have a single responsibility or a single job or a single purpose. The responsibility of a module should have one and only one reason to change, meaning that a module should have only one job. This means each of your modules or microservices should serve only one greater purpose and change only if the greater purpose changes. It doesn't mean each module or microservices doesn't require you to stick just one task or contain only one unit of work, but these tasks or units or elements all need to cohesively relate to the greater purpose of the microservice.

If a microservice has multiple responsibilities, there is a possibility that it is used all over the place. When one responsibility changes in the microservices, then we need to test the entire set of responsibilities whether it is changed or not.

This principle is related to the separation of concern principle; as concerns are separated from each other, it facilitates the creation of microservices that have a single responsibility.

Applying Single Responsibility to Microservice Design

Microservices serve a single responsibility in a domain. As shown in Figure 3-38, each domain like Customer Account, Payment, or Quote is considered to be a microservice, so these domains serve a single responsibility. This domain model is from the Auto Insurance domain.

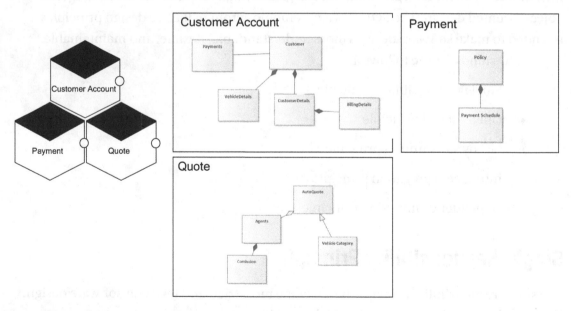

Figure 3-38. *Single responsibility principle in microservices design*

The Customer Account provides the functionality of customer account management like customer profile, vehicle details, payment details, customer details, etc. The Customer Account microservice invokes payment microservices to process a payment for insurance purchase based on the quote created.

Open-Closed Principle

The open-closed principle states that software entities should be open for extensions and closed for modification. When functionality changes, the entity can allow its code to be extended without modifying the existing code that has already been developed.

At a code level or class level, you should be able to extend the class's behavior without modifying it. This extension can be done by extending the class, either using inheritance or using composition.

At the architecture level, we are not modifying the functionality of an existing module but always add new elements by using the existing design.

Applying Open-Closed to Microservices

Even though this principle was created for object-oriented programming, this principle is still relevant in cloud native architecture.

In cloud native, you expose your functionality through either APIs or event-driven messaging. These APIs are contracted with the consumer, and you cannot modify the existing contract; instead, you extend it.

Let's move on to the specific example of insurance. As shown in Figure 3-39, imagine we work in an Auto Insurance domain, and you are building a new cloud native application. During the insurance process, the customer requests insurance by providing vehicle details and other customer details; your user experience invokes the customer microservices through APIs. You define an API contract between your customer account microservices and user experience (web and mobile native application) and to the third-party agent application.

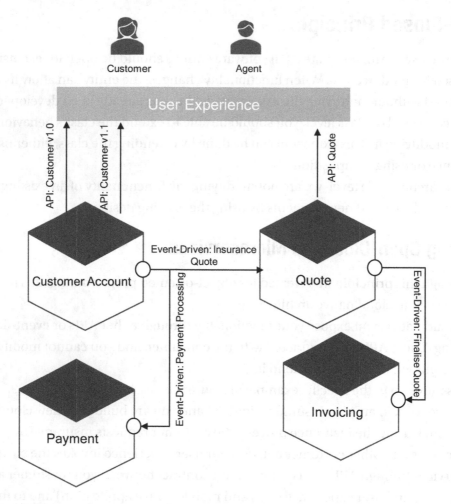

Figure 3-39. *Open-close principle in microservices*

Your business team would like to add new functionality for the existing one; in this case, are you going to modify a customer account microservices or add new functionality into the customer account? You will extend the functionality and provide a new API with the new version. Here you are doing open for extension and close for modification.

Liskov Substitution Principle

The *Liskov substitution principle* (LSP) defines that objects of a superclass will be replaceable with objects of its subclasses without breaking the application. This principle allows subclasses to inherit from a superclass, which includes the properties and methods of the superclass. This principle is like the design by contract concept defined by Bertrand Meyer.

In cloud native architecture, the design by contract is part of the API contract and relies on preconditions, postconditions, and invariants. The API contract is the contract of messages between your API provider and the consumer that will be used across channels.

Applying Liskov Substitution to Microservices Design

The LSP in OOP is to enable your code using type T1 to use type T2 instead, as T2 is a subtype of T1. In other words, you don't want to break existing code but alter behavior. If you apply LSP to microservices, you don't want to break existing clients of the service but replace them with better or enhanced ones.

We will use the same example as shown in the open-close principle with the modification of the API contract.

In the example shown in Figure 3-40, you need to find a way to replace the microservices Customer Account version 1.0 with version 1.1, not only breaking existing consumers but having them utterly unaware of these changes.

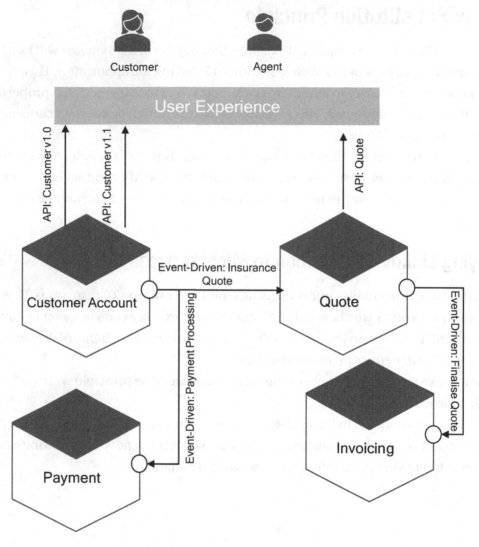

Figure 3-40. *Liskov substitution to microservices design*

The API contract for the Customer Account version 1.0 and the API version 1.0 of Customer Account is as follows:

> *GET https://mydomain/customer/resource-a*
> *Accept: application/json; version 1.0*

Some consumers want to add new features to the Customer Account microservice; here you need to extend it without affecting the existing customer. Here you need to introduce version 1.1, the API contract for the customer Account version 1.1, the API version 1.1 of customer Account as follows:

```
GET https://mydomain/customer/resource-a
Accept: application/json; version 1.1
```

Interface Segregation Principle

Interfaces in OOP define methods and properties but do not provide any implementations. Classes that implement interfaces provide an implementation. Interfaces define a contract, and consumers can use them without concerning themselves with their implementation details. The implementation can change, and if interfaces are not modified, the consumer does not need to change their logic.

In a cloud native architecture, an API is the interface between the consumer and implementation; the API provides the interface with properties and HTTP methods. Microservices that implement APIs provide an implementation.

The *interface segregation principle* (ISP) states that consumers should not be forced to depend on properties and methods that they do not use. This is exactly what an API implementation provides, you design APIs to provide an optional property with HTTP methods so that consumers can use only relevant properties and HTTP methods.

Dependency Inversion Principle

The *dependency inversion principle* (DSP) is a specific form of decoupling software modules for handling dependencies between modules and writing loosely coupled software systems.

The principle states the following:

- High-level modules should not depend on low-level modules. Both should depend on abstractions.

- Abstractions should not depend on details. Details should depend on abstractions.

In cloud native architecture, you can use DSP to design your microservice's internal layers and decouple dependencies between the API, database, and infrastructure. It has nothing to do with your domain but is related to the application microservice design. This principle allows you to decouple the infrastructure layer from the application's deployment layers.

Summary

In this chapter, you learned various cloud native architecture principles and how to adopt these principles in a cloud native architecture.

To design the best cloud native architecture, several principles can be applied, such as API first, polylithic and polyglot, consumer first, a culture of automation, digital decoupling, evolutionary design principles, etc. After you design services, you must run these services in production. For effective runtime efficiency, several principles can be applied, such as isolate failure principle, deploy independently, be smart with the state, design for failure, etc.

Security is the most important part of any application, and cloud native architecture is no different. To implement effective security in an application, several principles can be considered, such as defense-in-depth, shift left in security, security by design, etc.

Once you design an application, the next most important part is how you develop and deliver the software, and a number of principles such as agility, shift-left, products not projects principles must be adopted.

The container is the de facto standard for cloud native applications; the effective configuration of containers in a cloud native architecture is important. Therefore, you need to apply container principles for your deployment using principles such as SCP, HOP, LCP, IIP, PDP, SCP, and RCP.

You learned that to design orthogonal software systems that can be extended while minimizing the impact on existing and new functionality, you need to focus on loose coupling and high cohesion. Complexity is an important concept in software application; architects and designer think they need to build the Taj Mahal or Eiffel Tower. But the customer wants something else; therefore, you need to apply these principles to make sure you deliver what the customer wants: KISS, DRY, information hiding, YAGNI, and SoC.

The SOLID design principles, which include SRP, OCP, LSP, ISP, and DSP, can be used to design and develop code that addresses maintainability, reusability, testability, and flexibility concerns. Several practices, such as agility, product centric, decentralization, and shift-left, improve the quality of software systems.

Cloud native architecture patterns are reusable solutions that can be used to solve recurring problems. In the next chapter, we will go over some of the common cloud native architecture patterns so that you will be aware of them and can apply them appropriately to your services.

CHAPTER 4

Cloud Native Architecture and Design Patterns

The *Pattern Language* is an organized and coherent set of patterns, each of which describes a problem and the core of a solution that can be used in many ways within a specific field of expertise.

When architects and designers work on a particular problem, it is unusual for them to think of a new solution that is completely distinct from existing ones. They often recall or remember a similar problem they already solved and reuse the essence of that solution. Their problem may in fact recur again and again in various projects and implementations. Using the earlier solution to solve this recurring problem has a name; it is called using a pattern.

A software pattern is a solution to a recurring problem within a given context. Each pattern describes a context, a problem, and a solution. Patterns reflect how the code or components are developed and interact with each other. Using patterns simplifies design and architecture problems.

Each pattern describes a problem that occurs over and over again in our environment and then describes the core of the solution to that problem, in such a way that you can use this solution a million times over, without ever doing it the same way twice.

Software architects and designers who know available software architecture and design patterns can recognize when one can be applied in a design scenario. This chapter explains the details of patterns with real-time problem scenarios.

This chapter begins by explaining what software architecture patterns are and how they can be used in your design. It then briefly covers all the commonly available patterns and provides detailed information on cloud native-related patterns including Gang of Four patterns, enterprise integration patterns, microservices patterns, etc.

127

© Shivakumar R Goniwada 2022
S. R. Goniwada, *Cloud Native Architecture and Design*, https://doi.org/10.1007/978-1-4842-7226-8_4

In this chapter, I will cover the following topics:

- Evolution of software architecture patterns

- Software architecture pattern usage

- Architecture styles

- Gang of Four patterns, including the enterprise integration pattern

- Details of cloud native and microservices patterns

- Infrastructure patterns, testing patterns, database patterns, and transactional patterns

- Anti-patterns

- Do's and don'ts of pattern usage

Evolution of Design Patterns

Economic changes in the 19th century provided the catalyst for the rise of modern architecture and the creation of some iconic buildings. Christopher Alexander was a vocal critic of utilized space and developed theories for architectural and urban design. He published a theory of architecture: *The Timeless Way of Building in 1979, A Pattern Language in 1977 and the Oregon Experiment 1975.*

This *Pattern Language*, as it's called, details 253 patterns that serve as generic guiding principles for design.

Design patterns in computer science achieved prominence when *Design Pattern: Elements of Reusable Object-Oriented Software* by the "Gang of Four" was published in 1994 by Erich Gamma, Richard Helm, Ralph Johnson, and John Vlissides. The *Design Pattern* book used objects and interfaces instead of walls and doors, but at the core of both kinds of patterns are solutions to a problem in a context.

The next progression in the pattern world was *Studies in Computational Science: Parallel Programming Paradigms*, a book about programming techniques written by Per Brinch Hansen. He was a Danish-American computer scientist known for his work in operating systems, concurrent programming, and parallel and distributed computing. The author's main point is that the lack of proper programming techniques is the source of many difficulties in computing. This book mainly addresses concurrent programs, divide-and-conquer paradigms, parallel parallelism, etc.

The next progression in the pattern world was *Pattern-Oriented Software Architecture: A System of Patterns, Volume 1*, which was written in 1996 by Frank Buschmann, Regine Meunier, Hans Rohnert, and Peter Sommerlad. This book details how to design application and middleware software to run in concurrent and networked environments, event handling, synchronization, services access and configuration, and concurrency.

The next progression in the pattern world was *Smalltalk Best Practices Pattern* written by Kent Beck in 1997. This book is all about choosing names of objects, variables, and methods; how to break logic into methods; and how to communicate your implementation. Smalltalk is one of the most influential programming languages and was one of the first object-oriented programming languages, so all other languages that come after Smalltalk like Java, Python, Ruby, etc., were influenced by Smalltalk.

The next progression in the pattern world was *Pattern-Oriented Software Architecture, Volume 2: Patterns for Concurrent and Networked Objects* written by Douglas Schmidt, Michael Stal, Hans Rohnert, and Frank Buschmann in 2000. It is the second volume in the Pattern-Oriented Software Architecture series. This book focuses on networking and concurrency.

The next progression in the pattern world was *Pattern of Enterprise Application Architecture* written by Martin Fowler in 2002. This book is about enterprise architecture patterns like how to layer an enterprise application, how to organize domain logic, how to design web-based applications, and how to implement distributed design.

The next progression in the pattern world was *Enterprise Integration Pattern: Designing, Building, and Deploying Messaging Solutions* written by Gregor Hohpe and Bobby Woolf in 2003. This book covers enterprise integration and messaging with both synchronous and asynchronous loosely coupled patterns.

The next progression in the pattern world was *Head First Design Pattern* written by Eric Freeman, Elisabeth Freeman, Bert Bates, and Kathy Sierra in 2004. In this book, the authors illustrated already available patterns in a graphical way with simple understandable terms and with examples.

The next book in the pattern world was *Software Architecture Patterns* written by Mark Richards in 2015. In this book, the author provides details of modern-day architecture patterns such as event-driven architecture, microservices, layered architecture, etc.

The next book in the pattern world was *Microservice Patterns* written by Chris Richardson in 2018. In this book, the author provides the details of microservices patterns such as event-driven architecture, microservices, etc.

There are various other books available on the market about patterns, and each author gives details based on their experience with the best possible examples. In this book, I am not covering the entire set of patterns but providing brief details of existing patterns that are relevant to a cloud native architecture.

This chapter covers the details of relevant cloud native patterns, including object-oriented, enterprise application, and enterprise integration patterns. It also provides some examples.

What Are Software Patterns?

A *software pattern* is a solution to a recurring problem within a given context. Each pattern describes a context, a problem, and a solution. Patterns reflect how code or components are developed and interact with each other. Using patterns simplifies design and architecture problems. Some people interpret what is and isn't a pattern differently. One person's pattern can be another person's architecture style or building blocks. In general, a pattern has a pattern name, problem, solution, and consequences.

When an architect and designer work on a particular problem, it is unusual for them to think of a new solution that is completely distinct from existing ones. They often recall a similar problem they have already solved and reuse the essence of that solution in the new situation. In fact, the same problem may recur again and again in various projects and implementations. Using the earlier solution to solve this recurring problem is called using a *pattern*.

- Patterns can be seen as building blocks of more complex solutions.

- Their function is a common language used by technology architects and designers to describe solutions.

Architecture Style, Architecture Pattern, and Design Pattern

The architecture style, architecture pattern, and design pattern are not mutually exclusive but complement each other, and all of them can provide some insight into the development of a solution. There are small differences between all three and, again, different interpretations from person to person. Some say architecture styles and architecture patterns are the same, but others say they are different. I will try to highlight the differences based on my experience, and the rest I leave to you to judge.

An architecture style describes how to organize components of the architecture and code. It is the highest granularity of architecture, and it specifies the layers and high-level modules of the application, as well as how they interact with each other.

Architecture patterns help to specify the fundamental structure of an application.

Design patterns are more localized and solve a particular problem within the codebase. Examples include the factory pattern, singleton pattern, etc.

Anti-pattern

An *anti-pattern* describes a recurring solution to a problem that generates negative consequences. An anti-pattern is about applying a wrong solution to the right problem without having knowledge or analysis of either problem or applying patterns. The term was coined in 1995 by Andrew Koenig.

An anti-pattern from the developer's perspective is comprised of technical problems and solutions that are encountered. From an architecture perspective, it resolves problems in how systems are structured, and from a managerial perspective, an anti-pattern addresses common problems in software engineering.

In a nutshell, leveraging patterns is a valuable approach, but that doesn't mean you have to use a particular pattern. A common mistake by architects and designers is when they engineer a problem by using patterns. You need to understand the context and solution to the problem before applying the pattern in your context.

Cloud Native Data Management Pattern for Microservices

The following are cloud native data management patterns for microservices.

Event Sourcing Pattern

The event sourcing pattern is not new; Martin Fowler wrote about it in his book *Pattern of Enterprise Application Architecture* in 2002. The event sourcing pattern has not been used much, but it gains a lot of importance with the emergence of cloud native event-driven architecture. According to Fowler:

> *"Event Sourcing ensures that all changes to the application state are stored as a sequence of events. Not just query these events, we can also use the event log to reconstruct past states, and as a foundation to automatically adjust the state to cope with retroactive changes."*

In your application, when any activity occurs, it should be through an event. Without an event, the system may not function. The event can be anything such as clicking a button, clicking the back button, sending a request to an API, scheduling a job, transferring a payment, withdrawing a certain amount, purchasing a product, viewing reviews, etc. You need to use these events to track, audit, log, and restore marketing, etc. These events are difficult to store in the database by using create, read, update, and delete (CRUD) operations. You need a special type of data store to store all kinds of events.

The event sourcing pattern defines an approach to handling an operation on data that is driven by a sequence of events, and each of the event records is stored as a new record. The event-driven services publish the list of events with a description like an event name, time, date, user, etc., to the event store. It uses the event-centric approach to persist data. A business object is persisted in an event store with the sequence of state-changing events. Whenever an object's state changes, a new event happens to the sequence of events. The event store publishes events to the consumers, so the current state is derived from the event store.

Stream

The stream (the event store allows you to define and create as many streams as required for your domain) comprises a log of all events that have occurred during the state of an object. The event store can provide output as in a traditional database, and it provides much more such as time traveling through the system and root-cause analysis. The data in the event store is immutable and provides methods for audit logs.

Event Store

Figure 4-1 shows an overview of an event sourcing pattern, including storing events, externally consuming an application of an events, and querying an event for a specific state or current state. For example, the user performs various activities in an ecommerce application like logging in, searching for an item, selecting a brand, adding a brand or removing a brand, etc. These user activities are called *events*. The e-commerce application publishes all the user activities to the event stream by using event-driven systems like Kafka and stores them in the event store database like EventStoreDB.

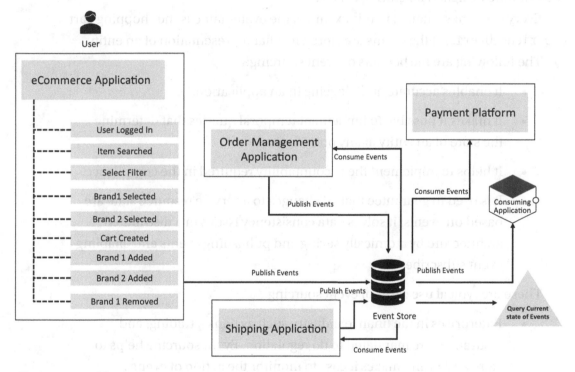

***Figure 4-1.** Event source*

All the events are immutable and stored using an append-only operation; the event capture and event store are published seamlessly in the background without affecting the performance of an application or the user experience. All the events are simple event objects with characteristics such as timestamps, user IDs, etc.

The event sourcing enables the following:

- You can do a complete rebuild of an application or service state by rerunning the events from the event log on a system or service.

- Temporal queries can be used to determine the application state at any point in time. This can be achieved by initializing a blank state and rerunning all the events up to a particular point in time.

- Event replay can be used to repair a corrupted state of an application or service due to an incorrect event being received. This can be done by initializing a blank application or service state and replaying all the events while replacing the incorrect with the correct one.

There are multiple databases such as EventStoreDB, IBM DB2 Event Store, and NEventStore designed for storing events.

Every event has a name; in this example, the event name is the shopping cart experienceUser1. All the events are stored in a flat representation of an entity.

The following are the benefits of event sourcing:

- It enables accurate audit logging in an application.

- It makes it possible to implement temporal queries that determine the state of an entity at any point in time.

- It helps to implement the accountability required in the compliance.

- It is used to guarantee that all changes to a service resource state are based on events; it solves data consistency issues in a distributed architecture by atomically saving and publishing events and enabling event subscribers.

These are typical use cases of event sourcing:

- Enterprises in the finance industry such as banks, trading, and insurances are mandated to do regulation. Event sourcing helps to store audits and makes it easy to monitor the action of events.

- Up-to-date record-keeping in government agencies.

- User activity in the retail application for marketing.

These are some considerations necessary when using event sourcing:

- Event sourcing typically improves the performance of updates, but it takes time to construct an aggregated state. Using a snapshot may decrease the amount of time needed by taking a snapshot and replying to the events from that point on.

- The event structure may change over time. Therefore, the application or service should have a versioning strategy and be able to handle events with different versions.

Command and Query Responsibility Segregation Pattern

The *command and query responsibility segregation* (CQRS) pattern isolates the updated operation data from reading operation data. Implementing CQRS increases the system performance, provides low overhead on the command database, and provides a higher degree of security.

In a traditional architecture, as shown in Figure 4-2, usually the system uses a single model for both command and query operations.

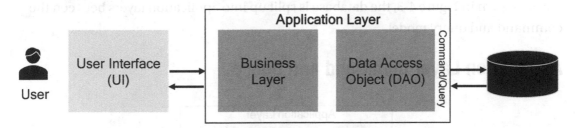

Figure 4-2. *Traditional architecture data operations*

In Figure 4-2, the application layer consists of business logic and DAOs and uses the same database for all CRUD operations. This type of architecture works well for basic CRUD operations. In more complex or legacy applications, this approach becomes unwieldy.

In one of my projects in early 2012, the client had a Temenos T24 core banking application, and it was very old and unable to support the business expansion; sometimes it failed to scale to meet the demand, which impacted the bank business. All the services from various channels like web, mobile, and branch were requesting both command and read operations from the same application with one monolithic database. Both read and write workloads are often asymmetrical, with very different performance and scale requirements.

The following are the drawbacks of this kind of architecture:

- Data conflicts can occur when both read and write operations are performed on the same sets of data.

- Performance degradation may occur due to the load on the data store and data access objects.

- Security becomes complex for security at rest and security in transit.

As our needs become more sophisticated, we are steadily moving away from that model. We need to look at the storage differently.

Approaching CQRS in two different ways, you can do the following:

- Segregate the application layer based on the command and query responsibility. The write request and read request are handled by two different objects.

- Split up the data storage, having separate reads and writes by using the event source.

As shown in Figure 4-3, the database is split up into application layers between the command and query model.

Application Layer Command and Query

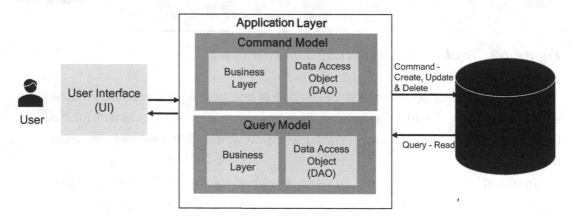

Figure 4-3. *Command and query model in the application layer*

Having separate models means different object models can be running in different processes and separate VMs or containers. There could be a separate request from the UI for commands (create, update and delete) and queries (read). This type of CQRS has both pros and cons, but it does not solve the industry problems. There is no change in the database load, and it may not improve the performance and security; however, complexity in the application layer is reduced.

Command and Query in the Database

As shown in Figure 4-4, we can split storage between the commands and queries by using event sourcing. These separate reads and writes go into different databases: the command database for creating, updating, and deleting and the querying database for read-only operations. The commands are usually task and transaction-based rather than data-centric. A query never modifies the data and returns a value object or DTO that does not encapsulate any domain knowledge.

For greater isolation, this model physically separates the read data from the write data. In this case, the read database can use its own data schema that is optimized for reading operations, and this type of architecture provides flexibility to choose the type of databases such as RDBMS or NoSQL, etc.

In the previous example of Temenos T24, we adopted the second model. We created the operational data store (ODS) from Temenos T24. We designed an event sourcing mechanism between the T24 database to the ODS database in near-real-time mode. From the enterprise service bus (ESB), we orchestrated all the read requests like statements, etc., to ODS with all the debit and credit orchestrated to the Temenos T24 system.

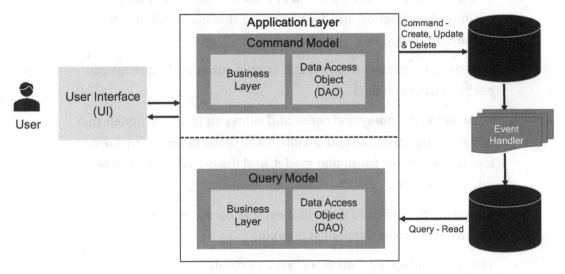

Figure 4-4. *Command and query in database*

As mentioned, the CQRS provides a separation of concerns. The command side is all about business or transactions and does not place much importance on queries or different materialized views over the data or optimized APIs from the nonrelational database, etc. On the other hand, the query side is all about read access. The main purpose is making queries fast and efficient. In many business systems, based on my experience, I can say approximately 70 percent of requests for read purpose from the users.

Separating the read side and the write side into separate models within a bounded context provides the ability to scale each one of them independently. The read data model could be de-normalized or could be a materialized view, which in turn increases the performance of the query execution.

The way event sourcing helps with CQRS is to have part of the application writing to an event store or stream topic. This is paired with an event handler that subscribes to the queue topic, transforms and cleanses the event, and writes the materialized view to read the store.

The following are the benefits of CQRS:

- CQRS allows the read and query workloads to scale independently.

- The query side can use a schema or materialized views that are optimized for queries, and the command side uses a schema that is optimized for updates.

- It is easier to manage security; that is, only command domains can perform writes on data.

- Segregating the query and command sides can result in models that are more maintainable and flexible. Most of the complex business logic goes into the command model, and the query model can be relatively simple.

- By storing materialized views in the query database, the application can avoid complex joins when querying.

- There are various options to use a query database, from RDBMS to NoSQL databases.

- The query database can provide data to the various analytical purposes.

The following are issues of CQRS:

- The idea of CQRS is simple, but the implementation is complex; you need very highly skilled resources.

- The best way to implement CQRS is to use event-driven architecture; you need to take care of data cleansing, message failures, etc.

- The query data may be stale due to replication time lag.

The following are the use cases for CQRS:

- You read more query-based use cases than command-based use cases, for example, social networking systems, retail bank applications, etc.

- In complex business logic, you want to simplify the understanding of the domain dividing problem into command and query.

Data Partitioning Pattern

A partition allows a table, index, or index-organized table to be subdivided into smaller chunks, where each chunk of such a database object is called a *partition*. Each partition has its name.

Data partitioning divides the data set and distributes the data over multiple servers or shards. Each shard is an independent database, and collectively, the shard makes up a single database. The portioning helps manageability, performance, high availability, security, operational flexibility, and scalability. This makes technologies an ideal fit for microservices data storage.

The *data partitioning pattern* addresses these issues of scale:

- High query rates exhausting the CPU capacity of the server

- Larger data sets exceeding the storage capacity of a single machine

- Working set sizes larger than the system's RAM, thus stressing the I/O capacity of disk drives

You can use the following strategies for database partitioning:

- *Horizontal partitioning (sharding)*: Each partition is a separate data store, but all partitions have the same schema. Each partition is known as shards and holds a subset of data.

- *Vertical partitioning*: Each partition holds a subset of the fields for items in the data store; the fields are divided according to how you access the data.

- *Functional partitioning*: Data is aggregated according to how it is used by each bounded context in the system.

You can combine multiple strategies in your application; for example, you apply horizontal partitioning for high availability and use a vertical partitioning strategy to store data based on data access.

The database, either RDBMS or NoSQL, provides different criteria to share the database.

- Range or interval partitioning

- List partitioning

- Round-robin partitioning

- Hash partitioning

Round-robin partitioning distributes the rows of a table among the nodes in a round-robin fashion. The range, list, hash partitioning, and an attribute called the *partitioning key* must be chosen among the table attributes. The partition of the table rows is based on the value of the partitioning key.

In range partitioning, a given range of values is assigned to a partition, and the data distributed among the nodes in such a way that each partition contains rows for which the partitioning key value lies within its range. The list strategy similar to the range, but a list of values is assigned one by one. The hash partitioning is based on the partition key and the hash values.

Horizontal Partitioning or Sharding

Applications in an enterprise require a database to store business data. When the business grows, the data size grows exponentially; at some point in time the database performs very badly with limited CPU, single storage capacity, performance, or query throughput. There should be a limit to increase the CPU, memory, etc. Therefore, you can't go beyond certain limitations.

Sharding is a common idea in database architectures. By sharing a table, you can store new chunks of data across multiple physical nodes to achieve horizontal scalability.

By horizontally scaling out, you can enable a flexible database design that increases the performance and high availability of data.

Figure 4-5 shows horizontal partitioning or sharding; in this example, user employee details are divided into two shards, HS1 and HS2, based on ID/key. Each shard holds the data for a contiguous range of shard keys. Sharding spreads the load over more nodes, which reduces contention and improves performance.

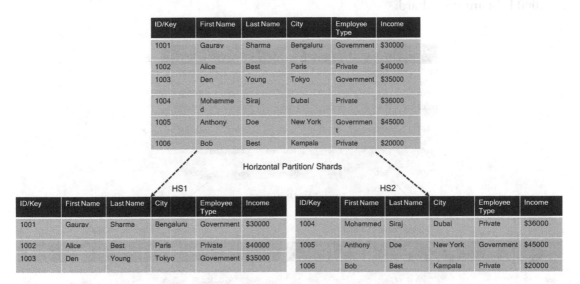

Figure 4-5.   *Horizontal partition/shards*

The shards don't have to be the same size. It's more important to balance the number of requests. Some shards might be large, and other shards might be smaller; you can choose the key based on the access operation. The smaller size is more frequent and faster; the larger size is less frequent and slow.

Besides achieving the scalability and throughput of service level agreements (SLAs), sharding can potentially improve unplanned outages, and each node collaborates to make sure always available. Some database vendors use the master-slave architecture style for sharding.

Range Based or Interval Partitioning/Sharding

Range-based sharding separates the date based on ranges of the data value. Shard keys with range values are separated into a separate chunk. Each shard in an architecture preserves the same schema of the master database. Interval partitioning is an extension to range partitioning in which, beyond a point in time, partitions are defined by the interval.

Range-based shards support more efficient range queries. Given a range query on the shard key, the query router can easily determine which chunks overlap that range and route the query to only to those shards that contain these values in a chunk.

Each partitioning, as shown in Figure 4-6, creates a dedicated partition for certain values or value ranges in a table. In the previous example, the partition is based on the income. The income less than $35,000 is shard into one, and the income greater than $35,000 is in another shard.

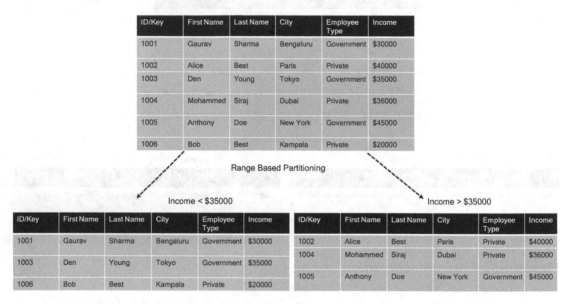

Figure 4-6. *Range-based sharding*

Partitions may be created or dropped as needed, and applications may choose to use range partitioning to manage data at a fine level of details.

The range partitioning specification usually takes a range of values to determine one partition, but it is also possible to define a partition for a single value. When one row is inserted or modified, the target partition is determined by the defined ranges. If a value does not fit one of these ranges, an error is raised. To prevent this kind of error, create another partition to accommodate these kinds of data that are not part of the range.

The range-based partitioning can result in the uneven distribution of data, which may negate some of the benefits of sharding.

Consider the range or interval partition in the following cases:

- Large tables are frequently scanned by a range predicate on a good partitioning column.

- You want to maintain a rolling window of data.

- You cannot complete any housekeeping activity on large tables in a required time, but you can divide them into smaller logical chunks based on the partition range column.

Hash Partitioning/Sharding

Hash partitioning is a partitioning technique where a hash key is used to distribute rows evenly across the different partitions.

Hashing is the process of converting a given key into another value and refers to the conversion of a column's primary key value to a database page number on which the rows will be stored.

Hash sharding takes a shard key's value and generates a hash value from it. The hash value is then used to determine in which shard the data should reside. With a uniform hashing algorithm such as Ketama (it is an implementation of a consistent hashing algorithm, meaning you can add or remove servers from the pool without causing a complete remap of all keys), the data with close shard keys is unlikely to be placed on the same shard.

In Figure 4-7, the table is partitioned by using the hash function on the ID/key column.

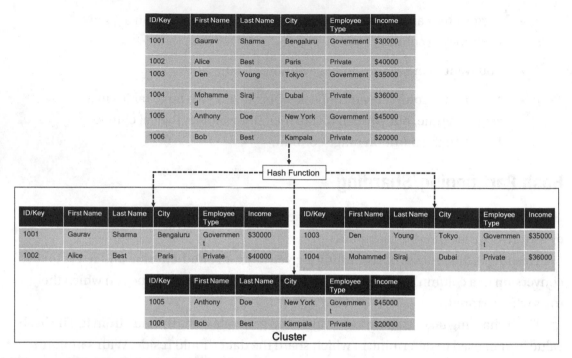

Figure 4-7. *Hash partitioning/sharding*

Partitioning by hash is used primarily to ensure an even distribution of data among a predetermined number of partitions and is focused on data distribution instead of data grouping.

As a rule of thumb, hash partitioning can be used in the following cases:

- To enable partial or full parallel partition-wise joins with likely equalized partitions

- To distribute data evenly among the nodes

- To randomly distribute data to avoid I/O bottlenecks

List Partition

The list partitioning concept is like range partitioning. As detailed, the range partitioning is done by assigning a range of values to each partition. In the list partition, we assign a set of values to each partition.

You should use list partitioning when you want to specifically map rows to partitions based on discrete values. For example, all users in Asia and Europe are stored in one partition, and users in America and Africa are stored in different partitions.

List partitioning is useful when we have a column that can contain only a limited set of values; even range partitioning can be used, but list partition allows you to equally distribute the rows by assigning a proper set of values to each partition.

Round-Robin Partitioning

The round-robin portioning is used to achieve an equal distribution of rows to partitions. With this technique, the new rows are assigned to partitions on a rotation basis. There is no partition key; rows are distributed randomly across all partitions, and therefore load balancing is achieved.

Vertical Partitioning

Vertical partitioning splits the data vertically to reduce I/O and the performance associated with fetching items that are frequently accessed.

In this example, as shown in Figure 4-8, different attributes of employees are stored in different partitions. VS1 holds data that is accessed more frequently, and, in another partition, VS2 holds the employee type and income, which are accessed intermittently.

ID/Key	First Name	Last Name	City	Employee Type	Income
1001	Gaurav	Sharma	Bengaluru	Government	$30000
1002	Alice	Best	Paris	Private	$40000
1003	Den	Young	Tokyo	Government	$35000
1004	Mohammed	Siraj	Dubai	Private	$36000
1005	Anthony	Doe	New York	Government	$45000
1006	Bob	Best	Kampala	Private	$20000

Vertical

Partition/Shards

VS1

ID/Key	First Name	Last Name	City
1001	Gaurav	Sharma	Bengaluru
1002	Alice	Best	Paris
1003	Den	Young	Tokyo
1004	Mohammed	Siraj	Dubai
1005	Anthony	Doe	New York
1006	Bob	Best	Kampala

VS2

ID/Key	Employee Type	Income
1001	Government	$30000
1002	Private	$40000
1003	Government	$35000
1004	Private	$36000
1005	Government	$45000
1006	Private	$20000

Figure 4-8. *Vertical partitioning*

The following are the benefits of vertical partitioning:

- Slow-access data can be separated from more dynamic data.

- Sensitive data can be stored in a separate partition with additional security controls.

- This strategy can reduce the amount of concurrent access.

Data Replication

Replication is the continuous copying of data changes from the primary database to the secondary database. The two databases are generally located in different servers, resulting in a load balancing framework by distributing various database queries and providing a failover capability. This kind of distribution satisfies the failover and fault tolerance characteristics.

Replication can serve many nonfunctional requirements such as the following:

- *Scalability*: Handling higher query throughput than a single machine can handle

- *High availability*: Keeping the system running even when one or more nodes go down

- *Disconnected operations*: Allowing an application to continue working when there is a network problem

- *Latency*: Placing data geographically closer to users so that users can interact with the data faster

In some cases, replication can provide increased read capacity as the client can send read operations to different servers. Maintaining copies of data in different nodes and different data centers can increase data locality and availability of the distributed application. You can also maintain additional copies of dedicated purposes, such as disaster recovery, reporting, or backup.

There are two types of replications:

- Leader-based or leader-followers replication

- Quorum-based replication

Leader-Based or Leader-Followers Replication

In leader-based replication, one replica is designed as a leader while another replica is a follower. Clients always send their write queries to the leader. Leaders write the data to its local storage first and then send the data change to its followers. When the client wants to read from the database, it can query either the leader or the follower. The leader is responsible for making decisions on behalf of the entire cluster and propagating the decisions to all the nodes in a cluster.

In Figure 4-9, there is a single leader with asynchronous and synchronous replication. The user sends an update request to update the first name to the leader. The leader updates first and then sends a synchronous request to Follower 1 and Follower 2. After the leader receives an OK response from Follower 1 and Follower 2, the leader sends an OK status to the user for a successful update. The leader replicates asynchronously to Follower 3, but the leader doesn't wait to receive any OK from Follower 3.

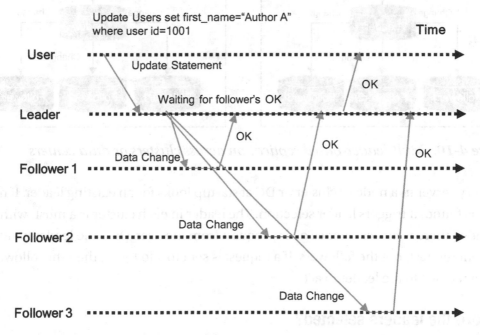

Figure 4-9. *Single leader with two synchronous and one asynchronous replication*

In a multileader example, there are two data centers (DCs) or clusters across geographies to provide high availability or latency to various users. In this model, you need to have two separate sets of leaders and followers in each cluster or DC and replicate each as mentioned in Figure 4-10; however, both need to synchronize and resolve any conflicts or inconsistencies. In this case, both leaders talk to each other over a conflict resolution object to sync each other.

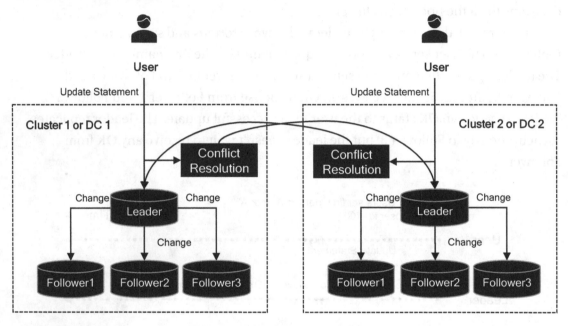

Figure 4-10. *Multileader-based replication across clusters or data centers*

Every server in a node or cluster or DC at startup looks for an existing leader. If no leader is found, it triggers leader selection. The leader in each cluster is a must; without the leader, there is no acceptance of any request from the user. Only the leader handles the client request, not the followers. If a request is sent to a follower, then the follower sends a request to the leader to act.

How are the leaders selected?

An election will be conducted to select a leader. If the existing leader is not available, then the database cluster uses the Raft consensus algorithm to choose the leader.

Raft is designed to select a leader by ensuring each node in the cluster agrees upon the same series of state transitions.

The Raft protocol was developed by Diego Ongaro and John Oosterhout (Stanford University) in 2014. Raft was designed for better understandability of how consensus can be achieved. The consensus is a method to involve multiple servers agreeing on one value; once they decide on a value, that decision is final.

According to Raft, each node in a replicated server cluster can stay in either leader, follower, or candidate. At the time of election to choose the leader, the servers can ask other servers to vote; hence, they are called candidates when they have requested votes.

Figure 4-11 shows the step-by-step process of how servers apply Raft consensus to choose a leader. A leader election is started by a candidate server; it starts the election by increasing the term counter, voting itself as a new leader, and sending a message to all other nodes. Here, Follower 3 is a candidate and sends messages to Follower 2 and Follower 1. A server will vote only once per term, on a first-come, first serve basis. If a candidate receives a majority vote, then it becomes a new leader. Here Follower 3 receives a maximum vote and then is selected as a new leader. Raft uses a randomized election timeout to ensure that split-vote problems are resolved quickly.

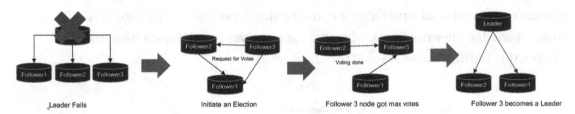

Figure 4-11. *Election process to choose a leader*

The high availability of leaders is achieved using a Failover pattern. A timeout with heartbeats is used to detect whether the replica is dead or alive. When one or more followers fall behind a leader by a certain configurable unit, it is called a replication lag and can cause strange side effects. Various consistency models can be used for deciding how an application should behave under replication lag.

Quorum-Based Replication

A cluster quorum disk is the storage medium on which the configuration database is stored for a cluster computing network. The cluster configuration database, also called a *quorum*, informs the cluster which physical server(s) should be active at any given time. The quorum disk comprises a shared block device that allows concurrent read-write access by all nodes in a cluster.

In this replication, the client is responsible for copying the data to multiple replicas. The nodes do not actively copy data among each other. The size of the replica group doesn't change even when some replicas are down. The client sends both read and write to multiple replicas. A cluster agrees that it received an update when a majority of the nodes in the cluster have to acknowledge the update. This number is called a *quorum*. The number of quorums will be decided by the following formula:

No of quorum = n/2+1

If you have five nodes in a cluster, then n=5 nodes, and then 5/2+1= 3 (round off). If you have a cluster of five nodes, you need a quorum of three.

In the quorum, how to decide how many failures can be tolerated equals the size of the cluster minus quorum. If you have five nodes and three quorums, then node-quorum = failure, 5-3=2. A cluster of five nodes can tolerate two of them failing.

You can use this formula to calculate nodes in a cluster:

2f+1

f=failure (2*2+1=5)

Figure 4-12 depicts a quorum-based replication pattern that shows quorum write, quorum read, and read repair after a node (replica 3) outage. In that case, it is sufficient to acknowledge the write. Thus, when the user receives two OK responses from the cluster, this satisfies the n/2+1 = 3/2+1=2.

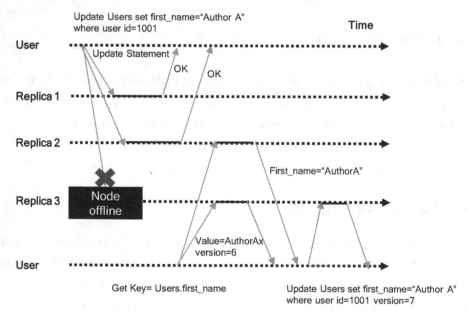

Figure 4-12. *Quorum-based replication*

If there are n replicas, every write must be confirmed by w nodes to be considered successful, and we must query at least r nodes for each read. The quorum allows the system to tolerate unavailable nodes as follows:

- If $w < n$, we can still process writes if a node is unavailable.

- If $r < n$, we can still process reads if a node is unavailable.

- With $n=3$, $w=2$, $r=2$, you can tolerate one available node.

- With $n=5$, $w=3$, $r=3$, you can tolerate two unavailable nodes.

The cluster can function only if the majority of servers are up and running. You need to consider the following:

- *The throughput of a write operation*: Every time data is written to the cluster, it needs to be copied to multiple servers. Every node in a cluster adds overhead to complete all the writes. The latency of data is a directly proportionate number of servers forming the quorum; therefore, if you increase the number of nodes, then it impacts the throughput.

- *The number of failures that need to be tolerated*: The number of failures tolerated depends on several nodes in a cluster; adding one more node doesn't give more fault tolerance. For example, 100 developers cannot complete the entire project in 1 day instead of 5 developers in 20 days.

Even if a client always performs quorum reads and writes, conflicts are likely to occur.

- Two clients may write to the same key at the same time (use concurrency control to manage this).

- If an error occurs during writing or if a node fails and needs to be re-created, a write may be present on fewer than w replicas.

The result is that replicas disagree about what a particular value in the database should be. In such a case, the application must be handled by using a concurrency algorithm.

Martin Fowler wrote in his blog about how to choose the optimal servers in a cluster, as shown in Figure 4-13. He says the decision is based on the number of tolerated failures and approximate impact on the throughput. The throughput column shows the approximate relative throughput to highlight how the throughput degrades with the number of servers. The number will vary from system to system. For further reading, refer to Raft Thesis and Zookeeper's paper (`https://raft.github.io/`).

Number of Servers	Quorum	Number of Tolerated Failures	Representative Throughput
1	1	0	100
2	2	0	85
3	2	1	82
4	3	1	57
5	3	2	48
6	4	2	41
7	5	3	36

Figure 4-13. *Deciding on the number of servers in a cluster*

In the quorum, write and read are not sufficient, as some failure scenarios can cause clients to see data inconsistency. Each server does not have any visibility of data on another server. The inconsistency can be resolved only when data is read from multiple nodes in a cluster.

Cloud Native API Management Patterns for Microservices

These are patterns for microservices.

Idempotent Service Operation

There are idempotent operations on HTTP methods. If a REST service is idempotent, the consumer of an API can make that same call repeatedly while producing the same result; in other words, making multiple identical requests has the same effect as making a single request.

When you design REST APIs, you must take into consideration that consumers can make mistakes. The consumer application can write client code in such a way that there can be duplicate requests coming to the API. In distributed architecture, failure may occur when invoking service. A lost request should be retired, but a lost response may cause unintended side effects if retired automatically.

These duplicate requests may be unintentional or intentional, you must design fault-tolerant APIs in such a way that the duplicate requests do not leave the system unstable.

The *idempotent service pattern* is used to provide a guarantee that service invocations are safe to repeat in the case of failures that could lead to a response message being lost. The idempotent requests can be processed multiple times without side effects.

When designing APIs, you must follow REST principles such as stateless, uniform interface, code on demand, etc. You will have automatically idempotent REST APIs for HTTP methods.

- GET, PUT, DELETE, HEAD, OPTIONS, and TRACE are idempotent.

- POST is not idempotent.

The GET, HEAD, OPTIONS, and TRACE methods should not have any significance when taking an action other than retrieval. These methods ought to be called "safe" methods. The POST, PUT, and DELETE are represented as "unsafe" requests and require special handling in the case of exceptional situation (e.g., state reconciliation).

POST is an HTTP method used to send data to a server to create/update data from the consumer. When you invoke POST requests many times, you will use the same resources on a server, so POST is not idempotent.

GET, HEAD, OPTIONS, and TRACE are used for requesting resources from a backend application; therefore, these methods never change a resource state on a backend application. They are purely for retrieving application data, so invoking multiple requests will not affect data on a server, so these methods are idempotent.

The PUT method is used to update a resource in a back-end application. If you call PUT multiple times, you are updating the existing record or overwriting the record. Therefore, it not changing any records; hence, PUT is idempotent.

The DELETE method is used to delete a record in a back-end application. The first request deletes a record in an application, and then the consumer will receive an HTTP response 200 (OK) or 204 (No Content) if the consumer sends the same request again and again, the DELETE method tries to find a record that was deleted earlier, or the HTTP returns 404 (Not Found) message. Here only the response is different, but there is no change in record status; hence, the DELETE method is idempotent.

Optimistic Concurrency Control in API

Concurrency control means an object will ensure the correct results are received for concurrent operations. Concurrency is required to avoid conflict between concurrent requests. There are two kinds of concurrency control.

- Optimistic concurrency control

- Pessimistic concurrency control

The *optimistic* concurrency control allows concurrency conflicts to happen. If they happen, the control makes sure the previously requested data is not changed. It doesn't lock any records to ensure the record wasn't changed in the time between the select and submit operations.

The *pessimistic* concurrency control blocks an operation of a transaction and does not allow another request to access a particular API or data.

Concurrency locking is not new; you, me, and everyone experienced concurrency issues in RDBMS, but how does the concurrency control impact our APIs? What happens when two users update the same record at the same time? Will you send any error messages? What response code will you use? In the REST API, several consumers interact with a single resource, each consumer holding a copy of the state. Let's imagine author A (you) and author B (me) are editing content on the same topic at the same time. You edit the content faster than me, and you submit the changes. When I complete my editing, I submit the changes, but I overwrite your changes. To avoid this type of conflict, you need a concurrency mechanism in APIs.

Conflict mostly occurs in response to the HTTP PUT method request as this method is used for the update operation. You need to use the concurrency control designed into the HTTP protocol to protect the integrity of your data.

An entity tag, specified by the ETag HTTP header, is an opaque token that the server associates with the particular state of a resource. It is an optional header in the HTTP request, and it is kind of like a version stamp for a resource. Whenever the resource changes, the ETag should change accordingly.

The API consumer and provider use the ETag value to determine whether a request to a resource is up-to-date by comparing the value of the ETag header on an incoming request to the value of the ETag header present on the server. If a value matches, then the consumer will get up-to-date information; if not matched, the consumer should refresh the request to receive the updated details.

With the previous example of content editing using an HTTP, imagine you want to modify some content in a server. What will you do? You use GET requests to fetch content and make a local modification and then issue a PUT request to update on the server.

With a single client, the interaction is happening without any issues. The concurrency is required when two or more requests try to modify same content, as shown in Figure 4-14.

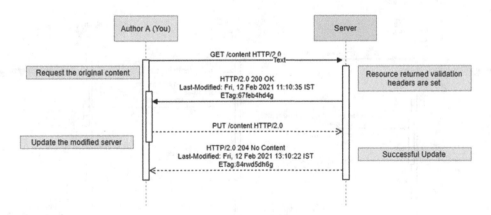

Figure 4-14. *Single request*

Say author A gets the content and modifies it locally, and author B requests the same content and modifies it locally. If both authors attempt to put their modifications back on the server, the modification of author A will be lost when author B's PUT overwrites, as shown in Figure 4-15. In this situation, both the authors are aware of this situation.

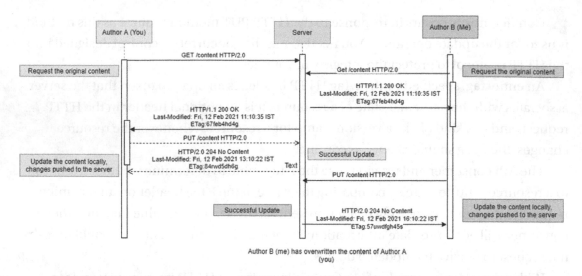

Figure 4-15. *Concurrency condition: author A updates lost*

To avoid these concurrency issues, as shown in Figure 4-16, you need to use the ETag header with the conditional request If-Match. This allows you to implement optimistic locking to avoid conflicts. With optimistic locking, each author is able to edit the content, and the author notifies with conflicts in a content.

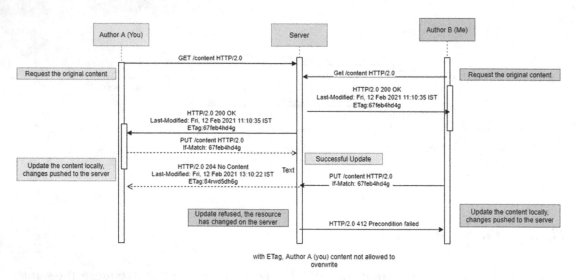

Figure 4-16. *Optimistic locking with ETag*

Figure 4-16 shows an implementation of optimistic locking by using an ETag and the If-Match header. If the ETag header does not match the value of the content on the server, the server rejects the change with 412 Precondition Failed. Author B is notified of the conflict and can try again after updating the local copy.

You need to make sure that when you are using optimistic locking, this condition is not suitable for everything, such as if both author A and author B update their photo at the same time on the same album. This is a feature, not a conflict.

Circuit Breaker

The circuit breaker pattern is used to check the availability of an external service, detect failures, and prevent them from happening constantly. In a distributed cloud native application, calls to remote resources and services can fail due to transient faults such as slow network connections and slow execution by microservices. These faults correct themselves after some time, and cloud and cloud native applications should handle this kind of situation.

For example, your mobile application needs to retrieve data from microservices hosted in the cloud platform. During business hours, your application might access 100 transactions per second (100 tps); in this case, your microservice is not available due to various faults such as network, slowness, etc. In this scenario, your microservice should be able to handle quickly and gracefully without waiting for each service request to time out.

The circuit breaker pattern was popularized by Michael T. Nygard in his book *Release It!*, which can prevent an application from repeatedly trying to execute an operation that's likely to fail. This allows it to continue without waiting for the fault to be fixed or wasting CPU cycles while it determines that the fault is long-lasting.

As illustrated in Figure 4-17, the idea of the circuit breaker is to wrap a protected function call in a circuit breaker object, which monitors failure. Once the failure reaches a certain threshold, the circuit breaker trips, and all calls to the circuit breaker return with an error, which means the circuit breaker acts as a proxy for operations that could potentially fail.

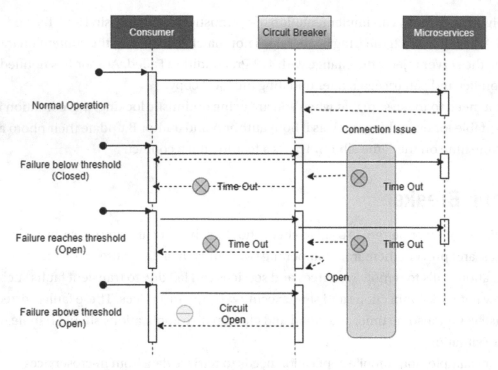

Figure 4-17. *Circuit breaker sequence diagram*

As shown in Figure 4-18, the circuit breaker pattern is implemented as a state machine that mimics the state of an electric circuit breaker.

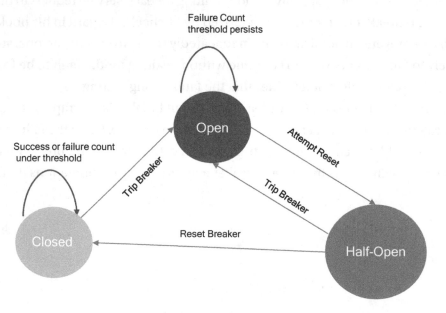

Figure 4-18. *Circuit breaker pattern states*

Closed: The operation executes normally. The circuit breaker maintains a count of the recent failures. If the number of recent failures exceeds a threshold within a given period, the proxy is placed into the open state. At this point, the proxy starts a timeout timer, and when this timer expires, the proxy is placed into the half-open state.

Open: The request from the application fails immediately, and an exception is returned to the application.

A half-open state is used to prevent a recovering service from being hit with a large number of requests. As a service recovers, it may be able to support a limited volume of requests until the recovery is complete, but while recovery is in progress a flood of work may cause the service to time out or fail again.

The circuit breaker pattern should be implemented asynchronously to offload the logic to detect failures from the logic to execute the actual operation. The implementation requires some form of persistence (to record the number of successful and unsuccessful operation execution). There are various tools are available in the industry like Istio, Hashicorp Consul, etc., to support the circuit breaker implementation.

Use this pattern in the following case:

- To prevent an application from attempting to invoke a remote service or access a shared resource if this operation is highly likely to fail

This pattern might not be suitable for the following:

- For handling access to local private resources in an application, such as in-memory data structure. In this environment, using a circuit breaker would simply add overhead to your application.

- As a substitute for handling exceptions in the business logic of your applications.

Service Discovery

The API gateway needs to know the location (IP address and port) for each microservice with which it communicates. In a traditional architecture and system, you could probably hardwire the location because this application is not dynamic. In a cloud native modern application like microservices, finding the needed location is a nontrivial problem.

Infrastructure services such as MQs usually have a static physical location that can be specified by using server OS environment variables. However, in cloud native microservices, determining the location of an application is not easy.

Application services are assigned a location and set of instances of service changes dynamically because of autoscaling, container orchestration, etc. Consequently, the API gateway needs to use the system's service discovery mechanism either in server-side discovery or in client-side discovery.

The service registry is a key part of discovery. It is a database containing the network locations of service instances. This is a single point of failure and therefore should be highly available and up-to-date.

Client-Side Discovery Pattern

When using this pattern, the client is responsible for determining the network locations of available service instances and load balancing requests across them, as shown in Figure 4-19. The client queries a service registry, which stores available service instances. The client then uses a load balancing algorithm to select one of the available service instances and makes a request.

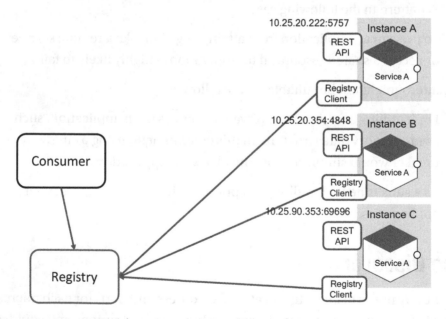

Figure 4-19. *Client-side registry*

The network location of a service instance is registered with the registry when it starts and removes when it terminates. The registration of services is refreshed regularly by using a heartbeat mechanism.

The client-side registry pattern has a few benefits and drawbacks. The following are the benefits:

- It is relatively simple, without additional components required except for the registry.

- The client can make intelligent, application-specific load balancing decisions such as using hashing consistently.

The drawbacks are as follows:

- The client is coupled with the service registry and potentially complicated with load balancing.

- You must implement client-side service discovery logic for each programming language and framework used by your service clients.

Server-Side Discovery Pattern

The client request to a service via a load balancer. The load balancer queries the registry and routes each request to an available service instance, as shown in Figure 4-20.

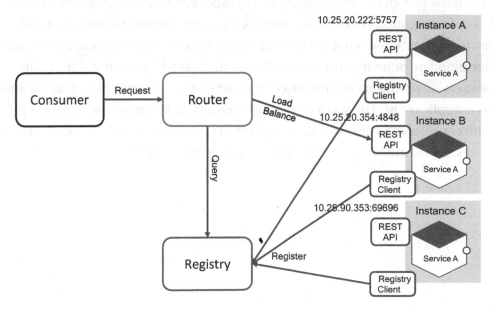

Figure 4-20. *Server-side registry*

As with client-side discovery, service instances are registered with the service registry.

The server-side pattern has several benefits and drawbacks. The benefits are as follows:

- Compared to client-side discovery, the client does not need to know how to deal with discovery. The discovery is abstracted away from the client. Instead, a client simply requests the router.

- This eliminates discovery logic for each programming language and framework used by your service consumers.

- Some cloud environments provide this functionality like cloud ELBs.

The drawbacks are as follows:

- Unless it is part of the cloud environment, the router is another system component that must be installed and configured. It will also need to be replicated for availability and capacity.

- More network hops are required than the client-side discovery.

Service Versioning

There are basic principles for designing an API exposed by microservices, the first of which is enforcing strong contracts. A microservice provides a versioned, well-defined contract to its clients and other microservices, and each service must not break it until it's determined no other microservices relies on it. Figure 4-21 illustrates the relationship between service producers like microservices and consumers such as web applications or mobile applications. The service producer registers all its services in service registries like Netflix Eureka and consumer contacts in the registry for service discovery, and later it connects to microservices for consumption of the service data.

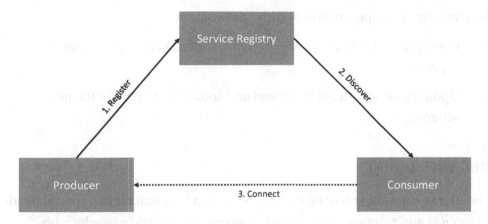

Figure 4-21. *Service registry*

There are two options for versioning the exposed API of a microservice. If you need to provide additional information on an HTTP method like a GET or POST or PUT operation, then the change is unlikely to be backward compatible. In that case, you need to look at ways of handling this problem.

The following are the two most common ways of handling versioning:

- Versioning in the URI

- Versioning in the header

URI Versioning

URI versioning is when you change the URI of the resource to contain version information, for example, /customer/v1.1/{id}. URI versioning gives you the ability to version an entire resource hierarchy. If you model a version like this, it enables resources for the automated navigation or discovery of resources.

The drawback of URI versioning is you need to change the resource name and location. This introduces a complex creation of URI aliases that make it difficult to track the production version, and it may break existing software links that do not include version information.

Here are two ways you can version in URI versioning:

- *Versioning at multiple hierarchy nodes (complicated)*: -/customer/
  version/2/account/version/2

- *Versioning as a query parameter*: /customer?version=2

163

There are multiple options to deal with this problem.

- Copy your old data into a new V2 database and keep the two entirely separate.

- Update your schema in place and add code to V1 to handle the new schema.

Header Versioning

In the header versioning, you need to include version information in a special header of each request and response. For example, say you need to add a header with `x-version:3.1`. In this approach, the resource name and location remain unchanged throughout your URL hierarchy, so you want to create URI aliases.

The drawback of the header versioning approach is that information can't be readily encoded into software links. It works only with custom clients that know how to encode the special header.

Based on the URI and header versioning mechanism, you can consider either forward- or backward-compatible methods.

- *Forward compatibility*: When developing a service, you make sure that this version will be compatible with future versions and won't be impacted when other services are updated (e.g., a new feature added). Achieving forward compatibility is a complex task since you have to deal with several unknown or unexpected features. The most common concept is to simply ignore unrecognized elements.

- *Backward compatibility*: The new version of a service is compatible with today's version, so existing clients can start using this new version as if there was no change. It can be verified by thoroughly testing the new version with old data sets.

There are a few different types of changes that are important for service versioning such as the major release, minor release, new capability, bug fix, etc.

You need a version number for each release. When a client requests a certain service, a service proxy forwards the request to a version of the service that is compatible with the version of the client. Therefore, all the clients have a single endpoint. While implementing the versioning, the governance of the API is of utmost importance to avoid any software breaks.

Cloud Native Event-Driven Patterns for Microservices

These are the event-driven patterns.

Asynchronous Nonblocking I/O

Compared to all the other characteristics of infrastructure such as CPU, memory, and disk, the network is slow.

- A high-end modern system is capable of moving data between the CPU and main memory at the speed of around 6 GB per second.

- A common local area network (LAN) of I/O is about 12.5 MB per second.

- Today's hard disk provides a lot of storage and transfer speeds of around 50–60MB per second.

- A CPU can execute approximately more than a billion instructions per second.

The I/O performance has not increased as quickly as CPU and memory performance, partially due to neglect and physical limitation. In a cloud native architecture, all system tasks are I/O-bound, and the I/O speed often limits the overall system performance.

According to Amdahl's law, as shown in Figure 4-22, improved CPU performance alone has a limited effect on the overall system speed. This law gives a theoretical speedup in the latency of the execution of a task at fixed workloads that can be expected of a system whose resources are improved.

$$\text{Execution time after improvement} = \frac{\text{Time affected by improvement}}{\text{Amount of Improvement}} + \text{Time unaffected by improvement}$$

Figure 4-22. *Amdahl's law*

Currently, the network is ubiquitous; it is the distribution of communications infrastructure and wireless technologies throughout the environment to enable continuous improvement. In the 5G world, network slicing enables the multiplexing of virtualized and independent logical networks on the same physical network infrastructure. Once the 5G network is rolled out, the speed of the network increases tenfold. Even though the network speed increases tenfold, it cannot match the speed of the CPU and memory. There are four fundamental performance metrics for I/O systems of your application.

- *Bandwidth (B)*: This is the amount of data that can be transferred in unit time from one service A to another service B, as shown in Figure 4-23. It is the capacity of the network like your Internet bandwidth of 1Mbps, 1Gbps, etc.

- *Latency (L)*: This is the time taken for the smaller transfer from service A to service B, as shown in Figure 4-23. The measuring units in time are transaction per second (tps), etc. For example, if the request that starts at service A is 0 seconds and reaches service B in 2 seconds, then your transaction rate is 2tps.

- *Throughput (T)*: This is the amount of data moved successfully from service A to service B in a given time period, as shown in Figure 4-23. It is measured bits per second as in Mbps and Gbps.

- *Response time (R)*: This is the time taken from the time service A sends a request to service B until the time that the service indicates the request has completed and reaches service A, as shown in Figure 4-23. For example, the response time is 4ms between your services, etc.

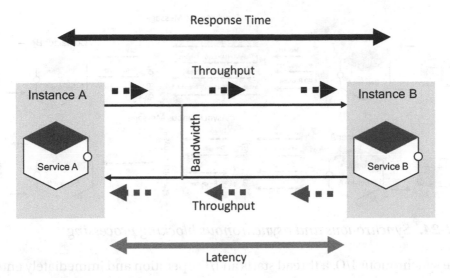

Figure 4-23. *Relationship of BLTR*

What is synchronous and asynchronous messaging?

As shown in Figure 4-24 A, synchronous messaging involves a sender that waits for the server to respond to the request with a message. The thread is blocked between the sender and the receiver. The sender cannot send another request until receiving a response from an earlier request.

As shown in Figure 4-24 B, asynchronous messaging involves a sender that does not wait for a message from the server. An event is used to trigger a message from a server. Even if the sender is down, the message processes the request. The server callback is sent once the server completes its execution. Here there is no blocking of threads.

Blocking I/O means that a given thread, after initiating an I/O operation, cannot perform further calculations until the result is fully received, which means when an API call is invoked to connect with the microservices, the thread that handles that connection is blocked until there is some data to read. Until the relevant operation is complete, that thread cannot do anything else but wait.

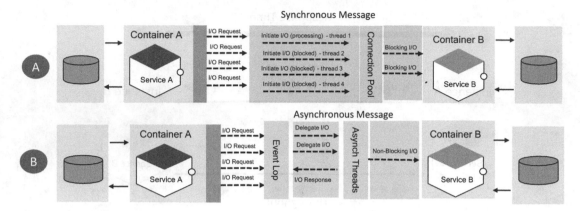

Figure 4-24. *Synchronous and asynchronous blocking processing*

In the synchronous I/O, a thread starts an I/O operation and immediately enters a wait state until the I/O request has been completed. This type of processing consumes a large number of resources.

The asynchronous nonblocking I/O pattern helps in saving the I/O cost where the total cost of I/O is more than the cost of the processing.

The asynchronous nonblocking I/O pattern immediately returns from I/O calls. On completion, an event is emitted, or a callback is executed. The interesting characteristic of this pattern is the fact there is no blocking or waiting at the user level. The entire operation is shifted to the kernel space. This allows the application to take advantage of additional CPU time while the I/O operations happen in the background on the kernel level. In other words, the services implementing nonblocking I/O can overlap the I/O operations with additional CPU-bound operations or can dispatch additional I/O operations in the meantime.

Use nonblocking I/O pattern for good performance under highly concurrent I/O. Most business use cases in modern architecture are based on asynchronous communication by using events; that is called *event-driven architecture* (explained in Chapter 6).

Stream Processing

Stream processing is a technique that lets consumers query continuous data streams and detect conditions quickly in a near-real-time fashion. Detecting the condition varies depending on the type of database and infrastructure you are using. Stream processing allows applications to exploit a limited form of parallel processing more easily. An application that supports stream processing can manage multiple computational units without explicitly managing allocation, synchronization, or communication among those units. The stream processing pattern simplifies parallel software and hardware by restricting the parallel computation that can be performed.

For the incoming data, a series of operations is applied to each element in the stream, and the operation can entail multiple tasks in the incoming series of data, which can be performed in parallel or serial or both. This workflow is referred to as a *stream processing pipeline*, which includes the generation of the data, the processing of the data, and the delivery of the analyzed data to the consumer.

Stream processing takes on data via aggregation, analytics, transformations, enrichment, and ingestion.

In the Figure 4-25 example, for each input data, the stream processing engine operates in real time on data and provides output. The output is delivered to a streaming analytics application and added to the output streams.

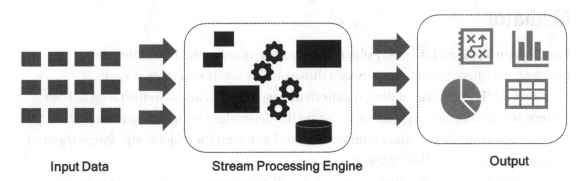

Input Data   Stream Processing Engine   Output

Figure 4-25. Stream processing

The stream processing pattern addresses many challenges in the modern architecture of real-time analytics and event-driven applications.

- Stream processing can handle data volumes that are much larger than the data processing systems.

- Stream processing easily models the continuous flow of data.

- Stream processing decentralizes and decouples the infrastructure.

The following are the typical use cases of stream processing:

- Trading

- Smart patient care

- IoT sensors

- Social media events

- Geospatial data processing

You can use tools such as Apache Kafka, Apache Flink, Solace, AWS Kinesis, etc.

Cloud Native Design Pattern for Microservices

The following are design patterns.

Mediator

Partitioning a system into many objects generally enhances the reusability, but proliferating interconnections between those objects tends to reduce it again.

Mediator is a behavioral design pattern and was written about in the Gang of Four pattern book. This pattern is about reducing the dependencies between two objects. This pattern restricts the direct communications between the objects and forces them to collaborate via the mediator object.

The mediator object (which encapsulates all interconnections), as shown in Figure 4-26, acts as the hub of communication; it is responsible for controlling and coordinating the interconnections of its clients and promotes loose coupling by keeping objects from referring to each other explicitly.

- Define an object (mediator) that encapsulates how a set of objects interact. Mediator promotes loose coupling by keeping objects from referring to each other explicitly, and it lets you vary their interaction independently.

- Design an intermediary to decouple many peers.

- Promote many-to-many relationships between interacting peers to full object status.

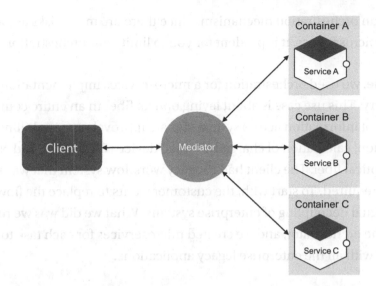

Figure 4-26. *Mediator pattern*

Services are not coupled with one another directly. Instead, each service talks to the mediator, which in turn knows and conducts the orchestration of others. The many-to-many mapping between colleagues that would otherwise exist has been promoted to full object status. This new abstraction provides a locus on indirection where additional leverage can be hosted.

Orchestration

Orchestration is like a conductor in a music concert. In a concert, an orchestrator takes a composer's musical sketch and turns it into a score of an orchestra, ensemble, or choral group, assigning the instruments and voices according to the composer's intentions.

Some say that orchestration is an anti-pattern. In the microservices world, based on my experience across industries, there are various use cases where orchestration is beneficial. Yes, orchestration is a single point of failure (SPOF) in an entire implementation, but that doesn't mean this is an anti-pattern.

Companies such as Netflix and Uber each created an orchestration tool. They are called Conductor and Cadence, respectively. Conductor is used in a workflow that adds Netflix idents to videos. (Idents are those four-second videos with the Netflix logo that appear at the beginning and end of the show.) You can use BPMN tools for orchestration, but with the caveat that you need to make sure of the context, use cases, etc., before you decide on an orchestration mechanism. Since there are many risks associated with orchestrating microservices, it is prudent for you to limit your orchestration to places that need it.

For example, we used orchestration for a microservices implementation in the telecom industry. This use case is about laying optical fiber in an entire country, which requires a flow of information across systems for an approval process, billing process, order progression, calculation of charged coupled device (CCD), V21, and NH21 validation of optical fiber. The client had a legacy workflow system that was very old and didn't scale as required. To start with, the customer wants to replace the flow system and later do digital decoupling of enterprise systems. What we did was we replace the flow with the orchestrator, and we created microservices for each task to connect synchronously with all the enterprise legacy applications.

Strangler Pattern

The digital decoupling of monolithic applications from scratch is a challenge. It consumes a lot of time and effort and involves a lot of risks. The main thing is to maintain the business continuity. You cannot apply the big-bang approach when decoupling legacy monolithic applications to microservices; it must be done incrementally, as shown in Figure 4-27. Feature of a legacy system can be replaced with microservices iteratively, but, finally, the new system with microservices eventually replaces all the features of the old system. You need to "strangle" the old system iteratively and allow the new system to evolve.

The fundamental strategy to adopt is event interception (i.e., the new microservices decide which events or requests will be passed on to the applications), which can be used to gradually move functionality to the strangler.

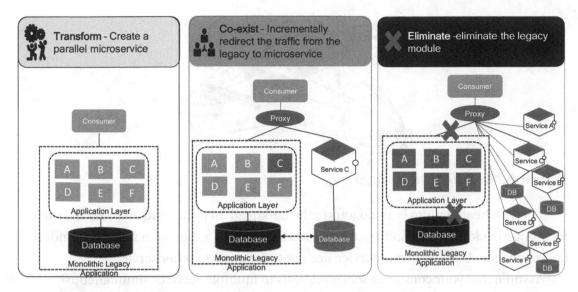

Figure 4-27. *Strangulation steps*

The proxy routes these requests either to the legacy application or to the new services. Existing features can be migrated to the new microservices gradually, and consumers can continue using the same interface, unaware that any migration has taken place.

This pattern helps to minimize the risk from decoupling and iterate the process smoothly. You can also set the percentage of users to an old or new application; once new microservices stabilize, then you route all users to new microservices. Over the time, as features are migrated to microservices, the monolithic legacy application is eventually strangled and gradually decommissioned.

Bulkhead Pattern

The bulkhead pattern is a type of application design that is tolerant of failure. It enforces the principle of damage containment and provides a higher degree of resilience by partitioning the system. In general, the objective of this pattern is to avoid faults in one part of a system taking the entire system down.

The bulkhead pattern, as shown in Figure 4-28, gets its name from cargo ship design. In a ship, a bulkhead is a dividing wall or barrier between other compartments. This means that if a portion of a ship hits a rock or iceberg, that portion fills with water, and the rest of the portion is unaffected. This prevents damage caused to the entire cargo ship and avoids sinking. If there are no partitions in the ship, the entire ship will sink. The bulkhead enforces a principle of damage containment.

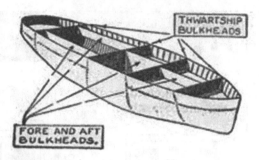

Figure 4-28. *Bulkhead in cargo ship*

The bulkhead pattern is analogous to the bulkhead on a ship and employs the same technique in cloud native architecture by separating your application into independent microservices. A failure in one service does not propagate to other services.

Assume that your consumer sends requests to multiple services simultaneously; during this time, your service is unable to respond in a timely manner due to various reasons. At that point, the request from the consumer to other services is also affected. Eventually, the consumer can no longer send requests to other services in your system.

In a microservices world, you cannot completely avoid dependencies across microservices to provide final responses to the consumers; therefore, you need to maintain intercommunication between microservices to complete the transaction.

To implement this pattern, you need to make sure that all your services work independently of each other and that failure in one will not create a failure in another service. The pattern also depends on what kind of faults you want to protect the system.

In Figure 4-29, service A and service B use service C, because both services depend on common functionality that resides in service C. Suddenly, service A becomes overloaded by multiple requests from the consumer; this will impact service C as service A needs dependent functionality from service C. In this case, service A is bombarded with requests to service C. In the meantime, the user sends a request to service B, so service B needs to call service C to fulfill a request to their consumers. However, service B is unable to get a response, or the response is very slow from service C, which will impact their consumer. This is all caused by both service A and B depending on service C and service C being unable to pool equally for both the services.

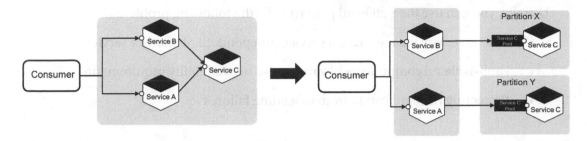

Figure 4-29. *Bulkhead in microservices*

To minimize this impact on service B, you need to adopt a bulkhead approach to partition service C into an equal pool of requests to serve its consumers. You don't need a separate database for service C; both instances of service C in each partition can share a database.

How does the bulkhead pattern work?

Figure 4-30 illustrates the bulkhead pattern with a connection example. This is a classic example for all synchronous connections, for example, in a database. The services request a connection to the database, and each head in this pattern has a single responsibility to manage the respective tasks. One component failing will not impact the whole.

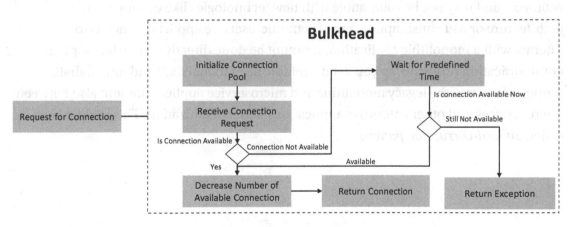

Figure 4-30. *Bulkhead pattern example*

While implementing the bulkhead pattern, you need to analyze the impact of the failure and how to minimize the damage caused by a failure. One more important thing you need to consider is to not generalize this approach for all your services as each service has its failures. Applying this pattern should be feasible both technically and financially.

Usually, you can use the bulkhead pattern to fix the following problems:

- Whenever you want to scale a service independent of another service

- Fault-isolated components of varying risk or availability requirements

- Protecting the application from cascading failures

Anti-corruption Pattern

The anti-corruption pattern, as shown in Figure 4-31, is a layer between the new modernized microservices and the legacy monolithic application. This pattern is useful in decoupling legacy applications into microservices.

In the journey of modernizing your monolithic application into a cloud native application, the journey cannot be done in one release or two releases; it takes many releases and takes months or years depending on the complexity of the system. Therefore, your approach should be iterative to decouple monolithic systems into microservices. In this case, you need to deploy both monolithic legacy applications and microservices to production, so your new microservices can't be executed silo without interacting with the legacy monolithic application.

A monolithic application was built on old technologies and communication protocols and may not be compatible with new technologies like event-driven architecture or API consumption, etc. If your microservice application needs to interact with a monolithic application, it cannot be done directly calling incompatible communication protocols, so you need a middle layer to marshall and unmarshall requests between the legacy monolithic and microservice applications and also between microservices and other enterprise applications in the organization. This middle layer is called an *anti-corruption pattern*.

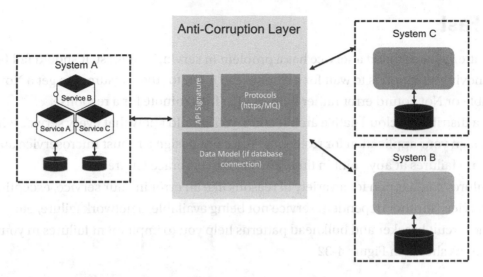

Figure 4-31. *Anti-corruption pattern*

Here is the functionality of an anti-corruption layer:

- Façade for other system; hides the implementation of service C and service D

- Establishing API contract signature

- Communication across systems with respective protocols like HTTP(S), MQ, etc.

- Data model interface if you are interacting with a database directly

- Translating the semantics

You can use any tools like ESBs and custom components as an anti-corruption layer. The following are some of the drawbacks of the anti-corruption layer pattern:

- This layer may add latency between the systems.

- Scaling of anti-corruption layer does not meet the requirements.

- The anti-corruption layer is a single point of failure and requires additional care to make sure it has high availability.

Cloud Native Runtime Pattern for Microservices

Here are the runtime patterns.

Fail Fast

This pattern states that if a service has a problem in serving a request, it should fail fast. An annoying situation is to wait for a response. It is OK for the consumer to get a Not Available or Not Found error rather than waiting for a minute for a response.

In a distributed cloud native architecture, you should know that every service will fail and design your application for resiliency. You can't design a robust microservice and expect no failures at any point in time. You need to embrace failures.

Failures can happen for a variety of reasons like an error in your service, exception in your service, another dependent service not being available, a network failure, etc.

The circuit breaker and bulkhead patterns help you to implement failures in your services, as shown in Figure 4-32.

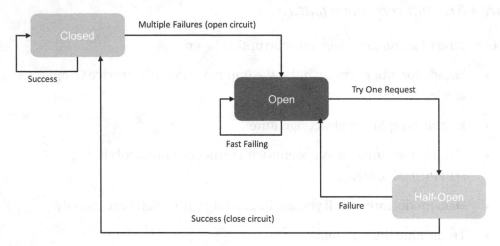

Figure 4-32. *Fail fast implementation*

Write an algorithm to detect the health of the system-based metrics. Certain metrics like the CPU usage of the containers will be evaluated for each scenario, and prediction methods are implemented that try to forecast failures based on these metrics. If the performance of the service is below the threshold, then you need to inject a boot request to the respective service to restart.

There are various online prediction methods to track failures and errors, such as symptom monitoring by using Bayesian predictors, co-occurrence predictors, pattern-based predictors, rule-based predictors, time-series predictors, and system model predictors. More details of failure management are covered in the "Microservices Architecture and Design" Chapter 5.

Retry

The *retry pattern* enables a cloud native application to handle transient failures when it tries to connect to services by transparently retrying a failed operation as mentioned earlier. The retry pattern improves the stability of an application by enabling the service consumer to handle anticipated, temporary failures of the service by retrying to invoke the same service operation that previously failed.

The retry approach is not new; you have been using the retry mechanism in all MQ-based applications. In MQs, you can configure several retries before sending to the dead letter queue. As shown in Figure 4-33, you need to adopt a similar approach in a cloud native application.

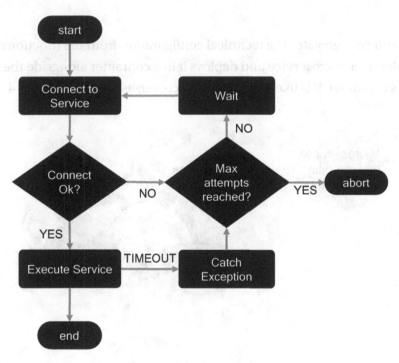

Figure 4-33. *Flow diagram of retry mechanism*

There are some considerations you need to consider when using this retry pattern.

- If you receive any indication that the fault is not transient or unlikely for a normal service request to be successful if repeated, for example, an authentication failure, then you should not use the retry mechanism.

- If the specific fault is unusual, it might have been caused by extraordinary circumstances such as a network packet lost in transit. In this case, the client code should use the retry mechanism immediately.

- If the fault is caused due to the unavailability of services, the service consumer should wait for a suitable time before retrying the request. Be careful here; you cannot retry a service infinitely.

- Set a retry count before you terminate or throw an error if the service is not available.

Sidecar

The sidecar pattern segregates the technical configuration from the functional implementation of a microservice and deploys it in a container alongside the functional microservices container. It is like a sidecar on a scooter, as shown in Figure 4-34.

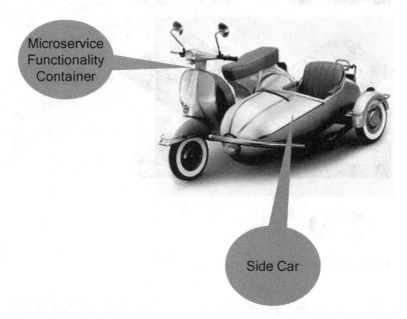

Figure 4-34. *Sidecar on a scooter*

This pattern allows you to add several configuration details from the third party without modifying the microservice. It is a single-node pattern made up of two containers. One container for the application container contains the core business logic, and another container is for the technical configuration details.

The objective of the sidecar container supplements and improves the application container without the knowledge of the application container. The sidecar container is co-scheduled onto the same machine through the container group, and it goes wherever the main container goes.

The sidecar container contains peripheral details of the application container such as platform abstraction, proxy to remote services, logging and configuration, etc.

There is no burden on the main microservices application logic container if you use the sidecar pattern as follows:

- Sidecar is independent of the main application container in terms of the environment, programming language, etc.

- It uses the same resources as the main microservice application.

- There is no latency when you separate the technical details to the sidecar; it runs on the same node.

- It reduces the burden on the application logic.

- There's no dependency on the platform code in the main logic.

The sidecar container uses a service mesh; refer to Chapter 5 for more details about service meshes.

Avoid the use of a sidecar when your application uses synchronous activity and your application code is small; it's not worth separating the technical functionalities from main components and also not suitable for microservices that undergo frequent changes.

Init Containers

Initializing logic for any program is common, if you remember how constructors work in an object-oriented program. The constructor will be called whenever an object gets initiated. The objective of the constructor is to prepare the object to execute the normal business functions.

Similarly, in a cloud native architecture, Kubernetes uses the same logic. There you are using constructors, but in Kubernetes, you need to use init containers.

A Kubernetes pod, as shown in Figure 4-35, can have multiple containers running microservices within it; similar multiple methods in a Java class also have one or more init containers, like the constructors in a Java class, and the init containers run before any application containers are started.

The init containers must complete successfully before the microservice containers start because the main microservice containers have prerequisites before they start. The prerequisites are setting up permissions on the file system, installing application seed data, initializing tools and libraries, etc. These prerequisites cannot be part of the main microservice containers; these prerequisites are part of the init containers.

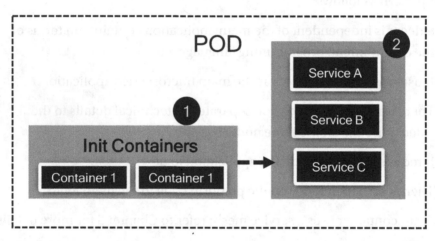

Figure 4-35. Init container

The init containers are small and complete the lifecycle very fast. For the pod to be successful, the init container must complete the initialization, or the entire pod will restart. The bottom line is that the init containers are mandatory for any pod to run successfully.

Saga Pattern

The saga pattern is an important pattern in the microservices world to ensure the consistency of the data in a distributed architecture without having a single atomicity, consistency, isolation, and durability (ACID) transaction. This pattern commits multiple compensatory transactions at different stages.

The two-phase commit transaction handles the ACID properties when the commit of the first transactions depends on the completion of a second. It is useful especially when you have to update multiple entities at the same time, like confirming the credit card transaction and crediting your account.

However, when you are working with a microservices transaction, then things get more complicated. Each service has its database, and you can no longer leverage the benefit of local two-phase commit to maintain the consistency of your whole system.

There are many scenarios such as the merchant payment, ecommerce application, etc., where the saga pattern is useful in a distributed microservices environment.

The saga pattern is a sequence of local transactions where each transaction updates data within a single service. The first transaction is initiated by a customer, and each subsequent step is triggered by the completion of the previous one.

In the order process use case, the saga pattern implementation looks like Figure 4-36. Each microservice depends on the other; there are sequences of steps of microservices.

Step 1: Order microservices (the order is created)

Step 2: Payment microservices (the payment is processed)

Step 3: Stock microservices (prepare order and inventory management)

Step 4: Shipping microservice (ship items by using the shipping address)

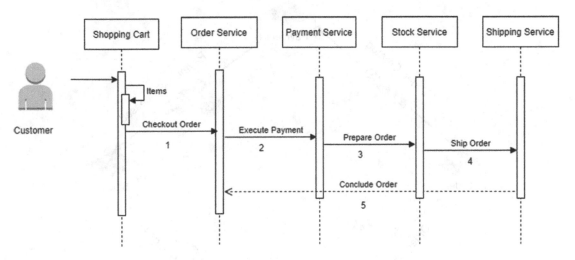

Figure 4-36. Sequence steps in order

To implement these use cases, you can choose from the following options:

- *Event-driven system with choreography*: Each microservice produces and listens to other microservices and self-decides whether an action needs to be taken or not.

- *Orchestration*: Central orchestration software or one microservice acts as an orchestration to coordinate saga's decision-making and sequence of business logic.

Event Driven and Choreography

In the choreography approach, as shown in the Figure 4-37, the Order microservice initiates a transaction and publishes an event, and payment services listen to these events and complete their local transaction. The Payment microservice publishes events, and the Stock microservices listens and consumes the payment event and executes its local transaction and publishes a new event. The final Shipping microservice consumes the event and executes the local transaction. The entire distributed transaction ends when the Shipping microservice completes its local transaction and there is no further publishing of events.

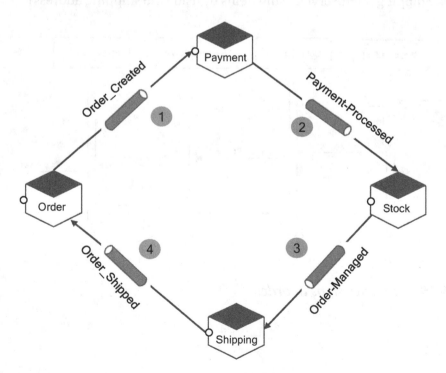

Figure 4-37. *Service interaction in choreography*

In the order process transaction, if the customer cancels its order or stocks are not available after a payment is processed, then you need to roll back the entire transaction and process a payment return to the customer. In this case, you need to implement another compensatory transaction.

In Figure 4-38, if an item is out of stock or a customer canceled an order, the Stock microservice publishes an event, and the Payment microservice consumes an event and processes a refund by compensating a transaction. The Payment microservice publishes an event, the Order microservices consume and update, and the order is canceled.

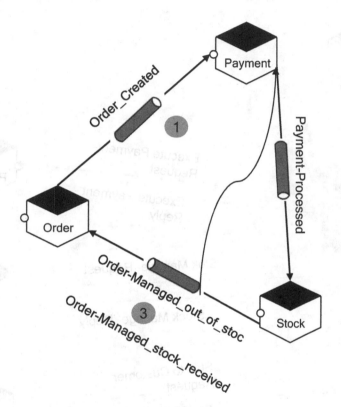

Figure 4-38. *Compensatory transaction*

Orchestrator-Based Saga Pattern

In this approach, either we use orchestration tools like Netflix Conductor/Apache Airflow/Uber Cadence or we create a new microservice with the responsibility of orchestrating each microservices. The saga pattern orchestrator communicates with participated microservices in a synchronous style or point-to-point messaging style with commands about an action.

As shown in Figure 4-39, the orchestrator sends a request to each service.

1. The orchestrator sends an Execute Payment to the Payment microservice, and it replies after execution.

2. The orchestrator sends Stock Manage to the Stock microservices and it replies with Stock Managed.

3. The orchestrator sends Process ship to customer to the Shipping microservices and replies after shipped.

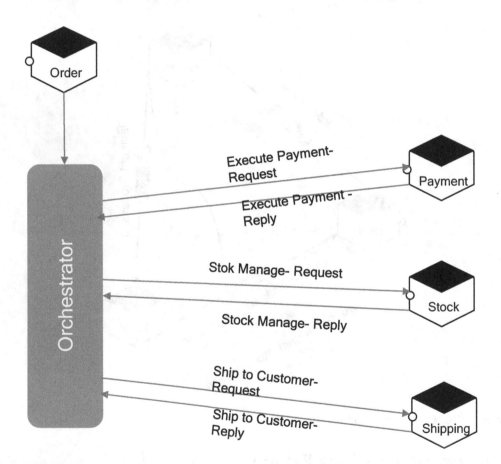

Figure 4-39. Orchestration saga

Rollback in the orchestration is easier. If the stock is not available or the customer cancels the order, then the orchestrator sends a command message to each service to compensate for the transaction.

Of the two, the chorography approach is the better and recommended approach to implement over the orchestrator approach.

Summary

Software architects must be familiar with software architecture patterns, as they are powerful tools when designing a cloud native architecture. Architecture patterns provide a proven solution to recurring problems for a given context.

Leveraging patterns gives architects a high-level structure of the cloud native system and provides a grouping of design decisions that have been repeated and used successfully. Using them reduces complexity by placing constraints on the design and allows us to anticipate the qualities that the cloud native system will exhibit once it is implemented.

In this chapter, you learned about some of cloud native patterns related to data, microservices, and event-driven architecture. You can use these patterns at design time and runtime.

The focus of the next chapter is how to architect and design cloud native elements such as microservices, event-driven elements, serverless, and data.

PART II

Elements of Cloud Native Architecture and Design

CHAPTER 5

Microservices Architecture and Design

Microservices are an architectural style for developing a single application as a set of domain services. Each service runs its process. The services communicate with clients and other services through synchronous and asynchronous protocols.

The microservices are highly maintainable, testable, loosely coupled, independently deployable, organized around business capabilities, and most important owned by a small team. This enables the rapid, frequent, and reliable delivery of large, complex applications. It also enables an organization to evolve its technology stack.

While much of the discussion about microservices has revolved around architectural definition and characteristics, their value can be more commonly understood through fairly simple business and organizational benefits: code can be updated more easily, and new features or functionality can be added without touching the entire application. This enables IT to develop and roll out new digital offerings more quickly and faster, making microservices an obvious choice for a cloud native application.

This chapter provides insight into implementing a microservices architecture for those who already have an idea of software architecture, design, and development. There are plenty of books and whitepapers available on microservices, and I will not duplicate that information; instead, I am covering microservices in the context of cloud native and showing some real implementations and problems you may face during implementation.

In this chapter, I will cover the following topics:

- Microservices architecture, the implementation and characteristics

- Decoupling

- How APIs are the de facto choice for microservices

- Hexagonal architecture and how to implement it

191

© Shivakumar R Goniwada 2022
S. R. Goniwada, *Cloud Native Architecture and Design*, https://doi.org/10.1007/978-1-4842-7226-8_5

- Reactive architecture and how to implement reactive microservices

- Resilience and fault tolerance in microservices

- Misconception of microservices

- Using AI and ML in microservices

- Case studies with real-time examples

Evolution of Microservices

Eric Evans wrote a book about domain-driven design (DDD) on how to modularize domains. This helped us to think about architecture, design, and code from a domain/business angle instead of just an IT angle. The concept of continuous integration showed us how we can automate our development and delivery process and efficiently move code to the production environment. We used to think that layering was the only approach for software development, but Alistair Cockburn's concept of hexagonal architecture changed the way we think of software architecture. The evolution of infrastructure from VMs to LXC containers to Docker containers helped us to better manage infrastructure. Martin Fowler and his team helped us to deliver software snippets by using agility.

DDD, agility, containers, DevOps, cloud, the microservices evolved from this world. No one invented microservices, but they emerged from the trends for solving business problems. Martin Fowler and his team from ThoughtWorks, Netflix, and Amazon helped us to build microservices. I started defining microservices in 2013, and I first developed a gaming client with the help of the former ThoughtWorks team.

In this chapter, I will explain a few important details of microservices for cloud native architecture and show some examples.

What Is a Microservices Architecture?

A microservices architecture, as shown in Figure 5-1, is an approach to developing one business application as a suite of domain services, with each domain service running on its container and communicating with a lightweight mechanism in a synchronous or asynchronous manner by using HTTP, GRPC, or messaging. These domain services are developed around business capabilities using independently deployable but fully automated deployment tools. Each domain service is decentralized in nature and developed with the polylithic and polyglot principles in mind.

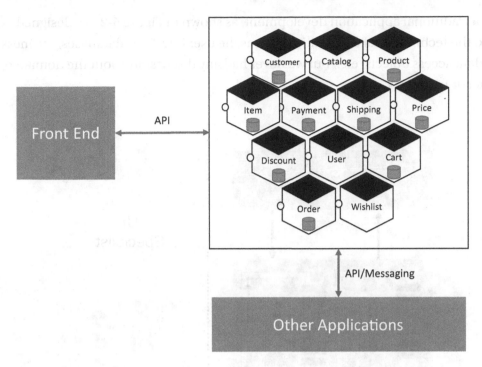

Figure 5-1. *Cluster of microservices*

Microservices can be adopted for any size and any type of business application irrespective of industry. Microservices are domain-based but have their unique characteristics. When you are considering building microservices, you need to make sure the following characteristics apply. Without these characteristics, whatever you are building is not a microservice; instead, you are building just a small monolithic application.

Characteristics of Microservices

The following are the characteristics of microservices.

Organized Around Business Capabilities

Before you start designing any microservices application, identifying and defining each microservice is important. What is the boundary of the microservice? What domain should it contain? What are the events and commands? What is the user role? Where will my microservices be deployed?

In a traditional application development, as shown in Figure 5-2, we designed around the technological capabilities such as the user interface, databases, business logic, data access objects, etc., but we never had any discussion about the domain or contract or boundary.

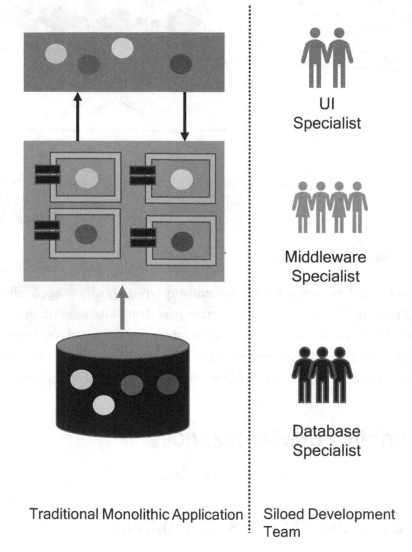

Figure 5-2. *Traditional architecture*

In a microservices development, as shown in Figure 5-3, each team owns the lifecycle of its services to production. Small teams act autonomously and are decentralized to build and own the microservices in production. This is called an *agile pod culture*. The structure includes all the resource capabilities to own and covers all the inception, construction, and operation-related microservices. This is the way that Amazon, Netflix, and Google are organized.

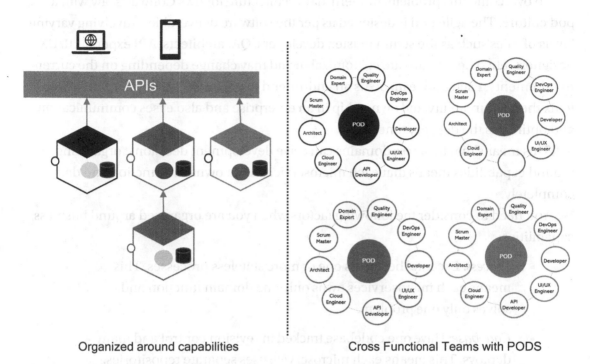

Organized around capabilities   Cross Functional Teams with PODS

Figure 5-3. *Microservices architecture definition*

When the architecture and capabilities are organized around domain business functions, the dependencies between the components are loosely coupled. As long as there is a contract between services, then each pod can run at its own speed. The structure of the agile pod was influenced by Conway's law.

Specifically, Melvin Conway mentioned the following in his book:

> "Organizations which design systems are constrained to produce designs which are copies of the communication structures of these organizations."

The meaning of this law is that communication is the key across teams; the teams belong to capabilities that require communication and collaboration to build an effective software system. If we work in silos like in a traditional development, there is no visibility across other teams. What they are doing, and how they are doing it? All these teams depend on well-structured documentation that consumes a lot of time, and there is no accountability and responsibility in teams. At the end, projects face too much technical debt and too many quality issues.

To overcome this problem, modern-day architecture follows Conway's law with a pod culture. The agile pod is designed as per the software deliverables, involving varying levels of roles such as the scrum master, developers, QA, architects, API experts, UI/UX designers, etc. These teams are customizable and may change depending on the current requirements. Each pod team owns an end-to-end microservices lifecycle, which helps to fix the accountability and ownership in an enterprise and also eases communication and optimizes the delivery time.

This means that business domains can drive development decisions; organizing around capabilities means that each microservices team owns the function and data completely.

You need to consider the following factors when you are organized around business capabilities:

- *Process*: Execute the app as one or more stateless processes. This means each microservices owns only one domain function and solves only one problem.

- *Codebase*: Have one codebase tracked in revision control and many deploys. This means each microservice uses separate repositories.

- *Build, release, run*: A codebase is transformed into a deploy through build, release, and run stages. This means each microservices has its own DevSecOps pipeline.

- *Admin process*: Run admin/management tasks as a one-off process; this means each microservices has its administrative tasks.

- *Config*: Store the config in the environment; this means each microservices has its containers, and it stores the config in a sidecar.

- *Disposability*: Maximize robustness with fast startup and graceful shutdown, which means each microservices is independent and has its lifecycle without affecting other services.

Autonomous

Microservices are a self-contained unit of functionality with loosely coupled dependencies across other services. The services are separate entities and deployed in an isolated container environment. All communication between microservices is through network calls by using HTTP, GRPC, and messaging protocols to enforce separation between the services.

These microservices can change independently and are deployed by themselves without requiring the consumer or other services to change, except for service contracts between consumer and other services. To create more autonomy in your microservices, you need to think about what services should be exposed and what they should have hidden. If there is too much sharing, our consuming services become coupled to our internal representations. This decreases your autonomy, as it requires additional coordination with consumers when making changes.

When you are adopting autonomous and DevSecOps in microservices, you need to consider the following design principles:

- *Communication independence*: Microservices constrains intraservice communication with other microservices as well as how your microservices communicate with external consumers. You must use nonblocking for all interservices communications. HTTP or the GRPC protocol is an example of blocking, and messaging is an example of a nonblocking technology; in addition, you should not consider using an external load balancer for interservice communication. All external communication negotiates its initial connection with API gateways for unified access control, and all subsequent communication is based on point-to-point communication with microservices and uses a round-robin load balancer to achieve equal distribution of load across microservices.

- *Agnostics*: The agnostic in your design dictates what should be provided by microservices. A pod team should be able to confer with the consumers of their service to determine what the contract should be and deploy it with no architecture configuration required and no concept of where and how the services are run.

- *Scalability*: The scalability principle governs rules for services configuration and implementation to ensure that the architecture is decentralized as much as possible and to ensure linear scalability. Microservices should not be aware of anything about other services' existence and their scalability. This means that any coordination of communication cannot be controlled above the service scope.

- *Independence*: All microservices are based on acting on incoming data and then responding to that by publishing their data. All services are equal; there is no master-slave concept. All services are terminated by themselves and not influenced by any other services.

Smart Endpoints and Dumb Pipes

This section discusses how your microservices effectively communicate with each other and what mechanisms need to be used. Communication across microservices is not an issue if you have only a few sets of microservices in your organization, but it becomes more complex when the microservices implementation grows in your organization.

If you go back to the SOA and ESB age, you used to implement services with BPEL or orchestration by central tool or process. The ESB is used to manage orchestration mechanisms to connect with various services or heterogeneous systems for intercommunication and managing logic. Now, with cloud native, there is no central tool, and we are not supposed to use one. The microservices are autonomous, decentralized, and distributed in nature; therefore, you need some kind of similar ESB mechanism in the microservices.

The alternative approach for an ESB-like mechanism in the microservices world is a smart endpoints and dumb pipes mechanism. The smart endpoints and dumb pipes simplify communication across microservices. In microservices communication, we use two types of protocols: synchronous and asynchronous with request/response and publish/subscribe, respectively.

The communication mechanism, security, and governance are often custom-coded into the microservice logic. Teams build in different languages and deploy to multiple environments, and organization services are typically siloed with a decentralized approach.

There are different approaches to solve communication complexity in microservices in which the endpoints are applications and the pipes are what connect them and allow them to communicate with each other. The following approaches are available:

- The first approach is to create custom code in the microservices logic as smart endpoints and use HTTP or message queues as dumb pipes. The drawback of this implementation is that you need to manage the code, implementation, and collaboration across various decentralized teams.

- The second approach is to create smart pipes like ESB. This is an anti-pattern. Microservices solve this anti-pattern. We are not suggesting that you implement this approach.

- The third approach is to externalize a communication mechanism to the sidecar proxy. In this case, the microservices concentrate only on the business implementation, letting the sidecar proxy manage communication at the network level. The drawback of this approach is you need to write custom configurations to manage communication across services by using sidecars.

- The fourth approach is an extension of the third approach. Use a service mesh and event mesh to communicate across services by using a sidecar proxy.

- The fifth approach is to use orchestration logic or software to simplify communication between microservices. Tools like Netflix Conductor or Uber or Zeebe, etc., provide an implementation of the orchestration mechanism. The drawback of these implementations is the single point of failure, and orchestration becomes too complex as microservices grow in an organization. This type of implementation is good for use cases like long-running services that are not best suited for choreography.

I suggest using the third and fourth approaches for implementing smart endpoints and dumb pipes, but the fourth approach is a clean implementation. This helps you to externalize the communication complexity and concentrate on the business logic.

What Is a Service Mesh?

In cloud native environment, a designing scalable and, independently deployable services are very much required. Services have grown largely in an organization, which creates a problem in the mesh of service-to-service remote procedure calls (RPCs) transported over networks. A service mesh helps you to design streamlined communication.

Service meshes provide intent-based networking for microservices and describe the desired behavior of the network topology. The service mesh pattern is used for microservices deployments and uses a sidecar proxy to enable secure, fast, and reliable service-to-service communications.

The service mesh provides the following:

- Provides a services-first network

- Removes the infrastructure concerns in the application code

- Provides declarative-based network behavior, node identity, and traffic flow through policy

Smart Endpoints and Dumb Pipes with Service Meshes

Using this approach, microservices deployed in a cluster interact with each other through a sidecar proxy, as shown in Figure 5-4. The sidecar intercepts both the synchronous and asynchronous communications of each service and acts according to the security and communication rules.

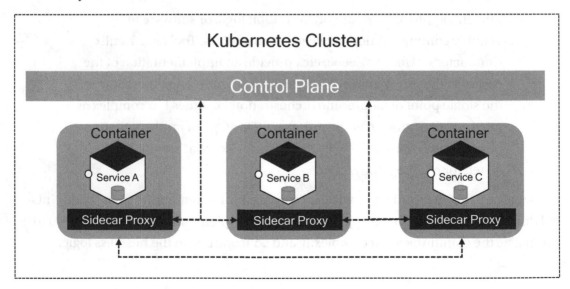

Figure 5-4. *Smart points and dumb pipes in a service mesh*

You can configure communication policies such as a circuit breaker, load balancing, service discovery, and security at the control plane level and abstract the governance considerations behind microservices from the service code.

A service mesh is used to abstract the governance regardless of the technology you are using to build microservices, and a service mesh is independent of the microservices architecture.

What Is an Event Mesh?

An event mesh handles the asynchronous event-driven routing of information between microservices. It intelligently routes events between the event brokers allowing the cluster or brokers to appear as a single virtual event broker.

A cloud native modern enterprise embraces an event architecture, and every application requires a robust central system to move events quickly, reliably, and securely from publisher to subscriber.

An event mesh is an architectural layer that dynamically routes events from one microservice to another irrespective of deployment location. The event mesh is a key enabler for event-driven architecture. An event mesh is a dynamic infrastructure that propagates events across disparate cloud platforms and performs protocol translation. You can find more details in Chapter 6.

Resilience in Microservices

Being *resilient* is the ability to provide the required capabilities in the face of adversity.

Specifically, it is the ability of a solution to absorb the impact of a problem in one or more parts of services while continuing to provide an acceptable service level to the business. A resilient application must thrive even when the unexpected happens; in other words, it provides the required capabilities despite excessive stresses that can cause disruptions. The residual defects in the software or hardware will eventually cause the system to fail to correctly perform a required function or cause it to fail to meet one or more quality attributes of microservices such as availability, security, performance, reliability, usability, etc. An unknown or uncorrected security vulnerability will enable an attacker to compromise the system.

Microservices resilience is more complex, and no microservice is 100 percent resilient to all adverse events or conditions. Resiliency is always a matter of degrees. Resiliency in microservices is typically not measurable on a single ordinal scale; in other words, you cannot say service A is more resilient than service B.

Resilience is not one component activity within microservices. The resilience must be composed of its parts. To exhibit resiliency, microservices must incorporate controls that detect a vulnerability and respond appropriately to these disturbances.

The service should be intelligent enough to detect changing conditions and act before it fails. Even if it fails, the service must self-heal by taking corrective action to ensure the availability of services at all time. Services must learn from past failures to predict eventualities and act to avoid cascading failures.

Resilience Capabilities

A resilient microservice protects its key capabilities from harm by using protective resilience techniques to resist adverse events and conditions or actively detect these adversaries, respond to adversaries, and recover from the harm they cause.

The following are the common adverse effects that require the resilient applications:

- Load-related failures

- Age-related failures

- Network failures

- Lost communications

- Input errors and defect-related failures

- Cyberattack

- Kinetic attack

- Nonavailability of dependency services

Figure 5-5 shows how these adverse effects impact a microservice's capabilities over some time. This scenario was captured for two microservices over a period of three days.

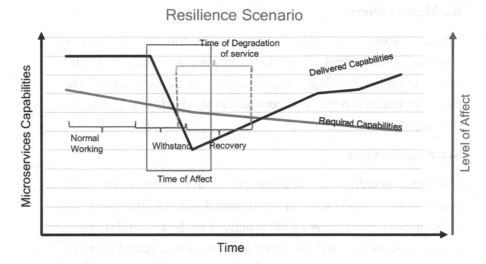

Figure 5-5. *Resilience scenario*

In the y-axis are microservices capabilities, and the x-axis is time. In the first few hours, the microservice performed with normal operation, and there were no adverse events. As time progressed and load increased, an adverse event occurred, and the microservices are encountered a fault and degraded the operation. This degradation exists for a certain time until response controls mitigate the faulty operation, and then the microservice will be in the normal working condition.

How to Build Resilient Microservices?

How do you design for automatic self-healing and application resiliency? As mentioned, with enough services and loads on the system, the microservices will always be in a partial failure status. But how can a designer approach microservices resilience? Approaching for resilience is not a one-time activity but is a continuous plan, culture, and work during the entire lifecycle of microservices.

The following patterns help you to design resiliency in microservices:

Circuit Breaker Pattern

The circuit breaker pattern prevents further damage to a failing system. The circuit breaker pattern detects the problem in the downstream system from timeouts and errors returned from the system. You can learn more details of the circuit breaker in Chapter 4.

Bulkhead Pattern

When designing your microservices application, sometimes you overload specific services within the application, and too much overloading leads to degrading of the service performance. This pattern isolates services and consumers via partitions. Learn more in Chapter 4.

Stateless Services

Use stateless services for designing resilient microservices. Stateless services depend on inputs and don't hold data; any copy of this service serves similar activity as the original services. These services spin off instantly depending on the condition of services such as CPU, load, etc. The load balancer can distribute load across microservice instances to improve resiliency and availability, and the load balancer can route based on the availability of instances.

Retry

Use the Retry option in your services; sometimes failures are short-lived for a few milliseconds, so retrying a few times may help in getting a response from the services. You can find more details in Chapter 4.

Fail Fast

Slow failure responses are the worst; it is better to have no response than a slow response. Implement self-restart by using the monitoring data. Use the container restart principle to autorestart your services. Learn more about how to restart a service in Chapter 3. Verify your service integration points early for downstream applications and other resources and send a validation request before processing.

Timeout

Use this pattern to design resilient microservices. When a consumer requests your services, there could be many reasons that your services might not respond or slow response. If there are too many requests during this period of slowness, this can cause a cascading impact, bringing the entire system down. Configuring connections and read timeouts at the client helps to release resources to the pool in case the microservices or database is taking more time than usual.

Throttling

Use this pattern for resilient microservices. The throttling or rate-limiting technique limits the number of incoming requests to be processed within a given time window. This approach helps to control the throughput meeting the SLAs and conserves the resource utilization by accepting only as many requests as it can handle.

There are various tools and software available to manage resiliency in microservices. Hystrix is a library designed by Netflix to isolate points of access to remote systems, services, and third-party libraries; stop cascading failures; and enable resilience in a complex distributed system where failures are inevitable.

Resilience4J was designed for functional programming; use this tool for managing resilience.

Elasticity in Microservices

Microservices and containers in a production environment need the adaptation of processes to enable elasticity. In a cloud native architecture, the microservices might receive unpredictable workloads and need to respond quickly to match the load and guarantee the quality objectives.

One of the most important characteristics of the cloud is elasticity. This is the degree to which a system can adapt to changes in demand by provisioning and releasing resources autonomously by autoscaling.

The following are the best practices you need to adopt for elasticity in microservices:

- Microservices must be stateless, and the states of an application must be stored outside of a container. The stateful application requires more care because a stateful data store will need to shard, replicate, and scale its state across the members in the cluster and know how to rebalance itself during scaling events.

- To keep costs to a minimum and meet quality objectives with agreed-upon service level objectives (SLOs), you need to configure the Kubernetes cluster to alter the required containers based on demand.

- For an event-driven architecture, each container instance is attached as a listener to the same request queue where the request arrived for processing. Use predictive approaches to set the arrival rate of the requests so that provisioning and releasing of resources take place beforehand. Here you need to add queues to the monitoring; you can configure the scale-up and down of resources based on the load on the queues.

Figure 5-6 illustrates how elasticity can be achieved in containerized microservices. I am using a payment processing example to show the elasticity. This example was captured during the first week of a month.

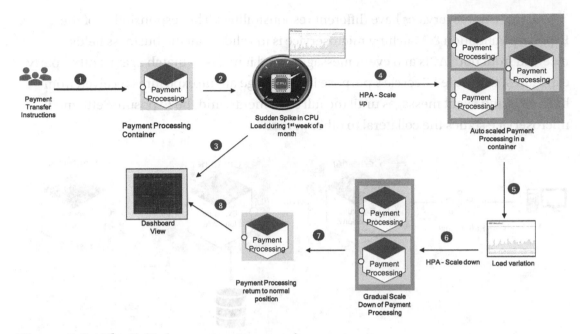

Figure 5-6. *Elasticity in payment processing*

More requests are always initiated during the first week of a month because the customer needs to use services for loan payment, payment of utility bills, etc. To meet the SLOs and quality attributes of microservices, the containers need to scale up and down based on the CPU load. When a spike occurs in payment services, the autoscaling option triggers and creates more instances of containers and scales down as CPU load decreases.

Distributed State

The state needs to exist within a bounded context of microservices. This is an ideal situation in a cloud native architecture.

In a distributed state across many microservices, it is difficult to say data is complete; only messages are being passed back and forth to create the whole transaction.

Let's see an example of collateral management in the capital market, as shown in Figure 5-7. It shows three bounded context microservices: Exposure Validation & Matching, Exposure Lifecycle, and Exposure Settlement. (Exposure is the entry point into the collateralization functions of multiple parties.)

All three microservices have different responsibilities. The responsibility of the Exposure Validation & Matching microservice is to validate all the business fields received from both APIs and event messaging, and it needs to match against other party exposures. Exposure Lifecycle's purpose is to manage all the exposures received from both APIs and event messages until the full settlements, and the Exposure Settlement microservice settles the collateral to other parties.

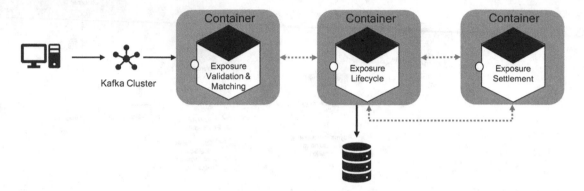

Figure 5-7. *State management*

In the classic SOA with ESB architecture, you might see the exposure is the common item and attempt to make it shared among these three microservices. This leads to functional bottlenecks. In fact, with these three examples of microservices, the only shared fields are the exposure business function. All the fields are unique to each microservice.

The state change of these microservices may be the result of many different inputs, and the inputs may come from other microservices with very low latency. The speed and scale at which the state is changing may make managing this with some sort of synchronous API call seem overwhelming. Changes to the state may be relevant and not just to the result. Synchronous API endpoints are not well suited for this type of change.

To manage various collateral types that are coming from different exposure services, the collateral management application is to keep track of changes in collateral in an ordered way, without having to lock or pause any other services. Everything must be asynchronous. Given these constraints, a service may need to retrieve the state as a whole.

How to Handle Distributed State with Asynchronous microservices

Nondistributed state is not an issue; it has one centralized, canonical representation of state. The state is accessible; you can manage the state without much complication. Distributed state is not easy because it has many dark corners, making it tricky.

In a distributed state, nothing is complete; only messages are passed between the services. These messages arrive out of order, are partially delayed, etc. You must consider failures when you are working with distributed systems.

As I explained in Figure 5-7, state change may be the result of many different inputs, and inputs might be user activity or other services. For either of these inputs, users are making relatively slow state changes or in a few service processes making high-frequency changes, so the state will be constantly moving. The speed and scale at which the state is changing makes managing this with API calls seem overwhelming. Changes to the state may be relevant not just to the end result but also along the way. Therefore, the synchronous API endpoints are not well suited to this type of change observation.

To meet these kinds of rapid state changes from various services, your architecture must be able to keep track of changes in an ordered way, without any pausing of services. Everything must be asynchronous.

Distributed state is vital to the management of various services. Anything backing the state should not be ephemeral for any outages, and the state should be able to be restored from the last known good position.

To solve the state management, the asynchronous APIs such as message queues or Kafka streams provide several capabilities for maintaining the global state of distributed microservices. In the collateral project, we used Kafka streams to build shared-state microservices that provide a fault-tolerant, highly available single source of truth about the state in our system.

As shown in Figure 5-8, exposure validation, match, and lifecycle services were built with Kafka stream instances with a source, processor with a persistent key-value store, and sink topic.

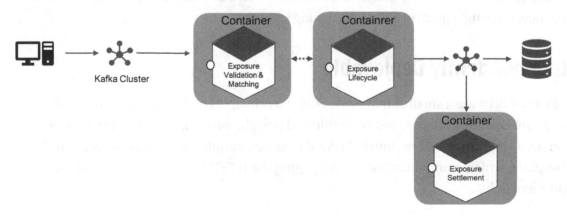

Figure 5-8. *Distributed state with Kafka streams*

In this example, an external system produces a message to the source topic in Kafka. Exposure microservices process the exposure messages using Kafka streams and writes calculated exposures to sink a topic in Kafka, and the consumer consumes new exposure messages. In this way, you can handle a seamlessly distributed state across microservices.

The second approach, as shown in Figure 5-9, is to use a distributed key-value pair caching technique such as Redis, Hezalcast, GemFire, etc., to handle distributed state across microservices.

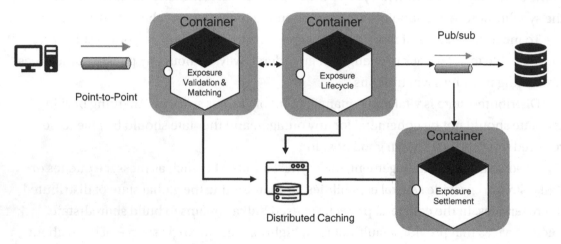

Figure 5-9. *Distributed state with caching*

In this example, the system sends a message in MQ, and exposure services consume and process and again publish the messages to exposure settlement and databases. The caching software stores session across microservices. The drawback of this approach is latency and single point of failure of caching software.

Independently Deployable

Microservices are a small unit of work, with the principles of the model related to the domain, bounded context, and polylithic and polyglot principles. Each microservice serves a single business responsibility and is loosely coupled with high cohesion and low coupling, which communicates across by using the HTTP, GRPC, and event messaging protocol only.

Microservices are owned by separate pod teams with their branching strategy and have less dependency on other microservices. These services to be deployed independently in a container and Kubernetes cluster. This type of deployment allows enterprises to test, modify, and add new business functionality independently without affecting other services in an application and allows them to scale up and scale down based on the load on a server, which helps to optimize the infrastructure cost.

Decentralization

You need to follow the decentralization principle for effective microservices. The main problem of centralization is to enforce central ideas, centralized technologies, etc., across the organization. My experience shows this approach is narrowing the thinking of team and innovation. Not every problem is a nail, and not every solution is a hammer. We need the right talent and the right software for the job.

Decentralization in microservices means the decentralization of governance, data, culture, team, and technology.

Decentralized Governance

Governance is a process to establish policies, standards, best practices, and guidelines to enable enterprise agility in an enterprise. In a traditional development methodology, we used to have a centralized governance team or centralized architecture board, etc., to make an entire decision on behalf of every unit in an organization irrespective of the team. This limited the speed, scale, innovation, automation, etc., and increased the cost of IT applications. Essentially, it did not support modern-day business.

In a cloud native, modern-day architecture, you need to encourage innovation and a culture of automation, scale, and speed. This can be possible only when you allow your team to work independently. The drawbacks of the decentralization approach are lack of control and duplication of development efforts, especially in midsize and large enterprises.

To succeed in the decentralization approach, you need to define effective collaboration, transparency, and well-defined standards, structures, and policies. Most important, your organization should embrace a culture of agility and automation. At Netflix, each team collaborates by sharing useful and tested code as libraries to encourage other teams to use them to solve similar problems and be open to picking up different approaches or modifying existing approaches. Similar to the Netflix model, you need to embrace a good model in your organization or develop a hybrid of your own.

Decentralized Data

In cloud native architecture, one of the microservice philosophies is the decentralization of data. A traditional monolithic approach uses a monolith database to store an entire application's transactional data in one RDBMS. In a microservice architecture, the best approach is to adopt a polyglot persistence architecture as defined by Martin Fowler's original microservices paper in 2014.

Correctly organizing data in the decentralization approach should be based on bounded context and API design. You are designing an API by providing a contract between your microservice and consumer, so in the database almost all the fields are related to your API contract, including operational fields and event storming events and related fields in the microservices. The design approach is to collect all API contract fields and events and group them in a related table and go through multiple iterations before finalizing the model.

The following are the main goals of a polyglot architecture:

- Remove scaling limits due to data access

- Avoid SQL joins

- Easier modeling of multipathing for performance

- Not restricted to one type of database; can use specific databases for microservices such as NoSQL or SQL

- Less potential for data model changes to have an application-wide microservices impact

- Simplified detection and correction of errors in production

One of the side effects of the decentralized approach is the ability to handle eventual consistency, synchronization of data, and latency.

Automation

Releasing microservices and new features to production rapidly and reliably with a single click is important for successfully managing microservice applications. You can achieve automation for the reliable deployment of microservices to production by using the principles of continuous integration (CI) and continuous delivery (CD). The fundamental building block of CI and CD is configuring a delivery pipeline with various tools, starting from the developer box to the production box.

In the delivery pipeline, an orchestrator like Jenkins configures various tools to run respective jobs starting from code check-in, code review, testing, security, performance, infrastructure as a code, and continuous monitoring. There are various good open source tools and cloud native PaaS services available to automate the entire pipeline.

Microservices are modular and intended to perform a single function. Modular software fits very well within the DevSecOps culture; thus, incremental code changes are easily pushed to production. Containerized microservices enable a quicker deployment, and services are immediately operational in production. Security in the pipeline for static code analysis (SAST) and dynamic code analysis (DAST) and container security both check for vulnerability at the early stage of the software. Automated operations and monitoring enhance the microservice approach to create an adaptable and scalable environment where deployment performs rapidly. Infrastructure as code automates the entire infrastructure, and containerization makes life easy for the entire development and infrastructure team, which reduces the cost and increases the quality of microservices.

By combining DevOps and microservices into development, testing will increase the efficiency of teams and reduce the cost. You can learn more about DevSecOps and get other automation details in Chapter 14.

Containerization

A container is a standard unit of software that packages up code and all its dependencies so the application runs quickly and reliably from one computing environment to another. It is a lightweight, stand-alone, executable package of software that includes everything needed to run microservices. Containers are built once and can be run on any infrastructure, meaning on-premises or with any cloud provider.

A container enables the fine-grained execution of microservices and provides isolation and a lightweight size. Virtualization is big and takes a long time to boot and run. Microservices are elastic and tend to experience highly unreliable workloads, and virtualization takes more time than a container takes to react to a spike. During this time, you may lose lots of transactions.

Containers enable continuous integration by streamlining the creation of new application environments and continuous delivery by allowing containers to run unmodified across environments.

The following are the benefits of a container:

- The developer concentrates on developing an application and leaves the rest to automation and the container.

- Containers can run on any infrastructure, such as private, hybrid, or public cloud.

- Containers increase resource usage and control infrastructure spend.

- Containers enable standardization practices and patterns.

- Containers offer a faster time to market for new services.

- Containers reduce deployment failures.

A microservices architecture does not dictate the use of containers, but using containers for a microservices architecture is better for implementing your applications. Container environments accommodate colocated application components in the same operating system instance and will help to achieve better service utilization rates. You can find more about container architecture in Chapter 16.

Design for Failure

Whatever system you use and however you design a system, you cannot avoid failure. Systems are bound to fail due to various reasons like network failure, server failure, catastrophic failure, natural disaster, a sudden spike in load, etc. An application needs to be designed so that it can tolerate the failure of services. If microservices fail, then you need to respond gracefully to the consumer.

Since microservices fail at any point in time, you need to design microservices to be able to detect the failure quickly and self-heal the failure. Microservices put a lot of emphasis on integrated real-time monitoring of application, infrastructure, and security and semantic monitoring. They need an early warning system so that you can use predictive analysis to heal the microservices

How Do You Design a Microservice for Failure and Stability?

The first design consideration is to use the circuit breaker pattern to avoid the effect. As I mentioned in Chapter 4, the circuit breaker pattern is commonly used to ensure that when there is a design failure, the microservice does not adversely affect other microservices in a system. This pattern works similarly to the electrical system of your home. It protects you from any adverse failure or power outage of your complex. Calls to microservices are wrapped in a circuit breaker object. When your microservice fails, the circuit breaker pattern allows subsequent calls to the service until a particular threshold of failed attempts is reached. At this point, the circuit breaker trips, and any further calls will be short-circuited and will not result in calls to the failed service.

The second design consideration is to use the bulkhead design pattern to avoid the effect. As we mentioned in Chapter 4, the bulkhead pattern is like a ship's hull that is composed of individual watertight areas. The reason for this is if one bulkhead fails, it does not impact the whole ship. You need to apply this kind of partition in your microservices design. Assume that your consumer sends requests to multiple services simultaneously. During this time your service is unable to respond in a timely manner due to various reasons; at that point requests from the consumer to other services are also affected. Eventually, the consumer can no longer send requests to other services. In a microservices world, you cannot completely avoid a dependency across microservices to provide final responses to the consumers; therefore, you need to maintain intercommunication between microservices. You need to make sure you follow independently deployable principles to avoid cascading failure.

The third design approach is integrated real-time monitoring to monitor the real-time health of your microservices. You need to configure all your services with event-driven architecture to send monitoring and traces of your services in real time to monitoring tools. This helps you with early detection to avoid failure. More details of integrated monitoring can be found in Chapter 19.

The fourth design approach is to apply machine learning predictive analysis to the health of the system. There are widely different failure prediction techniques available. The prediction algorithm can be created and trained based on the event log of a microservices, time-series data like CPU, etc. For errors captured in the event log, you can use pattern-recognition tools that run over log files to detect faulty behavior based on certain rules. Rule-based predictors derive failure in log files by gathering rules that indicate failure. The symptom monitoring method will detect symptoms of failure in the microservices based on several metrics collected in integrated monitoring. System model predictors use the CPU utilization and memory usage metrics to calculate the failure of a system. Once you gather the prediction, then you send signals to the container by using the container's lifecycle conformance principle and infrastructure as code to spin up a new container image of microservices and gracefully shut down the old.

The fifth design approach is to use failure as a service (FaaS). Failures are severe for any services, and customers cannot wait for you to fix the problem. The top ten digital trends in digital transformation believe the failure service influences how the software will be developed and tested. Use failure testing in your system; it is an approach that allows your team to discover weak spots that can lead to failure. The probability of failure parameter plays a major role in understanding the health of an application. Cloud service outages still take place. According to Netflix, there are many unknown real production scenarios in which a failure recovery might not work. Amazon has leveraged "game-day" exercises that inject real failures like EC2 failures, power outages, etc. There are many ways to test failures and failure as a service, such as the shift-left approach and chaos monkey. How failure services are tested will be explained in Chapter 12.

Living Continuous Design

In traditional development, the architecture and design could be planned at the start of the project or product. Once the team defined the architecture and design, the development should follow it, and there was very little room to change the defined plan. Now we have a rapidly changing environment to support unbelievable disruption in business and rapid changes in customer expectations. The team might not have any idea what next change comes and how your end customer interacts with your application. In a similar way, the technology is changing rapidly, and a lot of greater innovation is happening. Whatever the technology you use today to do development may become obsolete in the next two years.

You should always adopt a design mechanism that can manage change. The primary objective of a living continuous design is to enable your architects and engineers to have continual and incremental change support embedded in the application. The living design also ensures that your system is not fragile.

The living continuous design supports nonbreaking changes to ensure that we can adopt continuous design and derive various services. One of the evolutions of a living continuous design is the microservices architecture style. Microservices demonstrate a living design need.

Two features of living continuous designs are modularity and coupling. A living continuous design supports modularity, and microservices are decoupled from each other. Whenever there is a change in one microservice, it will not impact any other service in the system.

To get the benefits of a living continuous design, you must test the architecture and design. This test is done by adopting a fitness evaluation and identifying challenges and risks at the early stage. There are various fitness functions and methodologies that can be used to identify the fit of the architecture. How and what methodology and functions are used for fitness tests will be explained in Chapter 12.

Self-Healing

In an enterprise, there are several microservices that evolve daily. The management of these microservices becomes complex, which leads to a chance of failure that is very high even though you designed your microservices with the principles of failure and resilience. Therefore, you need to design your microservices to be self-healing at runtime. In normal circumstances, you can configure the services to send an alert if a service misbehaves so you can examine these alerts and fix the anomalies. You need to bring down the service, fix it, and deploy it, and this is a manual operation. What if your organization has more microservices across various systems? Is it possible to do that manually? If yes, how much effort and resources are required? Self-healing of services is one of the options to automate the failure process.

A self-healing microservices architecture, as shown in Figure 5-10, has the ability to continuously monitor the integrated operational environment, including the application, infrastructure, and security; detect and observe anomalous behavior; and provide a self-healing and self-tuning mechanism to adapt to sudden changes in its operational environment dynamically at runtime.

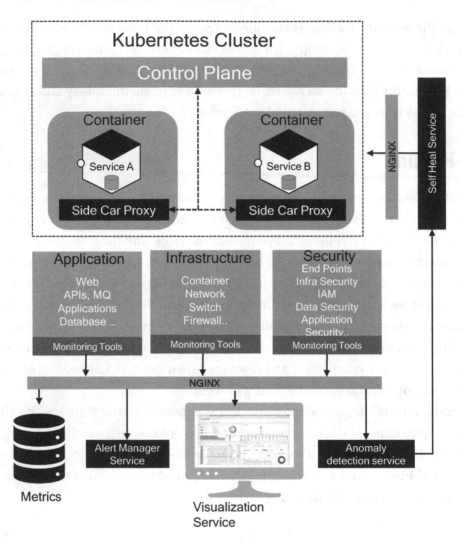

Figure 5-10. *Self-healing ability in microservices*

Metrics are collected continuously from the application, infrastructure, and security. The metrics are for cluster nodes, services, and containers and include CPU usage, memory, disk reads and writes, and network reads and writes. These metrics are streamed in real time into the metrics database. After you capture the service metrics, you need to run simple anomaly detection services continuously on the collected metrics and enable the training of a model with the collected metrics with simple rules.

The anomaly detection service provides the continuous detection of anomalous behavior and prediction about the microservice's performance based on the metrics collection. The identification of continuous detection is based on the parameters of

CPU usage, memory, disk, and network reads and writes against the normal behavior parameters of the microservice and health scores of different services. The scores are weighted by using a linear equation or a time decay function. Based on the score, a microservice is bucketed into three zones such as red, yellow, and green.

The scores are calculated based on the metrics you collected. Here are some examples:

- CPU utilization = 1

- Memory utilization = 1

- Error logging = 1

- Response time = 1

- Disk reads and writes = 1

- Network reads and writes = 1

Use the following formula to calculate the score of metrics:

- **Score of each metrics** = (current value – normal behavioral value)/ (critical value -normal behavioral value)

For CPU utilization, assume normal behavioral value is 0.5 and a critical value is 1.5.

- **Score of CPU Utilization** = (1-0.5)/(1.5-0.5) = 0.5/1= 0.5.

Here you can say your microservices are running normally.

Note   The critical and normal behavioral values will be different for every metric and every application.

The microservices score will be calculated as the summation of all the metrics scores:

- **Microservice score** = $\Sigma pi*wi$ / Σwi

If the microservice score is less than the critical score, then there is no need to take any action; if the score is above the critical level, take an action.

All this automated calculation is part of the anomaly detection service that calculates automatically in real time and sends a notification to the self-healing service to execute the action.

The self-healing service executes the outcome of the anomaly detection service algorithm by injecting the container principles detailed in Chapter 3. If the algorithm score is bad, it deletes its entry from the NGINX upstream list and kills the container by using the lifecycle conformance principle's `SIGTERM` and `SIGKILL` commands of the container. If the score is average, then reduce the load on NGINX for the respective microservices; if the score is good, then do not take any action.

Hexagonal Architecture

The hexagonal architecture, or ports and adapters architecture, is an architectural pattern used in software design. It creates loosely coupled application components that can be easily connected to their software environments using ports and adapters. This makes components exchangeable at any level and facilitates test automation.

The main idea of a hexagonal architecture is to provide interaction to the outside world at the edges of your design. The domain logic should not depend on what you expose as a REST or MQ, and your microservices should not depend on where you get data, whether through a database or NoSQL etc.

In a traditional layered architecture, you have a user interface, business logic or backend application layer, and database layer. All these layers are tightly coupled to each other. If you want to replace a database with another, then you need to change the data access layer within the application logic to accommodate the changes such as connections, SQL queries, etc. The hexagonal architecture addresses these concerns of tight coupling across various layers.

The concept of hexagonal architecture, as shown in Figure 5-11, is to create domain microservices without a UI or a database and run a test suite on domain services and later link the UI and services by using the adapters. It divides microservices into several loosely coupled and replaceable components, such as domain logic, adapters, platforms and infrastructure, test services, external systems, platform services, etc. Each component is connected with the other through a port and through communication with other applications or UIs or platforms through this ports.

This architecture allows you to isolate the core domain logic of microservices from the outside. This will help to change the data source details and API protocol details without a significant impact on code domain logic. The main advantage is to provide a clear boundary for testing. If data source changes, test only that part, entire your not microservice.

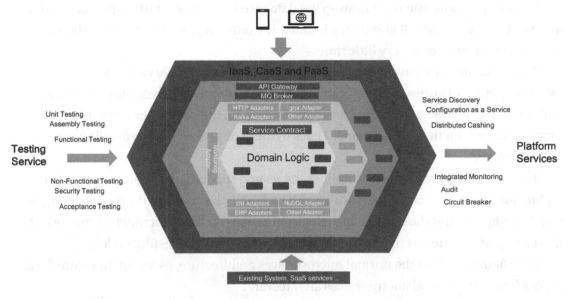

Figure 5-11. *Hexagonal architecture*

In Figure 5-11, the four layers to define business logic are as follows:

- Infrastructure layer where your microservices are deployed

- Platform layer where your API gateway, Kafka cluster, MQ broker, etc. are

- Adapter layer where your adapters are placed, which connects with external systems and your core domain logic of microservices

- Domain logic layer, where you construct the domain business functionality

With these four layers, you can define the business logic without any knowledge of where the data is kept and how the business logic is triggered and how consumers interact.

There are DB adapters for different storage implementations such as the RDBMS database or NoSQL adapter for document or key-value databases. A data source implementation method is defined in the adapters and stores the implementation of fetching and creating the data.

The communication adapters are input for your microservices. The communication adapters such as HTTP, GRPC, MQ, or Kafka, etc., include transport information from the consumers or requestors. All the interaction logic is constructed in the communication adapters and separated from the core domain business logic.

For some reason, you want to swap the database from existing RDBMSs like MySQL to a NoSQL like MongoDB and then without any trouble replace the MySQL adapter with the MongoDB adapter in very little time.

A new consumer wants to get some details from your microservices, but they listen only with MQ messages; you can bind the MQ adapter with your microservices and provide a queue name to the consumer. Therefore, the consumer can configure their system with a new queue name. That's it; they start receiving the details from microservices.

The hexagonal architecture simplifies the testing services. For seniors such as DB replacement and new consumers with an MQ adapter, the scope of the testing is only to test the adapters, not the core business logic, because you have not touched the code. In this case, just run the few regression test cases to complete the testing cycles.

Let's figure out how the normal microservices architecture, as shown in Figure 5-12, differs from a hexagonal microservices architecture.

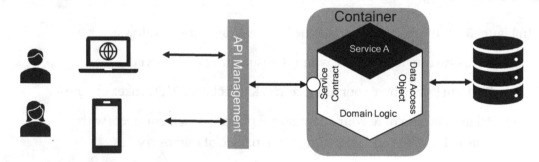

Figure 5-12. *Normal microservices architecture*

In the normal way, as shown in Figure 5-12, usually in the microservices architecture, you have domain logic created using any programming languages such as Spring Boot, Golang, .NET, Scala, etc., and it exposes the REST API contract between consumers and domain logic. Here the consumers can be a mobile application or web application or third-party application. The domain logic interacts with the repository to store or retrieve information from databases like NoSQL or RDBMS, etc., based on the consumer request by using HTTP methods like PUT, POST, GET, TRACE, etc. Here all service contract controllers and data logic are coupled in a single microservice with multiple subcomponents in it.

If you want to replace or modify the database, then you need to change the entire microservice and carry out entire regression testing of your microservices and for the new consumer with queues.

The following are the drawbacks of hexagonal architectures:

- Increases in the latency

- Additional complexities to manage adapters

Enterprise Microservices Examples

In previous chapters, you learned about certain patterns, and so far in this chapter, I have explained microservices, characteristics of microservices, etc. These topics cover how to solve various microservices problems. In the next few sections, I will cover how to wire all this together to explain the real-time microservices implementations. These are the examples from various industries, and I have been personally involved in architecture, design, and implementation of the real-life examples.

Case Study: Trade Finance

A trade finance project was implemented for Bank A. Bank A was doing millions of transactions with a value in the billions. They want a seamless and cloud native architecture for their new trade finance module. We proposed microservices and event-driven architecture and deployed them on the Azure cloud platform.

The following sections provide the details of the functional components and architecture components.

What Is Trade Finance?

Trade finance is the financing of international trade flows. It exists to mitigate or reduce the risk involved in an international trade transaction. In trade finance, an exporter requires payment for their goods and services, and an importer wants to make sure they are paying for good quality and for a specific quantity.

Trade Finance Ecosystem

As shown in Figure 5-13, the seller or exporter can require the purchaser or importer to prepay for the goods shipped, and the purchaser may want to reduce the risk by requiring the seller to document the goods that have been shipped. Banks may assist by providing various forms of support. The importer's bank may provide a letter of credit to the exporter, and the exporter's bank may provide a payment upon presentation of certain documents, such as a bill of lading. The exporter's bank may make a loan by advancing funds to the exporter based on the export contract.

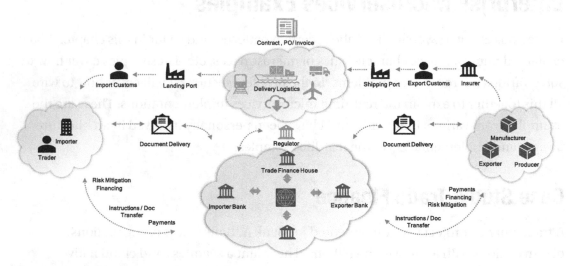

Figure 5-13. *Trade finance ecosystem*

Trade Finance Functional Architecture

As shown in Figure 5-14, the following are the functional components required to build a trade finance application for any commercial bank; these functional components are not limited to the ones shown in the diagram:

> *Letter of credit (L/C)*: As shown in Figure 5-15, in a documentary credit, a buyer asks a commercial bank to issue an L/C in favor of a seller. The issuing bank must pay the seller once it receives and verifies the proper documents for the trade.

> *Collections*: Banks act as intermediaries and present the sellers' shipping documents to the buyer as proof of transfer.

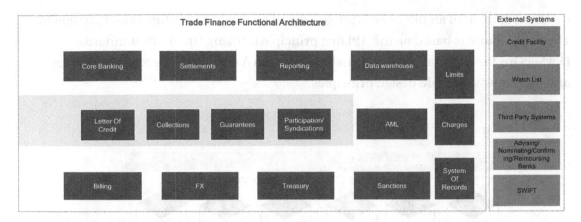

Figure 5-14. *Trade finance functional architecture*

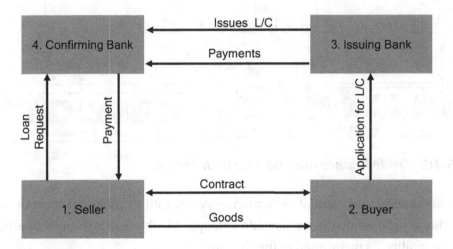

Figure 5-15. *Letter of credit flow*

Settlements: This is the transaction wherein the securities being trade are transferred into the buyer's account, and the monetary value of the security is deposited into the seller's account after the trade execution.

Guarantees: This is a way for buyers and sellers to prove their credit worthiness. It promotes confidence in a transaction that will greatly encourage the process. It is a promise to make a payment to a seller in certain circumstances, such as failure of obligation from the buyer.

The Figure 5-16 architecture is implemented for the previous functional architecture. The architecture is based on the API first principle by using Open API standards, DevSecOps for automation, cloud enablement with Azure Cloud, product principles, and frictionless upgrade design principles.

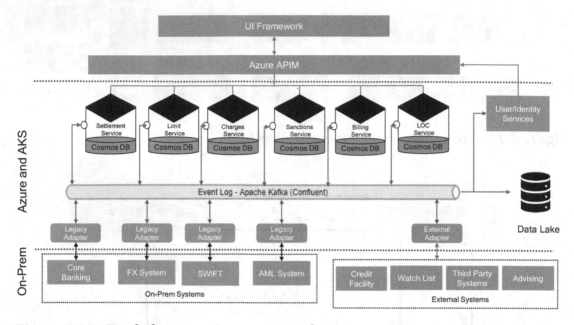

Figure 5-16. *Trade finance microservice architecture*

From an architecture point of view, microservices split a functional component into a service that is independently replaceable and upgradeable and is organized around a business capability, as mentioned in the diagram.

The architecture is implemented with microservices and event-driven architecture and with polyglot principles. Microservices such as settlement services, limit services, charge services, sanction services, billing services, and L/C services are deployed in the container by using Azure Kubernetes services, and each service interacts via an Apache Kafka implementation.

These architecture-provided APIs are the interaction mechanism with the external applications and UI dashboard. The architecture is provisioned in Kubernetes on Azure and with managed security on Spring Boot services using Helmet, Passport, and NGINX reverse proxies.

All trade finance services need to connect to various other existing bank applications such as core banking, Forex, SWIFT, etc., that reside in the on-prem data center and connect through legacy adapters by using a VPN connection. Anti-Money Laundering (AML) is an batch activity and audits every transaction in the trade finance industry and also connects to third-party systems like watch list, credit facility, etc., through the external adapter.

All events and transactions are sent to the data lake (Azure Blob) for further analytics and reporting.

Case Study: Collateral Management

As shown in Figure 5-17, the collateral management service aims to manage the collateralization of exposures resulting from bilateral trading activities between counterparties (repos, securities lending transactions, OTC derivatives, and so on) including activities subject to clearing.

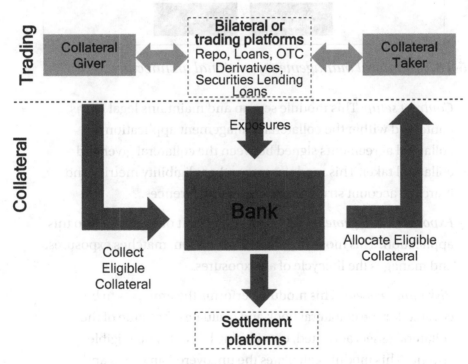

Figure 5-17. *High-level collateral interaction*

Processing between the collateral giver and taker (collateral selection, payment and settlement, and management during the life of transaction) is managed by the agents. These agents are the collateral portfolio managers of a bank.

Collateral Management Functional Architecture

As shown in Figure 5-18, the collateral management consists of several items.

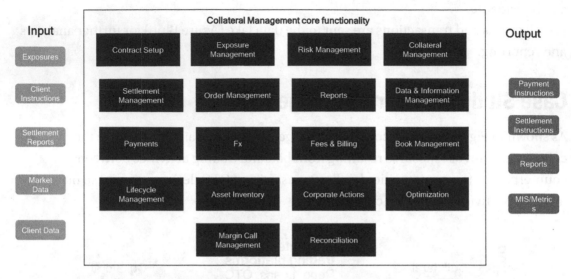

Figure 5-18. *Collateral management functional architecture*

Contract setup: This module sets up and maintains legal terms contained within the collateral management application for collateral agreements signed between the collateral giver and collateral taker. This module stores other eligibility metrics and haircuts, account structure, and client preferences.

Exposure management: This is an entry point of exposure into this application. This module performs validation, matches exposures, and manages the lifecycle of an exposures.

Risk management: This module performs the amounts to be covered for the collateral book and evaluates the value of the collateral assets allocated, considering haircuts and eligible criteria. This module calculates the uncovered amounts and triggers margin calls to the collateral application.

Collateral management: This module assesses the available inventory of collateralizable assets and runs an algorithm to determine the optimal collateral allocation based on given constraints, priorities, and preferences.

Settlement management: This module captures the required collateral movements and instructs the necessary settlement systems for execution and manages the settlement failures.

Order management: This module receives collateral status notification and updates the collateral books accordingly.

Reports: This module generates all the required data for all different consumers including data required for optimization algorithms.

The rest of the modules are standard such as collateral fees, billing, payments, Fx rates, book management, etc.

Collateral Management Architecture

Collateral management is a highly transactional and real-time processing of data. We decided to design collateral application with microservices and event-driven architecture principles because:

- Each component in collateral modules handles different types of transactions and needs to be scaled independently. For example, risk management requires highly scalable and robust services because it calculates and manages the collateral books in near real time based on the equity, Fx rates, etc. The contract module does not require much scalability because contracts are signed at the beginning of the collateral agreement.

- We adopted an event-driven architecture for publish-subscribe and real-time communication across microservices.

The technologies used for this application were Spring Boot, Active MQ, APIs, JRules, Data Grid Distributed Cache, and Postgres SQL.

As shown in Figure 5-19, all microservices are designed to deploy independently and scale independently. Each microservice was designed and developed with Spring Boot and deployed in the Red Hat Open Shift environment.

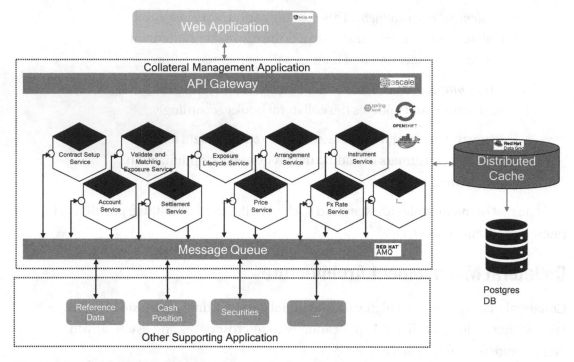

Figure 5-19. *Collateral management architecture*

All microservices are event sourced and stored in the distributed cache and eventually stored in a Postgres database. The state is stored in the Active Message Queue as events and then passed across microservices and stored in the databases. The microservices are deployed in the container in an Open Shift environment for the runtime platform and automatically deployed by using the Jenkins and Ansible Tower infrastructure as code solutions.

Microservices and User Interface: Micro Front End

There are two ways to implement the user interface of a microservice application:

- Front-end monolith, as shown in Figure 5-20
- Micro front end, as shown in Figure 5-21

A micro front-end architecture is a design approach in which a front-end app is decoupled into individual, semi-independent micro apps working loosely together. The micro front end is an extension of microservices.

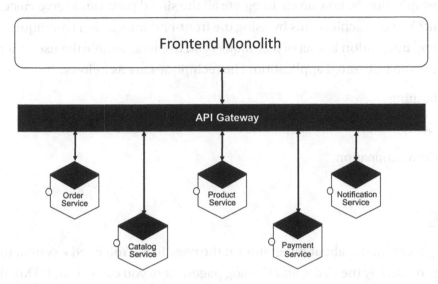

Figure 5-20. *Front-end monolithic with microservices*

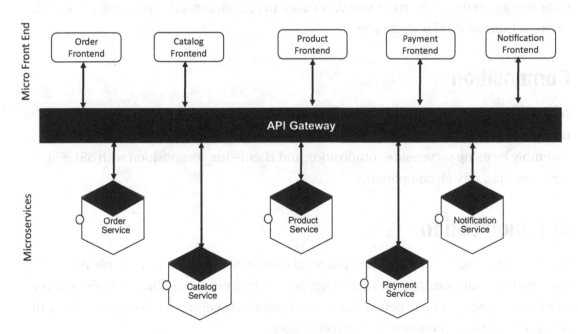

Figure 5-21. *Micro front end with microservices*

The micro front-end approach is different from other architectures in the way we think about and build features. Teams have an end-to-end responsibility for a given functionality and start building from the polyglot persistence, microservices, and micro front end.

The next question is, how do we integrate all the siloed pages and serve customers as a single unit? You can achieve this by using the front-end integration technique.

Front-end integration is a set of techniques you use to assemble the user interfaces of the teams into an integrated application. The techniques are as follows:

- Routing

- Composition

- Communication

Routing

The routing technique is about integration at the page level. You need a system to get from a page owned by the Order and Catalog pages. Here you can use an HTML link to integrate the Order and Catalog micro front ends. If you want to navigate from the Catalog page to the Order page, you don't need to reload; use a shared application shell or meta-framework like single-spa.

Composition

In the composition technique, each fragment in pages is collated and put in the right slot on a page. A separate composition technique does the final assembly. You can do that assembly by using server-side composition and client-side composition with SSI, ESI, iFrames, Ajax, or web components.

Communication

For interaction across applications, you need communication across multiple micro front ends. In our example, the Order page gets an update after adding an Order button to a Catalog page, and payment is done after the order is completed. You can achieve this integration by using communication techniques.

Pros and Cons of Micro Front Ends

The advantages of micro front ends are as follows:

- The individual team can choose their technology and ownership.

  - Combined with microservices, fully autonomous end-to-end teams can be deployed.

  - The business has flexibility to create teams focused on specific domains.

- Development and deployment are very quick.

- The benefits of microservices are leveraged in a much better way.

These are the challenges of the micro front end:

- UX consistency is an important aspect.

- User experience may become a challenge if each individual team goes in their own direction; hence, there should be some common medium to ensure UX is not compromised.

- Dependency needs to be managed properly.

- Multiple teams working on one product should be aligned and have a common understanding.

Microservice Architecture in Artificial Intelligence

You already know that some of the applications you use in day-to-day life use artificial intelligence (AI), such as Alexa, Google Home, Spotify, Siri, etc. These AIs are a set of programs developed to perform specific tasks.

AI will be a de facto standard and usage pattern for several objects in an industry, and it will grow spontaneously year after year. This will increase the number of objects or use cases and creates many challenges and opportunities for enterprises. In the broader vision of AI, every connected object in an industry will be reused in multiple AI application domains for enhancing the smartness and intelligence of the AI application.

The intelligence in AI is composed of the following five characteristics:

- Reasoning

- Learning

- Problem solving

- Perception

- Linguistic intelligence

When you define an AI application with this set of characteristics, the AI architecture must follow the pattern of separation of concern. If not, then it becomes a single, all-in-one, monolith kind of application. Then it follows the same approach for the provisioning of AI services. A better architecture for AI must be based on the microservice architecture style.

In the era of digital transformation, AI is emerging with improved data collection methods, data training sets, advanced data processing mechanisms, enhanced analytic techniques, and a modern service platform. If you separate the implementation into similar groupings, then it can be developed and maintained easily without much effort and risk.

The microservices style can be adopted in AI systems for marketing, banking, finance to predict future data, agriculture such as climate change, population growth, healthcare like medical care systems, clinical decision support systems, gaming, autonomous vehicles, and social media.

For all these kinds of AIs, microservices are the best approach for the activities such as data processing, data aggregation, and data transformation. They can be processed by using a pipeline with events.

AI Subcategories

The horizontally layered platforms do not address the issues of specific AI domains, but they support necessary technical solutions across the platform; however, the vertical components are used to resolve domain-specific problems. Figure 5-22 shows the vertical components.

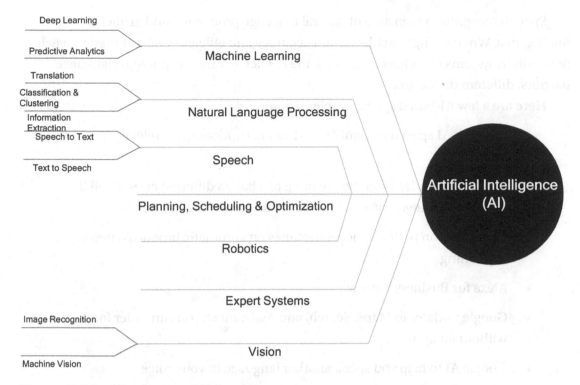

Figure 5-22. AI subcategories

Generally, the architecture of an AI component is modular and layered.

The first layer is to read the data and do data processing, data aggregation, data transformation, etc.

The second layer is to apply the execution layer like ML models and the execution layer for machine learning, foundation model and cognitive services for intelligent agents, automation engine and recognition engine for robotics, etc.

The third layer is for exposing the APIs like the Text/Speech API, Image API, Predictive API, Ecosystem API, etc.

The vertical components can be developed by using the microservice architecture style, which improves the service modularity, extensibility, availability, scalability, resilience, etc., for AI services.

Microservices Vertical Components: Speech AI

Let's look at an example of a Speech AI implementation to explain the details of microservices adoption; you can follow a similar approach for other AI implementations.

Speech recognition is an area of natural language processing and artificial intelligence. When trying to achieve good accuracy and efficiency of automatic speech recognition systems of various languages, the challenges are morphology, language barriers, different dialects, etc.

Here are a few AI-based speech implementations:

- Google's AI speech recognition to human captioning for television news

- AI that can understand the meaning of a baby's different cries to tell if the baby is hungry, tired, or in pain by listening to their cries

- Transcription performance milestones on automatic broadcast news captioning

- Alexa for Business Review

- Google updates to Maps, Search, and Assistant so you can order food without an app

- Google AI to help you speak another language in your voice

- DIY kid smart speaker that features a private voice assistant

- Google AI Translation to make anyone a real-time polyglot

If you search Google, you can find hundreds of different AI-based speech applications and implementations. Do you think all these application architectures are reusable, resilient, easily deployable, and easy to discard? No? How do you create new AI-enabled microservices speech software?

A speech recognition program works using an algorithm through the following:

- Acoustic modeling

- Linguistic modeling

In Figure 5-23, each blue box has its responsibility and can be developed with polylith and polyglot principles, and each box can scale and deploy independently; hypothetically, each box is a candidate for microservices.

For example, let's consider an example of any Indo-Aryan language that evolved from Devanagari script. Each language is spoken by more than a million people. Each language in India has a rich morphology and a complex structure of syntax. The diversity of dialects in the form of pronunciation, grammar, and vocabulary make speech recognition more complex. Converting speech into a text mechanism for Indian languages includes major limitations regarding accuracy because of the bulk corpora set, etc.

As shown in Figure 5-23, the basic architecture of speech processing, recognition, and modeling requires a well-thought-out and reusable design model to process many languages with accuracy and to encapsulate data.

The general architecture of speech recognition and write-to-text consists of several functionalities, and each functional box in Figure 5-23 can be developed as a microservice.

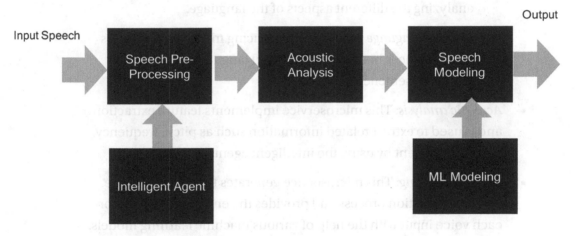

Figure 5-23. *Speech recognition modules*

- *Speech preprocessing*: Through the recording tool, the input speech data is stored in WAV format. The components of microservices are as follows:

  A. The external interface to read WAV file, AIFF, AU, or PCM files (either batch or near real-time with event-driven concept).

  B. Checks the quality, frame size, etc.

  C. Stores the data into the database and is handled by all kinds of interfaces either batch, event-driven, interfaces, etc.

- *Intelligent agent*: This microservice provides a cognitive capability and recognition capability that communicates in natural language with humans and provides an advisory using machine learning and NLP-like intelligence. It provides a set of services that enables services like NLP, speech to text, and text to speech to make an agent see, hear, speak, convert, understand, and interpret natural methods of communication. There are two components in NLP.

  A. *Natural language understanding*: Mapping the given input in the natural language into useful representations and analyzing the different aspects of the language.

  B. *Natural language generation*: Producing meaningful phrases and sentences in the form of natural languages like text planning, sentence planning, etc.

- *Acoustic analysis*: This microservice implements feature extraction and is used to extract related information such as pitch, frequency, and environment by using the intelligent agent.

- *Speech modeling*: This microservice generates the models for the speech generation process and provides the end output of text for each voice input with the help of various machine learning models.

- *ML modeling*: This microservice is used to make predictions about data; an algorithm together with the training data generates an ML model.

Figure 5-24 provides a high-level view of microservice architecture with domain objects and provides flow with events and objects.

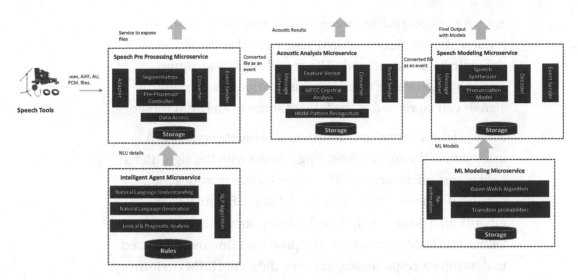

Figure 5-24. *AI microservices architecture*

Speech preprocessing microservices: This microservice is developed by using Python and components in the microservices that read various types of files and segment raw data speech signals into evenly spaced frames. The frame size can be selected based on rapid transition and enough resolution in frequency. This microservice uses intelligent agent microservices for the NPL process.

Intelligent agent microservices: These microservices use open source NPL processes like Apache Open NLP (`http://opennlp.apache.org/`), which supports tokenization, sentence segmentation, tagging, chunking, etc. These microservices follow the steps to provide NLP capabilities.

Acoustic analysis microservices: These microservices extend the details provided by IA microservices along with pitch, frequency, and environment for the statistical analysis. The MFCC (Multi-frequency Cepstral coefficients) Cepstral analysis is a standard technique used for feature extraction. All input files are converted into the MFCC files, which include a list of cepstrum coefficients.

Speech modeling microservices: These microservices use the hidden Markov model (HMM), represented as the simplest dynamic Bayesian network. The speech signals are quasi-stationary and stable for only a short period. The stability of signals can be viewed in the form of states in an HMM topology.

ML model microservices: The ML model microservice is an extension of the speech modeling process with the algorithms split across microservices. This microservice provides the capability of re-estimating the model of the Baum-Welch algorithm; it is used to update the active state with optimal values for HMM parameters. The pronunciation model is used to develop correspondence between different HMMs to form a model for each input. The decoding concatenating subword models are composed into a decoding network.

Summary

Software applications today have expectations and requirements that are different from traditional architecture. They have demands related to resilience, time to market, flexibility, failure, self-healing, and reliability.

In this chapter, you learned how microservices support agility in order to keep their software systems closely aligned with the business goals and market opportunities.

CHAPTER 6

Event-Driven Architecture

Event-driven architecture is not new; it has existed since the Unix operating system came on the scene.

Event-driven technology enables high-speed, asynchronous, machine-to-machine, or program-to-program communication with guaranteed, reliable delivery of events. Machines or programs exchange data each other. The queues or channels are the pathways that connect both the sender and the receiver. A sender or producer is a machine or program that sends events by writing data to the queues, and the receiver or consumer consumes the messages and sends an acknowledgment to confirm the message is received. The data exchange between the sender and receiver can be an object, JSON, XML, and byte. There are two ways to exchange information; the first is a point to point, and the second is publish and subscribe.

This chapter provides insight for anyone considering implementing an event-driven architecture; you should have a basic idea of software architecture, design, and development. There are plenty of books and whitepapers available on event-driven technology; I am not going to duplicate that information here. Instead, I will cover event-driven technology in the context of cloud native and real implementations as well as the problems you may face during implementation.

In this chapter, I will cover the following topics:

- What is event-driven architecture?

- What are events?

- Characteristics of event-driven architecture

- When to consider event-driven architecture

- What is complex event processing?

- Role of event-driven in microservices

- Case studies

© Shivakumar R Goniwada 2022
S. R. Goniwada, *Cloud Native Architecture and Design*, https://doi.org/10.1007/978-1-4842-7226-8_6

Evolution of Event-Driven Architecture

Most applications in enterprises are required to interact with each other by transferring data. In 1971, File Transfer Protocol (FTP) was introduced to transfer data across applications and machines on Network Control Program (NCP). In the early 1980s, the TCP/IP protocol was introduced to draw communication across systems. Later, applications can use a shared database, located in a single physical box; therefore, no data has to be transferred from one application to another. After the introduction of TCP/IP, applications were developed to start exposing some of their functionality so that they could be accessed remotely by other applications via a remote procedure. The communication occurs in real time and is synchronous with high coupling and low cohesion.

The FTP, TCP/IP, and Remote Procedure Call (RPC) protocols are slow and unreliable, and the interaction between applications needs to support the evolution of applications and keep pace with changes in the applications being connected. To overcome the slowness and reliability, the messaging infrastructure was introduced. Messaging is more immediate than FTP, better encapsulated than shared databases, and more reliable than RPC.

Tightly Coupled World to Loosely Coupled World

The messaging in applications and across applications in an enterprise became popular with the maturity of message brokers and message-oriented middleware (MOM). Messaging is a technology that enables high-speed, asynchronous communication with reliable delivery. Applications communicate by sending data called *messages* to each other over a pipe known as a *queue*.

Messaging capabilities are typically provided by a separate software system called *message brokers*. A *messaging system* manages the way the database handles the data persistence. Just like a database administrator (DBA) manages the database, the messaging administrator manages the messaging system. The messaging system coordinates and manages the sending and receiving of messages across systems. The main task of the message system is to manage reliability.

The primary features of message queues are storage, asynchronous messaging, and routing. The message queues store messages or some type of buffer until they have been either read by a consumer or expire or explicitly removed from the queues. The main advantage of a messaging system is loose coupling. The receiving application may not be available for a few seconds to receive messages, or the network is not available, but the receiving application can receive messages once it is available. The message broker keeps retrying to send messages to the receiving applications. This allows for asynchronous nonblocking communication that provides a higher level of tolerance against failure. Enterprise messaging technologies such as IBM MQ, Active MQ, Rabbit MQ, Zero MQ, etc., can be used to decouple your applications for the reliable and guaranteed delivery of messages.

Message queues allow subscribers to subscribe to a message from the message provider. Queues usually manage some level of the transaction to make sure the desired action is executed before the message is removed from the queues. The messages are delivered at least once. Even if the consumer is not available, the queues try to deliver by using a retry configuration. The queues send messages to dead-letter queues after a failure to deliver messages to consumers or the messages will expire. You can use a point-to-point or publish-subscribe model for communication across applications or machines or programs.

We looked at message queue systems, and we saw that message queue systems are used extensively for interapplication communication.

Message Broker World to Event World

Over the years, there has been an evolution of microservices and real-time integration with lightweight data interaction. We are moving from static to dynamic by accumulating data in data lakes to enable data in transit and keep track of it while it is moving from place to place. The shift to event-driven architecture means moving from a data-centric model to an event-centric model. In an event-driven model, the event is a more important component, whereas with service-oriented architecture (SOA) or message queue platforms, the highest priorities were to not lose any data while transferring, to deliver at least once to the consumer, and to have rest of the process leave it to the consuming application to take care of the data. With event-driven architecture, you can address the challenges of SOA and MQ, and the priority is to respond to events as they occur. The older the events, the less valuable they are.

Along with the processing of events, there is a need to persist a record and allow the application to process historical data and real-time data without the threat of deletion by a broker. All these characteristics are not possible in message brokers; there needs to be a streaming platform. The streaming application addresses one-event-at-a-time processing with nanosecond latency with stateful processing and joins and the aggregation of messages. Event streaming platforms can be used for both simple and complex event processing, allowing event consumers to process and perform actions based on the result.

Today, event brokers offer efficient and scalable publish/subscribe event distribution based on routing-labeled events and not just messages to a queue. They support the following:

- Dealing with a consumer that is too slow or offline by managing the state of events on the fly

- Decoupling which data to send to which consuming applications, getting it there reliably, and managing changes to this set of consumers over time

- Providing services such as priority delivery, load balancing to consumers, and more

Event brokers make cloud native services simpler and allow a more real-time, responsive, scalable, efficient, and fault-tolerant system.

There are various event streaming platforms in the industry such as Apache Kafka and Confluent, AWS Kinesis, Spark, Google Data Flow, IBM Cloud Park, Lenses, Hazelcast Jet, IBM Event Streams, SAS Event Streaming Process, Solace, and Azure Event Hub.

In the subsequent section, we will provide a step-by-step approach for designing and implementing event-driven architecture.

Event

Anything that occurs in enterprises or systems is an *event*, such as a customer request, batch update, data change, an employee swiping a credit card, a customer buying a product in a retail ecommerce application, someone checking in for a flight, etc. These events exist everywhere and are constantly occurring, and it does not matter what kind of application it is or what industry it is in. Events are pervasive across any business. There is value in knowing about an event and being able to react to it quickly. The more quickly you can get information about events, the more effectively your business can react to them. An event is separate from a message because the event is an occurrence, and the message is the carrier of the information that relays information about the occurrence. In an event-driven architecture, an event likely commands one or more actions or processes in response to its occurrence.

An event is not the same as an event notification, which is a message or notification sent by the system to notify another part of the system that an event has taken place. The source of an event can be internal or external inputs.

There are two types of events:

- Business events

- Technical events

Business Events

The business events are typically what we care about from a functional perspective. We can derive these from the event storming exercise of domain-driven design. These events are not always initiated externally but created by other business events. For example, an order-placed business event creates an order-shipped business event. Ideally, we should keep these business events around in perpetuity.

The following are examples of business events:

- The customer swipes their credit or debit card at the retail outlet.

- Employees enter the office premises by swiping an ID card.

- A bill is paid.

- An order is placed.

- The order management system sends details to update the inventory system.

- The source data changes for replication to the target operational data store (ODS).

Technical Events

The technical events are derived from business events; typically many technical events can be generated from a single business event. These events are used to communicate between services or systems. These events are technical in nature and are the only trigger to perform a specific action.

The following are examples of technical events:

- Database updated

- File uploaded successfully

- Email notification sent

Each of these events is like a command of one or more actions such as the authorization of payments, authorization of the employee entry, an update, a reduction of inventory, etc. The response is to log events for monitoring and analytics purposes.

Processing an Event

Events are recorded to an event log, as shown in Figure 6-1, and then processed by one or more services. Events do not "fall off" of the log; instead, they are persisted.

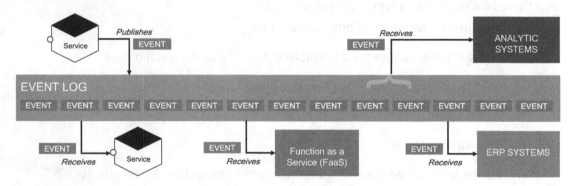

Figure 6-1. *Event processing in an enterprise landscape*

In event processing, the events are persisted on an event log, in a uniform schema, and events are typically organized by topics. Events of different types should not exist on the same topic. For example, customer payment and customer cart data are different topics, even though they relate to customer behavior like adding wish lists, etc. If you are interested in the order of events by customers across systems, consider creating a third topic of "customer actions" that relates only to the actions performed on a customer, discarding the rest.

Consider not defining the listeners in the first place. An event can have multiple listeners, and they may not all exist at the time of the event creation.

In Figure 6-1, the service publishes an event to the event log; the service, FaaS, ERP system, and analytics systems subscribe to an event from the log.

Event Handling in Domain Context

Events can be used for interdomain or intradomain communication. For example, as shown in Figure 6-2, in an ecommerce application, the ecommerce web and mobile applications make up one domain, and the back-end applications are another domain. If you want to send events between these two domains, you use business events.

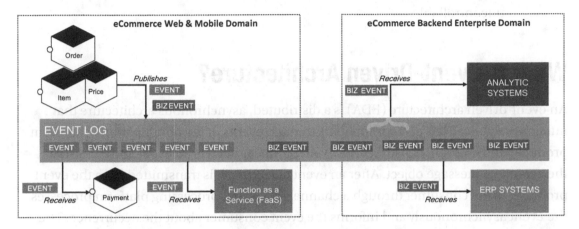

Figure 6-2. *Events across domains in an enterprise*

Within the same domain, the events can be technical or business events. Across domains, only business events are relevant. If you are using technical events, such as notifications, database updates, or requests received, across domains, then that could be a sign of ill-defined domains or a distributed monolithic system; in that case, it is not a cloud native architecture.

Event Governance

The following are the best practices for using events in an enterprise:

- Organizations should strive to make events discoverable to subscribers.

- Events should have a standard envelope that encloses them such as publisher ID, tracer IDs, etc., so that the events can stand alone as the systems evolve. I suggest using cloud event specifications.

- Events should be as small as possible, encompassing the data needed for that event. Topics should contain only one type of event. Smaller events and more topics are better suited to a distributed system.

- Within a domain, the team should design how to introduce new events, but across domains, you need to standardize namespacing and require a governance team to manage the events or they become uncontrollable.

What Is Event-Driven Architecture?

An event-driven architecture (EDA) is a distributed, asynchronous architecture that integrates applications and components through events. It is a combination of an event producer and an event consumer; an event producer detects an event and represents the event as a message object. After an event detection, it is transmitted from the event producer to the consumer through a channel. The event processing platform processes the event asynchronously and informs the event consumer about the occurrence. The event processing platforms will execute the correct response to an event and send it to the right consumers. For asynchronous communication, the consumer and the subscriber do not need to know or be aware of each other. EDA can be relatively complex given its inherent characteristics of asynchronous, distributed processing, issues that may occur due to a lack of responsiveness, failure of mediators, and brokers.

How Does Event-Driven Architecture Work?

As shown in Figure 6-3, event-driven architecture consists of four parts.

- Event producer/publisher

- Event consumer/subscriber

- Event broker or routers

- Event persistence (part of platform)

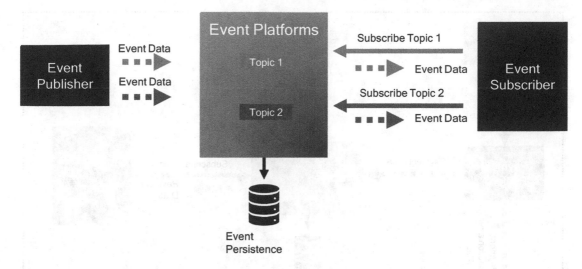

Figure 6-3. *Event-driven architecture components*

An event producer publishes an event to the router, which filters and pushes the events to the consumers.

Let's consider the example shown in Figure 6-4, showing payment processing in banks or a centralized payment platform in a country. You will receive a lot of credit and debit transactions, and you need to process millions of transactions. In these transactions, there might be a few transactions that are related to terror funding or anti-money laundering. How will you find these dubious transactions? If you scan these transactions offline, it leads to a delay in identifying transactions. The only option is to identify in real time just before completing the transaction. In this case, the event-driven architecture helps you to identify the dubious transactions in real time.

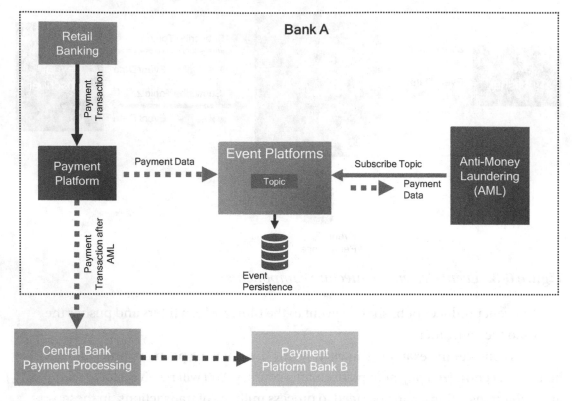

Figure 6-4. *Event-driven architecture example, payment platform*

Event-Driven Topologies

When you design an event-driven architecture, you may confuse which topology needs to be considered for your architecture and why.

In an event-driven architecture, there are two topologies. You need to choose the right topology for your use case.

- Mediator topology
- Broker topology

Mediator Topology

The mediator topology is like orchestration in an SOA enterprise service bus (ESB) or orchestrator components like Netflix Conductor or Uber Cadence. You use the mediator topology when you need to orchestrate multiple steps within an event through a central mediator. This topology is better suited for more complex situations where multiple steps are required to complete the process, thus requiring event processing coordination or orchestration.

The mediator topology consists of four components.

- Event queues

- Event mediator

- Channels

- Event processors

The event flow starts from the event originator by sending an event to event queues; these queues send events to the event mediator. The event mediator is the central component that controls the orchestration of services and is leveraged in a situation where a particular service needs to perform multiple steps sequentially to execute a certain business process. The event mediator sends asynchronous events to event channels to execute each step of the process. The event processor listens to each channel, receives an event, and executes the required business logic. The event mediator is not a business logic executer but is configured with orchestration to process an event.

As shown in the payment use case in Figure 6-5, the consumer makes a payment, and the "make payment" use case requires multiple steps to complete the payment process. The payment request is sent to the event mediator by the retail banking app or web application. The mediator orchestrates multiple steps like conducting AML, checking the payment, sending payment instructions to the central bank, etc. These steps are event processors to process the business logic.

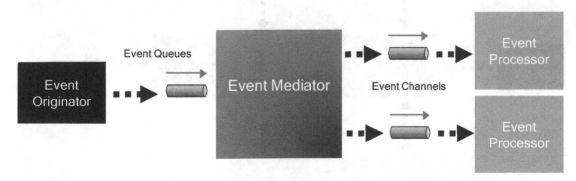

Figure 6-5. Mediator topology architecture

The software components are Camel, Fuse, etc., for the mediator topology along with Rabbit MQ, Active MQ, IBM MQ, or Kafka.

Broker Topology

In the broker topology, the message flow is distributed across the event processor components in a rope fashion through lightweight message brokers. It does not have a central component that controls the orchestration across processes as provided by the mediator topology. The broker topology mainly consists of a dumb broker and intelligent processor with dumb and pipe patterns.

There are two main components in the broker topology.

- Broker component

- Event processor component

The broker component can be centralized or federated and collaborates with all the events that are used within an event flow. The events contained within the broker can be message queues, topics, or a combination of both.

As you saw in Figure 6-6, there is no central mediator component controlling orchestration. In this topology, each event processor component is responsible for processing an event and publishing a new event indicating the action it just performed. The event processor acts as a broker for the rope of events. Once the event is processed by the processor, the other event is published so that another processor can proceed.

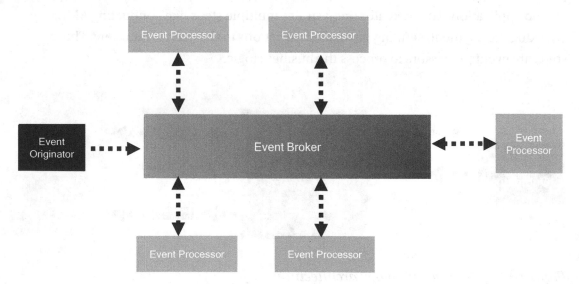

Figure 6-6. *Broker topology architecture*

In the same example of the payment processor that I mentioned, I have used a broker topology to integrate the payment process and to update the details in a banking application. Once the payment is processed, then we need to update the books to complete the transaction, and the payment services write the transaction to the Kafka broker. An event processor picks it up and inserts the record in MongoDB. The view transaction will retrieve the records from MongoDB and expose the API to users to view the transaction.

Choice of Topology

The rule of thumb is to choose the best topology for your use cases. The broker topology can be considered for a single event or chain of events requiring one task as their result. The mediator topology can be considered when using multiple tasks in response and thus requiring orchestration of each task.

Characteristics of Event-Driven Architecture

Almost all industry domains use event-driven architecture such as social media, financial markets, hospitality, Internet of Things (IoT), etc. Let's consider an example of IoT. Say your apartment building has installed sensors in each apartment to identify fire or smoke in the apartment building. The sensors send the details of events with a measurement of the average temperature of a room with a timestamp. The event-driven system will send events along with room temperature data to identify processes, and storing these events requires various EDA characteristics to complete the process. The following are the main characteristics of any event-driven architecture that you must follow:

- *Multicast communication*: The events are generated from the publishing systems, and event-driven systems can send these events to multiple event processors.

- *Real-time transmission*: The events are processed in real time to the event processors. The mode of processing or transmission is real time rather than batch processing.

- *Asynchronous communication*: The event does not need to wait for the event processor to be available before publishing an event.

- *Fine-grained communication*: Events are small units and are published as and when they occur.

- *Event ontology*: EDA systems always classify events in terms of some form of a group/hierarchy. This allows event processors to subscribe to a specific event or specific category of events.

Event-Driven Messaging Models

There are two basic models for transmitting the events in an event-driven architecture; you can use the right models for your use cases.

Event Messaging

In event messaging, the event consumers subscribe to the messaging published by the event originators. When an event originator publishes an event, the message is sent directly to all subscribers who want to consume it. The event broker handles the transmission of event messages between the originators and subscribers. The events will be deleted after all the consumers subscribe to them. An example of event messaging is the published/subscribe model. The event broker translates and routes messages to the subscriber.

Event Streaming

In event streaming, event originators publish streams of events to a broker. Event processors subscribe to the streams, but instead of receiving and consuming every event as it is published, event processors can consume events at any point and consume only the required events. The events are persisted and never deleted after the event processors consume them. The event streaming platforms are configured to persist events from a second to infinite time. This enables event streams to process real-time and historical data. The event streams can be used for both simple and complex event processing styles.

Event Processing Styles

Event processing is the process that takes events or streams of events, analyzes them, and takes automatic action. Each event processor must be independent and loosely coupled with other event processors. It tracks and processes streams of events so that opportunities and risks are proactively identified and optimized. There are three types of styles for event processing.

- Simple event processing (SEP)

- Complex event processing (CEP)

- Event stream processing (ESP)

Simple Event Processing

This event processing occurs when an event immediately triggers an action in the event processor. It is used to measure events that are related to specific measurable changes in conditions. SEP is used for real-time flow without any other constraint or consideration. Many events in architecture are simple, such as IoT sensors in your house that trigger when something happens in a house like a temperature change or smoke, etc. This type of event occurs when some notable, significant, and meaningful change of state or condition occurs. Typically this is used to take latency and cost out of the business process; simple event processing initiates action further down the application stream whenever a significant and meaningful change of state occurs in any hardware or software component of the system.

Event Stream Processing

In event stream processing, ordinary events that occur are filtered for notability and sent to event processors. This ensures that real-time information flows in and around the enterprise. This helps in real-time decision-making. In event stream processing, all the events are written to a log. Event processors don't subscribe to anything; they simply read from any part of the stream at any time. The following are the components of event stream processing:

- Event collect

- Event enhance

- Event analyze

- Event dispatch

This flow creates a process in which events are detected using components. These components detect relationships between multiple events, perform event correlation, and establish event hierarchies.

The event stream processing uses a data streaming platform like Kafka to ingest events and processes or transform the event stream. This can be used to detect a pattern in event streams. The event stream processing can be used in various use cases, for example, in order processing. If we consider the sequence of events in a jewelry shop, the RFID sensor generates an event for each item that moves out of the display. In this scenario, the retailer is to be informed when the item is sold and moved out of a store.

Complex Event Processing

This is a set of processes for capturing and analyzing streams of data as they arrive in real time. The objective of this processing is to identify meaningful events in real-time situations and respond to them as quickly as possible. It is used when multiple events must take place before final events are generated. Each event need not be like the others, nor do events occur at the same time. CEP waits until all criteria are fulfilled before generating an event message to communicate action instructions. To generate a finale event, the CEP requires the following components:

- Event interpreters

- Event pattern definition

- Event pattern matching

- Event correlation techniques

The CEP has a strong impact on future information systems and the way we subscribe to and consume information. It plays an important role in many domains like logistics, energy management, finance, etc. The usage of this style is expected to grow further with the increasing number of decentralized microservices, digital twins, etc.

CEP does not only mediate information in the form of events between providers and consumers but supports the detection of dependencies among events by using event patterns. The events are generated by the composition and aggregation of multiple events and can generate a final event.

CEP is used for a scenario in which there is a large volume of events occurring and latency requirements are very low, in milliseconds. Some of the use cases are stock trading, predictive maintenance (digital twin), real-time marketing, etc.

Event-Driven Architecture Maturity Model

IT in enterprise organizations needs to support business disruption by improving the speed and responsiveness of their internal and customer-facing processes and systems. Irrespective of what industries you are in, there is an increase in eventing capability across enterprise ecosystems. An EDA not only publishes and subscribes to an event but involves planning and maturity of EDA across portfolios in an enterprise.

The EDA concept becomes more broadly adopted, and enterprises progress through increasing levels of maturity. As shown in Figure 6-7, every organization has to undergo five levels of steps to reach maturity because the eventing is complex, requires special skills, and most important is part of the organizational culture. You can use assessment techniques to assess an enterprise's maturity level.

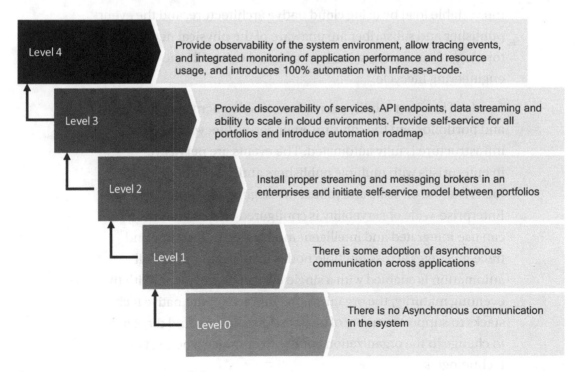

Level 4 — Provide observability of the system environment, allow tracing events, and integrated monitoring of application performance and resource usage, and introduces 100% automation with Infra-as-a-code.

Level 3 — Provide discoverability of services, API endpoints, data streaming and ability to scale in cloud environments. Provide self-service for all portfolios and introduce automation roadmap

Level 2 — Install proper streaming and messaging brokers in an enterprises and initiate self-service model between portfolios

Level 1 — There is some adoption of asynchronous communication across applications

Level 0 — There is no Asynchronous communication in the system

Figure 6-7. *Maturity model*

Level 0: There is no asynchronous communication in the enterprise. All integration is synchronous through APIs or TCP/IP or FTPs. Few applications in an enterprise are using some kind of ESB integration mechanism across the heterogeneous system.

Level 1: There is some adoption of an asynchronous exchange of information across applications. An example is a point-to-point interaction between related systems using messaging platforms like MQs, ESB, etc.

Level 2: Business and data event streaming and messaging are used with some level of high availability and initiating of self-services. Multiple application interactions are carried out by using messaging infrastructure with messaging characteristics.

Level 3: Discoverability, scalability, and failover are managed. The application-producing events are less aware that all the clients can subscribe to the messages and the same events can be used for various other observability. The message network can handle the variable load by using cloud native architecture, and the event publisher and subscriber are unaware of the physical network topology. Some automation is introduced to handle the software engineering lifecycle.

Level 4: The observability principle is enabled across applications and portfolios and the software engineering lifecycle, and the infrastructure is fully automated. The events are pervasive in enterprises with multiple publishers and subscribers. The focus is more on scale and robust messaging infrastructure. Enterprise-wide observability is configured so that administrators can use integrated and intelligent monitoring in real time and trace messages across multiple nodes in an event mesh. Full automation is enabled with a single click of deployment. With this eventing maturity, the organization embraces cloud native tech stacks to support a variety of business disruptions, and that leads to change in the organization culture to embrace a new set of technologies.

Decoupling Use Case by Using Event-Driven Architecture

The decoupling helps enterprises with legacy systems to engage customers in the following ways:

- Keeping legacy systems

- Making these systems accessible from the cloud native systems

- Shipping data to modern technology

- Enabling enterprises to access cloud native technologies

The era of the big transformation project is over; enterprises are not willing to invest in multimillion, multiyear efforts on transformation; they need to realize business value quickly. Instead of big fat projects, you need to imagine a world in which value is delivered quickly and accessible to customers after a short duration minimum viable product (MVP) and then continuously thereafter, with the freedom to pivot. On the journey to cloud native, you can't ignore legacy systems. There are tons of business transactions occurring in those systems; therefore, you need to keep evolving your architecture by using decoupling principles.

Decoupling is the process of using cloud native technologies, development methodologies, and migration methods to build systems that execute strategy on top of legacy systems. When you apply a decoupling strategy to the entire enterprise, it leads to exponential changes in IT and a scalable, flexible, and resilient architecture that gives companies the agility to continuously innovate.

Organizations are under constant pressure to deliver customer expectations. The following are the key drivers for organizations to embrace cloud native architecture:

- Changing customer expectations

- Technology innovation

- Cost pressure

- Extended enterprises

- New unicorn entrants

Figure 6-8 illustrates a step-by-step approach of how to conduct a decoupling of an existing system into the cloud native technologies. When your systems need to undergo decoupling transformation, you must adhere to the following principles:

- *Layering*: Apply layering to isolate from the old system, and layer within the new system.

- *Suitable fragmentation*: Fragment capabilities remove conflicts of interest and increase agility, enabling cloud native replacement.

- *4Events*: Make sure all data is accessible in real time.

- *Available, Real-time data*: Build out data meshes and data lakes with real-time eventing capabilities to support the objectives.

- *Automation*: Implement single-click automation from developer box to the production box with the use of DevSecOps and infrastructure as code.

- *Cloud*: Leverage cloud capabilities to isolate infrastructure and platform.

- *Intelligence built-in*: Add artificial intelligence and machine learning into your services and operations.

- *No SPOF*: Avoid a single point of failure (SPOF).

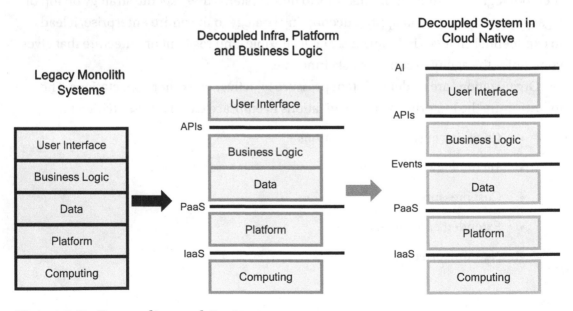

Figure 6-8. *Decoupling architecture*

Some of the myths of decoupling that you need to dispel for stakeholders are as follows:

- *A product alone solves a business problem*: Don't rely on someone else to solve our problems.

- *Perfect architecture and governance*: Avoid ivory tower thinking and focusing on overdesigned standards that don't drive business value.

- *End state is reachable*: Businesses don't stand still; what is valid today may not be tomorrow.

- *Old = bad*: Oftentimes, new technology is seen as the only way to solve problems.

- *All in one jar*: Oftentimes, a business uses one technology to solve all the problems.

When you want your application to be cloud native, then you need to apply the following modern-day approaches for decoupling your systems:

- Make data accessible (change data capture [CDC])

- Microservices

- Event-driven architecture

- Serverless

- Cloud

- Reactive interaction gateway

Make Data Accessible

If you look back at how application databases and data movement are designed traditionally, all are based on the pull-based model, with no information about changes. The data in the databases is static and reacts only when there is a request to modify the data by using SQL queries; it never reacts on its own. In the case of data replication, you should apply batch jobs to trigger a delta change in the source database and use extract, transform, and load (ETL) tools to load data in an (ODS) operational data store or data warehouse. Or use files to upload data to the ODS or data warehouse.

In event-driven architecture, events enable new real-time functionality to move data from the application and data store. You can apply replication either from business change events in an application or from technical change events in a database, as shown in Figure 6-9.

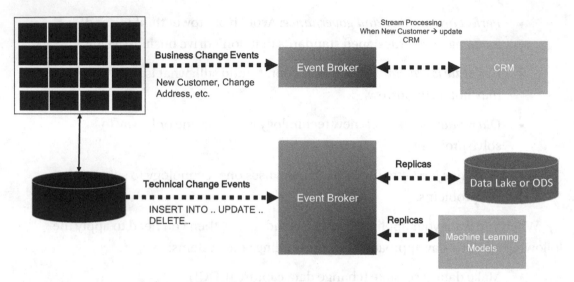

Figure 6-9. *Data accessible architecture*

How to Get Events and Make Data Accessible?

Many systems have native support for events. For example, databases like MongoDB, Couchbase, Cockroach DB, etc., and cloud services like AWS S3, Google Storage, and Blob storage in Azure, all these services provide an event when a file is uploaded. GitHub provides a webhook on all kinds of operations, and Salesforce provides change events.

If services do not support a native eventing capability, then you need to build that functionality yourself by using the following methods:

- CDC tools such as Equalum, Hevo, Infosphere, Qlik, Oracle, etc., allow you to integrate various legacy systems, such as Oracle and DB2.

- You can build your custom component that has central transaction logic points, allowing you to add code to publish events.

- If you are developing a new cloud native application, then you need to consider building an eventing capability right from the start.

Where to Store Events?

An event store is a database designed for tracking events as they occur and maintaining a record of those events. Relational databases such as MySQL, Postgres, SQL Server, and Oracle can be used to track events but have certain limitations for this use. A relational database stores data in a tabular structure and isn't a good match for event data; in addition, facts stored in a relational database can be changed. You can present up-to-date data from a relational database, but the limitation is to track every action.

Event stores record each event as it occurs, and no event may be overwritten or deleted. For example, as shown in the Figure 6-10, ecommerce may allow each customer to browse catalogs and items as a set of events. Adding each item to a wish list or shopping cart, adding payment details, entering a shipping address, and checking out are all events that should be recorded as they happen, and records of these events never change. Events recorded in an event store are immutable. Facts derived from those events change over time; in the same example, the customer enters different payment methods for each purchase.

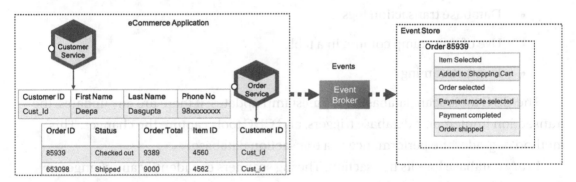

Figure 6-10. *Event store*

Event stores are ideal for applications where an audit trail, a machine learning model, a record of actions, etc., is desired. This is common for all event-driven transactional applications.

How to Get Data?

Getting data is often the hardest part; there are several ways to replicate data such as the following:

- Using CDC
- Replicating data to a log and using the log as a source of truth
- Using connectors, either industry tools or custom made

CDC

CDC is a process for identifying and capturing changes made to a data store; those changes can then applied to another data repository such as a data mesh or data lake or a data warehouse or event log by using event-driven architecture or other types of integration tools like ETL. CDC is the basis for another system with the same incremental changes or to store an audit trail of changes. The audit trail may subsequently be used for other uses such as updating to a data lake or data warehouse or running machine learning models across the changes.

CDC replicates data that has changed with database functions such as INSERT, UPDATE, and DELETE and makes a record of the change available to the CDC tool and event hub so it's available for other sources. CDC tools rely on database logs, which keep track of record changes internally for system recovery.

There are different approaches that a system can use to capture changes in the transaction databases, such as the following:

- Database transaction logs

- Use of timestamp column in a table

- Event streaming

The CDC tools scan databases for timestamp updates; if there are any updates, the transaction implements database triggers, and CDC tools capture the changes. This method degrades the performance of a transaction database.

Every database logs its transaction. The log scanners can identify any changes in these transactional logs, and the log scanner interprets and captures the changes in these transaction logs.

Event streaming is commonly used and relevant in cloud native architecture. It uses the publish/subscribe model of CDC, where a database triggers a log or publishes change events to a table and shares those changes with the CDC tool. The series of updates is sent to CDC in streams to be used to capture the changes in the CDC.

The event streams start the process of taking action on a series of data that originates from a data-driven application in an enterprise that continuously creates data. The term *event* refers to each data point in an application, and *stream* refers to the delivery of those events. During the streaming, there are many actions or logic that can be applied such as aggregation, analytics, enrichment, transformation, and ingestion. Event streaming is the real-time processing of data as soon as changes occur.

As shown in Figure 6-11, event stream processing works by handling a data set as one data point at a time rather than as a whole data set. Event streams are about continuously created data. In an event stream processing setup, there are two parts.

- The event storage

- Technology to take actions on changes in the database

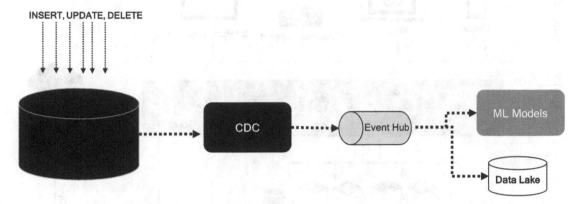

Figure 6-11. *Data streaming by using CDC and events*

The event storage stores data based on the timestamp. You might capture every action of users in an ecommerce application, and each action of the user is an event. This is handled by streaming technologies like Kafka, Kinesis, etc. The stream processors act on the incoming data. The enriched stream events are published to the steaming technologies for stream persistence.

Real-Time Interactivity

Real-time interactivity is the backbone of the modern-day customer experience. It establishes a scalable and agile event processing capability and generates new representation.

To provide real-time connectivity, as shown in Figure 6-12, you need to use event processing and data streaming to integrate services and systems in your enterprises and merge, transform, and enrich relevant data across an organization.

A batch process is always too late to respond to customers and introduces a bumpy load pattern. Distributed log systems offer very high throughput, strict ordering per log file, and independent reads from multiple systems, but they do not support the event streaming.

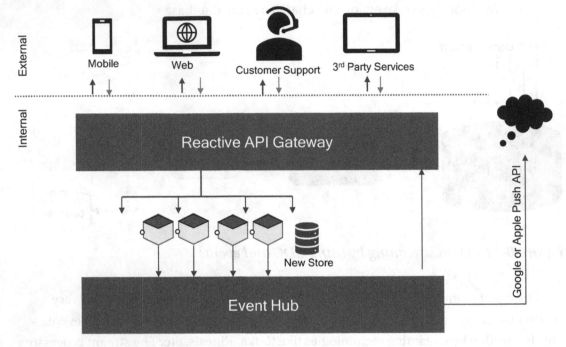

Figure 6-12. *Reactive architecture*

In an event hub or event streaming, a log is used instead of a service bus, and the service listens to the log and publishes messages to the log, typically on topics.

How to Use Existing Message Queues with Event Streams?

You can leverage your existing architecture, skills, and investments, and you can use event-driven techniques to offer more responsive and seamless integration with existing and new event streams. Event streams like Kafka, IBM Event Streams, etc., support connectivity to the existing MQs like Rabbit MQ, Active MQ, or IBM MQ. By combining the capabilities of event streams and message queues, you can combine your transactions in a combined application.

Let's consider a use case, as shown in Figure 6-13, in the travel and hospitality industry. The use cases are airline booking, car rental, hotel booking, flight status, and a weather report to provide a more personalized experience to customers. In these use cases, your client already developed part of the airline booking by using MQ, but you need to provide seamless and more personalized information to your customer.

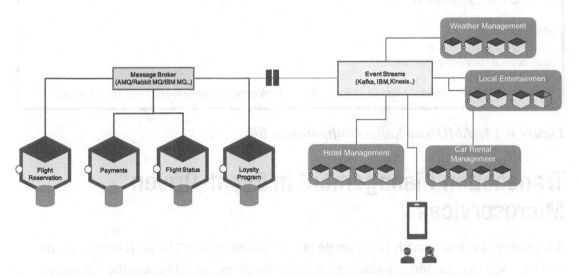

Figure 6-13. *Collaboration of eventing system with message queue systems*

Let's consider an example of a flight reservation; the management of flight reservation applications is already available in an enterprise with the decoupled architecture principles via MQ technologies. The airline management wants to enhance its business by providing a personalized experience for its customers. As mentioned earlier, the MQ is not meant for eventing and streaming. Therefore, I used event streaming technologies such as Kafka, IBM, or Kinesis to stream across various systems to provide seamless information to the customers.

To achieve interaction between MQs and event streams, you need to configure MQ to send and receive messages and events by using connectors. Event streams connect with various applications to manage a hotel reservation and location map, local entertainment details, and map and car rentals from the car booking management application.

For example, as shown in Figure 6-14, for the AMQ connection to Kafka, you need to configure a connector in the dependency file.

```
<dependency>

  <groupId>org.apache.camel.kafkaconnector</groupId>

  <artifactId>camel-activemq-kafka-connector</artifactId>

  <version>x.x.x</version>

</dependency>

use source connector for Kafka connector

connector.class=org.apache.camel.kafkaconnector.activemq.CamelActivemqSourceConnector
```

Figure 6-14. AMQ and Kafka configuration file

Transaction Management in Event-Driven Microservices

A legacy application usually has a single monolithic database. The ACID transactions can be easily maintained in a single monolithic database. ACID means the following:

- *A – Atomicity*: A transaction is an atomic unit. All the instructions within a transaction will successfully execute, or none of them will execute.

- *C – Consistency*: A transaction can bring the database from only one valid state to another, and data is in a consistent state when a transaction starts and when it ends.

- *I- Isolation*: One state of a transaction is invisible to another transaction. This ensures that concurrency is maintained across transaction and leaves the database in the same state.

- *D – Durability*: Changes that have been committed to the database should remain even in the case of failures.

As a result of ACID, your monolithic application and database can easily manage the database transactions.

When you decouple an application to a cloud native service or develop a new cloud native service, data access management becomes complex because of polyglot principles. Adopting a polyglot principle ensures that the microservices are loosely coupled and deploy and are managed independently of one another. If multiple services access the same data, then you need to handle coordination across cloud native services. One more obstacle is transaction management in polyglot microservices. The polyglot principle illustrates that each microservices can use different databases because a modern application stores diverse kinds of data, and one type of database is not always beneficial.

For some cloud native service, a NoSQL database might have a more convenient data model and offer much performance and scalability. It's similar for search microservices; you may be considering Elasticsearch for the graph-related store, and you might use graph databases like Neo4J, etc. In a nutshell, in one system, you might use multiple types of databases. Using polyglot persistence provides many benefits such as scalability, manageability, and high availability but introduces distributed data management challenges.

The following are the real challenges of using polyglot persistence in a cloud native service:

- Implementing a business transaction across services

- Retrieving data from multiple services

Let's analyze how these challenges impact your cloud native services.

The first challenge is implementing a business transaction that maintains consistency across services. Let's consider the example of an ecommerce application. The ecommerce application consists of hundreds of cloud native services to manage various business cases such as Order, Customer, Inventory, Catalog, etc.

In Figure 6-15, I am considering three cloud native services (Customer Service, Order Service, and Inventory Service) to illustrate transaction management.

- *Customer Service*: The responsibility of this microservice is to maintain customer information.

- *Order Service*: The responsibility of this microservice is the management of orders.

- *Inventory Service*: The responsibility of this microservice is to manage the inventory, and a new order doesn't give confirmation if the inventory is less than the number of product requested.

In the traditional monolithic application of ecommerce, the Order service can simply use an ACID transaction to check the availability in the inventory and confirm the order.

In the cloud native service architecture, the Customer, Order, and Inventory tables are aligned to their services, as shown in Figure 6-15.

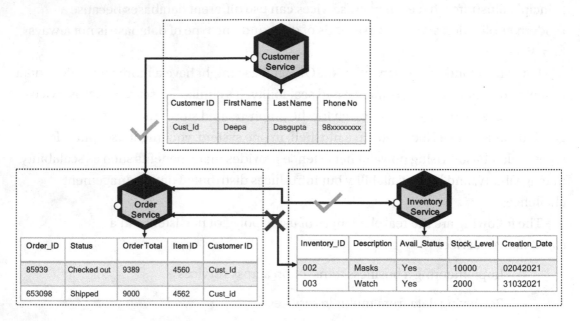

Figure 6-15. *Cloud native service polyglot persistence*

The Order service cannot access the Inventory service table directly and can be used only through the Inventory service's APIs or channels. When cloud native services such as Customer, Order, and Inventory services decomposes a monolithic system into self-encapsulated services, it can break transactions.

This means a local transaction of a monolithic application becomes distributed into multiple services. Figure 6-16 shows how the transaction could be handled in a monolithic ecommerce application; it shows a customer order example with a monolithic ecommerce system using a local transaction.

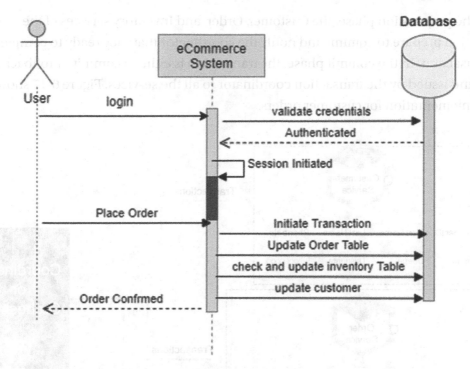

Figure 6-16. *Monolithic ecommerce system using local transaction*

As shown in Figure 6-16, the user logs in to the ecommerce system after authentication, and the system creates a session. The user places an order in the system, and the system creates a local transaction that manages multiple database tables by using an ACID transaction. If one step fails, the transaction can roll back.

Two-Phase Commit in Cloud Native Services

In the cloud native services architecture, the Order service could potentially use the Inventory service through a distributed transaction's two-phase commit (2PC). The 2PC protocol ensures a database commit is implemented in the places where a commit operation is divided into two separate phases.

- Prepare phase
- Commit phase

Let me explain how you can use 2PC for a cloud native services architecture for the Customer, Order, and Inventory services.

In the preparation phase, the Customer, Order, and Inventory services of the transaction prepare to commit and notify the coordinator that they ready to complete the transaction. In the commit phase, the transaction is either a commit or rollback command issued by the transaction coordinator to all the services. Figure 6-17 shows the 2PC implementation for customer orders.

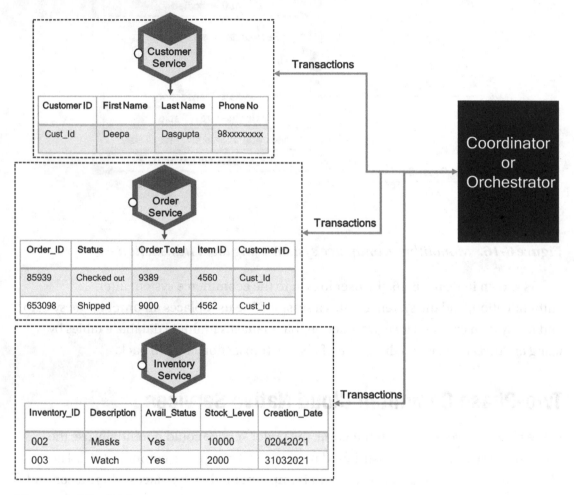

Figure 6-17. *2PC commit*

In Figure 6-18, when a customer creates an order, the coordinator or orchestrator creates a global transaction with all the context information. It will interact with the Order service to create an order, and the order replies to the coordinator after completion of order creation. Then the coordinator sends a request to the Inventory service the check the inventory availability by product ID. The Inventory service sends

OK, and the stock is available. The coordinator sends a message to the Order service to confirm the order, and at the same time the coordinator sends a message to the Inventory service to update it. At any point in time, if the service fails to process, then the coordinator will abort the transaction and begin the rollback process.

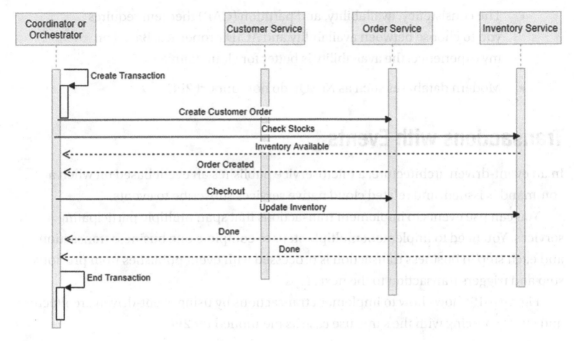

Figure 6-18. *Sequence steps of 2PC*

The benefit of 2PC is strong consistency.

- Prepare and commit 2PC phases to guarantee that transactions are atomic, either complete or none.

- 2PC allows read-write isolation; the changes are not reflected until the coordinator is not performing the commit.

The disadvantage of 2PC is that you can solve the transaction by using 2PC, but it is not at all a recommended approach for any cloud native architecture systems because of the following reasons:

- 2PC is synchronous (blocking); it will lock all the cloud native services until it completes the entire transaction. This could end up as a bottleneck in the whole system.

273

- This approach is very slow, due to the blocking of threads of all the participants' microservices.

- A coordinator or orchestrator is a single point of failure, and the whole system's transactions are based on the availability of a coordinator.

- The consistency, availability, and partition (CAP) theorem requires you to choose between availability and ACID properties. Based on my experience, the availability is better for cloud native.

- Modern databases such as NoSQL do not support 2PC.

Transactions with Events

In an event-driven architecture, a microservice publishes an event based on when a command is issued, and related cloud native services subscribe to events.

You can use events to implement transactions that span multiple participating services. You need to implement multiple steps to complete one business transaction, and each step in business transaction is processed with event publishes from previous step and triggers transaction to the next steps.

Figure 6-19 shows how to implement transactions by using event-driven architecture and event sourcing with the same use case as mentioned for 2PC.

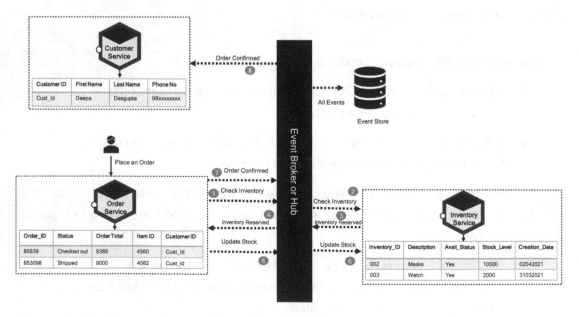

Figure 6-19. *Transactions with event*

As shown in Figure 6-20, the microservices publish and subscribe to an event via an event broker and event store. Each service publishes an event to the event broker, and other services subscribe to an event as and when it is published.

Here are the steps a place an order transaction:

1. The customer places an order, and the Order service initiates an order confirmation transaction, called Begin Transaction.

2. The Order service publishes an event to check the inventory by passing the product ID.

3. The Inventory service subscribes to an event from the event broker and checks the stock level against the product.

4. If the stock available, then the Inventory service publishes an event after reserving a stock.

5. The Order service subscribes to an event and confirms the order.

6. The Order service publishes an event to update a stock.

7. The Order service publishes an event for confirming an order.

8. The Inventory service subscribes to an event and updates the stock level.

9. The Customer service subscribes to the event for a confirmed order and updates the details.

10. The transaction ends.

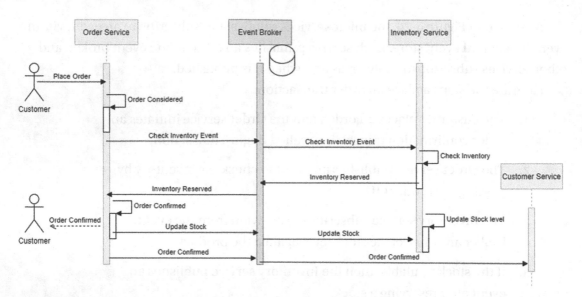

Figure 6-20. *Event transaction sequence diagram*

Here each service updates its database and publishes an event, and the event broker saves each event in the event store. All these transactions do not adhere to ACID properties, but all follow eventual consistency properties. Throughout this entire transaction, atomicity is important. To manage the atomicity of your transaction, your event store plays an important role. For example, for order creation, you need to store an order in the order service database and publish an event to the event broker; these two things should happen atomically. If the service fails after one task, then it becomes an inconsistency in a transaction. To achieve this inconsistency, you need to manage the event store table to store all kinds of events that occur in the whole transaction.

The event sourcing and event table persist all kinds of events in a transaction; if any transaction fails in between, the service can construct a state by using the event store, as shown in Figure 6-21, and each service publishes and subscribes to an event by using the event broker.

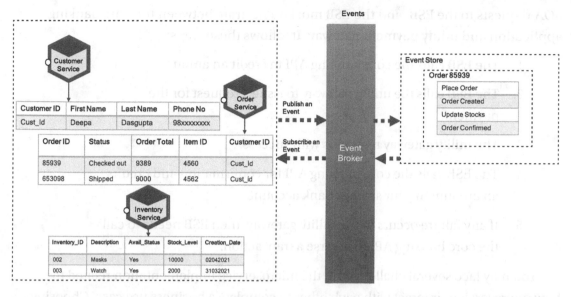

Figure 6-21. *Event store in a transaction*

One way of achieving an event-driven transaction is to use the saga pattern and CQRS, which are explained in Chapter 4.

Event-Driven Microservices Interaction

At a high level, there are two approaches to getting microservices to work together toward a common goal.

- Orchestration with synchronous

- Choreography with asynchronous

Orchestration entails actively controlling microservices like a conductor directing the musicians of an orchestra. Choreography entails establishing a pattern that microservices follow as the music plays, without requiring supervision or instructions.

The synchronous communication and orchestration across microservices are managed by the orchestrator. The orchestrator is not a new concept; it has existed since the SOA and ESB implementations were introduced. The ESB acts as an orchestrator and orchestrates across heterogeneous systems in an enterprise ecosystem. Let's look at an example of a utility payment from the banking web application. You want to pay an electricity bill through your web app, so you initiate the transaction by clicking the utility payment link. The web application sends

SOA requests to the ESB, and the ESB must orchestrate between the core banking application and utility payment gateway. It follows these steps:

1. The ESB calls the core banking API to credit an amount.

2. The ESB calls the utility gateway to issue a request for the payment.

3. The utility gateway responds with success.

4. The ESB calls the core banking API for confirmation and credits an amount in your savings bank account.

5. If any failure occurs in the utility gateway, then ESB needs to call the core banking API to reverse a transaction.

You may face several challenges in the microservice implementation related to how microservices interact with each other to complete a business use case. Choosing between orchestration and choreography will make a difference in how seamlessly the services function.

In an orchestra, each musician is awaiting a command from the conductor. They are each expert in playing their instrument, and yet they'd be collectively lost without the conductor. In orchestration, one service or any tools like Netflix Conductor or Uber Credence handle all communication between microservices and direct each service to perform the intended functions.

The downside of orchestration is the orchestrator is a single point of failure, and the controller needs to directly communicate with each service and wait for each service's response. These interactions are occurring across the network. Invocations and I/O blocking take longer, block threads, and impact service availability. In orchestration, each service is tightly dependent on other services, and they are synchronous, and each service must explicitly receive and respond to requests to make the whole service work; failure at any point could stop the process. The orchestration could rely on RESTful APIs. For some use cases, the orchestration is best suited; an example is Netflix using Conductor.

A choreography-based approach is like the dancers listening to the music and making the necessary moves because all dancers follow the same choreography. In this approach, you will avoid dependencies. So, each service works loosely coupled and independently.

In choreography, as shown in Figure 6-22, the event broker exchanges the information between microservices. It is like a fire-and-forget-it, decentralized way of broadcasting data known as *events,* and everything happens asynchronously, without waiting for a response. Each service observes its environment and subscribes to the message events to that channel and will know what to do from there.

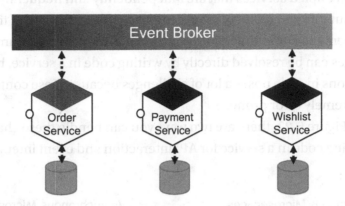

Figure 6-22. *Choreography in services*

The choreography isolates the microservices; this means if one service fails or fails to respond, it does not impact as a whole use case. You can use a various pattern like a circuit breaker to handle the failure.

The following are the advantages of choreography:

- Processing is faster as there is no requirement of the central conductor.

- There is no single point of failure.

- Each service is loosely coupled and is not aware of each service; therefore, it's easy to add and remove services.

- This resonated well with cloud native architecture.

- You can use several patterns like circuit breaker, CQRS, or event sourcing for effective management of interactions across microservices.

The disadvantages are that it is complex and requires special skills to configure and manage eventing capabilities.

Interaction Between Microservices

Managing across a few microservices is easy and does not require any extra management layer, but when microservices grow in your enterprises, you may face many challenges of managing services in a cloud native environment.

Many loosely coupled services that are independently and frequently changing do promote agility but introduce a lot of management challenges. Some of these challenges are traffic management, communication security, communication failures, etc. Many of these challenges can be resolved directly by writing code in a service, but embedding these configurations in code poses a lot of challenges because these configurations are complex and extremely error prone.

As shown in Figure 6-23, there are two ways you can handle these challenges without embedding code in a service for API interaction and event interaction across microservices.

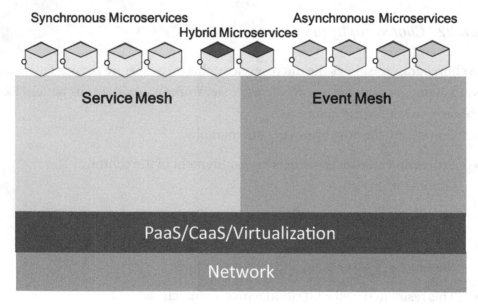

Figure 6-23. *Mesh architecture*

- *Service mesh*: Provides connection-level routing and traffic management for synchronous communication (HTTP(s)) interaction through sidecar injection into Kubernetes pods. The service mesh is focused on routing connections between endpoints by hijacking the connection requests and overriding the connection requests from the microservices.

- *Event mesh*: Handles asynchronous event-driven routing of information between microservices. It intelligently routes events between the event brokers, allowing the cluster or brokers to appear as a single virtual event broker.

The mesh frameworks allow you to observe, secure, and connect microservices. They don't establish connectivity between microservices but instead have policies and control applications on top of the existing network to govern how microservices interact. These frameworks shift the implementation logic out of the microservices code and move it to the network.

The service mesh and event mesh are not mutually exclusive, and you may consider implementing both depending on the use cases.

Service Mesh

A gateway centralizes the configuration and routes requests to the relevant microservices, and it can handle orchestration but with limitations.

The advent of cloud native architecture and the use of container and microservices platforms create a need for an orchestrator. The containers and orchestrators, coupled with the microservices for their speed to market and silos of the development pods, lead to service sprawl. The ability to run several distributed services requires a service mesh.

A service mesh solves the problems where microservices communicate using APIs. A service mesh uses the sidecar pattern to establish communication between microservices and ensures that the communication among containerized and often ephemeral application infrastructure services is fast, reliable, and secure.

Service Mesh Implementation

As shown in Figure 6-24, a service mesh will have a control plane to program the mesh and sidecar and serve as the control point for securing, observing, and routing decisions between services. The control plane transfers configurations to the proxies, and each proxy intercepts all inbound and outbound traffic. By intercepting traffic, the proxies will inject behavior into the communication flows between microservices.

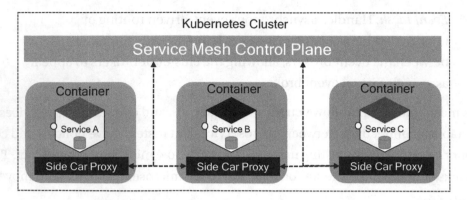

Figure 6-24. *Service mesh architecture*

The following behavior will be handled by the service mesh:

- Traffic shaping with dynamic routing controls

- Resiliency support for service communication such as circuit
  breakers, timeouts, and retries

- Observability of traffic between services

- Tracing of communication flows

- Secure communication between services

In Figure 6-24, all services A, B, and C are executed through sidecar proxies. By
having communication routed between the proxies, the proxies serve as a key control
point for performing a task such as initiating Transport Layer Security (TLS) handshakes
for encrypted communication with the previous behaviors.

Service meshes route data based on the connection URL and the ability to redirect a
connection based on the content routing rules against the URL and HTTP header
information.

Services meshes are one layer of your infrastructure and don't provide all that you
need. They do give you the ability to bridge the divide between your infrastructure and
your application.

Advantages and Disadvantages of Service Meshes

The advantages of service meshe is that they offer distributed debugging, provide topology and dependency management, participate in application lifecycle management, and participate in service and product management, offer deeper observability, provide multitenancy, have multicluster meshes, allow advanced circuit breakers with fallback paths, etc.

The service mesh provides a simpler network configuration for the microservices but with some caveats.

- The service mesh has no support for asynchronous events or stream processing.

- Most traffic and network services apply only to synchronous communication and the HTTP and GRPC protocols.

- A service mesh limits the connection-oriented routing and targeting of the transport connection, not the routing of actual data.

Microservices are using diverse message interaction patterns including publish/subscribe, point-to-point, push-with-reply, queuing, etc. In today's world, the microservices require a higher throughput and lower latency than you can meet by using Kubernetes clusters. It takes choreography rather than orchestration processing. In cloud native architecture, microservices require event-driven architecture because they require eventing capability, performance, and real-time processing that goes beyond a Kubernetes cluster. Here, you require an event mesh.

Event Mesh

A cloud native modern enterprise embraces event architecture, and every event-driven application requires a robust central system to move events quickly, reliably, and securely from publisher to subscriber.

An event mesh is an architectural layer that dynamically routes events from one microservice to another irrespective of deployment location. The event mesh is a key enabler for event-driven architecture. An event mesh is a dynamic infrastructure that propagates events across disparate cloud platforms and performs protocol translation.

A single event broker can handle only a certain volume of requests and microservices. There are different ways to scale, and one way is the event mesh.

In an event mesh, there is no underlying technology such as Kubernetes, and event brokers are designed to operate with or without a cloud. Event meshes route data based on topics and are transported with the event payload. It is a dynamic infrastructure that propagates events across multicloud platforms and performs protocol translations.

Figure 6-25 illustrates elements of an event mesh, and events can flow bi-directionally across the microservices irrespective of where they are deployed, whether it is in the same cloud, multicloud, or hybrid cloud.

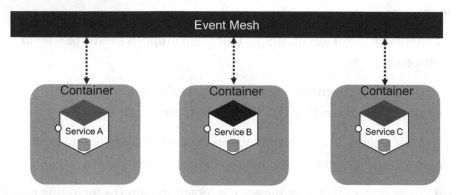

Figure 6-25. *Event mesh architecture*

An event mesh is configured along with an event broker. The event mesh translates any application into different languages and is deployed in different clouds. It publishes an event and lets the subscriber of another application deployed in a different cloud subscribe to that event . It also can be a different API altogether. This helps to separate the configuration from the business logic in microservices.

Characteristics of Event Mesh

The following are the characteristics of an event mesh:

- Made up of interconnected event brokers

- Environment agnostics; can deploy in any public cloud, PaaS, or non-cloud environment

- Dynamic and intelligent routing

- Security and WAN optimization

Event Mesh Capabilities

The following are the event mesh capabilities, and they are required for modern-day architecture:

- Supports publish and subscribe for events in various protocols such as Kafka, Knative, HTTP, AMQP, etc.

- Support for multiprotocol bridges between disparate events, microservices, and messaging platforms

- Supports on-premises and multicloud deployment to provide a uniform infrastructure

- Secure transmission of event messages

How Do Event Meshes Work?

Subscribers of events are connected to the event broker and register with the topic and configure the event type. When event messages arrive in the event broker, Event mesh routes them to the subscriber based on their subscriptions. In Figure 6-26, /Inventory would go to the Inventory service, the event with /Payment would be routed to the Payment service, and the /dispatch event would be routed to the Dispatch service.

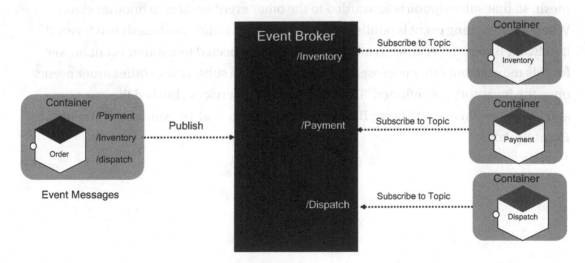

Figure 6-26. *Event mesh implementation*

The consuming microservices such as Inventory, Payment, and Dispatch are processing asynchronously and potentially in parallel. Each service uses processing overhead only when the event broker forwards an event based on the subscriptions. The event broker abstracts the routing of events between the publisher and the subscriber. All event brokers persist messages and don't need to be available when the event is initially published. They have the option of receiving events that were published while they were offline, but this impacts the customer experience.

Event Mesh in a Cluster of Brokers

I explained how the event broker manages the routing rules in a single broker. The complexity arises when you have a cluster of brokers, and each message is subscribed in a separate event broker. How will you manage this? The one option is to embed code in your microservices or configure them in the event broker to manage in a cluster. This is where an event mesh is useful to coordinate and collaborate across multiple event brokers to streamline the routing and publishing and subscription.

In Figure 6-27, the Order microservice sends a message to Event Broker 1 and asks for an order from the location to check inventory, local distribution, and local dispatch. All four microservices are deployed in the separate cloud with respective event brokers. For example, the Inventory microservice asks for any order microservices to check a local inventory where the order is originated. All brokers are connected with the event mesh, so that subscription is forwarded to the other event brokers in another cloud. When the matching event is published to Event Broker 1, the event mesh will forward it to Event Broker 2, because no microservices are connected to another event broker for this request, but other microservices are required to subscribe to other order events once the inventory is confirmed. The Inventory microservices checked the inventory and published an event to Event Broker 2 for availability and an event mesh is routed to Event Broker 1.

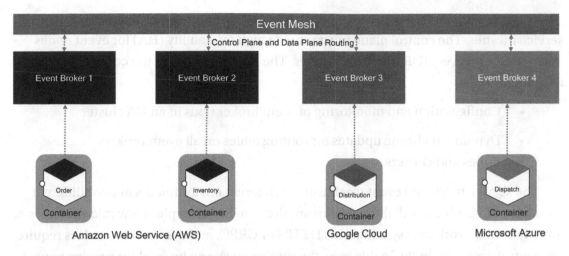

Figure 6-27. *Event mesh across cloud providers*

The Order microservice confirms the order and publishes an event called `confirm`. The event mesh routes to Event Broker 2, and the Inventory microservice subscribes to `confirm` events, updates stocks, and publishes an event called "confirm with the item" to Event Broker 2. The event mesh checks Event Broker 3 and Event Broker 4 for event subscription. The Distribution microservice subscribes to "confirm with the item," and the event mesh routes to Event Broker 3. The distribution microservice consumes and is ready for dispatch by publishing events to "dispatch" to Event Broker 3. The event mesh routes to Event Broker 4 for dispatch. All these microservices and event brokers are deployed in multicloud environments, and the event mesh can route within the cloud or multicloud environment.

While each event broker provides its local routing table based on topics, the control plane of the event mesh dynamically and transparently extends that routing information among all interconnected event mesh broker nodes like the Internet does for IP routes.

This is the way the event mesh makes many event brokers look like a single virtual event broker; it uses broker routing protocols to intelligently, dynamically, and efficiently route events.

Event Mesh's Control Plane

Not all event brokers enable an event mesh. The clustering of event brokers to provide high availability or local horizontal scaling is not an event mesh. If the local cluster does not provide intelligent routing between other clusters, then the event broker doesn't constitute an event mesh. Every event broker that does enable an event mesh provides a control plane.

The event broker must provide the tooling and capabilities like Kubernetes for service meshes. The control plane must provide high availability (HA) for event nodes and disaster recovery (DR) for broker nodes. The characteristics of the control plane are as follows:

- Configuration and monitoring of event broker nods in an HA cluster

- Dynamic real-time updates for routing tables on all event brokers nodes and clusters

The service mesh and event mesh work in different environments and for different use cases, but both can collaborate in an application. For example, a few microservices are required to work with synchronous HTTPS or GRPC, and a few microservices require an event-driven capability. In this case, the service mesh can be used for synchronous microservices, and the event mesh can be used for event-driven microservices

Box- and Port-Style Event-Driven Architecture

The *box- and port-style pattern* supports the observability of microservices or components. It provides a needed level of agility, timelines, information availability, and simplicity in a cost-effective way and provides the surrounding observability component to business services. This observability component can be deployed in the containers, cloud, and on-premises. Figure 6-28 illustrates how business components or microservices are wrapped with a componentless pattern and with observability.

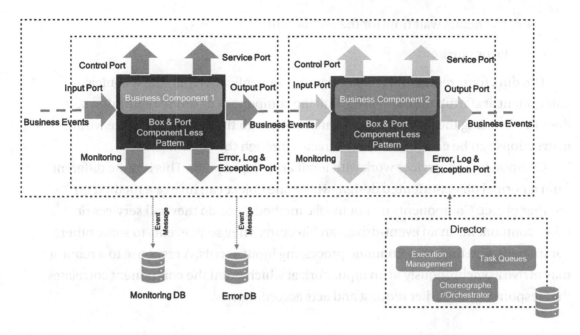

Figure 6-28. *Box- and port-style component less with observability*

On a distributed event-based platform, events are passed from one component to another component by using the message channels or events. This pattern externalizes all observability, interaction with other components, etc., from the core business logic. The ports are enabled for interaction between services or components.

As shown in Figure 6-28, the box and port are technical infrastructure components and support any kind of services irrespective of language and platform. The responsibility of this pattern is to convert message formats and capture errors and exceptions, log messages and traces, configure to topics, etc. This component supports observability to track each business component and supports multiple protocols to interact with business services. The only responsibility of the business service/component is business functionality, and the remaining technical details are maintained by the box and port.

The wrapper component provides an essential level of instrumentation, which means that it is possible to observe the processing of any component from outside. For example, the monitoring port is used to publish performance and other statistics to the dashboard. The operational monitoring includes but not limited to the following:

- Heartbeat monitoring

- The actual latency of every input-to-output event flow as well as average latency over a time window

- The actual wait time for the input event

- Error rates, etc.

The director is responsible for configuring an application into the technical component at startup time and lasts until the component or service shuts down. It does this by using the event delivery platform through the control port. The wiring instructions can be controlled by the director through the control port.

Components or services work with input and output ports. This is quite different from a normal object-oriented design, where one object can invoke a method on another object. Components do not invoke methods, nor do they call services or other components in an event-driven architecture. They send events to some other component, and then they continue processing input events. A response to a request may arrive asynchronously at an input port, at which point the component correlates that response to an earlier request and acts accordingly.

Characteristics of Box- and Port-Style Architecture

The following are the characteristics of box and port style:

- *Real-time operational behavior*: It can change the behavior of the system to dynamically react to incoming events.

- *Observations*: It observes all kinds of behavior and generates alerts when such behavior occurs and predicts failures based on the historical data.

- *Information dissemination*: It sends the right information to the right recipient with personalization.

- *Active and predictive diagnostics*: It can diagnose a problem that occurred based on historical data, predict the details, send alerts to the recipients, and send details to the dashboard.

- *Autoscaling*: Dynamic load distribution patterns such as queue with multiple subscribers are used to ensure that the workload is evenly distributed across all the components. The dashboard spins up the component by sending an instruction to the component with the manual intervention of the configuration file for Docker images.

This architecture style provides the most benefit to the existing legacy component-based systems where the observability details are hard-coded as part of the business logic in a service.

DevOps for Events

Event-driven cloud native architecture has gained a lot of attention; therefore, you need to have a DevOps pipeline for an event-driven architecture. Event-based systems could be comprised of many different enabling technologies such as Kafka, NATS, Solace, Confluent, microservices, serverless, CDC, etc.

The generic guidelines for DevOps are as follows:

- Treat events as API contracts; other systems may be reliant on event producer.

- Use schemas to encode events, with shared schema registries for access.

- Treat event configuration as code. The topics should be created by using scripts, and the event schema must be checked into your Artefactory tool.

- Use infrastructure as code to automate the configuration, installation, etc.

Event Security

In a distributed event-driven architecture, you must balance data democratization with the protection of sensitive data. The events must be encrypted between the publisher and the subscriber.

These are the types of encrypting events:

- Events in transit should always be encrypted using industry-standard encryption methodologies such as SSL/TLS.

- Disks/storage holding past events should always be encrypted in the file system or event store database.

- File-level encryption is the most secure way to encrypt the data, but it is more expensive; therefore, consider this only for sensitive data.

291

Field-Level Encryption Consideration

All data should be encrypted in transit and at rest. The level of field encryption depends on risk tolerance. If the topic contains no sensitive data, then do not use field-level encryption; therefore, you need a balance between security and performance. Figure 6-29 gives a clear strategy to choose what level of encryption is required in your system.

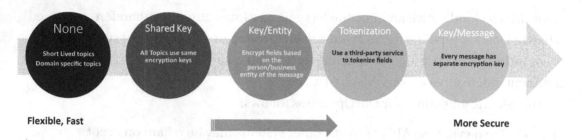

Figure 6-29. *Encryption level*

Cloud Events

In cloud native architecture, you can find events everywhere, and each event is published by a publisher with different event specifications. There is no common, standard way of publishing events in enterprises. This leads to constant learning across teams, leads to more error, and your Confluence documents might be full of event specifications across agile pods to refer to. This limits the potential libraries, tooling, and infrastructure to aid the delivery of events across systems in an enterprise.

As explained earlier in this chapter, an event includes context and data about an occurrence, and each occurrence is uniquely identified by the data of the event. The event represents facts and no destination, whereas the message conveys intent and transporting data from source to destination.

Events can be delivered through various industry-standard protocols, for example, AMQP, HTTP, MQTT, SMTP, and open-source protocols such as NATS, Kafka, or cloud vendor protocols, AWS Kinesis, Azure Event Grid, Google Pub/sub, etc.

The objective of the Cloud Events specification is to define the interoperability of event systems that allow services to produce or consume events, whereas both the teams can be developed and deployed independently.

The Cloud Events specification contains a set of metadata, known as *attributes*, about the event being transferred between systems and how those pieces of metadata should appear in messages. This metadata contains a minimal set of information for routing to the respective services and helps to process the events. Along with this metadata, there is also a specification to serialize the events in different formats like JSON, and protocols like HTTP, AMQP, etc.

The Cloud Events specification defines four kinds of protocol elements.

- *Base specification*: Defines abstract information of attributes and associated rules.

- *The extensions*: Includes use-case-specific and overlapping sets of extension attributes and associated rules.

- *Event format encoding*: Defines how the information model of the base specification with an extension is encoded for mapping the header and payload of a protocol

- *Protocol binding*: Defines the application protocol transport frame, in the case of HTTP to the HTTP messages.

As shown in Figure 6-30, the Cloud Events specification ensures a consistent approach to traceability, schema version, origin, etc. It is just a standard and extended to meet the needs of your enterprise systems. For more details, refer to `https://cloudevents.io/`.

```
{
  A  "specversion" : "1.0",
     "type" : "com.github.pull_request.opened",
     "source" : "https://github.com/cloudevents/spec/pull",
     "subject" : "123",
     "id" : "A234-1234-1234",
     "time" : "2018-04-05T17:31:00Z",
     "comexampleextension1" : "value",
     "comexampleothervalue" : 5,
     "datacontenttype" : "text/xml",
  B  "traceID" : "some-guid-4444-5555",
  C  "Schema" : https://schemaregistry.com/event-schema-1,
  D  "data" : "<much wow=\"xml\"/>"
}
```

Figure 6-30. *Cloud event metadata*

- *A*: The spec version is the version of the specification that the message is encoded to. This should match the Cloud Events specification. Between this marker and B are some of the Cloud Events spec fields you might find.

- *B*: This field is an "extension" of the Cloud Events specification. Here, the trace ID is used to track the event from place to place, usually tied to the origin. For example, a web request might be the originator of this trace ID, and all subsequent messages that are created throughout the system have this same trace ID. To define this tracer, consider the OpenTracing initiative.

- *C*: This schema is another Cloud Events extension, which declares how the data field is laid out. This allows the message to be decoded by services against a schema registry.

- *D*: The data field contains the actual important content, or business information, about an event. This data can be any format you like but should conform to a schema. The way data is structured within the data element is completely independent of the Cloud Events specification.

Summary

Constantly changing, real-time business needs demand cloud native transformation. The world is not slowing down, so your best bet is to identify ways you can cost effectively and efficiently upgrade your enterprise architecture to keep up with the times.

Events can float around on an event mesh to be consumed and acted upon by your microservices. Architects and engineers need real-time implementation details that help you to work together to achieve the real-time, event-driven goals. In this chapter, you learned all the details of an event-driven architecture and its implementation.

CHAPTER 7

Serverless Architecture

In the previous chapters, I discussed microservices and event-driven concepts and their architecture and use cases. In this chapter, I will explain serverless and function as a service (FaaS) and show how they are useful for your enterprises, and I will present some relevant use cases.

Serverless architecture allows the rapid development of cloud native applications that can handle various levels of traffic. The term *serverless* refers to the fact that the cloud provider provides a service without requiring you to manage or administer servers. Your code is executed on demand, as it is needed. You do not need to deal with physical servers, and the complexity of how compute resources are provided is hidden from you.

Serverless is a way to define the service, practices, and strategies to be agility in your development so you can embrace innovation and respond faster to business disruptions. With serverless computing, you don't need to worry about capacity management, infrastructure management, and so on.

Serverless architecture is still maturing, and all the major cloud providers offer various serverless services, including FaaS, databases, IoT services, and more.

In this chapter, I will cover these details of serverless architectures:

- Introduction to serverless computing and architecture

- Usage of serverless

- Journey to serverless architecture

- Relevant use cases

- The cost benefits of serverless

- Serverless in various cloud providers

© Shivakumar R Goniwada 2022
S. R. Goniwada, *Cloud Native Architecture and Design*, https://doi.org/10.1007/978-1-4842-7226-8_7

Evolution of Serverless

So that you can understand serverless better, I will explain how servers have evolved in the context of serverless. A more thorough history of servers in general has already been provided.

As shown in Figure 7-1, the deployment process has had several evolutions:

- Bare-metal technology is a large physical server with a single operating system.

- Virtualization technology virtualizes bare-metal servers into individual virtual machine resources.

- Each virtual machine is subdivided into containers.

- A service built on containers requires a function to run on managed services, called *serverless*.

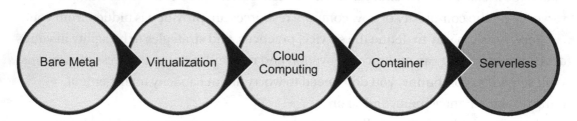

Figure 7-1. *Evolution of serverless*

The evolution of IT architecture has been driven by a series of technological innovations. In this process, the resources are broken down, operational efficiency is increased, and management of software is simplified. The innovation of IT architecture has followed a few characteristics:

- Hardware resources become more granular.

- Resource utilization increases.

- Operation management is gradually reduced.

- Automation and intelligence are increased.

- IT is more focused on solving business problems.

Enterprises are already getting the benefits of VMs and containers in a cloud including cost savings, operationalization, improved agility, etc. Although the cloud eliminates the need for enterprises to manage their own data center, any server-based architecture still requires enterprises to architect for scalability, high availability, reliability, fault tolerance, etc., and companies need to take responsibility for patching and deployment.

Serverless is designed to address these challenges by providing enterprises with a different way of approaching application design. It eliminates the complexity of managing the servers at all levels of the technology stack and implements effective pay-per request billing models.

What Is Serverless Computing?

Serverless is a way of describing the services, practices, and strategies that enable you to adopt agility in your development so you can embrace innovation culture and move faster to market.

Serverless computing is a method of providing back-end services on an as-used basis, and it allows you to write and deploy programs without worrying about infrastructure management.

The demand for serverless technologies is increased because it provides an opportunity for faster time to market by dynamically allocating the required compute and memory based on load.

Serverless services have built-in autoscaling, high availability, and pay-as-you-go billing models. This provides a cost savings through infrastructure management, which enables enterprises to use an IT budget for innovation and upskilling. The pay-as-you-go model with serverless technologies shifts from having capital expenditures to flexible on-demand consumption, allowing users to scale, customize, and provision computing resources as and when required.

As explained earlier in the book, for a traditional architecture, if you want to develop a web application or any software, you had to own the physical hardware, with it managed by you or managed a third party to run a server. This required a lot of management and resources, and in the end, it was expensive.

Serverless technologies effectively shift the operation management from you to the cloud provider. With a serverless operational model, there are no servers to provision, patch, or manage, and there is no management of software such as installation, operations, etc. Many enterprises that have embraced serverless as mainstream are adopting more frequent releases of services, resulting in a faster time to market.

Serverless architecture can be used for many types of software services. Some of the common types of systems that are suited to a serverless architecture include web applications, event-driven data processing, event workflows, scheduled tasks, mobile applications, chatbots, and IoT systems. Figure 7-2 shows an example of a system that has a serverless architecture.

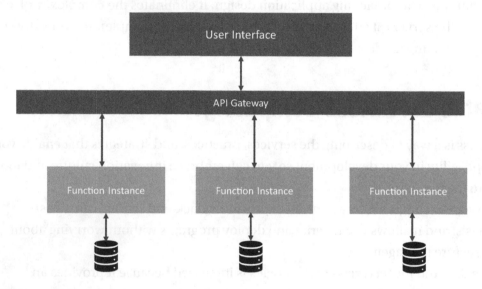

Figure 7-2. *Serverless computing architecture*

Serverless computing has three main benefits.

- *No server management*: There is no operating system to install or patch.

- *Flexible scaling*: Scale is managed for you or is done in a way that's defined in terms of the actual capacity of the application as opposed to having to consider things such as CPUs and memory and other kinds of server-based concepts.

- *Automated high availability*: All the serverless components of the overall platform have built-in high availability. You don't need to design for HA. Serverless gets HA out of the box.

To summarize, serverless computing still has the virtualized, containerized services underneath it, but people don't interact with those servers anymore. All those infrastructure tasks, such as provisioning, scaling, and cleaning up, are done by machines in a completely automated lifecycle.

Essential Components of Serverless

Serverless architectures dramatically simplify the development of event-driven applications and microservices by removing the need to develop and maintain many complex architectural resources such as service meshes, event meshes, dynamic discovery systems, load balancers, retries, circuit breakers, bulkheads, topics, and queues. Instead, you need to focus on four essential components, as shown in Figure 7-3.

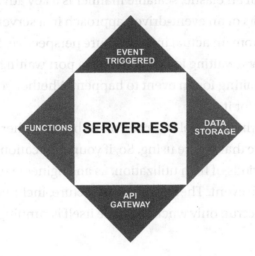

Figure 7-3. *Elements of serverless*

Event Triggered
The applications provide a constant stream of events to which functions subscribe and act upon. The details of the event are stored, and a trigger for the function occurs. Examples are triggers, orders placed, comments posted, setting changes, images uploaded, etc.

Data Storage
Storage ranges from simple disk storage to highly scalable data stores. Storage is always provided as software as a service (SaaS) by the cloud provider. Examples are details stored, state stored, etc.

Functions

Functions are the actual business logic that is spawned solely to process an event. As events come in, they are processed based on the request.

API Gateway

A light API gateway provided by the cloud platform may be in the form of streaming or REST calls to support endpoints for mobile devices. Examples are outcomes, notifications created, photos shared, analytics generated, etc.

Serverless and Event-Driven Computing

The event-driven architecture (EDA) of serverless computing means that every component is independent and decoupled. The ability to listen to events and react to them once they happen in an elastic, scalable manner is a key advantage of serverless.

One of the key benefits of an event-driven approach in a serverless architecture will help to eliminate waste from an actual infrastructure perspective. Most servers in cloud services are in data centers, waiting idle, listening to a port waiting for asynchronous requests to come in, or waiting for an event to happen. Whether your server is active or idle, you still need to pay for it.

With serverless, the whole model is turned on its head to where now you are paying only for the compute time that you're using. So, if your application goes through periods of low utilization and periods of high utilization, as an engineer you only need to worry about how to handle each event. Then your infrastructure, including your actual costs to run that application, accrue only when the code itself is running in response to those events.

Serverless Design Principles

Serverless eliminates a lot of common application architecture problems. When developing a serverless system, it's more important to follow modern-day architecture principles along with related serverless architecture principles. Several principles can be used to design your application with serverless architecture. These define what serverless architecture looks like and what the properties exhibit. However, serverless makes it easy for developers to design and develop applications more readily. This reduces a lot of operational overhead by adhering to some of the 12 Factor App principles that are inherited when adopting serverless frameworks. The following sections provide you with more clarity when designing an application using serverless architecture.

Stateless Functions

FaaS is ephemeral; hence, you can't store anything in memory because the compute containers running your code will automatically be created and destroyed by your application. Stateless is good to scale applications horizontally. Follow the single responsibility principle and only write functions that have a single responsibility and follow the right granularity. The appropriate granularity should be decided based on requirements and context.

Push-Based and Event-Driven Pipelines

Create push-based, event-driven pipelines to carry out complex computations and tasks. Use a choreography approach to interact between various serverless functions and try to build a way to create event-driven pipelines. Avoid polling or manual intervention where possible.

Config: Store Config in the Environment

FaaS providers such as AWS Lambda, Azure Functions, and Google Cloud Functions have separate environment variable sections where you can configure the key-value pairs that are made available to your functions at runtime. These configs can include resource handles, credentials, or environment-specific variables. So, by design, FaaS providers allow you to separate these from the code and eliminate the need to use any heavy frameworks.

Backing Services: Treat Backing Services as Attached Resources

FaaS frameworks inherently provide a clear separation between the business function code and the resources it accesses through the network. The framework does not allow you to run a dependent service or multiple processes inside the function.

Concurrency: Scaling Out via the Process Model

FaaS framework scaling comes out of the box as FaaS frameworks are designed to automatically scale in and out to meet the demands.

Disposability: Maximize Robustness with Quick Startup and Shutdown

FaaS frameworks are ephemeral. A container cannot be reused, so when a new function starts, it is not possible to start quickly, and there is some latency about setting up the execution context and bootstrapping. You need to follow best practices to keep your container warm. Usually, when you invoke frameworks the first time, it does download the dependencies, creating a container, and it starts the application before executing the code. The whole duration is known as the cold-start time. Once the container is up and running, for subsequent function invocation, the framework is already initialized, and it just needs to execute the function logic, called the warm-start time. You need to make sure you choose the appropriate steps to be the warm-start time.

Key Considerations for Serverless Computing

When you are considering the serverless platform, you need a culture of cloud and a culture of automation, and you need to embrace a nimble architecture. The following are a few guidelines that will help you to take full advantage of serverless computing:

Leverage the entire platform in the cloud appropriately.

The best result occurs when an enterprise starts by identifying the use cases that will optimize the dynamic serverless platform. To help enterprises achieve this goal, cloud providers offer a rich set of tools that integrate effectively with the serverless platform. A large independent software provider like open source or commercial software (COTS) also provides deployment, monitoring, and storage solutions with great support for serverless applications on the cloud. These include NoSQL database partners such as MongoDB, Atlas, Couchbase, etc.; continuous integration (CI) and continuous delivery (CD) partners such as

CodeShip and CloudBees for managing automated deployment pipelines; and monitoring partners such as Dynatrace, SignalFx, and I/O pipes with deep integration available for serverless platforms like AWS Lambda, Azure Functions, Google Cloud Functions, etc.

Don't try to reuse existing application code in a serverless environment.

You may have a ready application that was developed earlier and would like to repurpose it. But if you do that, you'll end up having way more code and heft than what the serverless environment is designed for. The suggestion is to refactor your code to adopt serverless characteristics such as stateless, function, ephemeral, etc.

Use existing platform components from providers for nonbusiness logic application functionality.

Serverless computing already has all the execution components you need already designed to work with serverless computing. For anything that is not related to business logic, the platform components always are your first choice; otherwise, there is no point in using serverless.

Create a reference architecture to guide all application development.

By creating a solution blueprint for what the system should look like, you ensure consistency across your application. This helps to create standardization and socialization across teams and resources, and it avoids mistakes.

Support DevOps.

Your development must create a DevSecOps pipeline before you begin your process.

Make a culture shift.

In my experience, you may need to be ready to do as much work restructuring organization and culture as you devote to the building of serverless applications.

303

Be idempotent.

Functions should be designed to be idempotent so that multiple executions of the same request yield the same result, and if the same request is processed more than once, there should be not any adverse effects.

Use an API gateway.

An important part of a serverless architecture is its API gateway. An API gateway is the entry point to a system. It is an HTTP server that takes requests from clients and routes to the relevant function containers.

Why Use Serverless Architecture?

The way you develop applications has changed dramatically in the past few years. As shown in Figure 7-4, in a legacy monolith architecture, you host a single application on the server. A few years back, the microservice architecture style started to evolve. In microservices, each component is an independent service that can scale horizontally and solves many problems of the day-to-day business. In a microservices architecture, you need to provision and configure the infrastructure. Serverless almost behaves the same as microservices, but you do not need to worry about any runtime environment or deployment environment.

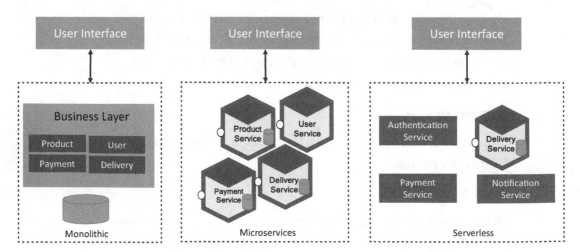

Figure 7-4. *Monolith/microservices/serverless*

Hosting a software application in a production environment involves a few parts. These parts are as follows:

- Code that solves a business problem

- Development and testing pipeline that automates the code build and testing lifecycle

- Deployment and infrastructure service provision, which creates containers, uses Kubernetes or provisions VMs, and configures the infrastructure and required software and runtime environment for your code

- Deployment of your code to a provisioned environment

Using an infrastructure from a cloud provider eliminates the physical hardware concerns but still requires the management of software installation and patches.

With a serverless architecture, you focus only on the code that solves the business problem, and serverless will take care of the rest of these points. This reduces the overhead of the agile pod team.

Best Practices of Serverless Architecture

After you build a serverless architecture, how do you grow an application and manage your source code repository for serverless? Usually, moving to serverless starts with FaaS and then you use the inherent functionality of scalability, etc., and move into production. Your application will grow more complex over time, performing multiple tasks to handle increasingly complex business logic, which leads to the following:

- A tightly coupled codebase

- Slower release cadence

- Poor discoverability

- Additional complexity

- Difficult to separate responsibility of ownership

- Difficult to maintain

Even though you added more functionality into an existing function, that will not be an issue. It still runs and provides the required output. The problem is that the function becomes monolithic, and you might face problems debugging and decoupling the function. To overcome all these traps, you need to adopt the following best practices:

- Design your function as an independent reusable function.

  - Each function is independent.

  - This reduces the impact of bugs or failures in one area of the code that affects the operation of other applications.

  - Allow a function to scale independently according to demand.

  - Share the logic, not the function, if two microservices access the same function.

  - Use contract testing and versioning.

  - Maintain a single source for libraries and dependencies for easier patching and updates in a serverless framework.

- Design your services for choreography.

- Organize source code repositories.

  - Group common functionality together for ownership and repositories.

  - Create repos around a group of functions and resources.

- Design your services with zero trust security.

  - Trust "no one" by default.

  - Build microperimeters around each resource to enforce strict verification of every person or service.

  - Execution role permissions can be limited by the application's permission boundaries.

  - Monitor for insecure flows and attempt to force a function into an unsafe code path.

  - Store secrets in a secret manager, not in environment variables.

- Do not reinvent the wheel; use already proven services in the cloud.

- Use custom resources to enable cross-account service referencing.

Types of Serverless Architecture

Serverless architecture is a way to build and run applications and services without having to manage infrastructure. Your application runs on servers, but all the management is done by the providers. Serverless is focused on any service category, be it compute, storage, database, messaging, API gateway, etc.

Serverless has two similar operational attributes that are frequently used together. The major cloud providers include both.

- Function as a service

- Backend as a service

Function as a Service

FaaS is a serverless way to execute a modular piece of code in a self-managed container and is focused on event-driven computing. It is a paradigm wherein a function is a computation that takes some input and produces some output. FaaS gives you a fast way to focus on building cloud native microservices by abstracting away the complexities of managing virtual machines or clusters of containers.

FaaS can be accessed through events or APIs that you define when you create a function. There are many functions in your architecture where you deploy outside of your service, and that service can be accessed through an event and API. Here are some examples:

- A function can take an input of an image and output a label of that image.

- A function can take a notification and output a personalized email.

- A function can take a YouTube video URL and output a statistic of that video.

- A function can take income numbers and output a total tax calculation.

Various cloud vendors provide the FaaS architecture, covered in the following sections.

AWS Lambda

According to Amazon, "AWS Lambda is a serverless compute service that lets you run code without provisioning or managing servers, creating workload-aware cluster scaling logic, maintaining event integrations, or managing runtimes. With Lambda, you can run code for virtually any type of application—all with zero administration." Lambda supports Node.js, Python, Go, Java, Ruby, and .NET.

You need to use AWS Identity and Access Management (IAM) to manage security in Lambda. For account-related tasks, you can manage permissions to access Lambda functions in the permission policy with users, groups, and roles.

You can call Lambda functions synchronously or asynchronously, with synchronous invocation. It is an I/O blocking service and will wait for the function to process the event and return a response. In the asynchronous invocation, it is non-I/O blocking. Lambda queues the event for processing and returns a response immediately. In cloud native architecture, I suggest going with an asynchronous invocation.

In serverless architecture, some use cases require a stateful nature and require running at the edge location. These are two features where the Lambda team is working.

Reference Architecture

The following section provides a few Lambda reference architectures; these reference architectures are just an example to show how Lambda can be used.

Ecommerce Reference Architecture

I will use the same ecommerce architecture as illustrated in the previous sections and will show how you can leverage Lambda for this. In the abstract version of Figure 7-5 of the ecommerce application (which included only the main services), I considered the following services:

- *User service*: Provides user management, authentication, and authorization

- *Product service*: Product information

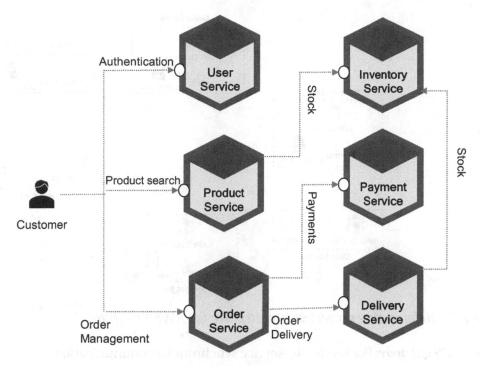

Figure 7-5. *Ecommerce system services*

- *Order service*: Manages the order creation

- *Inventory service*: Manages the stock management

- *Payment service*: Manages payment collection and refunds

- *Delivery service*: Manages shipping and tracking

Figure 7-6 illustrates how you can use the Lambda function along with other AWS services of these ecommerce services. Here I am not showing the entire architecture that includes data synchronization, third-party payment services, etc., and showing only high-level services and interaction across Lambda functions.

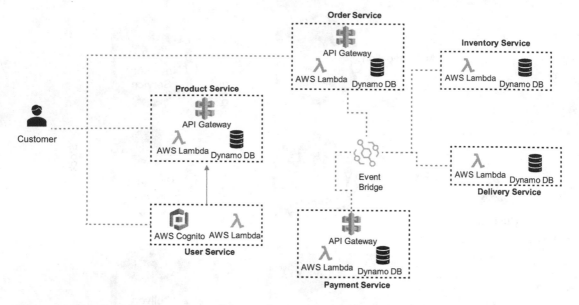

Figure 7-6. *Referencing serverless architecture for AWS Lambda*

- *API gateway*: For service-to-service synchronous communication and access from mobile and web applications, you can use any API gateways like Layer 7, Apigee, etc.

- *Event bridge*: For service-to-service asynchronous communication, you can use any event broker like Kafka, etc.

- *AWS Cognito*: For managing and authenticating users, this provides the JSON web tokens used by web services.

- *AWS Lambda*: The service implementation communicates with APIs and events.

- *AWS DynamoDB*: For storage service, you can use any service like MongoDB, Couchbase, Cassandra, etc.

Best Practices of Lambda

Here are some best practices of Lambda:

> *High availability*: By default, Lambda accesses S3 and DynamoDB in a VPC and won't access RDS, Elasticsearch, etc. To make these available to Lambda, select multiple subnets in different availability zones.

Concurrency: Lambda handles scalability on its own. Lambda can scale up to 1,000 instances per region as of writing this book. You should always consider the limitations of other integrated services so that you can adjust the concurrency limit for the function based on the maximum number of connections these services can handle

Throttling: The concurrency is limited to 1,000 requests as of writing this book. If a request exceeds 1000 requests, how will you handle your function? If the concurrency is synchronous, your service receives an error code with error details, and if the concurrency is asynchronous, service will retry before discarding the event. Therefore, you need to gracefully handle errors.

Performance: Design the function with a warm start.

Security: Design your function with zero trust security with one role per function.

Azure Functions

Azure Functions helps you develop and deploy serverless applications. It's a command-line interface (CLI) that offers structure, automation, and best practices for the deployment of both code and infrastructure, allowing you to focus on building business code that is event-driven. Azure Functions supports multiple programming languages such as JavaScript, Python, C#, F#, Java, etc., with extensive integration options. Durable functions provide stateful capabilities and bindings for Azure Event Hub, and Azure Event Grid helps you to build event-driven architecture.

Azure provides an online editor that is built on Visual Studio Online and provides a well-defined deployment pipeline. You can set up a continuous build and deployment using source code management software such as Team Service, GitHub, or Bitbucket.

Azure functions are logically grouped into an application container or environment called an *app service*. All the Azure functions within an app service share the same resources such as compute and memory. This enables the deployment as a whole application instead of individual functions.

The API gateway functionalities are built natively into Azure Functions, so they do not require any separate API gateway configuration.

Azure Functions supports several types of event triggers. Cron jobs enable timer-based events for scheduled tasks; for example, OneDrive or SharePoint can be configured to trigger operations in a function.

Reference Architecture

The following section provides a few reference architectures for Azure Functions; these reference architectures are just an example to show how functions can be used in your systems. I will use the same ecommerce services as illustrated in the Lambda example and will explain them from the Azure Functions perspective. Figure 7-7 shows only the logical application architecture, not the deployment architecture, as Azure Functions is combined with Azure App Services for deployment.

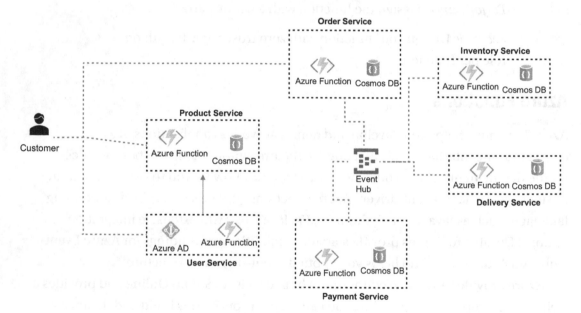

Figure 7-7. *Reference serverless architecture for Azure Functions*

- *API gateway*: There is no separate API gateway; the HTTP triggers are built in to Azure Functions.

- *Event hub*: For service-to-service asynchronous communication, you can use any event broker such as Kafka, etc.

- *Azure AD*: For managing and authenticating users, this provides the JSON web tokens used by web services.

- *Azure Functions*: The service implementation communicate with APIs or events.

- *Cosmos DB*: For storage service, you can use any service like MongoDB, Couchbase, Cassandra, etc.

Best Practices of Azure Functions

The following are the best practices of using Azure Functions:

- *Avoid long-running functions*: Large, long-running functions can cause unexpected timeout issues.

- *Cross-function communication*: Use Azure Durable Functions and Azure Logic Apps. These were built to manage state transitions and communicate between multiple functions.

- *Stateless*: Functions should be stateless and idempotent wherever possible. Associate any required state information with your data.

- *Write defensive functions*: Design your function so it has the ability to continue from a previous fail point during the next execution.

- *Organize functions for performance and scaling*: Optimize Azure Functions within the function app.

- *Organize functions by privileges*: Apply zero trust security and minimize the number of functions with access to specific credentials.

- Reuse connections to external resources wherever possible.

Google Cloud Functions

Google Cloud Functions is an FaaS offering from Google's serverless paradigm. It is a serverless execution environment for building and connecting cloud services. It is based on an open stack. A cloud function can be written using the JavaScript, Python, Go, or Java runtime, as of writing this book, but its programming language support is expanding.

Google Cloud Functions provides a connective layer of logic that lets you write code to connect and extend any cloud service. It augments existing cloud services and allows you to address various use cases with arbitrary programming logic.

From the security account perspective, it has access to the Google Service Account credentials and is thus seamlessly authenticated with the majority of Google Cloud services.

Google Cloud Functions has a good runtime environment that scales up well and cools down slowly and also has strong observability with the stack driver integration results in exceptional sets of telemetry. Data, files, and stream processing are done in real time using the Google platform. The other services in the Google Cloud help Google enhance time efficiency and simplify technology management and administration.

Google Cloud Functions is still catching up with its peers in terms of programming language support and efficiency.

Reference Architecture

This section provides a few Google Cloud Functions reference architecture examples, as shown in Figure 7-8. This reference architecture is just an example to provide how Google Cloud Functions can be used in your system. I will use the same ecommerce services as illustrated in Lambda and Azure Functions and will explain them from the Google Cloud Functions perspective. Here I am showing only the logical application architecture, not the deployment architecture.

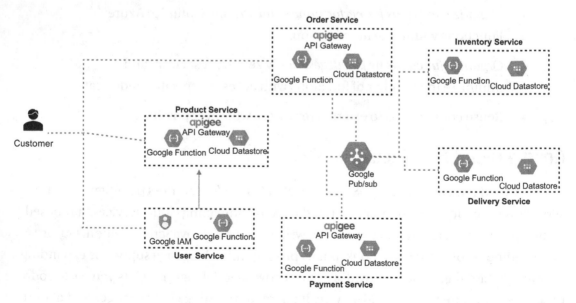

Figure 7-8. *Reference serverless architecture for Google Cloud Functions*

- *API gateway*: For service-to-service synchronous communication and access from mobile and web applications, you can use any other Apigee and also support third-party gateways such as Layer 7, Akana, etc.

- *Google pub/sub*: For service-to-service asynchronous communication, you can use any other event broker such as Kafka, etc.

- *Google IA*: For managing and authenticating users, this provides the JSON web tokens used by web services.

- *Google function*: The service implementation communicates with APIs and events.

- *Cloud datastore*: For storage service, you can use any service such as MongoDB, Couchbase, Cassandra, etc.

Best Practices of Google Function

This section describes general best practices for designing and implementing functions via Google Cloud Functions:

- *Write idempotent functions*: Your function should produce the same result every time it is called.

- *Do not start background activities*: Background activity is anything that happens after your function has terminated a function invocation finishes once the function returns or otherwise signals completion, such as calling a callback argument in Node.js background functions. Any code run after graceful termination cannot access the CPU and will not make any progress.

- *Always delete temporary files*: Have local disk storage in the temporary directory as an in-memory file system. Failing to explicitly delete these files results in an out-of-memory error.

- *Use dependencies wisely*: A function is stateless; the execution environment is often initialized from scratch.

- *Use global variables to reuse objects in future invocation*: If you declare a variable in global scope, its value can be reused in subsequent invocations without having to be recomputed.

315

FaaS Platform Evaluation Criteria

FaaS is a key element of cloud native architecture, and each cloud provider has an FaaS platform that is readily available to you, so everything may not be useful to you. Use the Table 7-1 criteria to evolve the FaaS platforms for your use and rate each framework against these criteria. One thing you need to remember is that not all the frameworks are 100 percent correct, and some frameworks score higher than others. Ask questions like these: What kind of use cases do you want. What are all the other architecture components. Where do you want to deploy them? One thing I would like to get straight is that the serverless technology is still maturing, and not all use cases can be serverless.

Table 7-1. *FaaS Platform Evaluation Criteria*

Step	Criteria	Details
1	Developer experience	How easy is it to create and deploy new functions? Is there any sample template available to develop a function and list of native development and deployment tools available?
2	Programming model	What does the programming model support? What is the state of the workloads (for example, stateless, long-running, etc.)?
3	Runtime execution environment	How do frameworks support building and deployment, and how do they manage cold and warm starts? What are the configuration options, and how easy is it to configure with business code?
4	Observability	What observability options does the FaaS framework provide (for example, logs, metrics, etc.), and how are machine learning models integrated for predictive analysis?
5	Integration	What are the various options that frameworks provide for integration? What kind of events can it subscribe to and publish? Is there support for event meshes and service meshes? How are APIs integrated?
6	Security features	How is access management done? How does it manage serverless specific threats such as denial-of-wallet attacks?
7	Extensibility	Can it support multicloud vendor configuration?
8	Testability	How is the framework support for nonfunctional testing such as performance, scale, etc.?

(continued)

Table 7-1. (*continued*)

Step	Criteria	Details
9	Roadmap	What is the release and upgrade strategy of frameworks?
10	AI and ML support	How does the framework support artificial intelligence and machine learning models?

Backend as a Service or Mobile Backend as a Service

Backend as a service (BaaS) is a cloud computing service model that serves as the middleware that provides developers with ways to connect their web and mobile applications to a cloud-based service. BaaS creates a unified application programming interface (API) and software development kit (SDK) to connect mobile apps to back-end services like cloud storage. This includes key features such as push notifications, social networking integration, location service, and user management, etc., which reduces the development cost and time, as a team does not have to write their code for the various functions. BaaS offers to use existing services.

The BaaS architecture consists of infrastructure as a service (IaaS), platform as a service (PaaS), APIs, and SDKs.

In the traditional architecture or microservices architecture, what steps do you take during mobile or web application development? Usually, you develop a back-end microservice process that contains business logic, authentication, authorization, data storage, integration, etc. There are a lot more other services involved, for example, user analytics, content management, push notification, etc.

BaaS is gaining popularity among enterprises; it is a new model for application development and can lower development costs, allowing the developer to focus on the development process by using APIs or SDKs. It accelerates mobile development and transforms back-end capabilities into services.

The back-end architecture in the cloud empowers the front-end architecture, i.e., mobile and web applications. It comprises hardware and storage located on the cloud service. The cloud service provider manages all the back-end services on behalf of enterprises and acts as a serverless platform. In the Figure 7-9 architecture, the other services of BaaS are push notification, user management, search functionality, visual development, and file management.

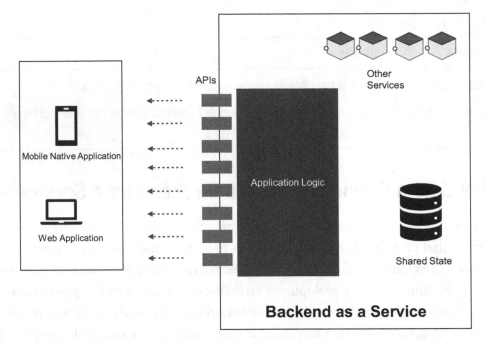

Figure 7-9. *BaaS architecture service*

BaaS eliminates the need for engineers to construct their back-end services and provides the customization features outfitted with common and necessary back-end features.

Is BaaS an advanced version of PaaS? The answer is yes and no. PaaS provides a platform through the cloud for engineers to build their applications. Like BaaS, the PaaS eliminates the need for the developer to build and manage the application back end, but PaaS does not include prebuilt server-side application logic, such as push notifications or user authentication, etc. PaaS offers you more flexibility, while BaaS offers more flexibility and functionality.

Various companies provide BaaS offerings; some are open source, and some are proprietary. The open source BaaS options are Parse, Back4App, Kuzzle, Couchbase, Deployed, etc. The proprietary ones are Pubnub, Appcelerator, PlayFab, Firebase, Kinvey, etc. All these services are hosted on any of the cloud providers or can be downloaded and hosted on any cloud.

Pros and Cons of BaaS

BaaS solves the complexity of cross-platform development and makes it easier to learn the skills needed to create effective back-end processing. You save time on technical use cases such as authentication and authorization, search, data storage, etc., and you don't need to manage the servers. Also, there is virtually no back-end servers to manage. The whole BaaS platform improves the time to market and reduces the cost of testing, management, etc.

The downside of BaaS is related to vendor lock-in and lower coding flexibility, but most BaaS providers offer an easy way to migrate to others, but in reality, it is not the same. BaaS provides full back-end fixed functionality; therefore, you are losing flexibility to move code from the front-end logic to the back-end logic. From the security front, the platform is isolated and multitenant, so there is a challenge on sensitivity, compliance, regulations, etc.

Function Deployment

When your function is deployed in a serverless system, you need to use a deployment pipeline, as shown in Figure 7-10. While the steps in the pipeline can vary depending on the cloud provider, a few fundamental steps are common to all.

You need to upload the function definition, which contains metadata about the function as well as the implementation code. The metadata includes a unique identifier, name, description, version identifier, runtime language, resource requirements, execution timeout, created date/time, and last modified date/time. When a function is invoked, it is invoked for a specific function version. The version identifier is used to select an appropriate function instance.

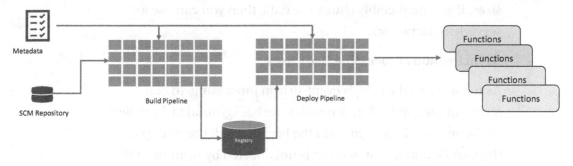

Figure 7-10. *Function deployment pipeline*

Along with the metadata, the code and dependency must be provided. Once the metadata is uploaded to the cloud provider, the build process uses it for compilation to produce an artifact. The resultant artifact may be a binary file or a container image.

The starting of an instance function can be a cold or warm start. With a warm start, one or more function instances have already been deployed and are ready to be executed when needed. A cold start takes longer since the function starts for an undeployed state. The function must be deployed and then executed when it is needed.

When to Use Serverless

As I explained earlier, the serverless work is based on a single function and is ephemeral and stateless. In terms of computing resources, serverless functions have provided good support in terms of memory and available duration. The duration and memory vary from each cloud vendor, and your function should work within the upper limits of memory and duration.

There are various concerns that serverless architecture gives cloud providers complete control over your services. There are many advantages and use cases that make this a good decision that can benefit the overall outcome of a solution. The following are the best use cases for going serverless:

Data Transformation

In the data transformation function, you take input, transform it, and provide different output. In this process, no state is required to execute, and the execution is simply based on few rules. The only thing you need to manage is that the data comes in different sizes. If you predictably chunk the data, then you can use a serverless framework.

Asynchronous Processing Use Cases

As mentioned, the FaaS is event-driven processing. In real terms for an application, it enables the background tasks to be well-connected and remain in the background. For example, the mobile application request is not affected by running in the background and still interacts with an application. You can use it in flight searches, hotel searches, etc.

Multimedia Processing Use Cases

The function can be created for multimedia processing such as image processing, file upload to the storage, etc.

Parallel Compute

In parallel computing, you require multiple instances to spin up and execute in parallel to meet the requirements. Using a serverless framework, you can configure with a concurrency model, which essentially translates as one function handling at any one time to scale thousands to meet the parallel processing.

Notifications

You can create notification functions to work with container-based microservices. The notification can be an email notification or SMS notification, or it can upload any image into the storage notification.

Building Restful APIs

Serverless frameworks provide a seamless way in which to create a scalable endpoint that processes data in real time. It has the ability to scale and fluctuate as demand changes without the need to maintain the servers.

Advantages of Serverless Architecture

Using a serverless architecture provides many important benefits, which explains why it is becoming increasingly popular.

Reduced Operational Cost

With a serverless architecture, your code is executed only when it is needed, so you are charged only for the actual compute resources that are used. Organizations moving to a serverless architecture will reduce hardware costs, as they no longer have servers and network infrastructure to support and do not have to hire staff to support all of that infrastructure.

The following are the reductions in the operational costs of serverless systems:

- Savings on the hardware
- Infrastructure management
- Managing the development and deployment of software

Optimized Resource Utilization

Serverless empowers you to design an application that scales up and down as per the demands. Serverless will take care of the optimum utilization of resources by managing the technical concerns effectively. This enables saving costs and reducing the impact on the environment.

Faster Time to Market

You need to concentrate only on solving business problems by writing good software code. Serverless abstracts away the infrastructure, deployment, and plumbing and wiring activity in an environment. The time to market is greatly reduced and avoids lots of unnecessary issues.

Ability to Focus on User Experience

Abstraction from servers allows companies to dedicate more time and resources to developing and improving customer-facing features.

Fits with Microservices

The serverless platform paradigm helps design a microservices architecture either by deploying a service in the serverless platform or by collaborating with the container-based microservices by deploying reusable functions as an FaaS.

The Drawbacks of Serverless Architecture

Although there are many benefits to using a serverless architecture, there is a potential downside to using serverless, and each vendor comes with their own set of drawbacks that need to be considered by architects creating such systems.

Standardization

There is no standardization across various vendors. Each vendor's serverless implementation has a different approach. For example, API gateway's features are part of Azure Functions, but AWS Lambda is an external feature. This requires locking into a vendor. If you want to move, then you need to rewrite your code.

Operations Management

It is more challenging to debug or do other operationalize activity. Implementation is a black box to you, and you will be unable to find any internal details of serverless. Understanding, anticipating, and predicting these operations is challenging. There are operation limits typically enforced on the duration of execution, size of the function, network utilization, storage capacity, memory usage, thread count, request and response size, etc. The vendor documentation does not have clear details on the operationalization of serverless.

Tooling Support

As I mentioned, serverless is still evolving, as compared to the containers. The containers have a lot of support tooling from the various industry players and also from open source other than the cloud vendors. Testing and deployment tools are limited, and the industry may come up with various tools as serverless adoption evolves.

Security

As the implementation of serverless is not transparent and is entirely managed by the cloud vendors, you need to rely on the vendor's security management. You do not have visibility into compliance, regulations, etc.

Long-Term Tasks

Serverless platforms are ephemeral functions that execute in a time-boxed manner. Each function must have a well-defined execution boundary. So, the ideal use cases to run as FaaS are deterministic computations that return execution results in a finite amount of time. You need to be careful when architecting your solution for long-running, probabilistic jobs. Running such jobs can incur more costs, which defeats the purpose of adopting serverless.

Future of Serverless

In recent years, serverless computing has gained a lot of traction, which has had a large influence on the computing industry. Serverless vendors are constantly innovating and enriching their offerings with better tools such as deployment, testing, and monitoring tools.

323

In the future, complex technical solutions will move from container to serverless computing and will be implemented and fully managed. The cloud services will provide capabilities in serverless computing platforms in the form of APIs and events.

As I explained in earlier chapters, the adoption of cloud native services has increased, especially after the pandemic. Cloud native services are mainly connected with other services through events. In the future, all services on the cloud and on-premises ecosystem are connected through events. All events related to the enterprise and extended enterprise business can be processed in a serverless manner, regardless of where the event occurs.

VMs and containers are two virtualization technologies with different orientations with strong security and high overheads. Serverless computing requires the highest security and minimum resource overheads and compatibility at the same time. For example, the serverless platform must be able to support arbitrary binary files. This makes it impractical for users to build serverless computing with language-specific VMs. Hence, new lightweight virtualization technologies, such as AWS Firecracker and Google gVisor, have emerged. For example, AWS Firecracker provides a minimal required device model and optimizes kernel loading, enabling startups within 100 milliseconds and minimal memory overhead. As the scale and influence are constantly expanding, it becomes important to implement end-to-end optimization at the framework level, language, and hardware levels based on the load characteristics of serverless computing.

Summary

Serverless approaches are designed to handle idle servers that affect enterprises' balance sheets without offering value; they also remove the cost of building and operating a fleet of servers.

Various cloud vendors offer serverless solutions for long-standing problems by eliminating the servers, containers, disks, and other infrastructure. Serverless is the easiest and fastest way to architecture a reactive, event-based system with a cloud native architecture.

In this chapter, you learned about the design principles, patterns, and use cases of serverless.

CHAPTER 8

Cloud Native Data Architecture

In previous chapters, we discussed the application side of cloud native architecture and showed use cases. In this chapter, I will provide details of the data part of a cloud native architecture. As you already know, data is a vast subject; in fact, you can find hundreds of blogs, articles, and books about data. Here I am not covering the topic, but only what's relevant to cloud native architecture.

Enterprises are continuing to move to cloud native architectures, and data plays a pivotal role in that. Data is everywhere; however, the importance and usage of data has changed over time.

Bad data can have significant consequences in an enterprise. Poor-quality data is often pegged as the source of operational problems, inaccurate analytics, and ill-conceived business strategies. According to Gartner, recent research has shown that organizations believe that poor data quality is responsible for an average of $15 million per year in losses. This is a huge loss incurred because of data quality.

Almost every enterprise today is seeking to position itself as a data-driven organization. Businesses are aware of the myriad benefits that can be leveraged when making intelligently empowered decisions and providing customers with top-notch, hyper-personalized experiences, often using artificial intelligence and machine learning models.

This chapter covers the following details of data related to the cloud native phenomenon:

- How has data gained importance?
- How useful is data in your day-to-day business?
- Data storage types and polyglot data architecture
- Data replication strategies

325

© Shivakumar R Goniwada 2022
S. R. Goniwada, *Cloud Native Architecture and Design*, https://doi.org/10.1007/978-1-4842-7226-8_8

- Data lake and data mesh usage

- Data streaming and change data capture

- Data processing for an analytics platform

Rethinking Data in a Cloud Native World

When dealing with disruption in both business and technology, one area that cannot be forgotten is the data layer. Enterprises must rethink their data layer strategy as they move their landscape to cloud native technologies.

In today's digital world, if an IT application lags for even a few seconds, it can have an enormous downstream impact on the end customer experience and on the business's success. Data processing must be quick enough to keep up with the real-time business-critical applications and today's consumer demand. If travel aggregator apps, maps, food delivery apps, etc., don't provide data instantly, customers will stop using them.

Cloud computing has made a big impact on how we build and operate software today, including how we work with data. More and more companies are embracing the cloud on a daily basis, especially after the pandemic, and shifting their data centers to the cloud, decentralizing their organizations, and making their application architecture more cloud native distributed in nature to enable the pace of innovation necessary to service real-time user needs.

To deliver a consistently fast, satisfying customer experience, the data is very important and must be modernized, moving from batch to streaming and data lake to data mesh, etc. Your enterprise's application is generating more and more data. The traditional way of handling data is simply too slow and does not meet the customer's business goals. In cloud native architecture, the data store must follow the polyglot principle explained in Chapter 5. Just storing static data is not enough; the polyglot principle and analytics principles are required for future data analysis. Enterprises need to make real-time decisions and predictions.

Organizations continue to face a range of complexities in transforming to a data-driven approach and leveraging its full potential. While migrating legacy systems, shunning legacy cultures, and prioritizing data management are all valid goals, the architectural structure of data platform initiatives can prove to be a major roadblock.

The need for traditional data storage functions such as backups, replication, and security don't go away in cloud native data services; they are just initiated and managed in new and real-time ways. With data replication, you often pull data from multiple sources to carry out a task, and increasingly such aggregation is on demand. Earlier you were doing nightly batch jobs, but in the cloud native world, you use data streaming techniques in real time.

In the data storage part, there are no changes in the storage and the create, read, update, and delete (CRUD) operations, but there are various options available to store data by using polyglot principles. You can choose from various storage mechanisms such as traditional RDBMS, NoSQL, caching, etc.

There is no change in data visualization. Earlier we generated reports by using classic reporting tools; now you have more options to choose from with rich functionality.

In a nutshell, the changes are in the way you are adopting the data and using it for various analytical decisions.

Cloud Native Data Persistence Layer

For a lot of businesses and enterprises, cloud computing has made a big impact on how they store data. The cost of storing data has significantly decreased. The management of database systems requires less work with the advent of cloud vendor-managed and serverless data storage. This makes enterprises choose various data storage types based on the data classification.

A polyglot persistence principle encourages cloud native services to decentralize the data; it is also common that data is replicated and partitioned in order to scale the system. Figure 8-1 shows how a typical cloud native architecture applies the polyglot persistence principle with data spread across the architecture.

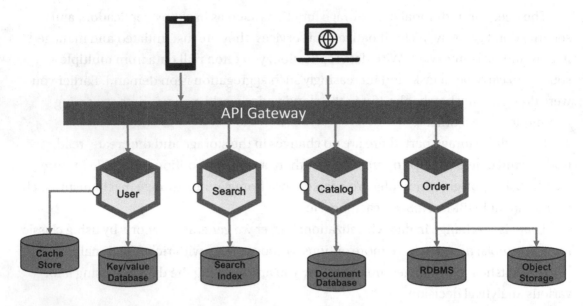

Figure 8-1. *Cloud native polyglot persistence*

Cloud native applications use managed and serverless data storage and processing services; all major cloud providers offer several different managed services to store, process, and analyze data. In addition to cloud providers, various database companies provide managed services on the cloud. For example, MongoDB provides managed services with Atlas, Redis provides managed cache storage, etc. By using managed cloud storage, you can focus on developing business logic that uses the data and database instead of spending time and resources managing the database.

Cloud Native Data Characteristics

For a cloud native application, you can use a blueprint like the 12-factor criteria to design it, as mentioned in Chapter 4, but for the data design, you need to consider the following key characteristics:

- Prefer a cloud native database that shards, tolerates faults, and is optimized for cloud storage.

- Prefer cloud native data that is independent of fixed schemas.

- Cloud native data can be duplicated for ease of access.

- Prefer managed data storage and analytics services.

- Use polyglot persistence, data partitioning, and caching.

- Embrace eventual consistency and use strong consistency when necessary.

- Cloud native data integrates through service and event streaming.

- Adopt a data mesh wherever possible instead of a data lake.

- Prefer real-time analysis to batching.

- Deal with data distribution across multiple data stores.

How to Select a Data Store

Selecting the right database is important for the successful completion of your project. There are about 347 databases available including RDBMS, NoSQL, event stores, etc. It can be difficult to determine which products to use, and sometimes you may choose the wrong database for your application that limits your whole application. I have witnessed projects change their database after pushing it into production. This might cause heavy loss to enterprises because you need to migrate, test, etc., so choosing the right database from the start is important. I will provide as many details as possible to help you to choose the right database.

I will first start with various types of data.

Objects, Files, and Blocks

Objects, files, and blocks are storage formats that hold, organize, and present data in different ways. Object storage manages data as an object and stores data with metadata and a key that is used as a reference for the object. File storage organizes and represents data as a hierarchy of files in folders. Block storage chunks data into arbitrarily organized, evenly sized volumes.

Note   Objects are considered images, documents, and files.

The major cloud providers such as AWS, Azure, and Google provide inexpensive object storage, and the data can be accessed through APIs. Each object is stored in a key-value pair with metadata linked into it, and it is stored with versions and globally available. The object storage tools are AWS's S3, Azure's blob storage, and Google Cloud storage.

Every document in a file is arranged in some type of local hierarchy. Network-attached storage (NAS) is a file-level storage architecture. Use it when using a library or service that requires shared access to files. Various NAS providers are available in cloud environments including natively from cloud vendors. A few major NAS vendors are NetApp, Dell EMC, HPE, Hitachi Vantara, IBM, Cloudian, Qumulo, and WekaIO.

Block storage breaks data into smaller blocks and stores the blocks separately. Each block of data is given a unique identifier, which allows a storage system to place the smaller pieces of data wherever is most convenient. Use block storage for applications for persistent local storage. For this kind of data, use any database to store it.

Databases

A database is a collection of data stored in an orderly manner, as shown in Figure 8-2. It is a structured set of data hosted on the hardware. There have been some new players in the database world over the past few years, and the number of databases available for us to choose from continues to grow every year.

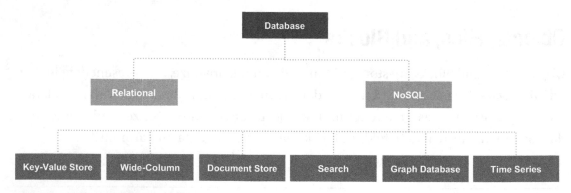

Figure 8-2. *Database types*

Many of these databases have been designed for specific use cases; some store graph-related data, some store financial models, etc.

Note   I have not covered caching technology because it is part of the key-value store family. Relational and object databases are part of the relational family.

Relational Database

A relational database is a collection of data items with a predetermined relationship between them. This data is organized into a set of tables, columns, and rows. A relational database provides access to data points that are related to one another. Each column in a table holds a certain kind of data and fields to store the actual values of an attribute. Each row in a table can be marked with a unique identifier called the *primary key*, and the rows in multiple tables can be made related using foreign keys. This data can be managed with CRUD operations.

Relational databases have been around for a long time. The most popular commonly used database, as of today, is still a relational database. The relational model is the best for maintaining data consistency across application and database instances. The relational databases support atomicity, consistency, isolation, and durability (ACID) properties with strong consistency.

Several factors can guide your decisions when choosing among relational database types. You need to ask the following questions before choosing a vendor:

- What is our data accuracy requirement?

- Do we need scalability? What is the anticipated growth?

- How important is concurrency?

- Where are we hosting the database?

- What kind of application are we developing?

Use Figure 8-3 to decide whether you need an RDBMS for your application.

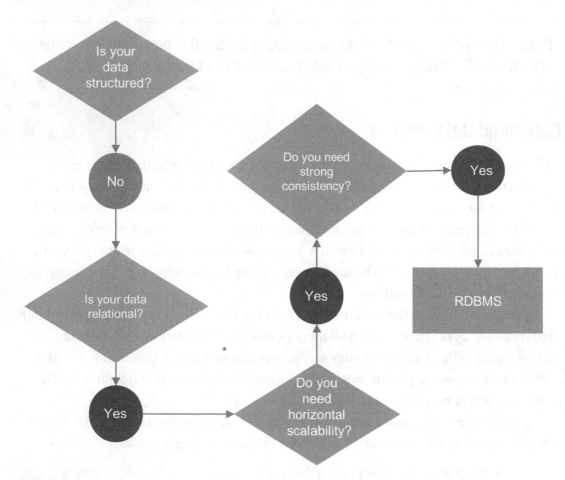

Figure 8-3. *RDBMS decision flow*

Key-Value

A key-value data store is a type of nonrelational database that uses a simple key value to store data. In key-value pairs, a key serves as a unique identifier. Both keys and values can be anything, ranging from simple objects to complex compound objects, and they can store dictionary/map/array objects.

Key-value databases use compact, efficient index structures to be able to locate a value quickly and reliably by its key, making them ideal for systems that need to find and retrieve data in real time. Key-value databases allow programs to retrieve data via keys, which are essential names, or identifiers, that point to some stored values.

Key-value databases are scaled out by implementing partitioning, replication, and autorecovery. They can scale by maintaining the database in RAM and can minimize the effects of ACID guarantees by avoiding locks, latches, and low-overhead server calls.

Several factors can guide your decision when choosing among the key-value database types. You need to ask the following questions before choosing any type of database:

- What kind of data do we want to store?

- Do we need scalability?

- Do we want our data to share across microservices?

- What kind of application we are developing?

Use Figure 8-4 to decide whether you need the key-value type for your application storage.

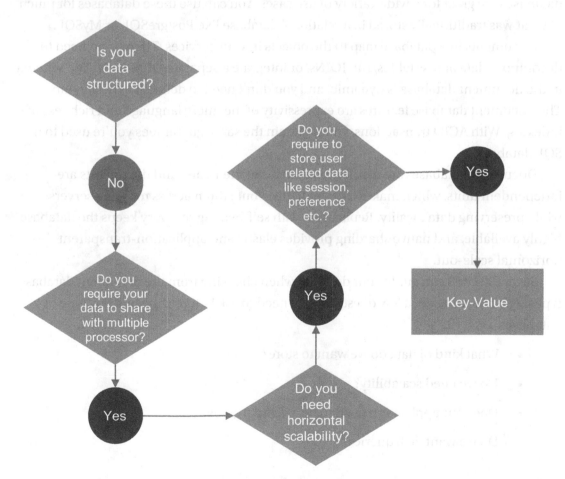

Figure 8-4. *Key-value store decision flow*

The following are key-value stores: AWS Dynamo DB, Redis, Riak, Couchbase, Berkeley DB, Cassandra, etc.

Document Database

A *document-oriented database* is a way to store data in JSON format rather than simple rows and columns. A document store does assume a certain document structure that can be specified with a schema. A document store is the most natural way of storing data among NoSQL-type databases, which are designed to store the document as is.

Each document in a store contains pairs of fields and values. The values can typically be a variety of types including things like strings, numbers, Booleans, arrays, or objects, and their structure is aligned with the application developer working with the code. Because of their variety of field value types and powerful query languages, document databases are great for a wide variety of use cases. You can use these databases for much of what was traditionally stored in a relational database like PostgreSQL or MySQL.

Documents in a database map to the objects in your services. There is no need to decompose data across tables, run JOINs, or integrate a separate ORM layer. The schema in the document database is dynamic, and you don't need to define it at design time. The document database features are expressivity of the query language and richness of indexing. With ACID transactions, you maintain the same guarantees you're used to in SQL databases.

Document databases are distributed systems at their core, and documents are independent units, which makes it easier to distribute them across multiple servers while preserving data locality. Replication with self-healing recovery keeps the database highly available, and native sharding provides elastic and application-transparent horizontal scale-out.

Several factors can guide your decision when choosing from the document database types. The following are a few questions you need to ask before choosing any type of database:

- What kind of data do we want to store?

- Do we need scalability?

- Does our application need to be available globally?

- Do we want SQL queries?

- Do we want a flexible schema?

- Do we want to store all kinds of data like modeling, semistructured, and unstructured data in one database?

- What kind of application are we developing?

- Do we want to store content or catalogs?

Use Figure 8-5 to decide whether you require a document database for your application storage.

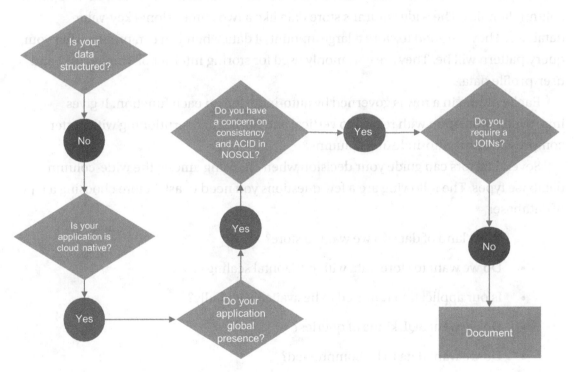

Figure 8-5. *Document store decision flow*

The following are a few major players in the area of document databases: MongoDB, CouchDB, Couchbase Server, Cosmos DB, Document DB, MarkLogic, Oracle NoSQL, etc.

Wide-Column Database

A *column database* organizes data into rows and columns and can initially appear very similar to a relational database. It stores data in tables, rows, and dynamic columns. A columnar database stores each column in a separate file. One file stores only the key column, and the other stores the remaining fields. Wide-column stores provide a lot of flexibility over relational databases because each row is not required to have the same columns.

Each column holds a set of columns that are logically related and typically retrieved or manipulated as a unit. Other data that is accessed separately can be stored in separate column families. The wide columns store data like a two-dimensional key-value database. They are good to store a large amount of data when you can predict what your query pattern will be. They are commonly used for storing Internet of Things (IoT) and user-profile data.

Each column in a row is governed by auto-indexing on each function. It gives improved automation with regard to vertical and horizontal partitioning with better compression and auto-indexing columns.

Several factors can guide your decision when choosing among the wide-column database types. The following are a few questions you need to ask before choosing a type of database:

- What kind of data do we want to store?

- Do we want to store data with horizontal scaling?

- Is our application required to be available globally?

- Do we want SQL kinds of queries?

- Do we want data to be compressed?

- What kind of application are we developing?

- Do we want to store IoT or geographical map data?

- Do we want a database for analytics?

Use Figure 8-6 to decide whether you require a wide-column database for your application storage. The major databases are Cassandra and HBase.

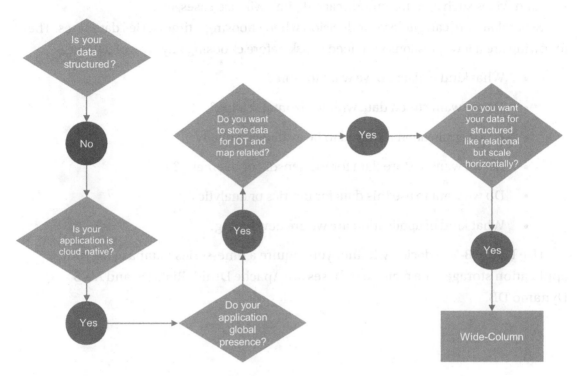

Figure 8-6. *Wide-column decision flow*

Time-Series Database

Time-series data is a sequence of data points collected over time intervals, giving you the ability to track changes over time. Time-series data can track changes over milliseconds, days, or even years. This could be server metrics, application performance monitoring, network data, sensor data, trades in the market, etc.

The time-series database is optimized for a time. It is built specifically for handling metrics and events or measurements that are time-stamped. These databases generally need to support a very high number of writes. Time-series databases are commonly used to collect large amounts of data in real time from many sources. Updates to the data are rare; more common are inserts and bulk deletes.

The size of the data structure is small for time and other coordinates. Time-series data is good for storing telemetry data; popular uses include Internet of Things (IoT) sensor devices such as autonomous cars, digital twin use cases, etc.

Several factors can guide your decision when choosing a time-series databases. The following are a few questions you need to ask before choosing any type of database:

- What kind of data do we want to store?

- Do we want stored data with horizontal scaling?

- Is our application required to be available globally?

- Do we want to store data for IoT sensors or telemetry?

- Do we want to use this data for metrics or analytics?

- What kind of application are we are developing?

Use Figure 8-7 to decide whether you require a time-series database for your application storage. The major databases are Apache Druid, Riak-TS, and AWS Dynamo DB.

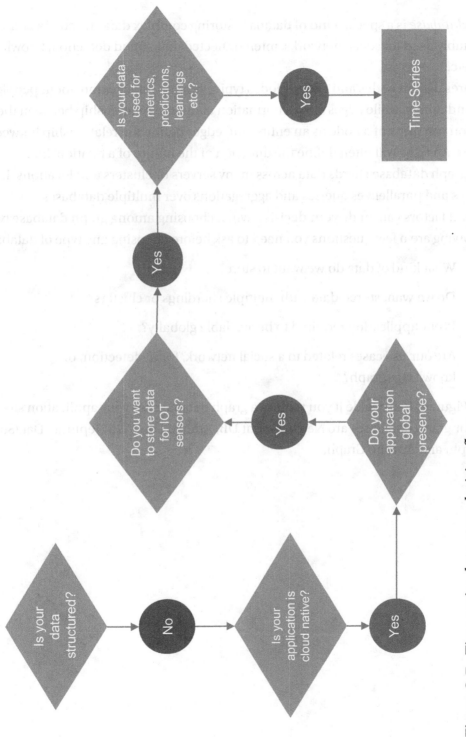

Figure 8-7. *Time-series data store decision flow*

Graph Database

A *graph database* is a special kind of database storing complex data structures and most notably used for social networks, interconnected data, fraud detection, knowledge graphs, etc.

It stores data in nodes and edges. Nodes typically store information about people, places, and things, while edges store information about the relationship between the nodes. You can think of a node as an entity, and edges define the relationship between the nodes. An edge will often define the direction of the nature of a relationship.

The graph database shards data across many servers or clusters and locations. It distributes and parallelizes queries and aggregations over multiple databases.

Several factors can guide your decision when choosing among graph database types. The following are a few questions you need to ask before choosing any type of database:

- What kind of data do we want to store?

- Do we want stored data with multiple shardings or clusters?

- Is our application required to be available globally?

- Are our use cases related to a social network, fraud detection, or knowledge graph?

Use Figure 8-8 to decide if you require a graph database for your application storage. The major graph databases are Neo4J, Orient DB, Arango DB, AWS Neptune, DataStax, IBM Graph, and Apache Graph.

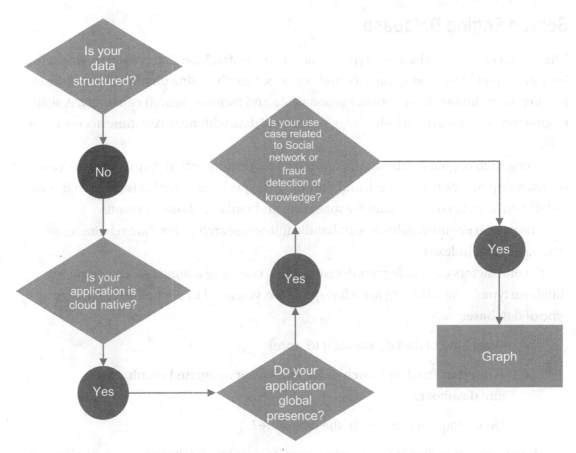

Figure 8-8. *Graph data store decision flow*

Event Store Database

In event-driven architecture, streams and queues are required to store events and messages (more details are explained in Chapter 6). In an event stream, the data is stored as an immutable stream of events. All the events in the event store are new records and do not allow updates; also, you cannot remove or delete an event.

The data in an event store is used to validate an aggregate sequence numbers of events, event snapshots, event sourcing details, etc.

There is various event store data store available such as IBM DB2 Event Store, Event Store DB, and NEventStore.

Search Engine Database

The search engine database is a type of nonrelational database that is used to search for information held in other databases and services. Search engine databases use indexes to categorize similar characteristics among data and facilitate search capability. A search engine index database can index large volumes of data with near-real-time access to the index.

The search engine databases are optimized for dealing with data that may be long, semistructured, or unstructured, and they provide specialized methods for search such as full-text search, complex search expression, and ranking of search results.

The search engine databases can handle full-text search faster than relational databases with indexes.

Several factors can guide your decision when choosing among search engine database types. The following are a few questions you need to ask before choosing any type of database:

- What kind of data do we want to store?

- Is our data used for search or log analysis or integrated monitoring and dashboard?

- Do we require indexing in the data store?

Use Figure 8-9 to decide whether you require a search database for your application storage. The major databases are Elasticsearch, Splunk, ArangoDB, Solr, AWS Cloud Search, Alibaba Cloud Log Service, and MarkLogic.

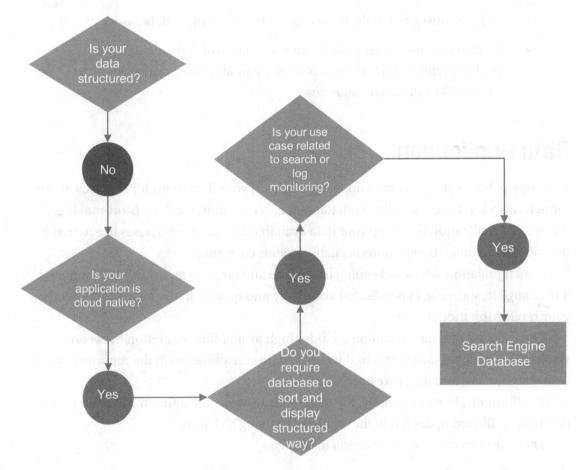

Figure 8-9. Search engine data store decision flow

Selecting a database is confusing when you have a vast number of options available today and new ones are constantly improving and adapting to cloud native. A website that tracks database popularity, DB-engines (`https://db-engines.com`), lists 347 different databases as of this writing. As you are moving toward cloud native architecture, you have the flexibility to choose a specific database based on your use cases. When choosing the specific use cases, you need to consider the following aspects:

- Consider the skillset of the team.
- Go for the managed serverless database from cloud vendors or individual database vendors (for example, MongoDB offering Atlas).

- Go for lightweight databases instead of big monolithic databases.

- Analyze your use cases and ask questions as provided for each database type; nowadays most NoSQL databases offer similar features like relational databases.

Data Replication

Data replication is the process of updating copies of your data in multiple places at the same time to improve reliability, fault tolerance, accessibility, and decision-making. The goal of replication is to keep your data available for various purposes like to make decisions or to make transactions available to your customers.

Data replication works by keeping the source and target synchronized. That means any change in source data is reflected accurately and quickly in the target data based on your replication model.

The use case of data replication includes high availability, migration between systems, operational data stores or data hubs, data consolidation in the reporting system, data warehouses, and data lakes, etc.

Traditionally, in an enterprise, the data replication occurs either from database to database or file are uploaded to the database by using ETL tools.

There are two database replication methods.

- Physical database replication

- Logical database replication

Physical Database Replication

Physical database replication is a block-based replication that uses a binary format to keep an exact database copy in sync with the primary database. Using the binary format for database replication provides completeness: the replicated database is an exact copy of the primary database including tables, relationships, indexes, triggers, stored procedures, etc. This kind of replication is common in disaster recovery use cases.

Logical Database Replication

This is a method of replicating data objects and their changes based on their replication key. Logical database replication is the most common method of replication in a cloud native architecture. It uses the publish/subscribe paradigm to replicate data from source to target databases. The logical replication of a table starts by taking a snapshot of the data on the publisher database and copying that to the subscriber.

In the logical database replication, you can do full database refreshes or logical refreshes or change data capture (CDC).

Full Data Refresh

In the full load refresh replication, all the data in the publisher loads data to the subscriber at an interval and overwrites all the data in the subscribed database. This method is very resource-intensive; usually enterprises adopt this approach only for the initial load.

Partial Data Refresh

In the partial refresh replication, use a column in the table that is modified for every change to the row with the timestamp. Use a filter when retrieving the data from the publisher instead of selecting full data. This approach is reliable only when data is not truncated.

Change Data Capture

CDC is a replication solution that captures database changes as they happen and delivers them to the target database. CDC typically starts by taking a snapshot of the data on the publisher database and copying it to the subscriber database, as shown in Figure 8-10. Once that is done, the changes on the publisher are sent to the subscriber as they occur in real time.

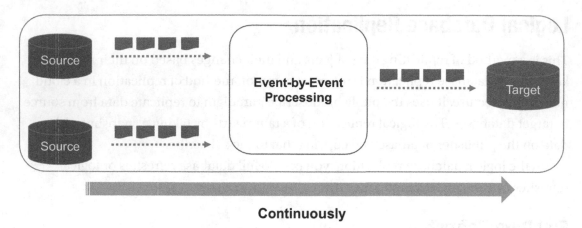

Figure 8-10. *CDC process*

The subscriber applies the data in the same order as the publisher so that transactional consistency is guaranteed for publication with the same subscription.

There are many techniques available to implement CDC depending on the nature of your implementation.

- *Timestamp*: The Timestamp column in a table represents the time of the last change; any data changes in a row can be identified with the timestamp.

- *Version number*: The Version Number column in a table represents the version of the last change; all data with the latest version number is considered to have changed.

- *Triggers*: Write a trigger for each table; the triggers in a table log events that happen to the table.

- *Log-based*: Databases store all changes in a transactional log to recover the committed state of the database. The CDC reads the changes in the log and identifies the modification and publishes an event.

The most preferred approach is the log-based technique. In today's world, many databases offer a stream of data change logs and expose them through an event.

Log-Based CDC

The log-based approach provides real-time asynchronous data integration and provides continuous integration through database logs. This approach allows the solution to transfer and integrate changes to the data incrementally as they occur, rather than making larger updates all at once.

Database transaction logs that store all database events allow for the database to be recovered in the case of a crash. The changes in the source database are captured without making application-level changes and without the overhead on the database and without having scans on operational tables, all of which add workload and reduce source system performance.

In the Figure 8-11 example, service A writes data to a database, and the database writes a change to the logs. The change is then managed by CDC tools and written to a stream of events and subscribed to by multiple consumers; the consumer could be a target database, data lake, or real-time analytics.

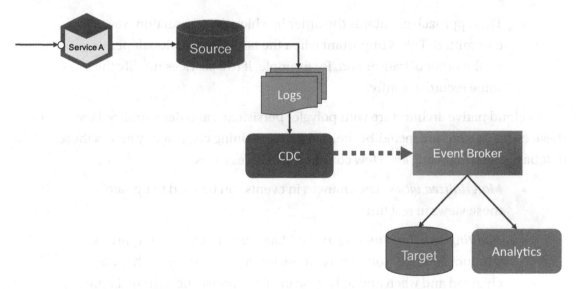

Figure 8-11. *Log-based CDC*

There are a few areas where you need to aware of, such as the following:

- *Concurrency*: Most CDC tools manage the order.

- *Data consistency issues*: In a microservices polyglot architecture, transactions span multiple databases. You need to write a set of changes to the changelog and then apply those changes. All the changes can be written to a stream maintaining order.

- *The compensating transaction*: Apply multiple techniques like saga and CQRS to manage the transaction (refer to Chapter 6 for more details).

The following are the advantages of log-based CDC approaches:

- This approach has a minimal impact on the transactional database.

- This works in near-real-time asynchronous event streaming; it helps you to manage analytics on the fly.

- This approach maintains the order in which the transaction was committed. This is important when the target application depends on the order of transaction, for example, if two services modify the same record instantly.

In cloud native architecture with polyglot persistence and decentralized datastores, these event streams are incredibly helpful in maintaining consistency across these databases. The following are a few common CDC uses cases:

- *Materialized views*: The changes in events can be used to update these views in real time.

- *Auditing and fraud management*: Many transactions are required to conduct auditing. You can use these log changes to track what was changed and when and to help scan all the transactions in real time for anti-money laundering and fraud management.

- *Analytics*: You may require data analytics both on the fly and off the fly. This approach will apply a machine learning model on the event streams and will use the fly analysis from a data lake or data mesh.

- *Decoupling*: When you consider moving from a legacy monolithic application to microservices, your approach should be iterative by applying strangulation. In this case, you need to use this approach to decouple legacy applications and their databases.

Extract, Transfer, and Load

ETL is a process that extracts data from different source systems, transforms the data, and finally loads the data into the target database. This process is not new; you have been using this approach for very long time. As the name indicates, ETL has three steps, as shown in Figure 8-12.

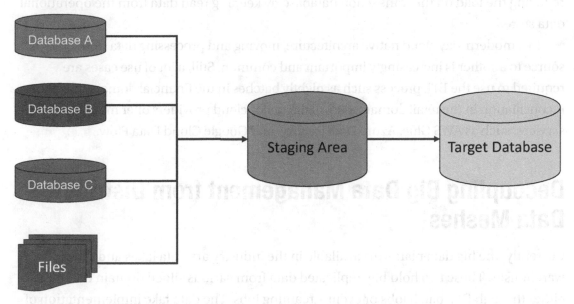

Figure 8-12. *ETL process*

Extraction

In this step, data is extracted from heterogeneous systems and files into the staging area. The source data is transformed in to the staging area without impacting the source system. The staging area is where you can check and apply rules before loading the data into the target database. During the data extraction, the ETL tool will do a sanity check of the data such as type check, duplicates, keys, etc.

Transform

Data extracted from the source databases is in the source database format and needs to be cleansed, mapped to the target, and transformed. This is the key step in the ETL process. In this transformation, you will apply a few rules such as aggregation, etc.

Load

Loading data into the target database is the last step of the ETL process. In batch mode, you need to load a huge volume of data in a short period; hence, the load process should be optimized for performance.

The ETL process is increasingly important to help your organization to analyze data, reducing the load on the transaction database by keeping read data from the operational data store.

In a modern-day cloud native architecture, moving and processing data from one source to another is increasingly important and common. Still, a lot of use cases are required to use the ETL process such as nightly batches in the financial domain, inventory reconciliation in the retail domain, etc. All the major cloud providers offer managed ETL services, such as AWS Glue, Azure Data Factory, and Google Cloud Data Flow.

Decoupling Big Data Management from Distributed Data Meshes

Currently, the big data platforms available in the industry are data lakes and data warehouses. These two hold big, replicated data from various siloed domain databases either through ETL batch jobs or event streaming jobs. The data lake implementation of your organization or client's organization has unclear responsibilities and ownership of the domains in a lake.

In modern-day business, disruption is happening like never before; therefore, we need to make sure that our technology supports the business. Data lakes and data warehouses are good but have their limitations such as centralization of domains and domain ownership. To overcome these challenges, the concept of a data mesh provides a new way to address common problems. Zhamak Dehghani from ThoughtWorks coined the data mesh and wrote a detailed paper on it.

The data mesh essentially refers to the concept of breaking down data lakes and siloes into smaller, more decentralized parts. It is like shifting from a monolithic legacy application toward a microservice architecture. In a nutshell, the data mesh is like a microservice architecture in application development.

You are already familiar with the microservices architecture and the decoupling approach from legacy monolithic services to microservices based on domains by using the domain-driven approach The domain-driven design approach addresses the problems in an application domain and in the transactional data related to that domain, but usually we are not addressing the domains or ownership of the data. The data mesh addresses data domain-driven design.

In a data lake and data warehouse, you might have observed the ownership issues. There might be an owner who can manage and operationalize the big data platforms but not from the domains. The ownership is important. For example, in your organization, you might have seen each vertical tower for finance, healthcare, retail, etc. There is someone in charge of that tower who owns the entire team and is responsible for delivering it and related clients. Similarly, you need an owner for the domain.

The data mesh implementation is based on the four principles shown in Figure 8-13. These are as follows:

- *Domain-oriented decentralized data ownership and architecture*: This principle is about implementing the data domain-driven concept to decouple and decentralize the data and ownership.

- *Data as a product*: This principle is about addressing a concern around accessibility, usability, and harmonization of distributed datasets.

- *Self-service data infrastructure as a platform*: This principle is about services and skills required to operate the data pipeline technologies and infrastructure in each domain.

- *Federated computational governance*: This principle is about data governance and standardization for interoperability, enabled by a shared and harmonized self-service data infrastructure.

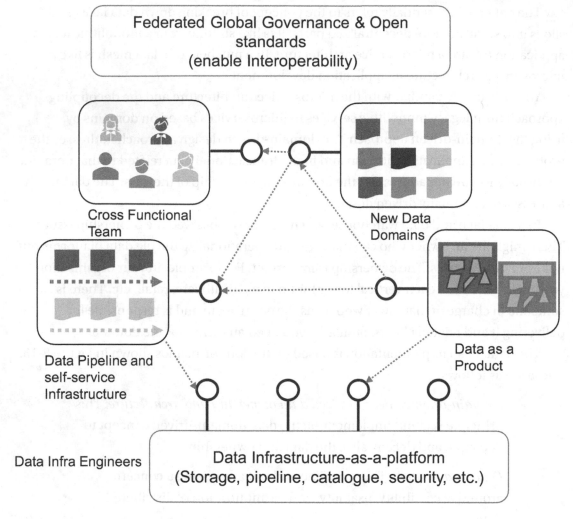

Figure 8-13. *Data mesh architecture*

A *data mesh* refers to the concept of decoupling data lakes and siloes into the smaller, decentralized domain-based model. The analytical scale can scale in the way the microservices and polyglot persistence have allowed transactional data to scale. Zhamak Dehghani explained all four principles in a detailed way at `https://martinfowler.com/articles/data-monolith-to-mesh.html`. I will cover them in a more structured way with an example of how you can implement data meshes in your project. I am using an example of an ecommerce application to explain data meshes.

Figure 8-14 shows the example data architecture. It's a centralized data lake architecture whose goals are to ingest data from all corners of the enterprises; cleanse, enrich, and transform data to the data lake; and serve the dataset in a data lake to diverse requests.

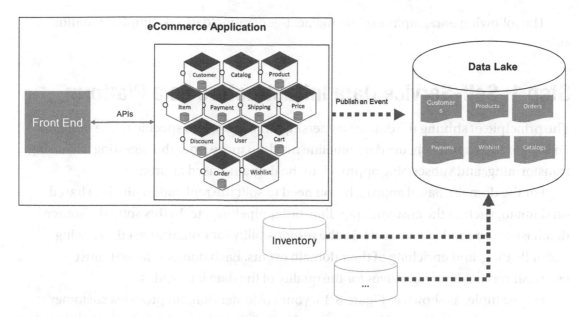

Figure 8-14. *Current data lake architecture*

The monolithic data lake platform contains and owns the data that belongs to different domains, e.g., customers, sales KPIs, inventory, payments, orders, etc., with the business changes. This kind of implementation is no longer helpful to support the required business growth, because of the diverse customers, more adoption of the cloud native approach in an application landscape, and the minimum viable product (MVP) approach.

On the replication side, you are streaming from diverse sources to the data lake, usually any in the organization. You are not building all the replication at once. You might follow an iteration model to build as the business grows. For this replication, you may use an ETL approach or streaming based on the events approach. Both approaches include ingestion, cleansing, transformation, and loading or subscribing to events. In this approach, if you want to add a new domain replication, then you need to change the whole set of replications, which leads to maintainability and testability problems.

The data ownership of today's monolithic data lake platform is based on who builds the data lake. In a nutshell, the ownership is based on technology and skills, not on the domain. The data mesh approach provides a solution to most of the problems you are facing with today's monolithic big data approach.

The following paragraphs explain the next-generation data lake implementation steps.

Step 1: Self-Service Data Infrastructure as a Platform

The principle of shifting the dataset ownership from the tool is specific to the domain. To support this approach, the data pipeline needs to move from the ingesting, cleansing, transforming, and subscribing approach to the domain-based approach.

For the domain-based approach, you need to split the replication pipeline based on domain, such as the customer pipeline, order pipeline, etc. In this split, the source database is required to own and take the responsibility for domain-based cleansing, deduplicating, and enriching of their domain events. Each domain dataset must establish service-level objectives for the quality of the data it provides.

For example, as shown in Figure 8-15, your customer domain provides customer demographic details. The "add product to wish list" domain can include cleansing and standardizing the data pipeline in the customer domain pipeline, which provides a stream of de-duped, near-real-time add product events. The aggregation of domains is responsible for the new data domains.

- Customer demographics + add the product to wish list = customer domain pipeline

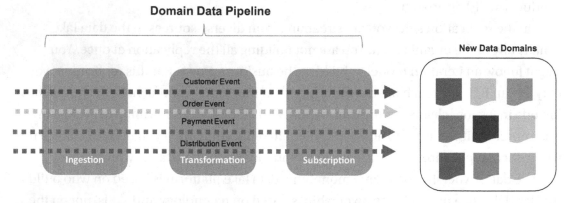

Figure 8-15. *Domain-based pipeline*

To summarize, the source side of the domain data pipeline has the responsibility to provide domain-related events, such as cleansing. The target side's responsibility is to subscribe to data, shown as New Data Domains.

Step 2: Data as a Product

Based on the previous step, the data ownership and data pipeline implementation are the responsibility of the business domain, as shown in Figure 8-16. This raises an important concern around the accessibility, usability, and harmonization of these new domain datasets.

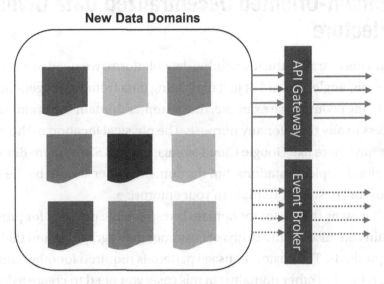

Figure 8-16. *Data as a product with a "as-a-service" model*

This is where you can implement data domains as a service by creating domain capabilities as APIs and make them available to the rest of the consumers in an organization. As part of the as-a-service approach, you need to create a set of well-designed APIs and events with discoverable, well-documented, and well-tested sandboxes.

Step 3: Data Infrastructure as a Platform

The main concern of distributing the ownership of data to the domain is the duplicated effort and skills required to operate the data pipeline's technology stack and infrastructure in each domain. Harvesting and extracting domain-agnostic infrastructure capabilities into a data infrastructure platform duplicates the effort of creating a domain-related pipeline, storages, and domain-specific streaming engines. The data infrastructure as a platform should be domain agnostic and configure the platform to be domain specific.

To build the data infrastructure for data meshes, you can use the existing available infrastructure; for example, you can use AWS S3, Google Cloud Storage, or Azure Blob Storage to store domain models, and for the "as a service," you can use standard API stacks and event stacks. For the data pipeline, use event brokers and ETL tools to create a separate pipeline and codebase for each domain-related replication.

Step 4: Domain-Oriented Decentralized Data Ownership and Architecture

To decouple and decentralize the monolithic data platform, we need to start thinking from a data domain angle, instead of just replicating data from heterogeneous sources to target data. In my ecommerce example, the customer domain owns and serves the dataset for access to any team for any purpose. The physical location of the customer domain can be anywhere like Google Cloud storage or AWS S3 or Azure Blob storage on the respective cloud implementations, but the domain owner should be the same team that owns the overall customer domain in your enterprise.

The team that owns the customer domain is responsible not only for providing the business domains but also for the truths of customer demographics and their likes and dislikes of the products. The customer usage pattern is required for other transaction details that are related to other domains; in this case, you need to create a domain-specific data set that requires consumption.

Step 5: Data Governance

The data mesh platform should be designed with a distributed data architecture, under the centralized governance and standardization for interoperability, and enabled by a shared and self-service data infrastructure. Once the data infrastructure is matured, then you can apply a centralized with decentralized governance concept to improve the innovation, independence, etc.

Data Processing with Real-Time Streaming for Analytics

Big data architecture is designed to handle the processing and analysis of data. Over the years, the data processing landscape has changed, and the business dependency on data processing has grown dramatically. Every business in any industry is relying on data processing for key decisions and also to provide a better experience to their customers. Therefore, you can say that managing big data processing is becoming the main interest of the CIO office because there are business deadlines to meet.

In data processing, some data arrives in real time, and some arrives in a batch with large chunks. Figure 8-17 shows the classic data processing of any data. You can choose whichever option you want, either batch or stream processing, based on the requirements. Real-time processing requires qualities such as scalability, fault tolerance, predictability, and resiliency.

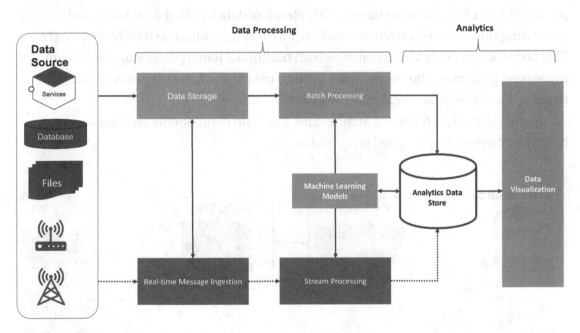

Figure 8-17. *Classic data processing*

The following are the main components of data processing for analytics platforms:

- *Batch processing of data source*: Processing of data files using long-running batch jobs

- *Real-time processing of data*: Processing of data in real-time stream processing

- *Machine learning models*: Applying various ML models on data analytics for predictive analysis

- *Proceed data storage*: Processed data storage for data visualization

- *Data visualization*: Generating various reports and dashboards for business and leadership

To support your organization's need for data analytics, you can choose from the following available industry architectures.

Lambda Architecture

The Lambda architecture is a reference architecture for scalable, fault-tolerant data processing and is designed to handle a big chunk of data by using both batch and stream processing methods. This reference architecture was first introduced by Nathan Marz. This architecture helps you to combine both traditional batch processing and stream processing pipelines. The Lambda architecture tries to solve the concerns around latency, data consistency, scalability, and fault tolerance.

In the Figure 8-18 reference architecture, the main components are data source, batch layer, serving layer, speed layer, and query.

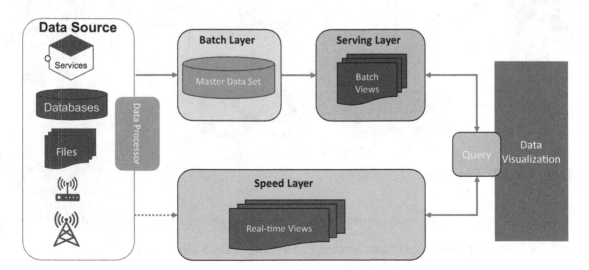

Figure 8-18. *Lambda architecture*

Data sources can be combined with various sources in an enterprise. This source can be designed by adopting ETL methods using streaming technologies. This data will be delivered simultaneously to both the batch and speed layers.

> *Batch layer*: The batch layer saves all the data coming into the system as batch views in preparation for indexing. The data is treated as immutable and append-only to ensure a trusted historical record of all incoming data. The objective is to maintain accuracy by being able to process all the available data when generating views. This layer can fix any errors if they occur by recomputing based on the data set; the output of this layer is stored in the read-only database. A technology like Apache Hadoop is often used as a system for ingesting the data as well as cost-effectively storing the data.

> *Serving layer*: The serving layer incrementally indexes the batch views to make a query by the data visualization. This layer can customize the indexes depending on the use cases. The objective of this layer is to make queries fast and serve them parallelly. While an indexing job in the service layer is for indexing data and service layer creates a new job for every new data processing.

> *Speed layer*: The speed layer processes data streams in real time and handles the data that has not already been delivered to the batch layer due to the latency of the batch layer. It also processes the latest data to provide a complete view of the data. Technology like Apache Stream, Flink, Spark streaming, etc., can be used to design a speed layer.

How Does the Lambda Architecture Work?

The batch and serving layers continue to index incoming batch data in batches. There will be latency in the indexing of all batches. The speed layer complements the batch and serving layer by indexing in real time all the new and also delayed batch indexes. Both the batch layer and speed layer collaborate to provide a large consistent view of data in the batch/serving layers that can be re-created at any time.

Once a batch indexing job completes the newly indexed data available for visualization, the speed layer's copy of the same data is no longer needed and is deleted from the speed layer. The serving layer processes the data that is already indexed by the speed layer.

Kappa Architecture

The Kappa architecture is a reference architecture for data processing for analytics and is used for processing streaming data. The reference architecture was introduced by Jay Kreps. The objective of this reference architecture is to process both real-time and batch processing for analytics, with a single technology stack. It is based on streaming immutable architecture in which data is stored in a database. The stream engine reads the data, transforms it in an analytical format, and finally stores it in analytical database for query and data visualization.

The Kappa architecture provides real-time analytics based on data availability. This helps the business team to reduce the decision time. It also supports historical analytics by reading the data stored in the data lake in the batch process. Kafka, AWS Kinesis, Azure Stream Analytics, Azure Event Hub, Google Pub/Sub, and Confluent are stream processing engines. For more information on the streaming, please refer Chapter 6.

The Kappa reference architecture shown in Figure 8-19 is considered simple compared to the Lambda architecture as it uses the same layers and technology stack for both streaming and batch processes. In a nutshell, the Kappa architecture is a simpler reference architecture for data processing.

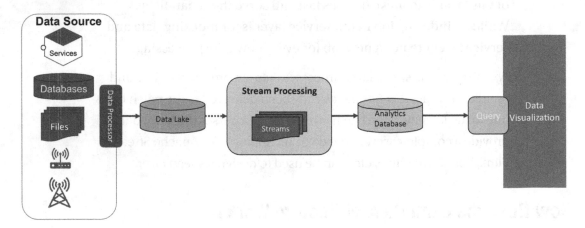

Figure 8-19. *Kappa architecture*

Microservices in Data Processing with Real-Time Streaming for Analytics

In the previous sections, I explained the real-time data processing reference architecture for the data analytics platform. You are already familiar with the microservices decentralized polyglot persistence principle. One challenge of dealing with decentralized data in a microservices architecture is the need to collate data for analytics. A common way to approach this is through data movement, meaning aggregating the data into a centralized data lake by using the Kappa architecture to provide data visualization, as shown in Figure 8-20.

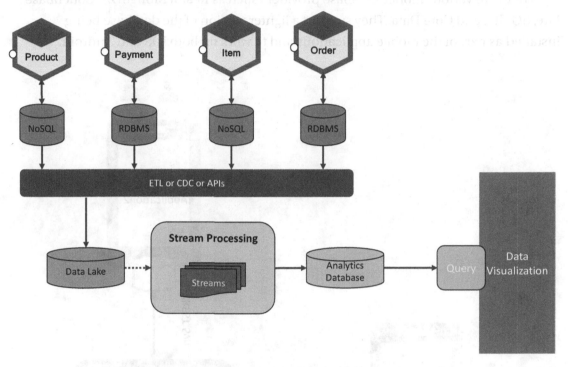

Figure 8-20. *Polyglot persistence with Kappa architecture*

Both the service and data analytics team can collaborate with each other to replicate data from each service to the data lake through ETL, CDC, or APIs.

Mobile Platform Database

Mobile computing applications need to store information locally to make your applications more responsive and less dependent on network connectivity. The trend of offline usage, or less dependency on the network, is gaining popularity. The use cases are a list of contacts, price information, distance traveled, etc.

A mobile application keeps the database locally or makes a copy of the database over the cloud onto a local device and syncs with it as required, as shown in Figure 8-21. This will help create faster and more responsive applications that are functional even when there is no or limited back-end connectivity.

There are various mobile database providers such as Realm MongoDB, Couchbase Lite, SQLite, and Core Data. They support a lighter version of the database being installed as part of the mobile applications and to work on both iOS and Android.

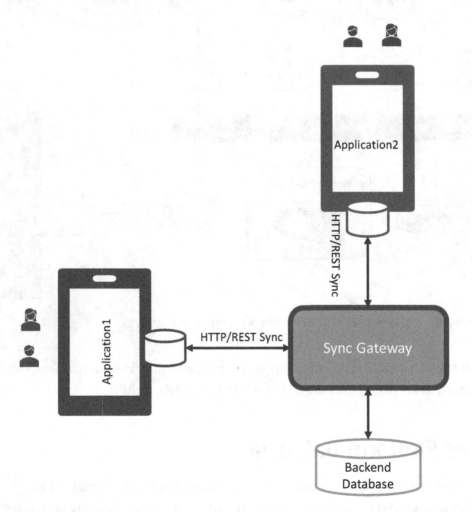

Figure 8-21. *Mobile database architecture*

The mobile databases must be installed along with your app, and they store all the data that is required to provide a customer experience on a slow network or offline. These databases will sync often to your back-end databases through sync gateways. The data synchronization is done via asynchronous data syncs and synchronous data syncs.

The asynchronous sync manages data events asynchronously without blocking any app functionality through reactive REST APIs.

In synchronous, the sync services are responsible for syncing data from a remote server to a mobile device and then storing the data locally in the mobile databases.

The data synchronization in the mobile application is achieved by using a sync service, sync adapter, and sync gateway. A sync adapter is a plugin that handles background syncs along with sync gateways.

A mobile database needs to have the following characteristics:

- Fast and secure
- Very lightweight
- Can work with low memory and power
- No server requirement
- Must work efficiently with mobile app code

There are various mobile databases available to choose from, such as Realm from MongoDB, Couchbase Lite from Couchbase, SQLite, and Core Data.

Intelligent Data Governance and Compliance in the Cloud Native World

Digital transformation in cloud native architectures is disrupting business. Along this journey, quality data is becoming an organization's most strategic asset for business decisions and better customer experiences that support business growth.

Why Data Governance?

With the exponential growth of data, a strict regulatory environment, and cyberthreats on the rise, protecting and extracting the value from your most strategic asset are imperative. These tasks are also a formidable challenge. The cost of failing to comply with stringent regulatory requirements may be a legal battle. Regulations such as General Data Protection Regulation (GDPR), Securities and Exchange Commission (SEC) regulations, and the legislation and regulations of each country are outpacing the capabilities of existing IT infrastructure investment. Data complication further increases as the IDC predicts global data will grow to 163 zettabytes by 2025.

Data governance helps organizations better manage the availability, usability, integrity, and security of their enterprise data. The objective of data governance is not just to bring data at rest under control but also to know where data is located; how it originated; and who, where, and access to data. Effective data governance must be self-governed irrespective of which country is compliant.

In the modern digital economy, anyone can access data anywhere at any time, on any device. The CxO demands easy access to data with tight regulations with the best-in-class compliance process. To satisfy these regulations, you need more than just strong governance; you need governance based on the data analytics with intelligence embedded.

What Is Data Governance?

Data governance helps you to better manage the availability, usability, integrity, and security of your enterprise data. Data governance moves beyond information management to support business processes and encompasses a broad set of data strategies and functions including the following:

- *Data delivery and access*: Any actions related to storing, retrieving, and acting on data.

- *Data integrity*: Ensuring the veracity, accuracy, and quality of data.

- *Data lineage*: Managing the movement of data.

- *Data loss prevention (DLP)*: Ensuring sensitive data isn't sent outside your organization's network and controlling what data can be transferred.

- *Data security*: Protecting unauthorized access or data corruption.

- *Data synchronization*: Ensuring data consistency.

- *Master data management (MDM)*: The complete collection of process, policies, standards, and tools for defining governance and managing data.

- *Data profile*: Reviewing the source data and understanding the structure, content, and interrelationships.

- *Data quality*: Measuring the condition of data based on factors such as consistency, completeness, accuracy, and reliability.

- *Data standardization*: Bringing data into a common format that allows for further analysis.

- *Data General Data Protection Regulations (GDPR)*: This is a privacy and security law that states that personal data is any information that is related to an identified or identifiable natural person.

Governance Framework

Figure 8-22 illustrates the overall framework for intelligence data governance. This framework is based on these five pillars:

- Change management
- Intelligent tooling
- Secure
- Decentralize
- Operating model

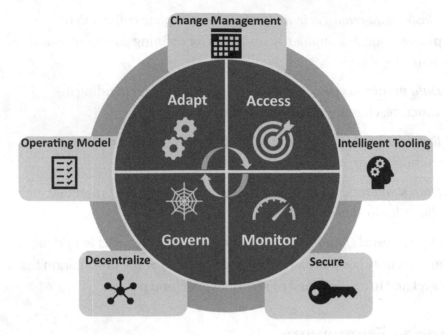

Figure 8-22. Governance framework

Change Management

Change management is the approach to planning, designing, and implementing data governance without any unintended disruption of the business. As part of the change management plan, the following key practices need to be adopted:

- *Leadership engagement*: Enabling leaders and sponsors to champion the transition.

- *Communication and stakeholder management*: Information, announcements, and updates through various channels; the updates include where and how the changes are impacting the organization.

- *Training and performance support*: Data governance process, policy, roles, and competency training.

- *Organization alignment*: Recommendations for new roles, performance measures, responsibilities, and workgroup structures.

- *Measurement and readiness*: Preparing the business and measuring its readiness to adopt the changes.

Intelligent Tooling

In intelligent tooling, you need to adopt best-in-class technology and accelerate business value from data assets. The following are the different tooling strategies that need to be adopted for data intelligence governance:

- *Rapid discovery and recognition*: Rapid discovery and recognition of personal and sensitive data across the ecosystem

- *Smart tagging of metadata and lineage*: Smart recommendations for business tagging of technical metadata and lineage using multi-metadata stores

- *Intelligent data quality rule recommendations*: It is based on the corpus and usage of ML models

- *Auto-remediation of data*: Learning from data curation actions and auto-remediation suggestions

- *Intelligent workflow triggers*: Automated workflow triggers based on user behavior

Operating Model

In the operating model, you need to manage the roles, responsibilities, processes, policies, and standards required to manage and govern the data ecosystem. In the operating model, you need the following teams:

- *Executive governance council*: This council is the ultimate authority in defining program-level scope, arbitrating escalated resolutions, and approving data governance strategy with a centralized and decentralization approach.

- *Business data owners*: The owners play a leadership role in championing data management and data governance efforts.

- *Data governance council*: The cross-functional and cross-entity leadership team provides direction and oversight to the overall data governance structure.

- *Data governance organization*: This organization provides overall non-IT support to the council.

Decentralization

In the decentralization approach, this framework embraces each portfolio in an organization to set its subgovernance under the guidance of the central governance framework. This helps an organization to decentralize the responsibility and accountability and helps to fasten the decisions. Each portfolio follows the same tooling and structure as central governance and tweaks it based on the nature of data.

Secure

The security of data is of utmost importance. As mentioned, you need to have a set of country-specific compliances in place and always conduct an audit across the organization.

You need to consider the following points when you execute this framework:

- Data governance should be viewed as an ongoing program, not as just a project.

- Data governance must have executive sponsorship, and they must take significant ownership of the initiative.

- Data governance councils must have real authority to resolve overall organization issues so the portfolio governance council can resolve the portfolio issues.

- There should be a clearly defined set of data governance and quality metrics published regularly and reviewed regularly.

- There must be a clear and timely communication method for data governance initiatives.

You must train your team regularly.

Summary

The cloud has made a big impact on how we work today, including with data. The cost of storing data has been significantly reduced; it is now cheaper and more feasible for companies to keep vast amounts of data. The operationalization of data has reduced significantly due to managed services and serverless data storage; this has made it easier to spread data across different storage types.

In this chapter, I explained five main requirements of your data layer. The first is how to choose the database based on the use cases, the second is how to replicate the data, the third is to decouple the data lake to a data mesh, the fourth is data for analytics, and finally the fifth is the governance model.

In the cloud native world, one thing you cannot forget is the data layer. To deliver a consistently fast, satisfying customer experience, the data layer must also be modernized along with your application. You must embrace all five requirements of data modernization.

Although there are many reasons to adopt governance approach, it enables data accessibility, data confidence and understanding, and data activation. Some of the benefits are as follows:

- Data consistency ensures completeness and accuracy.

- Proactive data quality checks ensure data alignment.

- It removes confusion over the data meaning.

- You can make fact-based decisions in real time with accurate data.

CHAPTER 9

Designing for "-ilities"

So far, we have discussed cloud native principles, patterns, and elements of the cloud. In this chapter, I will explain the quality attributes for designing a system, i.e., how to design for your "-ilities" in a cloud native environment.

Developing the functional requirements in your application means addressing the business use cases, but what about the nonfunctional requirements? How will you address them? Developing your application to meet the nonfunctional requirements is as important as for the functional ones. In the cloud native world, you must prioritize the "-ilities" and address them at the beginning of the project like with the functional user stories.

You are responsible for cross-cutting concerns and making sure that the individual components of a system can work together seamlessly to meet the overall objectives.

In this chapter, I will explain what you need to consider when designing your system for the following "-ilities":

- *Designing for security*: This is vital for a modern system in the digital economy, with the exponential growth across the globe, strict regulatory environments, and cyberthreats.

- *Designing for resiliency*: This is vital for modern-day, distributed applications, where any individual component could fail. The overall application should remain functional.

- *Designing for integrated observability*: This means providing the required behavior of an application across applications, infrastructures, and threat landscapes.

- *Designing for portability*: This helps you to design for multicloud and hybrid cloud environments across containers, VMs, and FaaS platforms.

© Shivakumar R Goniwada 2022
S. R. Goniwada, *Cloud Native Architecture and Design*, https://doi.org/10.1007/978-1-4842-7226-8_9

- *Designing for sustainability*: The whole world is talking about global warming. In IT, we need to help the world reduce its carbon footprint by minimizing the compute usage or utilizing more sustainable cloud hosting options.

- *Designing for availability*: The application must be available to serve your customer, either from the application logic or database storage or from the deployment environment.

- *Designing for reliability*: The designed application must be reliable to serve all the requests in the stipulated time.

- *Designing for business*: However you design an application, you need to ask the question, for whom are you designing this application and for what reason?

Why Do You Need "-ilities"?

Developing an application has always been a complex task. Cloud native, modern-day architecture and distributed systems that are built using microservices, with event-driven architecture, and that are deployed onto a container with a serverless infrastructure yield many benefits but also introduce several new challenges.

Decoupling allows teams to iterate faster by adopting agility and automation, which provides flexibility to increase the quality, release faster to market, etc. However, there is an accompanying increase in the number and level of code changes, testing, and deployment required.

Along with the domain requirements of your system, you need to consider numerous factors, some explicit and some implicit, of a system and balance all concerns optimally.

The following "-ilities" help you to develop quality systems, offer customers a great user experience, implement security, and meet customer vision.

Partial List of "-ilities"

Business and domain requirements exist along with "-ilities." These "-ilities" can alter the decision process for what and how to develop a system. Table 9-1 is the partial list of "-ilities." When developing a system, you must determine the most important of these "-ilities." However, many of these "-ilities" oppose one another. For example, achieving both high performance and high security can be difficult.

Along with the traditional "-ilities," I have given equal importance to sustainability and ethics to support our planet and humans.

Table 9-1. *List of "-ilities"*

Security	Scalability	Availability	Operability	Sustainability
Performance	Fault tolerance	Integrity	Testability	Maintainability
Extensibility	Usability	Portability	Agility	Debuggability
Interoperability	Simplicity	Ethics	Flexibility	Stability
Resilience	Inspectability	Robustness	Efficiency	Tolerance
Modularity	Coupling	Cohesion	Degradability	Cloudability
Self-healing	Self-sustainability	Observability	Autonomy	Auditability
Learnability	Changeability	Provability	Durability	Composability

Designing for Security

Designing and developing cloud native systems that are secure is of vital importance. A system that does not follow secure practices creates vulnerabilities that can be exploited by various threats. The result of a threat can be unauthorized access to your system. A secure system can prevent and protect against malicious attacks and unauthorized access to the system. It is your responsibility to design a system that protects against malicious attacks.

Cloud native is fundamentally new, and using an existing approach to designing and building applications raises a security challenge, because different systems have different security requirements. It is important to understand the security needs of the system, so your approach should be radically different.

Cloud native security necessitates a refocusing on security that operates in step with the overall cloud native strategy of your organization. The key emphasis of cloud native security needs to ensure that vulnerabilities are identified and remediated during development. The approach you are adopting must be holistic and should be baked in through the software engineering lifecycle including operations. You should strive to create cloud native applications that are secure by design.

Using the following proven and new concepts of security principles and methods can make your application more secure.

Defense in Depth

Security is more effective when each layer of the system architecture implements its own security techniques, so your strategy should be to adopt different methods for each layer. This redundancy ensures that if an outer layer is breached, then the subsequent layer can potentially thwart an attack.

In cloud native architecture, all components have asynchronous and synchronous communication. Therefore, each layer must be configured with well-matured security controls. If one security control fails, a threat may be prevented by another security control. Security controls in each layer with independent methods will make it much more difficult to exploit a vulnerability.

The CIA Triad

The CIA triad is the governing principle for information security and the protection of assets. The CIA triad, as shown in Figure 9-1, summarizes the attributes that you want your system to exhibit. CIA stands for confidentiality, integrity, and availability.

Confidentiality

Systems must protect confidentiality. The information that a system manages has value to users, and you must prevent unauthorized individuals from accessing information. The system must protect the data, APIs, etc.

Figure 9-1. *CIA triad*

Integrity

The system must ensure integrity. The objective is to prevent
unauthorized individuals from modifying the information. You
must design your application to ensure that the data has not been
tampered with by unauthorized individuals.

Availability

Systems need to maintain availability, and you must design a
system that allows authorized individuals access to information
in a timely and reliable way. Securing data serves no purpose if
authorized users cannot access it.

Policy as Code

The technology landscape is becoming more complex and agile, and manually
managing each policy has become more erroneous. Therefore, security needs to be
implemented with automation and well-defined engineering practices. When you are
developing a new cloud native system, you need to take into consideration the security
policies, which are the rules and procedures to protect your systems from threats and
disruptions.

Policy as code codifies the security policies, for example, access control, so this
policy can be treated as a test. When I say code, you do not need to write the code
yourself in a programming language; you write the code in a configuration file and apply

practices such as keeping the code under version control, configuring these files as part of your DevSecOps pipeline, automatically deploying by using infrastructure as code, and configuring observations to your software artifacts.

Tools such as HashiCorp, Open Policy Agent (OPA), istio, and all the major cloud vendors support policy as code.

Zero-Trust Security

Traditional network security is based on the castle-and-moat concept, where external individuals are restricted and everyone inside the network is trusted by default. The downside of this approach is that sometimes internal individuals become offenders. Or, if external resources gain access, then they can get access to your application and code. In cloud native applications, your systems are decoupled into multiple microservices and communicate synchronously and asynchronously. To secure your systems from all kinds of network threats, you need a zero-trust model.

A zero-trust model is a network security model, based on a strict identity verification process. This model doesn't trust anyone either internally (inside your network) or externally (outside your network) or a machine to access your application and code. In this model, you need to create a strict identity verification for every individual and device.

You need to adopt the following methods to implement zero-trust security:

- Implement a strong verification mechanism by using identity and access management for both system and network access.

- For the principle of least privilege; each access is granted only much as needed. To implement this, you need to categorize your application components based on access privileges.

- Segment your network into microservices by breaking up security perimeters into smaller zones to maintain separate access for separate parts of the network.

- Use multifactor authentication to require more evidence to authenticate a user.

- Use strict control for device access and implement the strict monitoring and auditing of every access.

Decentralized Identity

Challenges of the current centralized identity provider are all-access ties to the single centralized identity and access management with the top-down approaches. This was good for traditional IT, where your applications are deployed in a single monolithic and one data center.

In a cloud native architecture, elements like microservices, data meshes, and event meshes enable decentralized implementations, but identity management remains centralized. In a decentralized approach, discrete identifiable units such as people, organizations, and things are free to use any shared root of trust.

This is an emerging concept in a cloud native world; here you will give back control of identity to consumers through the use of an identity wallet in which they collect verified information about themselves from certified identity issuers such as a Social Security number (SSN) in the United States, Aadhar number in India, etc. The Decentralized Identity Foundation is leading the way to conceptualize the implementation.

Validating Input

A software vulnerability can be avoided by being diligent about validating input from any untrusted sources. Whether it is user input or APIs or events, your application must validate all the input before processing it further. In the case of external integration, that system may have security policies and standards that differ from yours, so the system much check the data that it receives from external integration or extended enterprises.

Design for Threats

Threat modeling is a structured approach for analyzing security in your system. A threat is the most vulnerable to the system and may cause serious harm to it. Therefore, you need to create a threat model during design time. Threat modeling is a process that identifies and prioritizes potential security threats so that you can develop and test potential threats. Threat modeling evaluates threats to reduce a system's overall security risks.

For cloud native and modern architecture, use threat modeling to focus on security from the attacker's viewpoint.

Naive Password Complexity Requirements

All enterprises are set up with a password policy that has a mix of capitals, lowercase, and special characters, a length from 8 to 15, and more. In this policy, people will forget to remember this complexity and end up using a more insecure password. According to the National Institute of Standards and Technology (NIST), password length is the primary factor in characterizing password strength. Passwords that are too short or too common will encounter brute-force attacks as well as dictionary attacks using words.

Compliance as Code

This is about building compliance into development and operations and writing compliance policies and checks and auditing into the DevSecOps pipeline so that regulatory compliance becomes an integral part of automation. How to implement compliance is described by James DeLuccia and his team in "DevOps Audit Defense Toolkit." This toolkit provides many details with real implementation scenarios.

The Chef Compliance tool from Chef scans infrastructure and reports on compliance issues, security risks, and outdated software, etc.

Shift-Left Security

Shift-left security applies to functional, security, and performance testing and related processes, techniques, and tools to be integrated as part of the DevSecOps and developer integrated development environment (IDE).

Shifting the security review process left requires a new way of developing the application compared to the traditional approach. These changes are not significant deviations. You need to add the following process for shift-left security:

- Involve an information security expert in the early lifecycle of the project.

- Use security tools.

- Integrate security tools as part of the continuous integration and as part of the developer IDE.

Configure static application security testing (SAST) and dynamic application security testing (DAST) as part of the DevSecOps pipeline, and implement container security to check the vulnerability at the early stage of the software development lifecycle.

Single Pane of Glass for Audit

Logs are essential components for helping to secure cloud native applications. Design your application for integrated centralized log management, operations, searching, and analysis. With this, you can use logs for detecting security threats, alerts, and notifications in an environment.

Through a single pane of glass, the tools provide you with holistic, business-level visibility across all environments. I will explain more about integrated monitoring in Chapter 19.

Homomorphic Encryption

Most encryption schemes such as Advanced Encryption Standard (AES), Rivest-Shamir-Adleman (RSA), Triple Data Encryption Security (DES), and Twofish consist of key generation, encryption, and decryption. Symmetric key encryption schemes use the same secret key for both encryption and decryption, and asymmetric key encryption schemas use a public key for encryption and a secret key for decryption. Both symmetric and asymmetric encryption can be used to secure data at rest and transit. Any outsourced computation will require such encryption layers to be removed before computation can take place. Therefore, cloud services providing outsourced computation capabilities must have access to secret keys and implement access policies to prevent unauthorized employees from getting access to these keys.

Homomorphic encryption (HE) refers to encryption schemes that allow the cloud to compute directly on the encrypted data, without requiring the data to be decrypted first. The result of such encrypted computations remains encrypted and can be decrypted only with the secret key of the data owner. Do not use HE for everything. It is a generic technology, so use only wherever computation data is possible on encryption. You can consider using federated machine learning results. Still, the industry is researching to standardize it. There are various software available for HE like SEAL, Lattigo, and HElib.

Fail Securely

Failures are bound to happen for any kind of system; therefore, you need to design your system to fail securely. This involves several things, such as using secure defaults, restoring to a security state, and always checking return values for failure. The confidentiality and integrity of your system should remain even though availability has been lost. Access must be restricted to privileged objects during failure. Application code should be written in such a way that there is proper exception and error handling and predictive analysis to alert required stakeholders.

Secure APIs

Your APIs are exposed outside of your network to transfer data. Broken, exposed, or hacked APIs are behind the major data breaches. You need to secure your API, but not all APIs require some kind of security. Open Authorization (OAuth 2) or Open ID Connect are open standards for authorization. They allow an application to be granted access to resources from the consumer. Open ID is an identity layer that sits on top of OAuth2 and OpenID Connect to enable authentication and authorization. Use a JSON Web token (JWT) along with your APIs to securely transmit information between the provider and the consumer as a JSON object.

There are no silver bullets when it comes to implementing security; however, there are proven principles and practices you need to secure your application. There are more techniques other than these; refer to the respective techniques in more detail while designing an application.

Designing for Elasticity

Elasticity is the degree to which a system can adapt to changes in demand by provisioning or releasing resources autonomously. The microservices, containers, and Kubernetes are built for elasticity. You need to design microservices to enable a view on resources as an infinite pool and give the ability to scale the deployed containers out and in depending on demand. To keep the costs to a minimum and quality objectives as promised in your client SLOs, an adaption process must exist that alters the number of container instances based on demand.

While you design an application, you should adopt the following principles:

- Design for stateless.

- Adopt a sidecar pattern.

- Make it independently deployable.

- Use the sharding principle for a database.

- Use autoscaling options from cloud providers.

You can find more information about elasticity in Chapter 5.

Designing for Resilience

Resiliency refers to the ability of a solution to absorb the impact of a problem in one or more parts of services while continuing to provide an acceptable service level to your business. A resilient application must thrive even when the unexpected happens. In other words, it provides the required capabilities despite excessive stresses that can cause disruptions. The residual defects in the software or hardware will eventually cause the system to fail to correctly perform a required function or cause it to fail to meet one or more quality attributes of microservices such as availability, security, performance, reliability, usability, etc. An unknown or uncorrected security vulnerability will enable an attacker to compromise the system.

The question is how to design for automatic self-healing and application resiliency. As mentioned in Chapter 5, microservices are always be on partial failure with more load. But how can the designer approach microservices resilience? Approaching for resilience is not a one-time activity but is a continuous plan, culture, and work during the entire lifecycle of a microservices.

The following patterns can help you to design resilient microservices:

- Circuit breaker pattern

- Bulkhead pattern

- Stateless services

- Retry

- Fail fast

- Timeout

- Throttling

You can find more detailed information on resilience in Chapter 6.

Designing for Sustainability

"Sustainability consists of the strategies and actions your enterprise takes to reduce its carbon footprint and consumption of the planet's resources so that it is not sacrificing the health and happiness of future generations to meet its own needs today."

—*Forrester Research*

Designing for sustainability is an innovator trend, and people are realizing the software industry is responsible for a high level of carbon usage comparable to the transportation industry. Some of our day-to-day activities are directly measurable, as compute usage is highly correlated to energy consumption.

In IT, energy is needed in the following areas:

- Creating, testing, launching, and maintaining applications

- Hosting and serving applications

- Interacting with users in applications

The JEVONS Paradox in Cloud Native

The Jevons paradox is an economic term coined in the 19th century by economist William Stanley Jevons.

The Jevons paradox, as shown in Figure 9-2, occurs when technological progress or government policy increases the efficiency with which a resource is used and increases the demand and subsequent consumption due to what he called the *rebound effect*: when something is cheap and convenient, more people want it. This theory was for coal usage, and he observed that technical advancement increased efficiency and reduced prices.

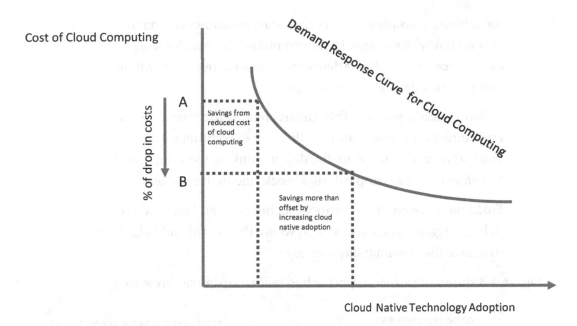

Figure 9-2. JEVONS paradox theory

His original theory was about coal, but his paradox can be applied to almost all resources and is especially relevant in present-day cloud native architecture.

Sustainability Approaches

The following approaches will help you to design your system for sustainability, as shown in Figure 9-3:

> *Net zero transitions*: Net zero carbon targets are no longer optional. The challenge is making them real and visible. Your organization must be rapidly progressing toward goals. You unleash the potential of cloud native to transform business models for the better.

> *Sustainable IT and technologies*: Cloud native technology is a true enabler of sustainability, but its energy consumption footprint is vast. You must use technology more sustainably, as well as use technology as a vehicle for being more sustainable.

Sustainable consumer experience: Today, consumers demand sustainability. Your organization combines deep technology experience to help clients deliver consumer experience without compromising the user experience.

Culture of sustainability: This means creating the mechanisms and cultures that bake sustainability into everything we do. Your organization must use the design thinking workshops and transform the way people design, work, and deliver systems.

Sustainable assessment: Use tools, techniques, and methodologies to help organizations understand where they stand and help them to realize the sustainability journey.

Figure 9-3 shows the six-step approach to build a sustainability system.

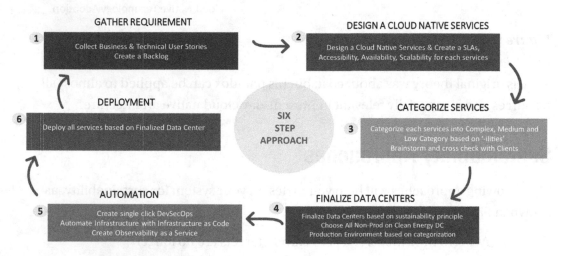

Figure 9-3. *Six-step approach*

Deployment Environment

Where you deploy your application is a significant part of sustainability. In a cloud native architecture, usually the cloud environment will be a deployment environment. All the major cloud vendors have data centers across the globe, but not all data centers are running with clean energy. So, you need to design your application to use the respective cloud environment appropriately and choose clean energy data centers.

In your application, not all use cases are highly critical, so you need to categorize the use cases as critical or noncritical with higher latency. The noncritical use case can be deployed in any data center that runs with clean energy, and the critical use cases that require low latency can be deployed in nearby data centers, which may or may not run on clean energy. For effective deployment management, you need to create infrastructure as code to automate your service based on criticality.

Software Engineering

The software engineering methodology plays a critical role in sustainability; I am talking about how you develop, test, and maintain your system. Use agility, next-generation automation, and AI-driven development to minimize the time and resource usage for software development.

UI Architecture

Web pages: According to the HTTP Archive and its page weight report, the average size of a website is around 2MB, and the average load time is 4.7 seconds for desktop and 11.4 seconds on mobile apps. When served up on a sluggish Internet connection with 2G, 3G, and 4G or mobile devices with slower processors, these pages waste time and energy and frustrate users. We are inclined toward high resolutions and multi-image carousels.

Social media: According to Statista, the average daily time spent on social media by users is around 145 minutes per day.

Video streaming: With more than 4.5 billion Internet users in the world as of this writing, YouTube streaming around 260MB/hour worldwide, and Netflix accounting for around 12.6% of total Internet traffic as of writing, the subscriptions for OTT platforms are increasing daily.

The total energy consumed by cloud computing is more than many countries in the world. You need to design your application effectively based on what you need to display and how much data you need to show to the user.

Sustainability Assessment

You can consider the previous design adoption for new projects. What about existing applications? How can you assess and improve the sustainability?

Assess the existing IT estate with the existing technology portfolio to establish comprehensive technology-driven sustainability. Follow these four steps to conduct an assessment:

1. *Current state assessment*: The objective of this initial step is to identify the current system landscape and deployment model: interview stakeholders, consolidate systems and criticality, and write a regulatory landscape report.

2. *Gap analysis*: The objective of this step is to consolidate the report of the existing landscape and map against a sustainability chart: list and define projects and criticality, map them against the sustainability data centers, and list automation gaps.

3. *Financial constraints and sustainability*: The objective of this step is to consolidate the sustainability report and financial constraints: list the carbon and sustainability measures per workstream, benchmark reports, list ambitions and target values, and set a sustainability transformation scope.

4. *Roadmap, project charter, and recommendations*: The objective of this step is to define a path for a roadmap to project realization, including project cost estimates and project organizations.

You need to conduct an audit by asking the following questions:

- What are you trying to accomplish? List the objectives and SLAs and SLOs for each business use case.

- What are we trying to assess? Do an inventory of all use cases and categorize them.

- What is the impact of our inventory? Do the impact assessment. List the present inventory and what changes are needed to apply sustainability, include how much CO_2 is generated based on where it is deployed, and check whether the hosted environment uses fossil fuels or green energy.

- What does the data tell us? Create a target architecture and create a plan to move from fossil fuels to a clear energy hosting platform.

Designing for Failure

A cloud native architecture might fail for a variety of reasons, such as bugs in your code, unstable deployment, poor underlying infrastructure, resources saturated by load, unhealthy underlying nodes, faulty data center, or network between services failing. Lastly, human error can lead to major failures. You might have seen recent outages on Google services, Azure India availability zones, etc.

It is impossible to eliminate failure in a cloud native architecture; the cost of that would be infinite! Your focus should be on designing services that are tolerant of dependency failures and that are able to gracefully recover from them to mitigate the impact of those failures on their responsibility. You need to understand the different types of failures they might be susceptible to. Understanding the nature of these risks and their likelihood is fundamental to both architecting the appropriate mitigation strategies and reacting rapidly when an incident occurs.

These are the following areas of failure you need to consider while designing your services:

- *Infrastructure*: The underlying infrastructure on which your service operates such as containers and VMs

- *Communication*: Collaboration and coordination between various services through APIs and events

- *Dependencies*: Failure independent services

- *Internal*: Errors within your service

Infrastructure

Regardless of where your services are deployed, the reliability of services depends on the infrastructure that underpins them. The sources of failures in the infrastructure are hosts, data centers, networks, operating systems, etc. The failure in the infrastructure may affect the operations of multiple services in an application. You need to design your application with redundancy to mitigate infrastructure failure that might happen in one availability zone. You need to balance the redundancy because it incurs additional costs to your project.

Communication

Communication between services or external third-party services may fail. The source of communication failure might be firewalls, messaging, network, etc. These failures are common. You need to design your service to maximize availability, correct operation, and recovery when it occurs. To mitigate these errors, you need to configure your services with a retry mechanism for asynchronous or proper error mechanism for API implementation. Along with this, consider using circuit breaker, communication brokers, fallback, and other patterns.

Dependencies

Failure can occur in other dependent services or databases. Failures are related to timeouts, external dependencies, overload on other services, etc. You need to use various patterns such as a circuit breaker, timeout, retry, etc., to mitigate dependencies on other services and to provide the consumer experience as a whole system.

Internal

Inadequate software engineering practices might lead to failure. Services might be poorly designed or developed, inadequately tested, have improper deployments, etc. This leads to memory leaks, improper CPU usage, erroneous programs, etc., which leads to performance degradation. You need to design your service with software engineering best practices like shift-left, automation, testing, etc., and also adopt self-healing, graceful degradation, etc.

Designing for Reliability

Reliability is the probability that your system will continue to work normally over a specified interval of time, under specified conditions. For example, your Payment service might have a reliability of 99 percent during business hours; it has a 99 percent chance of working normally during this time. A more reliable system requires less maintenance. The reliability is design-centric, i.e., how reliable your system is comes from how you design your system. This is the reason we collect the reliability measurement at the start of the architecture and design it as a nonfunctional requirement.

Failures in your services are normally distributed as shown in Figure 9-4. Different services and failure rates will apply to different kinds of services, but generally, all services behave like Figure 9-4 irrespective of what kind of services you have.

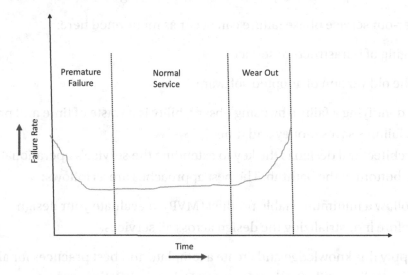

Figure 9-4. *Bath tub curve*

As shown in Figure 9-4, the graph goes by the name the *bathtub curve* because of its characteristic shape. The highest failure rates correspond to premature failure and end-of-life wear-out. Your services might fail after some time due to various conditions; this is understandable, but what about premature failure? The premature failure is the result of bad design and development. This can be eliminated by identifying and adopting good design practices.

The premature failure can occur as mentioned here:

- Services are designed and developed well but inappropriately deployed.

- Services are not built properly in the DevSecOps pipeline.

- Services are not managed by the operation team.

- Overall, service design is not good and introduces unnecessarily high throttling.

The normal service phase failure can occur as mentioned here:

- Failure due to natural calamities

- A sudden spike in a request, for example, during Black Friday time

The wear-out service phase failure can occur as mentioned here:

- Aging of infrastructure services

- The old version of adopted software

Simply identifying a failure by using observability is a waste of time and process. Eliminating failures saves money and time.

Good architectural design is the key to extending the service's operational lifetime, which is the bottom of the bathtub. The best approaches are as follows:

- Follow a minimum viable product (MVP) to evaluate your design before industrializing the design across all services.

- Apply this knowledge and create a template and best practices for all the services' agile Product Oriented Delivery (POD) teams.

- Create automation in every step; this helps to quickly pivot if any failure occurs.

- Create redundancy like a disaster recovery (DR) and replica set for databases.

Pareto Chart

Apply Pareto analysis (the 80/20 rule), where 20 percent of service faults in the system are responsible for 80 percent of the failure cost. Prioritize to identify this 20 percent and provide an early remedy. Use a Pareto chart.

Fault rates under specific headings are tabulated and calculated and converted to graphical form, as shown in Figure 9-5, so you can examine the individual cost of running the services. The individual faults that are responsible for the highest operation cost are the ones to remedy first, either rectifying errors or creating new ones. One of the useful principles of cloud native services is that it is easy to create a new microservices if the operation cost is more than the new development cost.

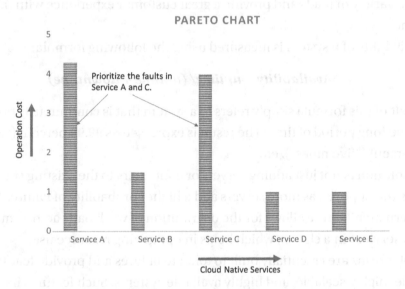

Figure 9-5. Pareto chart analysis

Although the software services are not subject to wear-and-tear, the bathtub curve and Pareto chart provide us with insight into the operational lifecycle. The bathtub curve and Pareto chart enable software systems to understand the reliability of your services. This helps you to strategy your operationalization of services.

Designing for High Availability

High availability configuration is an approach for defining the services of your system, which ensures optimal operation performance, even at times of high loads. Although there are no fixed rules for implementing high availability (HA) systems, there are a few good practices that you need to follow to make your system highly available.

For any kind of system, there are two types of downtime: scheduled and unscheduled. Scheduled downtime is a result of maintenance like a software update or patch update. You can't avoid this. Unscheduled downtime is caused by some unforeseen event, like hardware, software, or network failure.

The main objective of implementing an HA architecture is to make sure your system can handle a variety of loads and provide a great customer experience with minimal or no downtime.

The availability of a system is measured using the following formula:

$$Availability = uptime/\ (uptime + downtime)$$

The result of this formula simply refers to a system that is continuously operational for a desirable long period of time. The result is expressed as 99.99 percent ("four nines") or 99.999 percent ("five nines"), etc.

An HA solution is not just adding servers or containers to the existing stack, but actually, it is the opposite as more servers add a higher probability of failure. The cloud native modern architecture allows for the distribution of workloads across multiple instances of services in a cluster, which helps in optimizing resource use.

Cloud platforms are essentially built to tolerate failures and provide features to help build reliable, highly scalable, and highly available systems. Such features include the following:

- Infrastructure as a service (IaaS) is available across geographic locations.

- Availability zones are engineered to be isolated from failures in other zones.

- Your services can be deployed across availability zones across geographic locations to provide HA.

However, you cannot leverage the previous benefits just by moving your application to the cloud. To achieve HA in a cloud, consider these best practices:

- Design your application to be cloud native.

- Design your application for availability and recoverability.

To achieve HA, you need to strategize all the layers of the application equally. Let's examine each component of your application.

High Availability of Databases

You use can both SQL databases and NoSQL databases in your architecture, but they will run on a separate server. You need to configure databases for redundancy. This can be achieved with a master and slave strategy. If the master fails, the voting technique will be carried out to choose a master and also can be made highly available by using a sharding strategy. More details of horizontal scalability are explained in Chapter 4. I have extensively covered database partitioning with various patterns such as horizontal partitioning or sharding, list partition, round-robin partition, vertical partitioning, leader-based replication, and quorum-based replication.

High Availability of Services

Applications can scale automatically by using containers and Kubernetes based on the load across multiple availability zones and geography. You can find more details in Chapter 16 Cloud Native Infrastructure.

To design an HA cloud native solution, you must remove the single point of failure at each layer, all the way from the infrastructure to software applications. The HA is usually accomplished with the redundant deployment of your systems. The deployment strategy can be chosen as either active-active or active-passive. Each strategy comes with cost and effort.

Active-Active Deployments

In an active-active deployment, application instances are actively running simultaneously.

- The load balancer distributes incoming requests across application instances.

- Instances are always running and ready to receive a request.

- You can achieve a recovery time objective (CTO) close to zero.

- Write messages simultaneously for both the data center for event-driven architecture by using messages queues or Kafka streaming.

Active-Passive Deployments

In active-passive deployments, one instance will be active, and the other will be in standby mode.

- The request sends only to primary instances.

- If the primary fails, then it routes to secondary instances.

Follow these best practices to make a system highly available:

- *Data backups, recovery, and replication*: Plan your databases to take regular snapshots and create read replicas to server requests to help recover if the primary fails.

- *Clustering*: You cannot avoid failure. HA is all about serving consumers regardless of failure. An HA cluster includes multiple nodes and shares information across nodes depending on the type of your architecture, like event-driven or synchronous calls. In an event-driven use, message queues or Kafka clusters share information across nodes as mentioned for active-active deployments.

- *Load balancer*: Use a load balancer to route traffic to the available instances. You can configure the load balancer to route request with the percentege or near location.

- *Geographic redundancy*: You can use a cloud location to deploy your application across geographies to make your application highly available.

- *Self-healing*: Apply a self-healing mechanism to heal your services automatically without human intervention; you can find more details about self-healing in Chapter 6.

- *Design your systems with stateless as much as possible*: Service states are not stored in one instance; the loss of an instance will impact availability and performance. Always store the state outside of the container.

- *Design your application to handle disruption gracefully, without customer impact*: Deploy the application in multiple AZs and automate the load balancer at every layer.

- *Observability*: Implement integrated observability across all services to monitor the health of services.

- *Prediction machine learning model*: Use ML models to predict your service health and the load; therefore, you can manage your system effectively.

Designing for the Customer

In the age of the digital economy, we are undergoing a lot of business and technology disruption. The customer can become impatient and want something new. Therefore, as an architect, you need to always think about the customer and business while designing your system.

With cloud native, IT services that can quickly build and deliver solutions in response to customer needs will attract and retain your customers and build enduring success. The methodology that you adopt must enable your engineering team to iterate faster and release software rapidly so that you can respond more effectively to customer needs and events.

When you designing your system, you need to focus on the customers and their needs in each phase of the design process. The team must involve users throughout the design process through a variety of research and design techniques to create highly usable and easily accessible applications.

Adopt the following best practices for customer-centric design:

- Cloud native microservices allow you to deliver continuously and be agile. There is no final version of services. It's an approach where you see action every day.

- You need to constantly update the code based on customer feedback, regardless of whether it's voiced directly, comments on social media, etc.

- Rather than the software engineering team working in a silo, you need to enable the engineering team to engage proactively and regularly with the business team through design thinking workshops.

- Adopt hypothesis-driven development to get early feedback from customers and use their feedback to make valuable real-time improvements.

- Adopt A/B testing, which helps you to discover if a customer-suggested change represents the majority opinion and whether any services can be modified and deployed in production without a business impact.

- Adopt continuous integration and continuous delivery to turn around quickly on changes and also create infrastructure as code to automate infrastructure.

- Follow a decentralized governance approach, which allows agile Pod teams to work independently and embrace customer-centric innovation.

- Follow canary deployment. Test a new version of the software before the version is introduced in the main production environment. Make small releases available to a small group of people to get early feedback.

- Collect customer data, analyze it instantly, and apply changes to your software.

Designing for Interoperability

Interoperability can be understood in multiple ways, like data transfer from one system to another without transformation loss or the ability of different applications to interact with each other dynamically, facilitating the smooth exchange of information. In this section, I am use the second interoperability definition.

Each system in your enterprise is different, and systems do not interact with each other out of the box. You need to create an integration mechanism between two systems to work. In cloud native architecture, each domain is designed as a microservice, and you need to implement interoperability across multiple microservices to complete a unit of work. For example, completing payment processing with a debit or credit card requires multiple services to perform. The degree of interoperability of a system or service can be measured as its cost of integration. The cost of integration of your services should be considered over its lifetime, not just at its point of first use. Changing to a service interface implies a need to re-integrate it with other services. The lifetime cost of a service whose interface changes will be considerably more than its initial cost. A service should have well-defined interfaces that do not change over time and are backward compatible.

For an ecommerce application, as shown in Figure 9-6, you are required to develop various services and also required to integrate with various third-party applications to fulfill the orders. In Figure 9-6, ecommerce services like order, customer, discount, item, partner, shipping, and distributions are part of your application. The delivery partners and selling partners are extended enterprises where you need to partner with them to complete the order lifecycle.

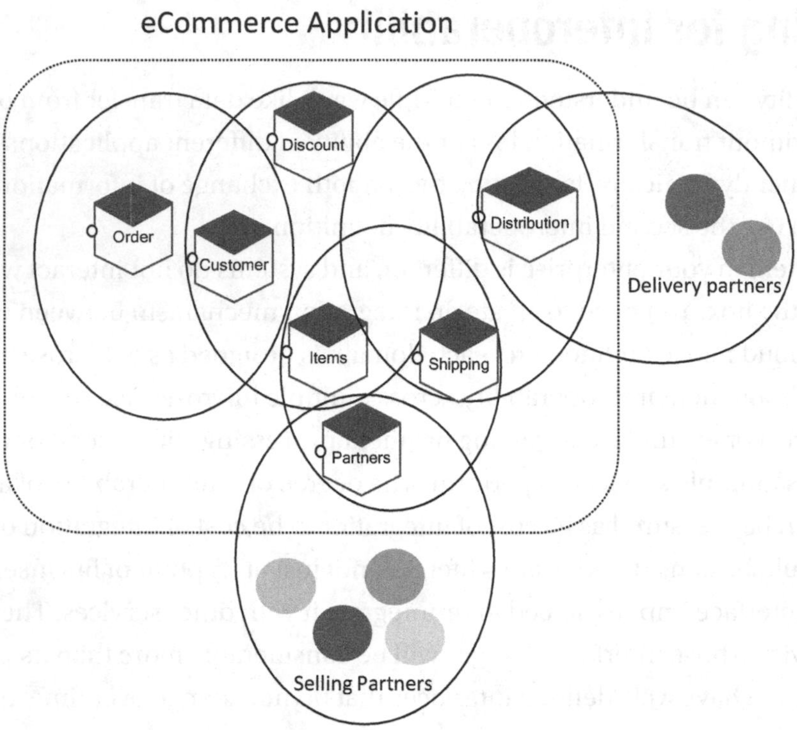

eCommerce Application

Figure 9-6. *Interoperability of services in an enterprise*

For your services to be interoperable, they must be able to exchange data and subsequently present the data in a way that is understood by other services.

In the exchange of messages among services, communication can be weaved through many services, across many security domains. Your service must be agile in nature, and your system must be able to modify interoperable conversation across involved services. The robustness of the conversation depends on well-formed message exchanges. For a well-formed message, the services must know each other for a well-defined contract. As messages are exchanged among services, the services must cross boundaries of local knowledge.

The interface of your service must be clearly described, and the description should be human-readable and also machine-readable. The human-readable description is essential for the developer to understand and integrate. Machine-readable descriptions enable dynamic discovery and composition of your software components.

Designing for Events

Anything that happens in enterprises or systems is an event. Examples include customer requests, batch updates, data changes, employees swiping a card, the customer swiping a credit or debit card, the customer buying a product in a retail ecommerce application, or someone checking in for a flight. Events exist everywhere and are constantly happening, no matter what the application is and what industry it is. Events are pervasive across any business. There is value in knowing about an event and being able to react to it quickly. The more quickly you can get information about events, the more effectively your business can react to them. The event is separate from the message because the event is an occurrence, and the message is the carrier of the information that relays the occurrence. In an event-driven architecture, an event likely commands one or more actions or processes in response to its occurrence. The following are the decisions you need to be aware of while designing an event-driven architecture:

- Prefer domain events to technical events, consider only technical events within a domain, and use domain events within and across domains.

- You should consider event-driven architecture for everything by replacing HTTP calls.

- Replicate data with ownership. Create governance for who is responsible for what; have only one data owner per domain entity (explained in data mesh) so that only the responsible person may write and changes to an entity and must be requested by the data owner.

- Do use distributed tracing, because distributed systems are difficult to observe and they use conversation IDs to track business-relevant interactions over time and in multiple bounded contexts.

- Use the Cloud Events specification for the interoperability of events across enterprises.

- Use event sourcing and write events to a journal table in the same transaction; instead of publishing them, use sidecar track events from that journal and publish them.

- Design with security and privacy concerns in mind from the beginning.

Designing for Observability

Observability is the extent to which you can understand the internal state of services based on the behavior. Making the system observable involves the practice of combining context, information, and specific knowledge about the system to create the conditions for understanding. In cloud native architecture, all services are distributed across various containers, which increases the need for observability because such architecture can fail due to interaction between multiple services.

The term *observability* originates in the mathematics of control theory, in which observability is a measure of how well the internal states of a system can be incidental knowledge of external outputs.

You might use monitoring tools to track the performance of infrastructure, networks, and services that support business use cases. As the organization is enabling cloud native architecture, the monitoring tools have shown limitations in their ability to adapt to the volatility of these architectures. Your existing static dashboards and manual thresholds do not scale, are not able to provide behaviors of systems, and are inflexible in assisting the resolution of unforeseen events. Using these tools, the business is unable to determine the state of its services with a high degree of certainty and to understand how its services impact key business indicators (KPIs).

Observability has evolved to solve the problems of present-day modern architecture. There is a need for observing techniques throughout the software development lifecycle. It encourages a shift-left approach starting from the developer laptop. It is an evolution of established monitoring, emphasizing visibility of the behavior of your distributed services in the traditional monitoring that focuses on individual services. To fully realize the promise of modern development methodologies, the application must be built with observability-driven development.

The monitoring relies on building dashboards and alerting to escalate known problem scenarios when they occur. The monitoring dashboards may not be able to provide the exact behavior of your services, such as when unknown problems happen frequently especially during request spikes. In these circumstances, the monitoring dashboards cannot get the entire picture of your services. Observability enables quick interrogation of services to identify the underlying cause of performance degradation.

Observability enables your system to reduce the time it takes to identify the root causes of performance issues. You can find more details of observability in subsequent chapters. The benefits of observability include the following:

- It improves the time to identify the issues, which helps to improve the application uptime and performance.

- The shift-left approach helps the developer to code for observability by implementing right configuration in a code.

Observability emphasis on collection and prediction of monitoring and, logging data.

Designing for Portability

Portability is the capability of running an application on the various platforms without any changes. Nowadays, many organizations are prioritizing a multicloud strategy and require you to move the application from one cloud provider to another cloud provider automatically without changing the application. But to achieve this, you need to design your application to be portable. Adopt a multicloud strategy for several reasons, including vendor lock-in, optimal utilization, reduced cost, SLA issues, etc.

Portability can be categorized into three ways.

- *Functional portability*: This is realized by describing the application's functionality details in a vendor-agnostic manner.

- *Data portability*: This is realized when the customer is able to access and save application data from the provider and to input this into a corresponding application hosted by another provider.

- *API enhancements*: API enhancement metadata is added through annotations; metadata provides information about other data.

In application portability, there are four areas of concerns that you need to take into consideration while designing an application.

- *Programming language and framework*: To build an application, the programming language plays an important role, and all cloud platforms have certain languages and frameworks that they support. For example, Google App Engine supports Java, Python, PHP, GO, and Node.js.

401

- *Platform-specific services*: Cloud platforms provide services through specific APIs, etc.

- *Data storage services*: There are two types of storage, SQL and NoSQL. The data that you designed for SQL will not work for NoSQL, and the data you designed for AWS Dynamo DB will not work directly Azure Cosmos DB, etc.

- *Platform-specific configuration files*: Platform-specific configuration files also exist on the cloud. For example, Google AppEngine, for instance, uses the "app engine web XML file." Adapting the configuration file to each target cloud platform affects application portability.

Along with these considerations, follow these techniques for your application design to adopt portability:

- Choose the right programming language.

- Containerize your services.

- Use a unified cloud API.

More important, create infrastructure as code for your application; this helps to deploy your application to any cloud vendors.

Designing for Ethics

You can find technology everywhere. Our society is more reliant on technology than ever before. Currently, without technology, nothing is moving. Therefore, it is everyone's responsibility to consider ethics when making decisions. Some in the society are misusing the advancement of technology and so we have fake news, cyberattacks, and technology wars against each other. The average person spends around 145 minutes per day on social media, and the average person usage of mobile is around 7 hours per day. Those fixated eyes never leave screens, which creates stress and anxiety.

As software engineers, it is natural that we spend most of the time focusing on how best we can serve users and how we can better compare to peers, which is perfectly fine. In some ways, we need to consider how we can use technology to create a better world. For example, Facebook never realized that it would grow to become a home of algorithmic propaganda and filter bubbles, YouTube didn't expect to become a conspiracy theorist, and Twitter hadn't anticipated the hate speech or trolling.

Let's look into another example that may occur if a company like Facebook purchases a major bank and becomes a social credit provider. What happens if artificial intelligence becomes a mainstream tool, spawning across terrorism, theft, and more?

While designing your system, you need to anticipate the long-term social impact and unexpected uses of the tech you create today. Your job is not only to create a fancy architecture but also remain ethical. So, ask yourself these questions before you make any design decisions:

- If the technology you're building will someday be used in unexpected ways, how can you prepare for this?

- What are the new categories of risk that you should give special attention?

- How can you react if any unforeseen risks occur?

There are various toolkits available for you to think through some of the future implications of the software you are building. They are the Ethical OS and Tarot Cards of Tech. Let's explore briefly what they offer.

The Ethical OS comes from a partnership between the Institute of the Future and Tech and Society Solutions Lab. It addresses social impact harms ranging from disinformation to a dopamine economy.

The Ethical OS toolkit helps manage the design process and manage risk around the existing technologies you are using and helps to identify dark spots of your architecture and design. It has risk zones and provides a checklist to identify the emerging areas of risk of your design. The following are the eight risk zones:

- *Risk Zone 1: Truth, Disinformation, Propaganda*: These risks have bad actors using the data and creating propaganda against individuals or companies, using the fake data to undermine the credibility of a company, etc.

- *Risk Zone 2: Addiction and the Dopamine Economy*: This risk zone is about addiction. As I mentioned, people are spending more hours on mobile and social media. This is not good for the mental or physical or social health of people. In recent times, we have seen many young have once lost their lives due to the PUBG game.

- *Risk Zone 3: Economic & Asset Inequalities*: This risk zone talks about inequalities in society. The people who don't have access can encounter setbacks compared to those who have access to it.

- *Risk Zone 4: Machine Ethics & Algorithmic Biases*: This risk zone talks about how you use machine learning models and create a bias against individuals or the marketing of a product.

- *Risk Zone 5: Surveillance State*: This risk zone provides information about the use of technology by government bodies and military zones, for example, in the recent case of Philadelphia police action.

- *Risk Zone 6: Data Control & Monetization*: This risk zone is about data privacy, data share, and data monetization.

- *Risk Zone 7: Implicit Trust & User Understanding*: This risk is provided by collecting the data or use of technology without acceptance from the user.

- *Risk Zone 8: Hateful & Criminal Actors*: This risk zone helps to identify bullying, harassing, or stalking about people and financial fraud and illegal activities.

Each zone provides a checklist to evaluate your technology choice, tools, and features you're working on and choose the risk zone that is relevant to you. You can start investigating these checklists and mitigating these risks. After you understand the risk zones, carry out the following activities to be ethical in your software design:

- Use the relevant questions in each risk zone and design your system to mitigate these risks.

- Use this selected checklist as part of your agile backlog.

- Socialize these questions across your project team and client.

- Collect relevant resources and brainstorm with the right subject matter experts.

- Fine-tune your design by implementing ethics in your system.

Designing for Accessibility

Accessibility is a design concept that means your application will include accommodations to the user interface or for slow networking so it can reach all people without any discrimination. Accessibility is all about supporting that flexibility for different user needs. The following are a few incidents:

- 3,500 web and app accessibility lawsuits were filed in 2020.

- 1 in 5 adults in the world live with a disability.

- Around 70 percent of web users with a disability will simply leave a website that is not accessible.

- 100 percent of humans in the world will face temporary and situational impairments at some point in our lives either in touch, sight, hearing, or speech.

In the digital world, you may use a variety of technologies and strategies in several ways to access and use digital content depending on your needs. Human-centered design focuses on the specific needs of individuals, including people with disabilities and elders, who most need accessible content. Designing and creating accessible content benefits all of us, while it is essential for some of us. Accessibility encompasses all disabilities that affect access and engagement to digital content including physical, speech, visuals, auditory, cognitive, learning, and neurological disabilities.

People across the organization use different technologies and strategies to access and navigate content based on their needs and preferences. You can adopt two approaches.

- *Assistive technologies*: This includes any technologies that aid in the usability, perception, comprehension, and navigation of digital content, such as screen readers that read content aloud, screen magnifiers, voice recognition software, and selective switches.

- *Adaptive strategies*: These are techniques that people use to improve interaction with digital content, such as increasing text size, reducing mouse speed, and turning on captions.

People who have multiple disabilities need a combination of assistive technologies and adaptive strategies to interact with content.

Accessibility Guidelines and Standards

The Web Accessibility Initiative (WAI) of the World Wide Web Consortium (W3C) develops guidelines that are widely regarded as the international standard for web accessibility. The Web Content Accessibility Guidelines (WCAG) is the set of technical standards and recommendations developed by WAI that defines requirements on how to make digital content such as text, images, multimedia, structure, and presentation accessible. The WCAG is organized around the POUR principle (Perceivable, Operable, Understandable, Robust). There are two WCAG standards; they are WCAG 2.0 and WCAG 2.1.

These standards are categorized into three levels of conformity.

- *Level A*: This is the basic level; you must consider all the guidelines included at this level as "MUST SUPPORT" requirements.

- *Level AA*: It is a midrange level that satisfies all Level A criteria and more; guidelines included in this level of conformance are considered "SHOULD SUPPORT" requirements.

- *Level AAA*: This is the most comprehensive level of conformance and also the most restrictive. You consider guidelines at this level as "MAY SUPPORT" requirements.

You need to consider the following areas for defining and designing the template of a document with an accessibility checklist:

- *Readability*: Good readability should be guaranteed to all users, in particular with disabilities. Ensuring clear and flawless readability is key for rendering a material accessible. Some of the readability elements are screen magnification, actionable elements, and movement and animation.

- *Use of color*: Contrast is the difference between text and the background immediately behind it. High-contrast text benefits users with low vision, color blindness, or other visual disabilities. Ensure that good color contrast with at least 4:5:1 is established between text and images and the background color, and ensure a contrast ratio of 3:0:1 between text and the neighboring text when color is used to denote status.

- *Text formatting*: The readability of text can be affected by how the text has been formatted. Ensure that you choose a typeface that emphasizes clarity and readability, and use a font size between 12 and 14 points and use a 1.5 line space.

- *Navigation and orientation*: Well-organized content helps users to orientate themselves and to navigate effectively.

There are many more checklists available such as headings, interaction and feedback, repeated elements, metadata, images, and links.

There are different types of tools that need to be used by your quality assurance team to test digital content for accessibility such as evaluation tools, assistive technologies, and authoring tools.

Designing for Automation

Automation is always required for software systems, but the cloud makes it easier for you to automate, test, and build infrastructure. These are some common areas for automation in cloud native applications:

- Continuous integration and continuous delivery (CI/CD)
- Infrastructure
- Observability and automated recovery

The lifecycle of CI/CD is continuous definition, continuous integration, continuous deployment and release, and continuous operation of your packages into the cloud environments by adopting the following principles:

- Have cohesive teams with shared objectives.
- Test early and often test right.
- Implement zero-touch deploy and configuration.
- Automate everything.
- Embrace failure, recover automatically, and degrade gracefully.

In the infrastructure, you need to automate the creation of infrastructure using infrastructure as code. It is a process that allows you to treat your infrastructure provisioning and configuration in the same manner that you handle application code. The infrastructure configuration is stored in the source code repository and uses a CI/CD pipeline to automate infrastructure.

In the case of observability and automated recovery, you should add user stories from inception. Logging and monitoring observe the behavior of the system to give a measure of the overall health of your system and automate your application by applying self-healing, resizing the disk, etc. You can read more details about DevSecOps in Chapter 14, Enterprise cloud native operation, which explains the end-to-end DevSecOps pipeline.

Designing for Maintainability

Maintainability focuses on the ease with which a software system can be maintained. Maintenance of a system takes place as changes are made to it after it is in production. Changes are constant in the present-day world; it is inevitable that the system experience will change. It is important to build a maintainable system.

In cloud native architecture, your systems are built with microservice principles. The core principle is to make it easy to maintain and enhance. To achieve this principle, your microservices must be well designed with the use of domain-driven design.

Designing for Usability

Usability describes how easy it is for users to perform the required tasks using the system. User satisfaction is directly correlated to its level of usability. Users are more satisfied with a system that is easy to use and that provides a good user experience. Adopt a hypothesis-driven development approach to design for usability.

Summary

The main principle of architecting for cloud native architecture focuses on how to optimize system architecture for the "-ilities." In traditional architecture, we focus on the "-ilities" of a relatively small number of components, but in the cloud, that fixed infrastructure makes much less sense because it is easily available and on-demand usage. Therefore, cloud native architecture focuses on achieving the "-ilities."

You must pay attention to designing for the "-ilities" as they influence the architecture and design of your system. The system must meet the designated "-ilities" while identifying and specifying them in a way that they can be measured and tested.

The success of the system depends on how you are approaching each "-ility." Look at the holistic design of your system while designing your application.

Now you understand more about designing the "-ilities" and the fact that they influence your software design.

PART III

Modernizing Enterprise IT Systems

CHAPTER 10

Modernize Monolithic Applications to Cloud Native

So far, I have explained various cloud native architectures such as microservices, event-driven, and serverless. These architecture concepts can be used for both greenfield and brownfield projects.

Business requirements can change, which is why old legacy systems in an enterprise may not support or meet the needs of business disruptions. There are various reasons that your enterprise must embrace modernization and go on a decoupling journey.

- Changing customer expectations and behavior

- Technology innovation

- New market entrants like unicorns (privately held startup company valued at over $1 billion)

- Blurring industry boundaries

- Cost pressures

In this chapter, I will explain how you can modernize and decouple your enterprise's monolithic applications by using decoupling techniques.

In this chapter, I will answer the following questions:

- What does decoupling mean to you? Why do you need decoupling more than ever?

- What are the different approaches to follow your journey?

- What are the challenges you may face during the journey?

413

© Shivakumar R Goniwada 2022
S. R. Goniwada, *Cloud Native Architecture and Design*, https://doi.org/10.1007/978-1-4842-7226-8_10

- How can you explore innovation while ensuring business continuity?

- How do you decide which systems require modernization?

- How will you plan the decoupling journey?

- What is the domain-driven design and approach?

What Is Decoupling?

In today's business environment and digital economy, organizations need to satisfy the existing customers and also need reach out to new customers across markets with more segments by expanding their digital offerings, without a comparable extension in IT and or market budgets.

Digital decoupling is the combination of strategy, approach, tools, and techniques to address speed to market at scale with designing for cloud native and when designing for a customer in an organization's IT estate burdened with years of technical debt. It is the concerted approach to exploit cloud native technologies to break down monolithic legacy IT, address technical debt, and transform to an ecosystem where IT changes are negligible.

Decoupling enables large enterprises to reassert competitive advantages against incubators or unicorns.

Decoupling involves replacing the technicalities of the IT system by keeping the business functionality to support revenue growth and add the greatest value to the customers. This way, your enterprises can respond to market forces and technological innovation while maintaining cost levels.

When decoupling at scale, this leads to @Scale IT, a scalable, flexible, and resilient architecture that gives your organization the agility to innovate at scale, streamline the IT estate and retire unused systems, and rationalize the portfolio to a singular function across the landscape. This helps your organization to compete with the unicorn companies on equal terms.

Decoupling embraces the use of cloud native architecture and software engineering methodologies to build new systems that execute on top of legacy systems.

@Scale IT is the emergence of cloud and cloud native technologies, various channels, artificial and machine learning with observability, and modernized software engineering with agility and AI-driven development. The more adaptive event-based architecture is called @Scale IT.

Technical Debt

"The price companies pay for short-term technological fixes hinders their ability to innovate and adapt in the digital age. One strategy to combat technical debt? Digital decoupling." —Adam Burden, Edwin *Van der Ouderaa, Ramnath Venkataraman, Tomas Nystrom, and* Prashant P. *Shukla*

IT is not new, and the systems in your enterprise are probably not new either. As the business expands, the systems in your IT department become legacy by the nature of the fact that the environment around them, such as people, process, and technologies, progress while the systems remain relatively static.

Organizations face intense pressure to meet the business disruptions, competition from unicorns, and customer expectations. To support this, enterprises are adding more features into the existing legacy systems, which results in technical debt that leads to more operation overhead. The decisions that resulted in technical debt were likely not wrong at that time; they were made to enable the business. However, if not properly paid attention to, the debt will continue to grow at an alarming rate. In the end, you need to spend more money on maintaining an application than on innovation and new technologies. Over time, the enterprise faces a lot of challenges when updating these systems. This becomes devastating for IT teams, and digital transformation becomes more difficult.

How Are Technical Debts Accumulated?

As explained, technical debt is a normal result of software engineering. Some debt occurs for good reasons, and some occurs unintentionally.

The first type of technical debt occurs when an enterprise IT team makes an informed decision to generate some technical debt and is fully aware of the consequences due to various reasons. The reasons can be to meet the delivery timeline, meet a resource crunch, create business functionality in production, etc. These decisions can accumulate quickly over time.

The second type is unplanned technical debt that arises due to poor practices, inexperienced teams, no review and checks, poor understanding, etc. This poor management, poor communication, or misalignment can accumulate over time.

The third type is business and technology change. These debts are unavoidable due to business disruption and better technology and solutions being available. It typically accumulates by adding more features to the existing systems to support the new business without changing the technology.

In a nutshell, the technical debt stems from everyone's carelessness, bad decisions, and other reasons. Figure 10-1 shows Martin Fowler's technical debt quadrant. I have modified the quadrant to suit present-day software engineering.

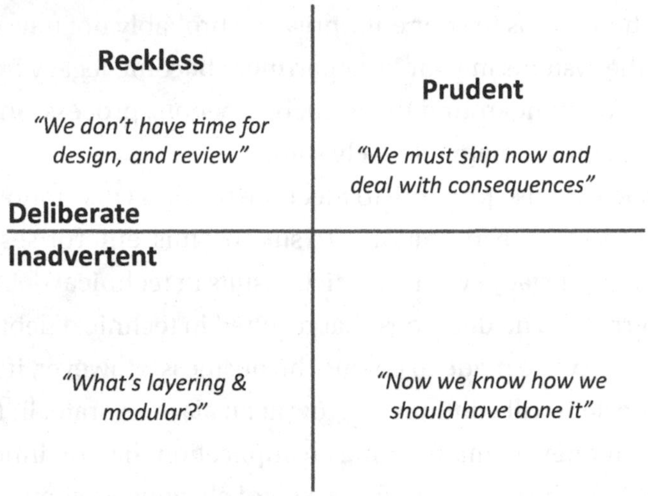

Reckless

Prudent

"We don't have time for design, and review"

"We must ship now and deal with consequences"

Deliberate

Inadvertent

"What's layering & modular?"

"Now we know how we should have done it"

Figure 10-1. *Technical debt quadrant*

How Is Technical Debt Impacting Your Enterprise?

Technical debt makes your enterprise uncompetitive against peers or unicorns; it makes it more difficult to add new business value to the software and makes fixing problems more challenging. This will reduce the overall asset value and create greater risk in managing the portfolio of assets. These are critical inflection points where constraints move beyond IT to threaten core mission, business, and operational programs. They occur when accumulated technical debt causes these critical systems to either chronically break down, decline, or become so inadequate, sluggish, or inflexible that your organization is forced to halt or significantly slow down investments on innovative new cloud native systems until it consolidates, replaces, or rearchitects existing systems into cloud native.

The leading causes of these events are legacy systems, lack of resources for maintenance, inability to add new features and integrate across enterprises, including poor maintenance and inadequate investments.

How to Decide on Decoupling?

As explained, technical debt can arise across enterprises irrespective of decision levels; everyone in an organization is responsible for technical debt.

Technical debt is a metaphor that, just like in finance debt, incurs interest payments. This means technical debt makes your enterprise's IT more expensive to maintain than it has to be. This is a direct impact on your business. The following section will help you to measure technical debt in your organization to decide on a decoupling journey of a system. I call this method the *decoupling model*.

Decoupling Model

Technical debt doesn't help decision-making if we can't do an analysis. Once we quantify technical debt, we can make an analytical comparison.

> *Legacy cost*: This is the largest debt in any organization, and it is easy to measure. It includes the cost to remediate and maintain in-house legacy and vendor products. Like financial debt, you make measurable progress in debt reduction by paying down the principal.
>
> *Variable cost*: These are the costs related to staffing, reviews, tools, delays, and duplicating systems that must be maintained. By not reducing the legacy cost, the variable cost is unavoidable and incurred.
>
> *Maintenance cost*: The legacy systems become fragile and vulnerable. Outages, breaches, and data corruption occur, leading to significant cost for the maintenance of replacing software, hardware, etc.

You need to consider many variables to determine the effect technical debt has on computation. Some of the variables include complexities, lines of code, maintainability index, Halstead complexity measures, etc.

Technical Debt Ration (TDR) = (Remediation Cost/Development Cost) *100%

Remediation cost is a ratio of the cost to fix a software system, and development cost is the cost of development.

Always keep the TDR below 5 percent. If the TDR is above 5 percent, then it's time for you to take action to decouple the legacy system.

Remediation cost (RC) is the maintenance cost of a system. The RC is directly proportional to the cyclomatic complexity of your code.

$$RC = k(\text{cyclomatic complexity})$$

Cyclomatic complexity is a metric used to indicate the complexity of a program. You can get cyclomatic complexity from review tools like SonarQube or CAST Software, and k is the constant.

Development cost (DC) is a variable cost for writing some lines of code. For example, if a file has 100 lines of code (LOC) and the average time to fix is 20 minutes to write one line of code, the cost per line of code (CPL) is 20 minutes.

$$DC = 25/\text{line} * 100 \text{ lines} = 2500 \text{ minutes} = 2500/60 = 41.66 \text{ hours}$$

To calculate whether your application requires a decoupling, use this formula:

LOC = 25,000
RC = 735 hours
DC = 0.42/line. DC = 0.42*25000 = 10,416 hours
TDR = (RC/DC) *100%
    = (735/10416)*100% = 7.05%

Your application TDR is 7.05 percent. In this example, this application requires you to undergo a decoupling method to move into the cloud native application.

Decoupling

Based on research from a leading consulting company, as many as 81 percent of organizations indicate that they would like to replace their legacy core systems with a cloud native architecture.

As mentioned, *decoupling* is the process of decoupling monolithic legacy applications by using new technologies, development methodologies, and migration methods to build new systems that execute on top of legacy systems. For example, by using application programming interfaces (APIs), agility, automation, and cloud native, you can gradually decouple core systems, migrating critical functionality and data to new platforms.

Decoupling is required in present-day architecture because of the following:

- *Changing customer expectations*: You need to connect more with the customer with meaningful customer relationships and provide a great user experience based on individual tastes to make a customer's life easier.

- *Technology innovation*: Your business must be accessed by any user on preferred devices without interruption, and your system should be able to provide real-time analytics based on real-time feedback.

- *New market entrants*: The rise of unicorns without any legacy baggage shifts the market share.

- *Blurring industry boundaries*: Your system must be able to adjust to real-time demands from the customers by rearranging the value chains and providing real-time analysis on pre- and post-sales.

- *Cost pressure*: Organizations are under immense pressure to deliver a higher level of services at lower cost and to remove legacy infrastructure, reengineering processes, and rationalizing workforces.

As I mentioned, 81 percent of organizations want to move to cloud native, especially after the COVID-19 pandemic, by removing the legacy applications, but organizations are taking too long to decouple legacy services.

Legacy services are the main drag force to innovation and digital transformation; however, as shown in Figure 10-2, making changes to legacy services is difficult because:

- We are dealing with tiered systems, designed to operate as a whole.

- Individual components are highly coupled and interdependent.

- Making any small change inevitably causes a ripple effect that must be mitigated or adjusted for.

- The change will take a long time and be expensive.

- It's hard to know where to start and exactly what to change. See Figure 10-2.

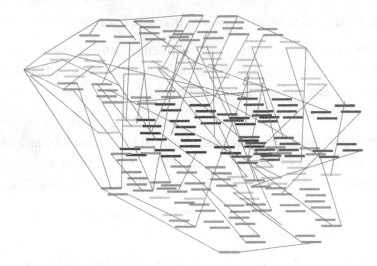

Figure 10-2. *Monolithic legacy application in an IT estate*

If you want to build cloud native technologies around a monolithic, it adds more complexities. With every addition into the monolithic system, the cost of testing, enhancement, and operation will increase.

As shown in Figure 10-3, legacy systems are typically dominated with a large and highly complex monolithic business layer. The legacy core is a tightly coupled monolithic architecture that acts as a brake on innovation, agility, and cloud native.

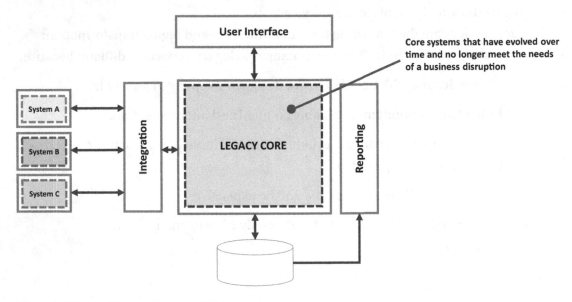

Figure 10-3. *Typical monolithic system*

A tightly coupled architecture increases delivery timelines, operations, and risks. The impact assessment on change requests, the lengthy testing cycle to test the entire legacy core for small change, and the complex code all add to the uncertainty.

Figure 10-4 indicates how organizations can change to cloud native systems. Usually, the organization puts in five to ten years of transformation, which leads to system flaws, complexities, and inefficiencies of a system. If you do not adopt decoupling early, then it will be too late to come out of the mess and you might lose the customer base.

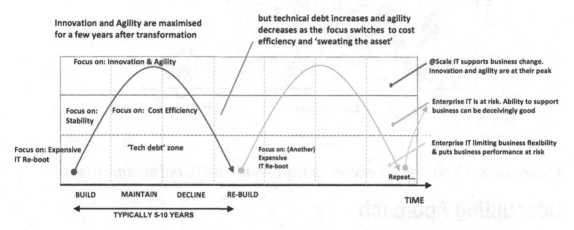

Figure 10-4. *Organization's approach on digital transformation without decoupling with cloud native*

As I mentioned, the digital economy has changed the competitive landscape, allowing new entrants to seriously challenge incumbents and change the market overnight. Figure 10-5 provides a high-level comparison of decoupling across unicorns, early adopters, and laggards. This is a lesson for you to adopt to cloud native early in the lifecycle by decoupling the legacy applications. This graph should open your eyes to the importance of decoupling.

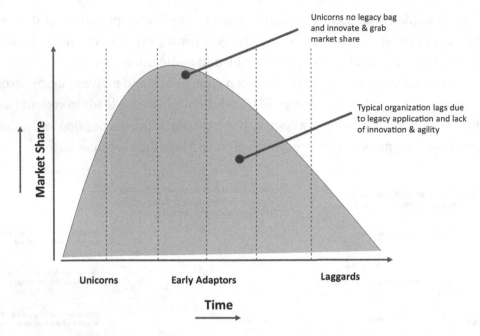

Figure 10-5. *Comparison between unicorns and traditional organizations*

Decoupling Approach

In the decoupling approach, the legacy core as shown in Figure 10-3 is evolved and provides the business transactions to the customer. But due to disruption in the business and changes in customer expectations, today organizations do not meet the needs anymore. A user interface is heavily relying on the legacy core as shown in Figure 10-3 with a tightly coupled architecture. An entire stack of the system is deployed on-premises on a virtual machine or bare metal.

As shown in Figure 10-6, the journey to a decoupled architecture starts with the implementation of automation for the existing legacy core. In parallel, the organization builds the cloud native services and deploys them on-premises and in the cloud, respectively, to exchange data. All the "Specific New" applications are converted into cloud native services with event-driven architecture and exposed as APIs to the web and mobile interfaces with real-time interaction. Those services are decoupled from the database by adopting the polyglot persistence principles and syncing them with the legacy core database for other transactions.

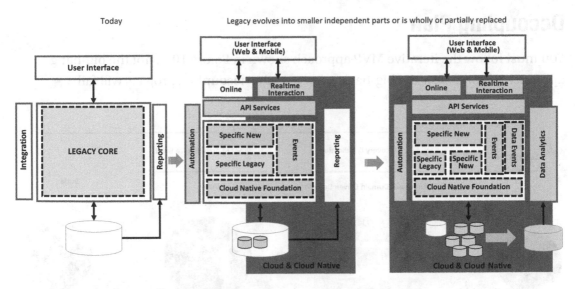

Figure 10-6. *Decoupling approach*

Finally, incrementally, the entire legacy core is decoupled into a cloud native system with polyglot persistence, and data is replicated to the data lake or data mesh for analytic purposes.

Following the decoupling approach, the organization introduces integrated monitoring or observability, real-time data lake integration, and systems of intelligence for smart interaction.

The end goal is to transform the monolithic legacy core system into a cloud native platform to fully unleash its value while eliminating current constraints. This requires understanding of future roadmaps, the business, and customer behavior.

Large-scale application modernization projects usually encounter overruns and failure. Adopting agility, automation, strangulation, iterative development, and incremental delivery can reduce risks while accelerating time to value.

The decoupling and continuous modernization for your organization is important because it allows enterprise IT to be more responsive to business changes and is easy to prioritize based on the demand. In addition, it helps to guard against the accumulation of additional technical debt through regular upgrades and follows the easy to create and easy destroy principle.

As you move toward @Scale IT, your enterprise can evolve toward a true service-based IT architecture that maximizes agility. This provides rules-based decision-making across the organization.

Decoupling Plan

You must follow the iterative MVP approach shown in Figure 10-7, not the big-bang approach. If you follow the big-bang approach, the decoupling projects will fail.

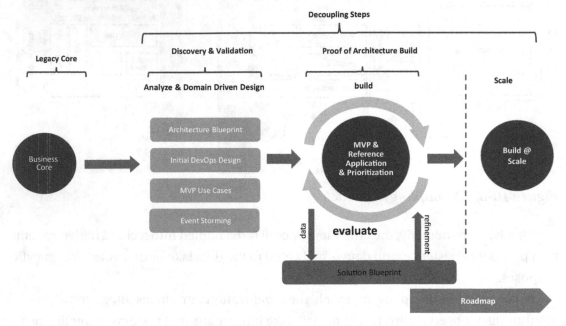

Figure 10-7. *Decoupling approach and plan*

Follow these steps for the decoupling approach:

1. Identify a system in your enterprise to start decoupling.

2. Create an architecture blueprint.

3. Conduct a design thinking session and domain-driven design with an event storming exercise to identify the microservices.

4. Initiate DevSecOps.

5. Identity an MVP use case.

6. Create a proof of concept (POC) and reference architecture.

7. Deploy the POC along with the legacy core and evaluate.

8. Once it is successful, create a solution blueprint.

9. Finally, go with scale to decouple the entire legacy.

Decoupling Principles

Use the following principles during the decoupling process:

- *Layering*: Apply layering to isolate parts of the core system.

- *Appropriate fragmentation*: Fragment capabilities to remove conflicts of interest and increase agility.

- *Simplification*: Simplify systems and keep differentiated logic separate from commoditized logic.

- *Differentiated services*: Build out the systems of differentiation to support reuse, automation, data analytics, and agility.

- *Cloud*: Leverage cloud native capabilities to quickly adapt and build services.

- *Intelligence built-in*: Build systems with AI and ML in them to enable smart interaction.

- *Event-driven*: Build an application that supports asynchronous events.

- *Real-time data*: Build data lakes or data meshes with real-time eventing capabilities to support the services.

- *Prediction-based model*: Add prediction across the application for self-healing and infrastructure prediction.

- *Observability*: Build a system with observability as a service.

Decoupling Business Case

When you consider decoupling the legacy core, you may be required to create a business case for your leadership before initiating @Scale IT.

You need to conduct the as-is assessment of the existing system and do a decoupled architecture assessment to compare the costs in order to determine the value of the decoupling.

For the as-is assessment, consider the following:

Overall, as-is cost = *Infrastructure cost + platform license cost (app server, DB etc.) + Resource cost (people) + Maintenance cost + deployment cost + opportunity loss (delay in future loss, sales impacted etc.)*

For the target state assessment, consider the following:

Overall target cost = *Infrastructure cost + License cost + People cost + Refactoring cost + Maintenance cost + Benefits*

Cost-Benefit Analysis = **Overall as-is cost ~Overall target cost**

Decoupling Strategies

The transition journey from the legacy core to a cloud native architecture requires an incremental approach to decouple the legacy core and integrate it back to the legacy core. The transition journey begins with a strategy. The following are the decoupling strategies you need to adopt for your journey:

- *Service decomposition strategy and roadmap*: This strategy identifies objectives, business context, and priorities. Assess the current architecture; you can refer to Chapter 11 for an assessment approach to incrementally refactor the legacy core into cloud native. Develop a high-level roadmap based on the business value impact. Identify the use of any relevant standards and adherence to cloud native governance and compliance requirements.

- *Decoupled architecture and integration planning*: This strategy defines the integration architecture for routing requests between the new services and the legacy core as well as enables the service to access data and functionality from the legacy core.

- *DevSecOps strategy*: This strategy defines the technical deployment infrastructure and delivery model required to build continuous deployment and defines infrastructure as code for automating the infrastructure service to deploy cloud native applications.

- *IT operating model*: This strategy defines an integrated intelligent IT operating model to organize around systems and value generation. Adopt a Intelligent Operation as explained in Chapter 18 to enable a faster time to market for decoupled services. Here you analyze the organizational impact based on the recommended changes to people, process, and technology for a decoupling journey.

- *Value case*: This strategy develops the business case to determine how a decoupled architecture can be implemented to deliver greater value to meet business disruption.

Domain-Driven Design

Domain-driven design (DDD) is an approach for developing software for complex needs. In this method, the implementation is a constantly evolving model to match the core business. The concept was first introduced by Eric Evans in his book *Domain-Driven Design: Tackling Complexity in the Heart of Software*.

Before getting into DDD, let's first understand why you need DDD and what are the difficulties of creating and maintaining a software system. Brian Foote and Joseph Yoder have defined a pattern called *big ball of mud* (BBoM). The definition of BBoM is "haphazardly structured, sprawling, sloppy, duct-tape and bailing wire, spaghetti code jungle."

A BBoM system appears to have no distinguishable architecture. The issue with allowing software to dissolve into a BBoM becomes apparent when routine changes in workflow and small feature enhancements become a challenge to implement due to the difficulties in reading and understanding the existing codebase.

Eric Evans describes such systems as containing "code that does something useful, but without explaining how." As shown in Figure 10-8, this is one of the main reasons systems become complex and difficult to manage, mixing the domain with technical complexities.

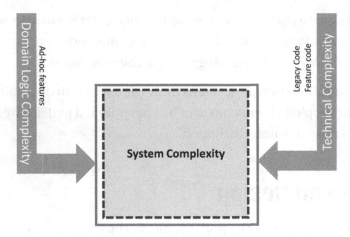

Figure 10-8. *Complexity in software*

A lack of understanding of the domain, the ad hoc introduction of code, and improper management in the source code repository makes the codebase difficult to interpret and maintain because translation between the design model and the development model can be costly and erroneous. Let me explain in a real-time example how improper management of code becomes very costly.

Continuing to persist with an architectural spaghetti-like pattern can lead to a sluggish pace of feature enhancement. When newer versions of the project are released, there can be mismanagement of the codebase. Over time, this problem grows and becomes unmanageable.

I was working as an architect with one client that had a monolithic tightly coupled web-based architecture. About 100+ software engineers were working on this huge complex platform, and they spent nearly two to three weeks identifying the right branch in the source for building and deploying changes to the production. When I conducted an analysis, I found nearly 2,000 branches in an SCM, and no one knew why they were created. This illustrates how code management can become complex over time if you do not manage it properly.

How Does Domain-Driven Design Manage Complexity?

DDD deals with the challenges of understanding a problem domain and creating a maintainable solution that is useful to solve problems within it. DDD uses strategic and tactical design principles to define a domain-based design.

What Is a Domain?

A *domain* is the knowledge and activity around which the application logic resolves; in other words, it is the business logic that is the core of the system.

There are three types of domains.

- *Core domain*: The core domains are the most strategic domains for the business at the enterprise level and program level. This is software that you build and is a differentiator.

- *Supporting domain*: The supporting domains are required by the core domain and are either built or are commercial off-the-shelf software (COTS) or SaaS.

- *Generic domain*: Generic domains are likely implemented by selecting commercial software/services or open source software, e.g., identity and access management.

Goals of Domain-Driven Design

The following are the goals of DDD:

- Build software that has a complex business process (business domain) while the knowledge is limited.

- Identify a bounded context and its patterns of interaction to enable independent deployment teams.

- Separate the business model (business logic) from the implementation details.

- Collaborate between technical experts and domain experts to implement a solution that works seamlessly.

- Create a ubiquitous language for each bounded context to use among business architecture and software engineers throughout all phases of development.

Domain-Driven Design Model

DDD is about distilling the legacy core into cloud native services. Figure 10-9 illustrates the various exercises needed to identify a service. DDD is distilled into strategic and tactical DDD.

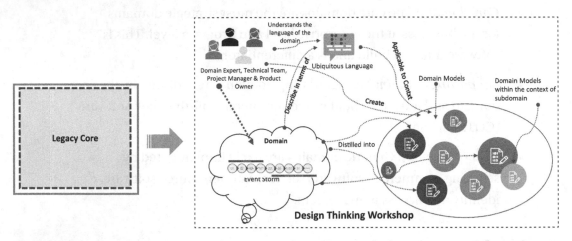

Figure 10-9. *DDD model workshop in a single diagram*

Strategic DDD

Strategic DDD distills the problem domain and shapes the architecture of an application. The technical team, product owner, and domain experts use the design thinking method to distill a large and legacy problem domain into microservices. DDD emphasizes the need to focus effort on the microservices as these hold the most value and the way forward.

Holding a design thinking workshop on the core domain helps the team to understand the domain in the legacy core and how important this domain is in the business. It will enable the software engineering team to identify and invest its time in the important parts of the system.

The outcome of DDD is to identify a well-defined cloud native architecture solution with microservices as its core and to identify the domain stories without changing the core domain business logic and rules.

The cloud native services are built through a collaboration of domain experts, product teams, and technical teams. Communication is achieved using an ever-evolving shared language known as the *ubiquitous language* to connect cloud native services efficiently and effectively to a conceptual domain model. The cloud native services are bound to the domain model by using the same terms of the ubiquitous language for its structure and class model.

Cloud native services sit within a bounded context, which defines the applicability of the services and ensures that their integrity is retained. Larger services can be split into appropriate services and defined within a separate bounded context where ambiguity in terminology exists or where multiple teams are participating in a design thinking (DT) workshop to further reduce complexity. Bounded context is used to form a protective boundary around services that helps to prevent software from evolving into a BBoM. This is achieved by allowing the different models of the overall solution to evolve within well-defined business contexts without having a negative, rippling impact on other parts of the service.

Tactical DDD

Tactical DDD is a collection of various cloud native patterns that help to create effective services for complex bounded contexts. Many patterns are explained in Chapter 4. You can use these patterns appropriately for each service instead of adopting them randomly.

Guiding Principles of DDD

There are practices and guiding principles that are key to the success of DDD.

- *Focusing on the core domain*: The core domain is the area of your system where most of the business logic resides. The behavior and functioning of your system depend on the core domain.

- *Collaboration across a team of experts*: This stresses the importance of DT workshops that allow brainstorming with the technical team, domain experts, and product owners. Without collaboration across teams, much of the knowledge sharing will not be able to take place.

- *Use domain terminology in the code*: DDD treats analysis and code as one, which means the technical code model is bound to the analysis model through the shared ubiquitous language. Use domain terminology in code to reflect the business language.

- *Communication*: The single most important facet of DDD is the creation of the ubiquitous language. Without a shared language, collaboration across teams would not be effective. It is the collaboration and construction of a ubiquitous language that makes DDD is more effective. It enables a greater understanding of the problem domain and more effective communication.

- *Continuous evolving*: Without the synergy between the code and domain language, you will end up with a codebase that is hard to modify, resulting in a BBoM.

How does it help you?

- DDD provides a logical approach for identifying subdomains to convert a legacy core system to multiple relatively independent cloud native services.

- DDD allows you to identify subdomains for specialized treatment based on specific needs.

- DDD enables the identification of core, supporting, and generic domains, with each domain capable of being deployed independently of others.

- The DDD process is a powerful tool for business and delivery teams to be on the same page regarding core code.

- The business process shares a common vision of what is important to the business.

Event Storming

Event storming is a design thinking workshop for the collaborative exploration of complex business domains and a modeling approach to domain-driven design. It was created by Alberto Brandolini in 2012 as a quick alternative to Unified Modeling Language (UML).

As shown in Figure 10-10, event storming in DDD consists of a four-step approach.

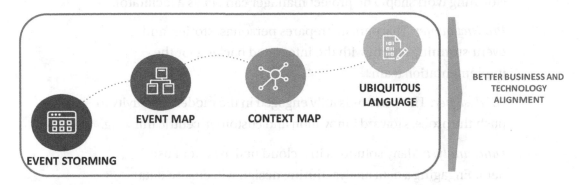

Figure 10-10. *Event storming in a DDD*

Event storming: This consists of design-level modeling and focuses on domain events and business process.

Event map: Business processes are documented using events, commands actors, and external systems.

Context map: This is a visualization of boundaries, dependencies, and communication paths between cloud native services teams.

Ubiquitous language: This is a clearly defined language used for all discussion between product teams, architecture, and engineering. It is a model that acts as a universal language. This is needed for understanding and communicating concepts in the domain in an unambiguous manner and improves collaboration with domain experts in order for everyone to be more creative and valuable. This must be expressed in the domain model to unite participants and eliminate inaccuracies and contradiction.

Key Roles in an Event Storming Workshop

These are the key roles:

Domain experts: These are the business representatives who understand the product vision and the target state's business process.

Architect: The architect and designer will be building the final solution.

Facilitator and DDD practitioner: This person facilities the event storming workshop. The project manager can act as a facilitator.

Product owner: This person prepares personas, stories, and event storming output with the integrated backlog for the implementation team.

UX designer: This persons is fully engaged in the modeling activity to push the process toward innovation and customer-centric thinking.

Data analyst: Many solutions in a cloud native system use data. Engaging a data analyst during design will ensure data implications are thought through at the beginning.

Event Storming Exercise

As shown in Figure 10-11, the event storm is a nine-step design thinking workshop that brings together domain experts, technology team, product owner, and project manager to model and understand the business process. It is *not* a technical design session nor an exploration of the current state of the architecture. The goal is to understand the ideal business process, *not* the current or future technical implementation.

Event storming is a:

- Conversation starter

- The evolving model of problem and solution

- Tool to gather requirements and build an event-based view of an event process

- A visual reference to view problem areas and possible solution paths

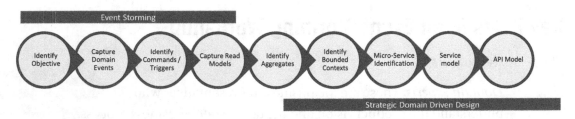

Figure 10-11. Event storming steps

The following sections cover the nine steps of the event storming process.

- *Identify objectives and capture domain events*: The event storming team can identify the domain scenarios and use cases and identify all the events that take place during the identified scenarios and then document and sequence events using sticky notes. The events must be in past tense like item purchased, invoice sent, invoice paid, etc.

- *Discussion*: Experts brainstorm by asking questions and clarifying details.

- *Identify commands and read models*: Identify the user and external systems that interact with the events.

- *Aggregates*: Identify aggregates by combining the events and commands

- *Bounded contexts*: Identify bounded contexts by using the events, commands, users, and systems identified in the event map.

Step 1: Identify the Objectives

In this step, as shown in Figure 10-12, you need to identify a domain scenario and use cases. In this example, I am choosing the auto insurance domain. Within the domain, there are value chains that are nothing more than the subdomains or departments in a portfolio of your organization. In the value chain, I am selecting the Policy Management value chain. Within the value chain, I am selecting the Quote & Policy Issuance use case to explain event storming further.

Within Quote & Policy Issuance, the objectives are quote generated, information provided, policy purchased, payment processed, account created, etc.

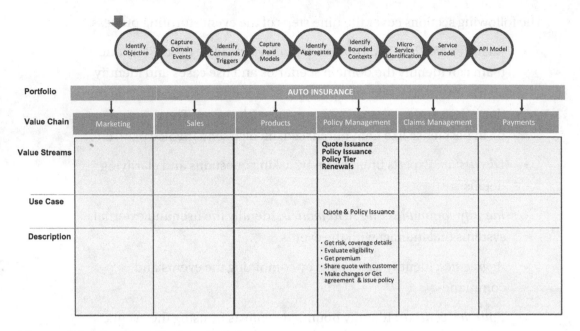

Figure 10-12. *Identify the objectives*

Step 2: Event Map: Capture Domain Events

In this step, as shown in Figure10-13, a team of experts discuss and identify domain events with a sequence. In the DT workshop, use orange sticky notes to identify all the events of an identified use case.

These are the key activities in this step:

- Document all events irrespective of minor or major occurrences for a given use case; events are written in the past tense.

- Rearrange events in a sequential order and resolve any. Group multiple events into larger, single events appropriately, and rearrange them based on time.

- Identify the actors responsible for each event.

- Capture questions, risk and warnings, assumptions, and conversation points.

Note   Any activity in a use case is called an *event*.

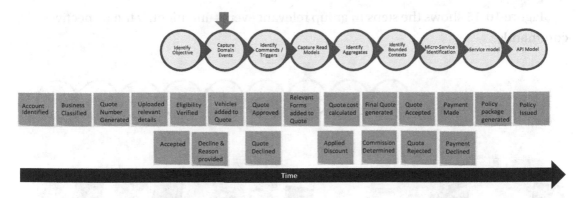

Figure 10-13. Domain events

Step 3: Event Map: Identify Commands, Triggers, and Read Models

With your events outlined, you can work on evaluating each event based on the behavior and what triggered this event. Without a trigger, there is no event. The trigger can be from external users or external systems or internal systems. The trigger of the event is noted as a command. Commands are documented by using blue sticky notes in the present tense and represent user interaction with the system.

Along with the commands, you need to add a user/role of the command and write it on a brown sticky note.

You need to capture the information about the commands such as the type of commands, how they are triggered etc., and write them on green sticky notes.

Figure 10-14 provides a clear view of the relationship between commands, events, users/roles, and read models.

Figure 10-14. Relationship between command and events

Figure 10-15 shows the steps to group relevant events and identify the respective commands.

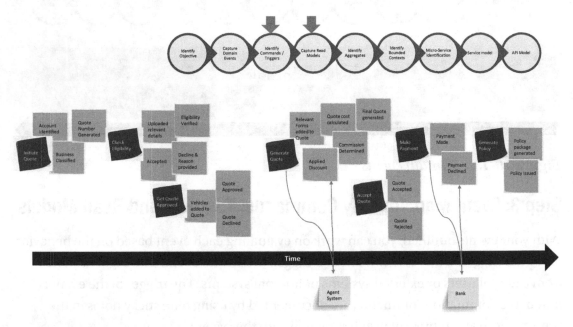

Figure 10-15. *Commands and events*

Step 4: Event Map: Identify Aggregators

An *aggregate* is a combination of domain events and commands that can be treated as a single unit. In an aggregate, one main domain event will be the aggregate root, and any reference from commands should go only to the aggregate root. The root can ensure the integrity of the aggregate as a whole. Don't mix a UML aggregate with a DDD aggregate. It is a domain concept, while collections are generic.

An aggregate consists of one or more entities and domain models that change together. You can consider them as a unit of data changes, and you need to consider the consistency of the entire aggregate for any changes. The aggregate helps you simplify the domain model by collecting multiple domain events under a single abstraction around domain variants and acts as the consistency and concurrency boundaries. The most important rule to define a boundary for your aggregate cluster is that the boundary should be based on domain invariants. Domain invariants are business rules that must always be consistent. The consistency boundary logically asserts that everything inside adheres to a specific set of business invariant rules no matter what operation is performed.

Entities inside the same aggregate should be highly cohesive, whereas entities outside aggregates are loosely coupled among other aggregates.

The aggregates have a local responsibility and receive commands and then emit domain events. The aggregates are documented by using yellow sticky notes in the form of a noun.

Figure 10-16 provides a clear view of the relationship between commands, events, users/roles, and read models and aggregates.

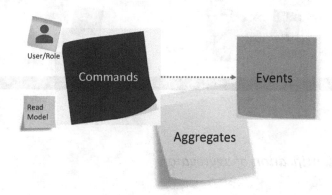

Figure 10-16. *Relationship between commands, events, and aggregates*

As shown in Figure 10-17, you can identify an aggregate from commands and events. The following are the rules to define an aggregate:

- Aggregates should be based on domain invariants.

- Aggregates should be modified with their invariants completely consistent with a single transaction.

- Aggregates represent domain concepts, not just a collection of domain events.

- Avoid having transaction across aggregates and consider them as a single unit of work.

- Try for smaller aggregates to support the "-ilities."

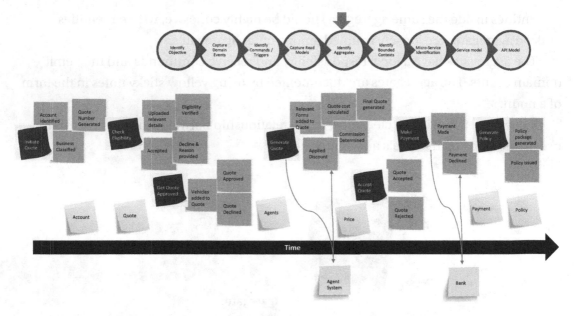

Figure 10-17. *Identification of aggregators*

Step 5: Context Map: Identify the Bounded Context

A *bounded context* is the logical boundary of a domain model that represents a particular subdomain of your system. It is the focus of the strategic design section to deal with domains and events. As I mentioned, the domain model represents the real things of the business, such as an account, insurance, policy, etc. It is the conceptual design of your system.

In an enterprise scenario, a bounded context is often based on ownership, with the bounded context being maintained by a team. For each bounded context, there will be a command and triggers along with the events produced. Typically, in strategic DDD, the bounded context is the last step you will define for a system. Each bounded context should be independent and owns its language and model. The rule of thumb is that each bounded context is a microservice.

Figure 10-18 shows the bounded context with domain events and commands.

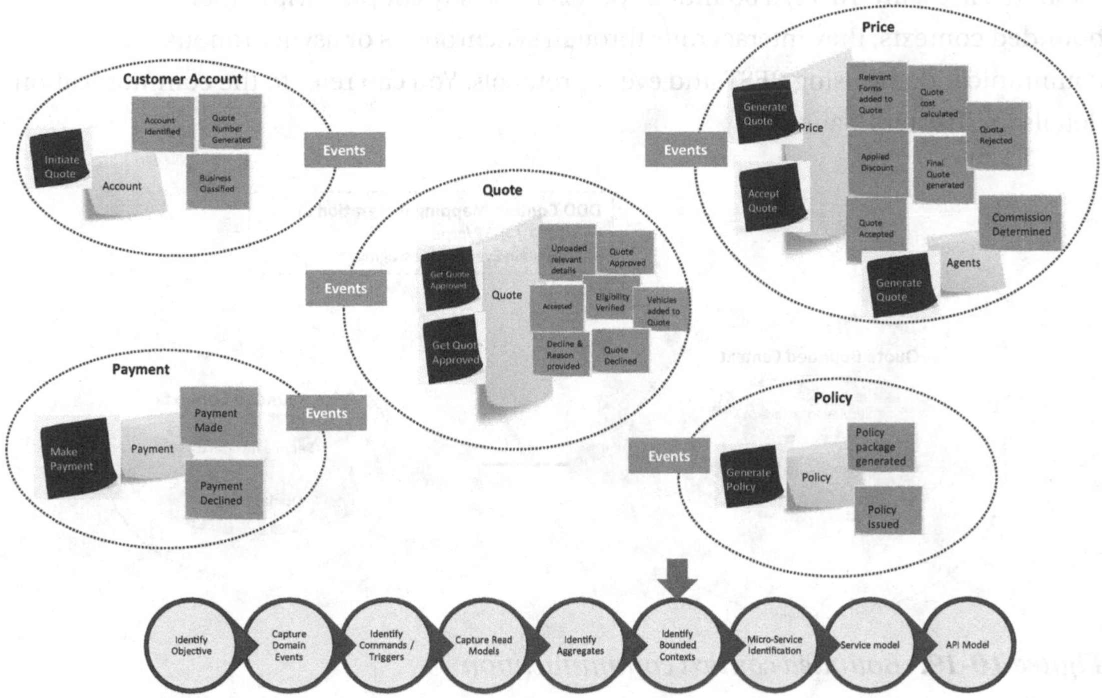

Figure 10-18. *Bounded context*

How do you identify a bounded context?

- Identify and collect the most meaningful domain events guided by domain knowledge based on business capabilities.

- Identify whether there's a clear cohesion required for certain domain events based on dependencies.

- A domain model has specific domain entities within a bounded context and delimits the applicability of the domain model and gives clear ownership to the pod team.

- Apply Conway's law to identify a bounded context; this law emphasizes that the system will reflect the social boundaries.

- Use the context mapping pattern to identify various contexts in your system and their boundaries.

How Does a Bounded Context Communicate?

As shown in Figure 10-19, a bounded context is loosely coupled with other bounded contexts; they interact only through synchronous or asynchronous communication by using REST and event protocols. You can refer to the communication details in Chapters 5 and 6.

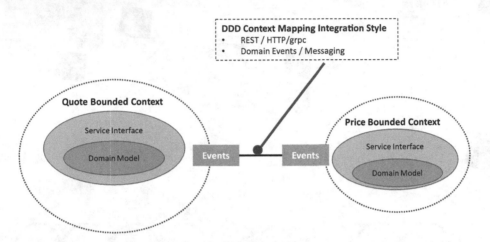

Figure 10-19. *Bounded context communication*

Ubiquitous Language

A ubiquitous language is a clearly defined language used for all discussion between domain experts, product teams, the architecture, engineers, etc. The ubiquitous language will also be used in the documentation, test cases, and code. Generally, each bounded context has its own ubiquitous language, and therefore a translation may be needed when communicating with another bounded context.

The following are the reasons why a ubiquitous language is needed:

- It is needed for understanding and communicating concepts in the domain in an unambiguous manner.

- It improves collaboration with domain experts to be more creative and valuable for all the teams.

- It is used for all the brainstorming between domain experts, product owners, architects, developers, testers, etc.

- It reveals the intention, not the implementation.

It helps to unite people in the project team and eliminate inaccuracies and contradictions. The domain model will evolve and will not end at a single meeting. You need to create a glossary of domain workshops to create a ubiquitous language.

Tactical Implementation of DDD

The goal of tactical DDD is to produce artifacts that are clearly defined and well understood by all team members. Identify the right thing to build.

- Tactical DDD occurs at a lower level typically within a team to support the service design.

- From a lean-agile perspective, this allows the team to share and align on what they need to align on.

- Create an integrated backlog and discuss epics, user stories, etc.

- Apply stories within a single bounded context.

Step 6: Microservices Identification

For microservices identification, look for entity and aggregators, as shown in Figure 10-20, which help you to identify the natural boundaries of the service. A general principle you need to consider is that a microservice should be no smaller than an aggregate and no larger than a bounded context.

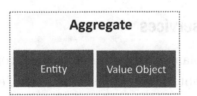

Figure 10-20. Microservice identification

Entity

An *entity* is an object with a unique identity that persists over time. For example, in an insurance quote, vehicle details and customer details would be entities.

- An entity has a unique identifier in the cloud native service, and the identifier is unique to the service and may span multiple bounded contexts.

- Objects have an identity that remains the same throughout the states of the software.

- An entity must be distinguished from other similar objects having the same attribute (e.g., customer account for an insurer).

- The attributes of an entity can change (mutable).

Value Objects

Value objects have no identity, and they are defined only by the values of the attributes. Value objects are the things within your model that convey meaning and functionality but have no uniqueness. These are used to pass parameters in messages between objects, and they are immutable. Attributes of value objects cannot change; they must be replaced with addresses, etc.

Aggregates

An aggregate defines a consistency boundary around one or more entities, and it is a cluster of entity and value objects. One entity is an aggregate of the root, and each aggregate is treated as one single unit that is retrieved and persisted together in a single transaction boundary. The root identity is global. The identities of entities inside are local, and the root is used for communication to the outside world. Internal objects cannot be changed outside the aggregate.

Domain Model to Microservices

In the previous section, I explained the bounded context, commands, and events, and explained how a bounded context is identified with a set of entities and aggregates.

As shown in Figure 10-21, here's an approach that you can use to derive microservices from the domain model:

- Let's start with a bounded context; in general, the functionality in a microservice should not span more than one bounded context. If you find a microservice that spans a bounded context, that's a sign that you may need to go back and refine your domain analysis.

- Look at the aggregates in your domain model; aggregates are often good candidates for microservices.

  - An aggregate must derive from commands and domain events.

  - An aggregate should have high function cohesion.

  - An aggregate is a boundary of persistence.

  - Aggregates should be loosely coupled.

- Finally, look at the "-ilities" and adopt Conway's law and an agile POD team structure for the ownership of a service. These factors may lead you to further decompose microservices.

- Each service must have a single responsibility and minimize transactions across services so there are no chatty calls between microservices.

- Each service is small enough that can build, manage, and destroy with small POD teams.

- Services have high cohesion inside and are loosely coupled outside.

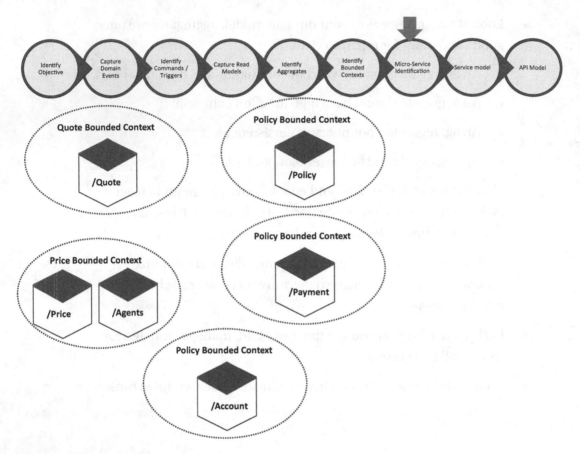

Figure 10-21. *Microservices model*

In the previous example, quote, account, payment, policy, agents and price are candidates of microservices.

API Model

A good API model has the same importance as a good design of microservices, because all data exchange between services occurs through APIs or events. APIs must be efficient to avoid creating chatty I/O. It is important to design and distinguish between public APIs and private APIs. Public APIs are exposed to the outside world, and private APIs are used for interservice communication or backend systems.

For public APIs, you need to consider REST over HTTP(s), and you need to consider various factors such as performance, backend systems protocols, etc. Depending on the granularity of services, interservice interaction can result in a lot of network traffic, and the service becomes I/O bound. For this reason, your services should be designed with the appropriate granularity. Serialization speed and payload size become more important. You can consider REST over HTTP and gRPC, Apache Avro, and Apache Thrift. Figure 10-22 shows the sample APIs of the previous example.

Resource	Method	Operation	Parameter	Response	Description
/Account	GET	Get Account ID	Business Info	[Account Info]	Search accounts based on accountName
/Quote	POST	Create Quote Number	Basic Policy No	Quote Number	Stores Basic Policy info
/Quote {QNum}	GET	Referral determination		Referred/Declined /Cleared	Based on Quote number provided referral determination check will be made

Figure 10-22. API model

Value of Domain-Driven Design

There are multiple benefits of DDD.

- It is an extremely flexible approach to software.

- DDD takes on the domain model to decouple the business cases or legacy systems, and the technology will follow to realize the business model.

- DDD understands the customer values and perspective on the issues. The collaboration between domain experts, product teams, and technical teams can help to create a domain model with a ubiquitous language.

- The ubiquitous language used for each model provides clarity, precision, and commonality between all the stakeholders.

The Business Value of DDD

There are many reasons why a business finds value in DDD.

- The objective of DDD is to provide value to businesses by modeling the software from the business paradigm.

- DDD provides a clear understanding of how the business works and provides an understanding of how the business runs.

- The users of the systems are able to contribute starting from day one as a domain expert; this helps each service be built with a rich domain.

- This helps to focus on core domains.

Drawbacks of DDD

Because of the modular nature of DDD and the strict following of the domain, the software itself requires significant insulation, and isolation is one part of the development.

- There are unfamiliar processes and rules in the legacy system; they are difficult to identify and may miss some circumstances that become costly for the service design.

- It is effective as a domain, but you may not get an advantage by applying it for small, simple business domains.

- Ubiquitous is the common language in DDD. If one person doesn't get it, then it could represent a bad design.

- DDD has a learning curve in an enterprise.

- DDD adds time to the entire DDD process; sometimes the engineering lifecycle is very short, so the team ignores the DDD process to identify a service. That becomes costlier later for the service management.

Where DDD Is Not Useful

There are some common misconceptions of DDD.

- DDD is not a set of patterns that exists for repurposing, and it is not code-focused and not an object-oriented concept. If your project is more suited toward those things, we suggest using UML.

- DDD is not for every enterprise architecture design; we also suggest using either TOGAF or the Zachman framework.

- DDD is not a solution for everything. Different organizations will have difficulties that require a paradigm shift that simply cannot be solved by using DDD.

- DDD is not an architectural pattern or design pattern; it is about how to design your application with a focus on the domain.

Summary

DDD is a domain language that is designed to manage the creation and maintenance of a system, and it is a collection of patterns and principles that can be applied to service design to manage complexity. Its emphasis on the distillation of large problem domains into subdomains can reveal the core domain, which is the area of most value. Using a ubiquitous language across teams can better manage collaboration.

The best pace of technological change in decoupling is as follows:

- *Architectural design*: By adopting a cloud native architecture, you can build out systems with greater flexibility. You can shift to lean architecture, APIs, cloud-based service platforms, etc.

- *Engineering practice*: The value of architectural change accelerates when you embrace newer ways of working that speed up development and delivery like DevSecOps, automation, design thinking, etc.

- *Talent evolution*: You need to upskill resources at greater speed and scale than ever.

You must adopt the following actions for decoupling to a cloud native architecture:

- Decoupling data from legacy systems

- Decoupling applications from legacy infrastructure

- Decoupling tightly integrated systems into loosely coupled systems

- Decoupling organizations from traditional structures and measures

- Decoupling essential differentiation from unnecessary differentiation

Modernizing your enterprise is not straightforward. One way to gauge the need for modernization is to look at the current level of technical debt, essentially the money it would take to upgrade legacy systems.

To make modernization a reality, you must do the following:

- Adopt decoupling as a rational approach to focus on modernization in a way that gradually migrates systems away from legacy while effectively managing the costs and risk.

- Conduct an application assessment to identify recommendations that help you to draw a roadmap that offers transparency and reduces risk.

- Socialize a modernization approach like DDD and event storming that has a high success rate across industries.

CHAPTER 11

Enterprise IT Assessment for a Cloud Native Journey

In the previous chapter, I explained how to modernize your legacy monolithic application to cloud native services by using decoupling, domain-driven design, and event storming.

Many enterprises fail or lose stream because they cannot demonstrate their business value to the customers and market. The modernization of a single system to cloud native technology does not show business value. So, you need to conduct an assessment that considers the following: application portfolio upgrade, technology modernization, optimization of the line of business, and the journey to the cloud to identify the maturity of the existing IT real estate.

An architecture assessment plays a vital role in both greenfield and brownfield application development, in the re-engineering of an existing application, and in the modernization and rationalization of portfolios.

Assessment is an activity to validate and review the existing IT real estate of an enterprise in terms of architecture, digital transformation, automation, software engineering, and cloud journey.

In this chapter, I will explain different ways to assess an enterprise by using various methods.

- What is an assessment?
- Different types of assessment
- Assessment strategic planning
- How to validate technical stability
- How to identify technology opportunities in an enterprise landscape

451

© Shivakumar R Goniwada 2022
S. R. Goniwada, *Cloud Native Architecture and Design*, https://doi.org/10.1007/978-1-4842-7226-8_11

- Architecture assessment maturity model

- Digital transformation assessment maturity model

- Automation assessment maturity model

- Cloud transformation assessment maturity model

Introduction

Digital-native companies across industries are fundamentally transforming every IT system to support business disruptions and embrace technological innovation. When confronted with large-scale digital disruption, enterprises must adapt quickly and lean into the cloud native by reimagining and elevating IT as a strategic core business function.

Large organizations are struggling to compete with new competitors and unicorns because of their own complex, tightly coupled IT real estate and aging technologies. Cloud native enterprises have invested heavily in cloud native technology platforms to create data-driven enterprises that provide business insight and that enhance the customer experience. Nimble new entrants like unicorns are leveraging new channels, scaling at an unprecedented pace, stealing market share, and rewriting the rules of the game by adopting a "culture of customer."

Many enterprises across geographies with rigid legacy systems, siloed data, old economy workforce skills, and outdated operating models can't compete with cloud native companies because emerging technologies scale quickly and can be delivered on demand by enabling machine learning and AI models. If you want to keep up with the digital disruptors, you must redefine IT by conducting as-is assessments. The assessment outcome provides a look at your landscape with recommendations. This helps you to strategize your transformation.

To reposition IT as a transformation engine, the leader of an enterprise should strive to change how IT engages with the business. For this journey, you need to know where your current problems are in the landscape and how to manage them.

Figure 11-1 illustrates why you need an assessment for your enterprise.

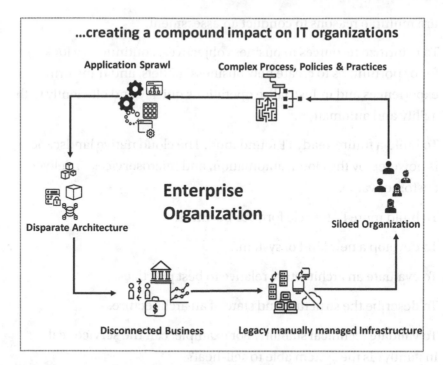

Figure 11-1. *Disconnected enterprise organization*

Assessment

An assessment provides a different way of conceiving, designing, and deploying technology across an enterprise. Assessment techniques help you to unlock unrealized streams of business value by optimizing your enterprise's current IT real estate to innovate with a set of new technologies that are cloud native.

An assessment is a structured study on a well-defined set of IT capabilities or elements focusing on the technology and business aspects. It is guided by the agreed-upon objectives of the enterprise to analyze and document the as-is state and to make recommendations on the to-be state.

What Is an Assessment Used For?

When you approach technology strategically, the core objective is to create business value for all aspects of the business, from the CxO to the back-office engineer and from software engineering to the customer experience. When you simplify your organization by using cloud native tools, you can better optimize your legacy estate.

There are multiple reasons to conduct an assessment.

- To prioritize resources to business objectives, continuously look for opportunities to create new business models, and transform experiences and industrialize operations quickly and efficiently with agility and automation.

- To build a future-ready IT foundation. The cloud native landscape is powered by the cloud, automation, and microservices to deliver customer value.

- To build more IT muscle for your business.

- To develop a new kind of system.

- To evaluate an architecture relative to best practices.

- To describe the structure and state of an architecture.

- To validate technical stability. For example, can the service scale instantly? Is the system able to self-heal?

- To identify technology opportunities, for example, cost reduction, agility, platform consolidation, portfolio rationalization, technology standardization, etc.

- To provide architecture for the due-diligence process, mergers and acquisitions, etc.

- To define the technology roadmap.

- To analyze the architecture's dynamic behavior in response to external events.

- To provide details of value proposition, cost reduction, and decreased cycle time.

Assessment Objectives

The objective is to identify the widening gap between the business and IT capability through an architecture assessment. Another objective is to improve the customer experience, by making it faster and with higher quality, as illustrated in Figure 11-2.

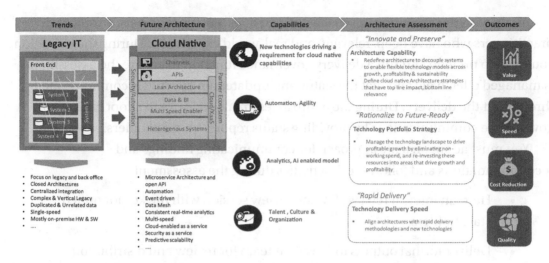

Figure 11-2. *Assessment objectives*

Assessment Execution Approach and Key Activities

What are the activities carried out during the assessment, and what are the deliverables of the assessment?

Based on the scope of assessment and type of assessment, you can decide how many weeks will be required to conduct an assessment and what key roles are required to conduct an assessment.

Figure 11-3 helps you to create a plan and deliverables for your client.

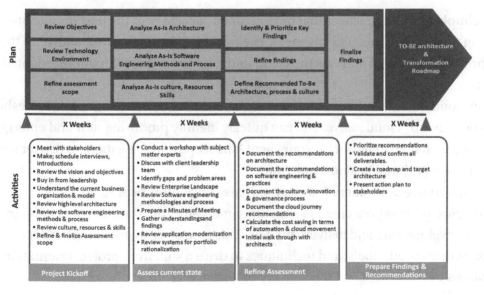

Figure 11-3. *Assessment plan and activities*

Along with the execution approach and activities, you need to have strong practitioners who have deep, relevant, and real-world experience. During the execution, you need to provide and run a delivery governance function to ensure the assessment is managed effectively and that the status and updates are effectively communicated throughout the delivery. During the entire assessment cycle, try to adopt critical governance communications by providing status reports to stakeholders.

You must adopt an agile approach for communicating findings and recommendations and follow these activities during the assessment:

- Hold an interim review /finding review session with the key identified stakeholders.

- Deliver formal outputs to the client team for review and distribution for early feedback.

- Create an execute summary pack for each workstream to give a high-level view of the approach, findings, and recommendations.

Along with this activity, you need to call out what you need from the client and who is required and how much time you require for workshops. The following sections cover different types of assessment.

Cloud Native Assessment

The technologies and practices that have enabled success over the past decade are reaching the limits of their effectiveness. The next big practice is cloud native. To thrive, enterprises must design and execute cloud native technologies with unprecedented agility.

The cloud, microservices, containerization, eventing, serverless, and data meshes are all powered by cloud native. You can quickly identify promising new and emerging technologies that are relevant for your client landscape and scale them to deliver new capabilities, value, and business outcomes.

A cloud native assessment is more than assessing enterprises against new technologies; it helps your client to shift fundamentally from traditional technology strategy, development, and delivery models. This type of assessment uses modern architecture methods, tools, and techniques to drive a shift from project orientation to continuous development and the delivery of systems.

As shown in Figure 11-4, each system adds complexity to the cloud native journey. The y-axis represents speed and efficiency, and the x-axis represents complexity. The complexity of an organization increases while the speed and efficiency to cloud native reduces, and vice versa. Therefore, you need to choose the type and level of system for a cloud native journey.

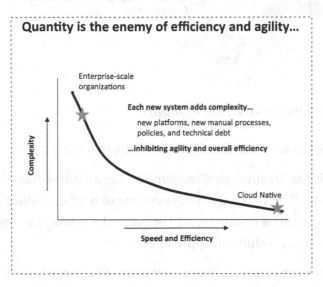

Figure 11-4. *Cloud native assessment comparison*

When to Consider a Cloud Native Assessment

As shown in Figure 11-5, in the cloud native assessment, you will assess the following:

- Methods and practices such as software engineering, automation, governance, deployment, etc.

- Technology and architecture such as cloud, microservices, event-driven, serverless, other cloud native elements

- Business alignment in terms of talent, innovation, culture

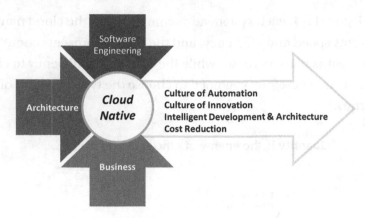

Figure 11-5. *Cloud native assessment model*

You can consider cloud native assessment for the following:

- *Responding to the strategic direction*: You see an immediate situation where your client is asked to improve time to market, reduce costs by optimizing various resources, and improve the quality by considering automation and a shift-left approach.

- *Enterprise team concerns*: Your client wants to change the way they are working and how they are working.

- *Enterprise estate*: An enterprise wants to move away from legacy monolithic applications, tight coupling, or poor delivery quality.

- *Manual delivery*: An enterprise wants to move away from old ways of working that result in manual builds, tests, and deployments that could be automated.

Cloud Native Maturity Assessment Model

A cloud native assessment is a model combined with quantitative analytics, gap assessments, and planning methodologies. It is the combination of existing practice area models, with a culture of automation and next-generation software engineering delivery concepts.

For each question in a cloud native maturity assessment, you must provide a rating based on the current practices and make recommendations based their maturity. The ratings are as follows:

- *Ad hoc*: With this rating, the process is not standardized, the architecture is not streamlined to cloud native, and agility is not followed. There is no vision available on cloud native adoption. This is like a one- or two-star rating.

- *Streamlined*: With this rating, the culture of automation exists but is not available across enterprises. Teams have started adopting cloud journeys but only in nonproduction environments, and few teams are following the agile approach with all 12 agile principles. This is like a three-star rating.

- *Optimized*: With this rating, a culture of automation exists but with only continuous integration, but there is no automation testing and no infrastructure automation. Few applications are deployed on the cloud, but they have started modernizing legacy monolithic applications to a cloud native architecture. This is like a four-star rating.

- *Matured*: With this rating, an agile pod approach is adopted across the organization, and most of the applications embrace cloud native architecture and collect real-time metrics. This is like a five-star rating.

You must prepare the questions for the cloud native assessment and evaluate each answer. Based on this evaluation, you will come to know where the current organization stands, and this will help you to make recommendations. One thing you need to remember, if the organization is ad hoc, don't recommend the matured approach. None of the organizations can go from one to five stars quickly. They need time, and therefore make your recommendations wisely. Always provide multiple iterations before the organization reaches the maturity.

Table 11-1 shows some sample questions with data from a cloud native assessment.

Note   The score and comments are illustrative, and the data is from a global life science client. I conducted a cloud native maturity assessment for the entire enterprise. I interviewed all the relevant stakeholders including the leadership architecture team, project manager, product owner, development team, and infrastructure team. I captured these details during my workshop with the global life science client.

Table 11-1. *Cloud Native Assessment Sample Questions*

Measure	Ad Hoc	Streamlined	Optimized	Matured	Current Score	Desired Score	Comments
Cloud Native Architecture Roadmap	There is no cloud native architecture roadmap.	There is a cloud native architecture roadmap that has some basic elements needed to build new capabilities.	A cloud native architecture roadmap is available and loosely followed.	A well-defined cloud native architecture roadmap is available, and teams across the organization have adopted it.	2	3	The organization has started a cloud native architecture journey and started creating a roadmap.
Hypothesis-Driven Development (HDD)	Teams uses observations and interviews to understand users but solely on quantitative studies.	Team follows HDD and uses both quantitative and qualitative analysis.	Team follows HDD and uses both quantitative and qualitative analysis.	Team follows HDD and regularly uses human-centered methods; involves users throughout the lifecycle of a project.	1	2	Some projects follow waterfall, and some follow the agile approach.

Methods & Process	Project teams do not follow any specific methods or process.	Team has followed some methods, but agile methods and process are not followed.	Most projects have consistent agile methods.	2	Most projects have consistent agile methods with @ Scale IT.	3	Some projects follow agile method but do not have product owners or detailed backlogs available.
Standards & Guidelines	Team does not follow any standards or guidelines.	A few guidelines are available, and some teams follow the guidelines.	Follows the guidelines and also uses the tools to document the guidelines.	2	Follows the guidelines and has a process to share them across enterprise.	3	Team follows the standard guidelines and procedures, but they are not updating regularly, and the entire team does not have visibility.

(continued)

461

Table 11-1. (*continued*)

Measure	Ad Hoc	Streamlined	Optimized	Matured	Current Score	Desired Score	Comments
Design Standards	No design standards exist.	Design standards have been created, but they are in static nature, and only a few in the project can access to them.	Design standards are available, and the project team is able to access them.	Design standards are available and are able to be accessed across team for reusability instead of reinventing the wheel.	1	2	No design standards are available.
Culture of Automation	Team does manual development and deployment.	Team does continuous integration, but testing and deployment are manual.	Team follows continuous integration and delivery and captures a few software engineering metrics.	Enterprise uses automation, and well-defined metrics are collected with infrastructure automation.	1	3	Team uses an ad hoc approach; there is no proper CI and CD pipeline.

Environment Strategy	There is no enterprise-wide environment provisioning; all are manual with require-based approach.	There is adoption of the cloud by a few teams in the organization but only for nonproduction environments.	There is adoption of the cloud across organizations for nonproduction environments, but few applications are running on the cloud.	1	There is a clear strategy available to adopt the cloud, and most of the applications are already in the cloud; some are on the cloud journey.	3	A few projects are adopting the cloud, but the majority of teams follow the on-premises approach.
Modernization	Organization has a lot of legacy applications and is running in on-premises virtual machines.	Organization started an application modernization journey by adopting cloud native but not for all the applications.	Organization has well-defined modernization roadmap and started adopting all cloud native elements.	1	Organization is already on the journey of modernization by adopting all the elements of cloud native.	3	Found huge technical debt, and 80% of systems in the enterprise are legacy monolithic systems.

Detailed Architecture Assessment

The detailed architecture assessment model provides quantitative analytics, gap assessments of detailed existing architecture, and planning methodologies. It is an instrumental technique to validate technical stability and to identify technology opportunities. It is an essential part of technology due diligence and technology roadmap definition.

The cloud native architecture assessment will be used to assess the maturity of existing enterprises against cloud native elements such as microservices, APIs, agility, automation, event-driven, serverless, and cloud, and the detailed architecture assessment will be used to assess the stability of the existing systems in terms of application architecture, integration architecture, the behavior of an application for the "-ilities," and more.

The outcome of this assessment helps you to decide whether the system is able to support modern-day business and can consider lift and shift to the cloud environment or whether the system can be modernized by using the domain-driven design technique.

Assessment Usage

The main purpose of this assessment is to assess an existing behavior of a system with the capabilities of the application architecture, infrastructure architecture, development architecture, and "ilities" architecture. This assessment can be used to conduct a review at each system level or enterprise level across portfolios.

In this assessment, you need to prepare a questionnaire with questions that should be asked to drive the assessment such as interviews, workshops, and Q&A sessions with all the relevant stakeholders.

Architecture Assessment Model

Figure 11-6 shows the assessment model. The following assessment model capture the current results and analyze the document findings and provide recommendations.

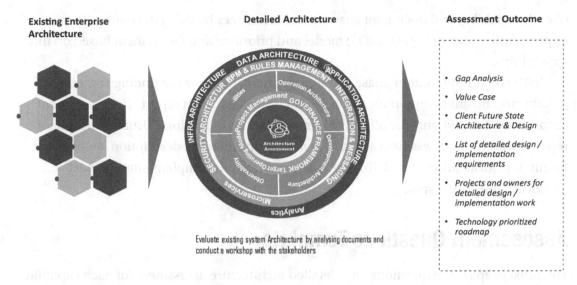

Existing Enterprise Architecture

Detailed Architecture

Assessment Outcome

- *Gap Analysis*
- *Value Case*
- *Client Future State Architecture & Design*
- *List of detailed design / implementation requirements*
- *Projects and owners for detailed design / implementation work*
- *Technology prioritized roadmap*

Evaluate existing system Architecture by analysing documents and conduct a workshop with the stakeholders

Figure 11-6. *Assessment model*

In the planning phase of the assessment, you need to identify the scope of an assessment, for example, if its scope is for only one system or one portfolio/department or the entire enterprise. Identifying the scope drives the accuracy, complexity, and costs of an assessment. In the planning phase, you also need to define a clear objective, investigation area, and capabilities. Once the scope is identified, you need to define a plan for how many resources are required, what skills are required, and how much time it will take.

In the workshop phase of the assessment, you need to work with the client team to identify subject matter experts (SMEs), and the time required from them, and make sure the client stakeholders are committed to this. One thing you need to remember is that you need seriousness and active participation from client SMEs and other stakeholders for a successful assessment. Based on their availability, schedule a workshop with the relevant stakeholders. Note: invite only the relevant SMEs. It is better to share the list of assessment questionnaires with the SMEs in advance so they can prepare before the workshop.

In the capture content phase of the assessment, you collect existing documents and review each of them. You document every discussion of the functional capabilities of a system, the technology capabilities of a system, the architecture styles used, the pain points, the software engineering capabilities of a system, the behavior of a system, etc. You need to conduct a thorough investigation by going through the questions

465

of each capability and document answers and references by using the issues, risks, opportunities, and strengths (IROS) model and prioritize and group them based on the capabilities.

In the recommendation phase of the assessment, evaluate the findings based on priority and business importance, and produce an assessment report. The assessment report must contain only the official recommendations of findings. Usually, the final report contains an assessment scope overview, scope element description, assessment findings, prioritization of each finding, roadmap, reference implementation, best practices, and conclusion.

Assessment Questions Template

You must prepare the questions on a detailed architecture assessment for each capability and rate each answer. The rating can be from 1 to 5 based on current industry and technology trends, and you can document the client feedback on each question.

For example, let's consider the rules management question, "Are you using rules management, and if yes, how are the rules managed?" If the client feedback is yes, then you need to probe further. What kind of rules? Are they using only action rules or decision rules? Are the rules are externalized? Are they using any ML-based model for rules? If they answer yes for all, then your rating will be 5. If they are using rules management and externalizing the rules, then your rating will be 4. If they are managing rules externally in the configuration, fine; then it should be 3. If they are hard-coding the rules in source code, then it is 1 or 2.

Similarly, you need to probe the client by asking more questions until the end.

You can find a few sample questions for the detailed assessment in Table 11-2 and prepare similar ones for a full-fledged assessment.

Note The score and comments are illustrative, and the data is from a global retail client. I conducted a detailed architecture assessment for a portfolio. I interviewed all the relevant stakeholders including the architecture team, project manager, product owner, development team, and infrastructure team. I captured these details during my workshop with the global retail client.

Table 11-2. *Detailed Architecture Assessment Sample Questions*

Capability	Question	Client Feedback	Current State (Rating)	Target State (Rating)	Best Practices	Comments
UI Architecture	What are the UI architecture components, and how do they communicate to the back-end system?	Some projects are designed with responsiveness, but the majority of applications are in old legacy technologies.	1	3	No best practices are followed.	Only a few projects use the latest technologies with responsive design, and the majority of the applications are client-server architecture.
UI Architecture	What technologies are involved in both web and mobile applications?	Web applications are using legacy technologies, and a few systems use responsive design.	2	3	Best practices are available, but teams are not following them properly.	There is no roadmap to adopt a responsive design.
Rules Management	Are you using rules management? If yes, how are rules managed?	Rules are part of systems.	1	3	No best practices are available.	Rules are not defined properly, and rules are not externalized; a few systems require frequent changes to update rules.

(*continued*)

Table 11-2. (*continued*)

Capability	Question	Client Feedback	Current State (Rating)	Target State (Rating)	Best Practices	Comments
BPM	Are you using a business process in your application? If yes, is this automated?	Few systems use the BPM tools.	1	3	Following a few best practices.	Systems are legacy, and there is no enterprise-wide approach.
Integration	What kind of integration are you using? Are you using APIs or event-based integration?	Few systems are APIs, and some systems use an MQ-based approach.	1	3	API standards are not available.	The APIs are available without any standards, and teams are using MQ for point-to-point.
Data Integration	How is data integrated across enterprises? Are you using any ETL or CDC approach?	All integrations are batch.	1	3	ETL standards are followed.	Teams want to move into real-time streaming from batches, but a roadmap is not available.
Data Architecture	How is the data stored in your system? How are transactions managed?	All systems are using monolithic database.	1	2	Data standards are available.	Teams are using a single monolithic RDBMS.

Area	Question	Answer				
Software Engineering	What methodology should you follow for development of a system? Are you using any DevOps pipeline?	Yes, few projects are using CI but no CD.	2	3	No best practices are available.	Teams are following only CI, but testing and deployment are manual; client wants to automate end-to-end lifecycle.
Software Engineering	How can you conduct testing? Are you using any automation frameworks or doing it manually?	Executing manual testing.	2	3	Test cases are available; using manual test data.	Teams are conducting manual testing for every release and need to automate CD as part of delivery.
Software Engineering	How are the issues and risks managed?	Uses Microsoft Excel.	1	3	Follows organization best practices.	Uses Excel but wants to automate risks and issues in AML tools.
Operation Architecture	How are you managing applications? Are you using bots to improve the operation capability?	All operations are manual.	1	2	Operation procedures are followed.	First wants to streamline operations and later wants to use AIOPs.

(continued)

Table 11-2. (*continued*)

Capability	Question	Client Feedback	Current State (Rating)	Target State (Rating)	Best Practices	Comments
Operation Architecture	Are you using any monitoring tools? If yes, what kind of tools? What are the metrics you collect?	Some systems are using monitoring.	1	3	Ad hoc; no standard available.	Few systems use the monitoring tools and capture the metrics, traces, etc., but the majority does not follow them.
-ilities	How is application and perimeter security is managed?	Security is very well established.	2	3	Yes, they have followed good security practices.	Follows security but wants to improve with the latest tools and configuration.
-ilities	Are there any pain points in the system behavior at runtime?	Yes, company is facing lot of issues in production environment.	1	3	No best practices are followed.	The client wants to automate the system bottlenecks and self-healing mechanism.
-ilities	How are you managing peak load? Is the system highly available? If yes, how many nines?	Majority of the systems are using on-premises.	1	3	No best practices are followed.	The majority of systems are legacy and deployed on-prem; wants to start cloud journey.

-ilities	Tell us about application performance. Are you facing any performance glitches?	Some systems behave very well, and some are unable to scale.	1	No best practices for performance tuning.	2	Wants an automated performance management.
Infrastructure Architecture	How is your application deployed? Is it deployed in VMs or containers?	90% of applications are VMs.	1	No best practices are available.	2	Few systems are deployed in a container; wants to improve container adoption percentage.
Application Architecture	Tell us about the application architecture of your system. What are the technologies used?	Legacy systems; some are very old.	1	No best practices are available.	3	Old legacy monolith applications, and some systems developed ages ago; wants to embrace cloud native.
Project Management	How is your application delivered? What kind of metrics do you collect? How do you report to leadership?	Some projects follow agile and waterfall and capture delivery metrics.	2	Delivery best practices are available; some are ad hoc.	3	Team wants to embrace agile and pod culture.

Automation Maturity Assessment

Automation is an essential part of every organization for a cloud native journey. Based on recent Gartner research, 39 percent of an organization wants to improve automation strategy and innovation, 23 percent wants to develop a stronger talent model, 23 percent feels their team lacks an understanding of automation trends, and 11 percent feels resistant to change.

There is some kind of automation that exists in almost all enterprises around the globe; However, these enterprises do not know whether they are following the right automation approach, what the gaps are compared to industry standards, etc. This maturity assessment helps you to find the client's concerns and the level of maturity of automation.

The automation maturity assessment framework is to assess the automation maturity of the organization to align with the enterprise's vision and industry standards. It will help you to understand the current gaps and identify a case for change.

To achieve the true potential of automation, you need to look for opportunities across the enterprise and cover every project of an organization. Automation can achieve the following:

- *Enhance user experience*: Customer satisfaction with the timely availability of data.

- *Optimize process*: Identify relevance in the current market and quick responsiveness, and optimize process components with the right process elements.

- *Drive cloud native journey*: Identify applications to connect better with the customer, and automate physical and virtual environments to support cloud native and shift left on security vulnerability.

- *Focus on generating revenue*: Reduce repetitive, standard work and enhance cost, efficiency, and reliability.

Automation Maturity Assessment Model

The maturity assessment model is a combination of capabilities, process, governance, technical stack, and performance management that enables the enterprise to deliver services to its customers. In the automation model shown in Figure 11-7, evaluate the current environment using the diagnostic and maturity model and create value cases for the automation journey. This model helps you to identify the impact of change assessment and the impact on people, process, skills, organization, and culture.

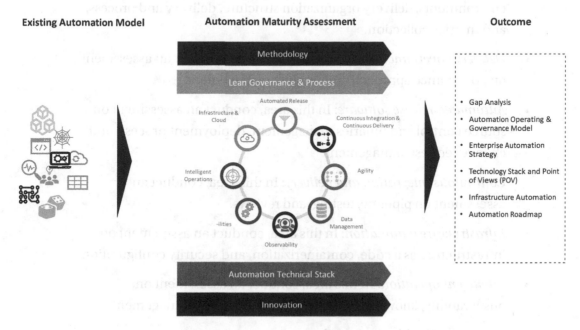

Figure 11-7. *Automation maturity assessment model*

To conduct a maturity assessment, you follow a similar approach as illustrated in the previous assessment types, like plan for workshops, capture the current state, analyze and document findings, and provide recommendations.

During the engagement, review the automation operating model's current state for the key technology elements, adoption of technologies, skills and talent availability, and change management model.

Automation Maturity Assessment Questionnaire Template

You must prepare the questions on automation maturity assessment for each capability and evaluate the answers. The rating can be ad hoc, streamlined, optimized, and matured (refer to the earlier cloud native assessment for details). Then document the client feedback on each question.

You need to consider the following areas for a maturity assessment:

- *Delivery organization and methodology*: In this area, conduct an assessment of release frequency to production and nonproduction environments, delivery organization structure, delivery and process, and metrics collection.

- *Delivery governance and process*: In this area, conduct an assessment on governance approach and product management.

- *Automated release software*: In this area, conduct an assessment on source control and binaries management, deployment process, and change request management.

- *Continuous integration and delivery*: In this area, conduct an assessment on pipeline, testing, and reviews.

- *Infrastructure automation*: In this area, conduct an assessment on infrastructure as a code, containerization, and security configuration.

- *Intelligent operation*: In this area, conduct an assessment on observability, knowledge management, and ticket management.

- *Innovation*: In this area, conduct an assessment, new process adoption, culture of automation, and culture of innovation.

You can find a few sample questions for an automation maturity assessment in Table 11-3; use them as a jumping-off point to prepare similar ones for a full-fledged assessment.

Note   The score and comments are illustrative, and the data is from a global retail client along with cloud native journey. I conducted a detailed architecture assessment for a portfolio. I interviewed all the relevant stakeholders including the architecture team, scrum manager, product owner, development team, and infrastructure team. I captured these details during my workshop with the global retail client.

Table 11-3. *Automation Maturity Assessment Sample Questions*

Area	Ad-hoc	Streamlined	Optimized	Matured	Current Score	Desired Score	Comments
Delivery Organization and Methodology: Release Frequency	Release process is poorly defined, with ad hoc change requests and long gaps between releases.	Release process is managed and has had multiple postponements of releases.	Release process is well-defined, and product backlog is stable.	Releases on demand; have a very good process; even small changes can be pushed to environments.	1	3	A few projects follow waterfall, and a few projects follow agile, but there is no backlog available; wants an integrated backlog.
Delivery Organization and Methodology: Process	Process and methodology are not defined.	Follows waterfall methodology.	Follows a mix of waterfall and iterative approach.	Follows agile with pod culture.	1	3	Wants to embrace both waterfall and agile with a streamlined approach.
Delivery Governance and Process: Governance	Governance process does not exist.	Delivery governance process is based on a traditional approach like waterfall etc.	Centralized governance approach.	Centralized with decentralized approach like federated approach.	1	3	Ad hoc governance and decisions are based on resources, not based on roles.

(*continued*)

475

Table 11-3. (*continued*)

Area	Ad-hoc	Streamlined	Optimized	Matured	Current Score	Desired Score	Comments
Delivery Governance and Process: Product Management	No product road map exists; follows ad hoc management.	Product management exists but limited to certain extents like defects, etc.	Product owner is empowered to make decisions.	Long-term roadmap available and fully controlled by product owner.	1	3	There is no roadmap for a project.
Automated Release Software: Source Management	Code merge is manual, and no proper management exists.	Code and binaries must be version controlled, and merge is semi-automatic.	All code and binaries are versioned by using tools, and auto merge exists.	Follows well-defined branching strategy; traces user stories and able to track.	1	3	Code merges are manual, and some systems and managing branches properly want to embrace feature branching.
CI/CD: CI	CI pipeline exists, but there are no proper jobs.	CI pipeline exists; has proper jobs but no automated review mechanism.	CI pipeline exists with all required jobs with review mechanism and quality gate.	CI pipeline exists with all jobs and follows the shift-left approach.	1	3	CI exists, but for few projects; wants to adopt cloud native best practices.
CI/CD: CD	Ad hoc manual testing.	Test scripts are defined and executed.	Automated test script available and executed as part of pipeline.	All tests are automated and run for all environments and run in live estate.	1	3	All testing is manual and wants automated approach.

Infrastructure Automation: Automation	Deployment of artifacts are done manually.	Artifacts deployment by using auto scripts.	Infrastructure configuration are done automatically by using infrastructure as code.	Configured with infrastructure as code across multicloud vendors.	1	3	All infrastructure is manual; wants to do MVP for few projects before embracing across organization.
Intelligent Operation: Observability	No monitoring tools available.	Tools in place, but not all application are configured.	Well-defined monitoring tools are available and configured properly.	Well-defined integrated monitoring; follows the observability as a service.	2	3	Tools are available but not captured with metrics, etc.
Innovation	Organization does not have roadmap on automation.	Few projects in an organization use automation; skills exist.	Well-defined roadmap available, and team follows the culture of automation.	Whole enterprise adopted the culture of automation and culture of innovation.	1	3	There is no enterprise-wide automation available and exists for only a few projects.

Summary

In this chapter, I explained different kinds of assessment and evaluation models and showed examples with illustrative data. These questions are sample ones that you need to add depending on the type of client and nature of assessment. By using these frameworks, you can evaluate the IT real estate maturity and provide recommendations with a clear roadmap for both tactical fixes and the strategic journey.

The following are the best practices when conducting an assessment:

- Find out the client's and stakeholder's commitment.

- Choose the right SME with deep skills.

- Interview the right stakeholders and pose the right questions.

- Capture all the details and take minutes at the meeting.

- Evaluate each question and rate them, and then prepare observations and recommendations.

- For each recommendation, provide industry best practices and references.

- Prepare a roadmap for separating tactical and strategic goals.

- Review your recommendations internally.

- Arrange regular meetings with a small group of stakeholders to discuss your observations and recommendations.

- Finally, read the final report to a larger audience.

Similarly, you can assess the client API maturity, software engineering approach, etc.

CHAPTER 12

"-ilities" Fitness Function

After designing a solution, you must evaluate your design by using the fitness function to ensure it can solve the problems under consideration. To check the functional requirements fitness, you might be using test-driven development, but what about the "-ilities"? How will you check the fitness function for the "-ilities"? This chapter gives you insight into the step-by-step approach for the "-ilities" fitness function.

In a modern cloud native environment, the architecture will evolve constantly to support business changes. How do you support evolution? You have everything to support and test the functional use cases, but what about the architecture, design, and the "-ilities"? Does your designed software support all the architecture elements and decisions, not with theory but with actual data points? For example, how do you shift left the PowerPoint version of the architecture block diagram into the real implementation?

In the age of cloud native and modern-day architecture, you need to predict the performance and behavior of your architecture during the development time, not at the end of the development lifecycle; it is about being proactive, not reactive.

In the previous chapter, I explained how to design the architecture for the "-ilities" and assess the health of a system.

In this chapter, you will gain more insight into how to conduct a fitness check of the designed "-ilities."

- What is fitness in architecture?

- How do you create a fitness function?

- How do you test the fitness function?

- How do you measure the fitness function?

© Shivakumar R Goniwada 2022
S. R. Goniwada, *Cloud Native Architecture and Design*, https://doi.org/10.1007/978-1-4842-7226-8_12

What Is a Fitness Function?

In evolutionary computing, a fitness function is a type of objective function that is used to determine how close a given solution is to achieving the desired result. The function returns the fitness of your architecture. These functions take the solution to the problem as input, and they produce as output details about how to fit and how good the solution is concerning the problem under consideration.

The fitness function is being used in genetic programming and genetic algorithms to guide simulations toward an optimal design solution.

A genetic algorithm is a machine learning technique that attempts to solve a problem from a pool of candidate solutions. These generated candidates are iteratively evolved and mutated and selected for survival based on a grading criterion, called the fitness function. For example, when using a genetic algorithm to optimize a driverless car, the fitness function assesses the identification of safety, signboards, objects, zebra crossings, and other characteristics that are desirable to create a 100 percent safe driverless car.

A fitness function can be applied to a cloud native architecture to determine how close the designed architecture is to achieving the desired characteristics. Fitness functions are an objective way to assess architectural characteristics.

In cloud native architecture, the fitness functions are used to evaluate the design for "-ilities," and the defined architecture must be evaluated using a fitness function algorithm to ensure its ability to meet the required service level agreements (SLAs), service level indicators (SLIs), and service level objectives (SLOs) under consideration.

The fitness function is not generic; each system's "-ilities" varies. Some systems require more security, some systems require high scalability and availability, and some might require more resilience to failure. Therefore, your input and output of a fitness function are system-specific.

As shown in Figure 12-1, a fitness function takes target input and applies the fitness algorithm for all the required "-ilities" based on input and generates the output with metrics. The fitness function represents every requirement of your system. You can consider the fitness function as a metric or test case. Some "-ilities" require a test case; for example, the performance fitness requires you to run performance test cases to identify fitness metrics.

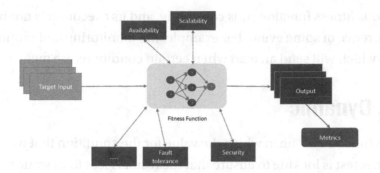

Figure 12-1. *Fitness function*

A fitness function should be clearly defined and provide a quantitative measure of how fit a solution is for a particular problem. A quantitative measure is how fit a solution is for a particular problem, while a quantitative result matrix is what will allow you to compare the architecture before and after a change is introduced.

Categories of Fitness Functions

A fitness function protects the various architectural constraints of the system. The constraints are not the same across the system. They vary depending on the nature of the system. You can check the fitness function in various dimensions such as scope, frequency, domain, global presence, architecture type, and other ways.

Atomic vs. Holistic

The atomic fitness function focuses on a single context and one architectural characteristic. For example, you can have a single "-ilities" unit test that is designed to test cohesion, coupling, etc., and is atomic.

A holistic fitness function takes multiple architectural characteristics into consideration at the same time, for example, by conducting security and performance fitness functions together and calculating the quantitative matrix.

Triggered vs. Continuous

Triggered fitness functions are executed based on some event. For example, the "-ilities" unit test is executed as part of the build.

A continuous fitness function runs constantly, and its execution is not based on some occurrence of some event. For example, the monitoring tool monitors continuously, which will send an alert when certain conditions are met.

Static vs. Dynamic

A static fitness function is one in which the value for the condition that we are testing for is constant. A test is looking to ensure that the result is less than some static numeric value or that a test that returns true or false returns the value that you expect.

The dynamic fitness function change is based on a different context. For example, the performance test might be different depending on the current level of scalability. At a much higher level of scalability, a lower level of performance might be acceptable.

Automated vs. Manual

Automated fitness functions are triggered automatically. They could be part of the automated unit test or part of the continuous integration (CI) pipeline. In cloud native, the preferred approach is automated. However, there are many times you may require executing fitness tests manually.

Temporal

The temporal fitness function is based on a designated amount of time. Other fitness functions are focused on architectural change but are triggered based on time. For example, the fitness function is created for a system patch on certain days. This executes based on time.

International vs. Emergent

Many fitness functions can be defined during the discovery phase of a project; these are known as *international* fitness functions. However, some characteristics of the architecture are not known right from the beginning but emerge as the system continues its development. These fitness functions are known as *emergent* ones.

Domain-Specific

Domain-specific fitness functions are based on specific concerns related to the business domain such as compliance, regulatory, security, etc. A domain-specific fitness function can ensure that the architecture continues to conform to these requirements.

All these categories are executed either during design or at runtime; they are further classified here.

Design-Time Fitness Function

At design time, you need to run fitness functions related to atomic elements like a unit of code or static security. For the code fitness function, you have to write a unit test specific to the architectural concerns such as coupling and cohesion, and write a domain-driven fitness function to check against the domain modularity of your system.

Runtime Fitness Function

In the runtime fitness function, you need to consider running a fitness function for the context of one "-ility" or implement a holistic approach by combining more than one "-ility." In the single context, you can examine the fitness of runtime security, that is, dynamic security testing (DAST) on OWASP vulnerabilities or scalability testing against the SLA.

In a holistic runtime fitness function, you need to combine more than one "-ility" to conduct a fitness function, for example, combining dynamic security and scalability, security, and performance. This helps you to identify whether your system can meet the target SLA holistically. Here you need to execute both security and scalability fitness together.

Execution of the Fitness Function

The fitness test can execute either as a single manual or as a continual part of the DevSecOps pipeline.

Manual Execution

The design-time and runtime fitness function tests are executed manually by the engineers either in the development environment or in the test environments. Many projects globally still follow a manual approach to developing, testing, and deploying; therefore, these systems are required to conduct fitness tests by using certain tools. For example, the "-ilities" unit test can be run by the developer on their machine or in a development environment, and the performance engineer can execute the performance test by using tools in a QA or performance environment.

Even though you are using automation in your project, some aspects of fitness functions resist automation; therefore, you require a manual execution.

Automated Execution

In the automated context shown in Figure 12-2, there are both-design time and runtime fitness test within an automated context, like a continuous integration (CI) and continuous delivery (CD) pipeline. In the pipeline, you can execute the "-ilities" test cases and implement a single and holistic approach of a runtime fitness test.

After collecting the fitness functions, configure them in a testing framework. Ideally, the fitness function should address the requirements of the "-ilities" in terms of an objective metric that is meaningful to stakeholders. Regular fitness function reviews can focus architectural efforts on meaningful and quantifiable outcomes.

You can configure unit test jobs and domain-driven bounded context test jobs as part of the CI/CD pipeline for the continual execution of design-time fitness. As a result of this automation, every new and major change in service is developed in a way to pass the fitness functions.

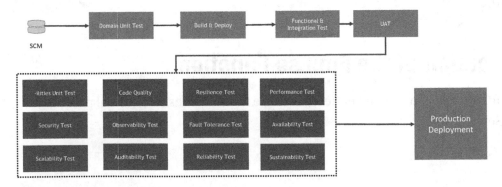

Figure 12-2. *Automated fitness function*

For a runtime fitness function, you configure a single-context approach to execute every "-ility" to make sure each one meets the SLAs and later executes a holistic approach by combining various "-ilities." For example, combine security cases like API authentication, security at transit, and data encryption along with the performance of state and intercommunication of services. Once you execute the functions, you can create a matrix of both and compare the results.

Fitness Function Identification

You need to define most of the fitness functions in the project discovery phase as they are characteristics of architecture and design, but this is not final. As your project evolves, you need to revisit your fitness function to accommodate evolution. As I mentioned, the fitness function is not generic; it has to be project-specific and industry-specific. For example, the financial industry has a lot more compliance than other industries, and an ecommerce application and trading platform has more spikes than other industries.

During the identification of the fitness functions, you need to categorize them based on relevance to your project because these fitness functions directly impact your design decisions. The categorization based on relevance is as follows. Each fitness function must have objectives and quantifiable results.

> *Key*: These categories of fitness functions directly impact your design decisions and architecture choice.

> *Relevance*: These categories do not directly impact the design and architecture decisions but relevance during the realization of a design.

> *Not Relevant*: These categories are not of much importance but are nice-to-have fitness functions.

Fitness Function: Coupling and Cohesion

To conduct a fitness test on coupling and cohesion "-ilities," you need to write a "-ilities" unit test that verifies against the developed code. Two strategies are available to conduct fitness test.

- By layer
- By feature

The layered classical approach is followed by the Model View Control (MVC) pattern; this strategy is based on horizontal layering. The by-feature strategy is when the features are organized by vertical layer. All domains or features related to a single domain reside in a single layer. This matches the layout of a cloud native service.

To illustrate the by feature fitness function, as shown in Figure 12-3, I have created a small Java project that contains a package structure with dummy classes and components.

```
✓ ⊞ com.cloudnative.fitnessfunction.ServiceA
    > 🗾 BusinessCoreA.java
    > 🗾 ControllerA.java
    > 🗾 ReposirtoryA.java
✓ ⊞ com.cloudnative.fitnessfunction.ServiceB
    > 🗾 BusinessCoreB.java
    > 🗾 ControllerB.java
    > 🗾 RepositoryB.java
```

Figure 12-3. *Code package of cloud native services*

As shown in Figure 12-4, I defined two services and defined the rules. If you write code that invokes service A and service B cyclically, the unit test fails. I prefer to write these test cases along with the domain test cases. You need to make sure that all these "-ilities" unit test cases are executed separately and owned by the architecture team.

```java
public class DesignFitnessTest {
@Test
public void VerifyDesignilities()

{
    DependencyConstraint fitness = new DependencyConstraint();
    JavaPackage serviceA = fitness.addPackage("com.cloudnative.fitnessfunction.ServiceA");
    JavaPackage serviceB = fitness.addPackage("com.cloudnative.fitnessfunction.ServiceB");

    serviceA.dependsUpon(serviceB);
    serviceB.dependsUpon(serviceA);
    jdepend.analyze();
    assertEquals("Dependency mismatch", true, jdepend.dependencyMatch(fitness));

}

}
```

Figure 12-4. *Jdepends verify of fitness function for coupling and cohesion*

To execute these test cases, you need to make sure to configure the CI pipeline as a separate job to track the metrics of the fitness function.

Fitness Function: Security

To conduct your architecture and design fitness function, there are two strategies. Each strategy evaluates various fitness functions for your architecture.

- Static security system testing (SAST)

- Dynamic security system testing (DAST)

SAST conducts a fitness test of your encryption, SQL injection, input validation, stack buffer overflows, and false-positive analysis. DAST conducts a fitness test of the OWASP Top 10 vulnerabilities like cross-site scripting, broken authentication, broken access control, and more.

To verify SAST, there are various tools like IBM App Scan, the Fortify static code analyzer, Code Scan, etc. To conduct DAST, tools like OWASP ZAP, Burp Suite, Checkmarx, etc., can be used.

The design-time fitness function is executed along with the CI pipeline, as shown in Figure 12-4. As I mentioned, you need separate unit test cases for functional requirements and the "-ilities," the both the test cases need to execute separately to get the execution metrics, and need to run SAST and DAST along with the pipeline.

The execution of functional testing before or after the fitness function depends on each pod team.

Fitness Function: Extensibility, Reusability, Adaptability, and Maintainability

A code quality test helps you identify fitness functions for extensibility, reusability, and maintainability. These tests are added to the pipeline to determine the relevant "-ilities." This set of fitness functions can serve as quality gates to prevent unmaintainable code in production.

Quality gate tools like SonarQube can be used to create fitness function for the "-ilities." You can configure a maintainability rating and reliability rating fitness function in the tool.

Fitness Function: Performance

The fitness function for performance should be defined during the discovery phase; not all services are required to perform in a similar way. Various tools and frameworks provide mechanisms to build tests and test load in a variety of scenarios. The performance fitness function should be executed as part of the CI/CD pipeline in a separate environment, and the configuration of the environment should mimic the production environment.

Tools like JMeter, Load Runner, etc., can be used to test the fitness function, and these tools should be configured as part of the CI/CD pipeline and use tools like Gatling to execute the fitness function early in the programmer development environment. Use a configuration environment that mirrors production for the performance fitness test.

Fitness Function: Resiliency

Use a fitness function for resiliency to identify and ensure the availability of an application during failure. This fitness function configures the code to handle tolerance and then retires. You can use load test tools to check the resiliency of your service. The metrics can be calculated as several successful versus unsuccessful requests. You can use Chaos Monkey tool to test the resilience fitness function.

Fitness Function: Scalability

Use a fitness function for scalability to ensure a service can scale based on user spikes. This fitness function configures containers and Kubernetes to handle the user load. The code must manage the state, configuration, etc., during the scalability of an application. You can use load testing to check the scalability fitness function. Create a matrix that shows the number of successful transactions versus unsuccessful transactions with the transaction round-trip time.

Fitness Function: Observability

A fitness function for observability ensures all the services in a system are monitored and send alerts, catch errors, and meet the architectural standards of observability. It will collect metrics across the application, infrastructure, and security environment. The metrics, such as all the observability parameters, are collected for successful versus missing parameters.

Fitness Function: Compliance

The fitness function for compliance ensures that domain-specific and country-specific compliances or regulations are met. A matrix can display whether compliance has been met or not (true or false).

A fitness function may come in the form of tests, monitoring, and the collection of metrics. Not all tests are fitness functions; only those that assess the "-ilities" are fitness functions.

The fitness function can be used to calculate various software metrics to determine whether an architecture continues to meet the "-ilities" requirements. For example, for cohesion, coupling, and maintainability, the fitness functions are cyclomatic complexity details and unit test as measurement to identify fitness. This fitness function helps you to identify whether refactoring is required.

Performance tests ensure that the architecture continues to meet your requirements and that any recent changes to the services have not negatively impacted its performance. Security tests can focus on the security parameters of your system to ensure that changes have not introduced any new vulnerabilities.

Using these various types of fitness functions provides an architect with information on the quality of the overall architecture as changes are introduced and it continues to evolve. These fitness functions provide a way to give a software architect confidence that the system continues to be capable and informs you if it is starting to decline in quality. Fitness functions facilitate the creation of an evolvable architecture.

For holistic fitness, the functions test multiple parts of the system all the time. An example of a continual holistic fitness function is Netflix's Chaos Monkey, which tests latency, availability, elasticity, resilience, scalability, and so on, in the cloud.

Fitness Function Metrics

Using the fitness measurements and a matrix of fitness functions provides a software architect with information about how fit the overall architecture is. The measurements give a software architect a way to calculate how fit their systems are. Table 12-1 provides insight into the requirements that can be collected for the fitness function test of one of my projects.

Table 12-1. *Fitness Function Metrics*

Fitness Function	Details	Requirement	Measurement
Cohesion and Coupling	Check coupling and cohesion through code quality.	Quality gates Unit test success: 100% Maintainability rating Reliability rating	Use SonarQube to measure against the quality gates. Write unit tests to check coupling and cohesion.
Availability	Check for high availability of your service.	Availability is 99.99% (four nines)	Measure by using **X=(n-y) *100/n** n = total number of minutes y = total number of minutes unavailable For example, 31 days/month N=31*24*60= 44,640 minutes, if a server is not available for 15 minutes in a month **X=(44640-15)*100/44640** **=99.96%**
Scalability	Scale in and out depending upon the load on your system.	Annual connection = 5,000,000 Average per day = 13700 Peak per day = 25000 Average day peak hour = 12500 Peak day peak hour = 13,500	Little's law: X=N/R The law says that if the box contains an average of N users and the average user spends R seconds, then the throughput is X. N = transaction R = seconds X = throughput transaction/per second (tps) X = 100/1200ms = 83.33tps
Performance	Check the overall performance of your system.	API server-side response time: <1 seconds DB calls: < 2 seconds Initial page load: < 4 seconds	Use load testing tools to measure the performance along with monitoring.

(*continued*)

Table 12-1. (*continued*)

Fitness Function	Details	Requirement	Measurement
Security	Check the overall security of an application; the security is different for each system.	OWASP Top 10 vulnerabilities Static security test Threat model Firewall Encryption	Use SAST and DAST tools to measure the security and use the threat model to create a threat analysis.
Observability	Monitor and alert across applications.	Integrated observability across application, infrastructure, and security.	Check observability dashboards, alerting, events, etc.

Review Function Metrics

After identifying and calculating the measurements of the fitness function, you need to schedule a meeting with the key stakeholders about the goal of conformance. In the meeting, you can check the relevance of the current fitness function, determine a change in the scale or magnitude of each fitness function, and decide if there is any better approach to measuring the fitness function.

Summary

In this chapter, I covered fitness functions and how they can be used in your product or project development. I covered how to determine whether the architecture continues to achieve the required "-ilities" and also provided a few examples on how to identify and measure the fitness functions.

You must adopt the following best practices when using fitness functions:

- You must define the fitness functions clearly with no ambiguity, and the relevant stakeholder must understand the fitness function for the project.

- The fitness function must be implemented efficiently.

- Each fitness function must be measured to demonstrate how fit a created architecture is when solving the problem.

- The fitness function must generate intuitive results.

PART IV

Cloud Native Software Engineering

CHAPTER 13

Enterprise Cloud Native Software Engineering

As a software engineer, you get to see your work being used in every aspect of life, and you are responsible for how it is developed and deployed in an environment. According to recent global surveys, a large percentage of software deployed around the world is poorly designed and executed and the people using it are unaware of the socially engineered risks of software exploitation. Software is not just about an executable deployed on a server; it is about adaptability, agility, accessibility, security, and intelligence.

A methodology is a set of guidelines and principles that can be tailored to a specific situation. It can also be a specific approach, with templates, forms, and even checklists used throughout the project or product lifecycle.

Note Consulting organizations use the term *project* for a work product delivered to enterprises.

Methodologies enable you to implement shared experiences and a ubiquitous language across diverse teams located geographically.

Agile methodologies introduced principles that put software development, quality, and collaboration above contracts and plans. This improved software quality and development approaches because now customers are involved in the requirements phase and development phase with a clear definition of what the business and customer wants.

© Shivakumar R Goniwada 2022
S. R. Goniwada, *Cloud Native Architecture and Design*, https://doi.org/10.1007/978-1-4842-7226-8_13

In previous chapters, you learned how to create a cloud native architecture and design cloud native systems. In this chapter, I will explain the methodologies you can use to develop cloud native systems. There are tons of books and articles on software engineering, which I am not going to rewrite or explain here. In this chapter, I will cover the details of how the software engineering methodologies relate to cloud native systems. In addition, I will explain how you can enable a culture of agility by using these development methodologies.

In this chapter, I will cover the following:

- Distributed agile methodology

- Feature-driven development

- Hypothesis-driven development

- Test-driven development

- Behavioral-driven development

Cloud Native and Traditional Application Engineering

The nature of the application development process has changed in recent years, especially with the evolution of cloud native services. This affects agility and automation of software engineering and, cloud native has pushed enterprises to adopt modern day technologies and process. This adoption of modern technologies help enterprises to meet the customer expectations and to develop faster to market.

This transformation in development methodology helps to move from the traditional to cloud native application development mindset and process.

The difference between traditional and cloud-enabled development methodologies is vast, and the application development process in a cloud environment provides larger operational and economic benefits by using platform as a service (PaaS).

Whether you are modernizing a legacy system or building a new one, you are likely using a PaaS environment. Enterprises are rapidly finding that cloud native application development offers numerous benefits over the traditional approach.

Cloud native is about how applications are developed and deployed, not where. Innovative software engineering is required to leverage all the benefits of cloud computing and mitigate its challenges strategically to push forward its advances.

As I mentioned in earlier chapters, cloud native systems are built upon using the cloud native elements with DevSecOps and agility, collaboration across global teams, and stakeholders.

The priorities of cloud native application development over traditional development are as follows:

- Speed to market, with an emphasis on quick turnaround of new services or changes to existing services. This is compared to slow traditional development methods, long-term development plans that assume underlying binaries, and business value that remains stable for a longer duration of time.

- Short, continuous development cycles, rather than long timeframes.

- Key pod culture with Conway's law compared to traditional resource mapping.

- Built on containers and services infrastructure utilized both in the cloud and on-premises rather than server-centric based on VMs and bare-metal servers.

- Feature-driven, hypothesis-driven, model-driven, test-driven, behavioral-driven compared to traditional requirements-based modeling.

Intelligent Software Engineering

As you know, 20th-century engineering is a thing of the past, and 21st-century engineering is evolving rapidly in all sectors of industry. For example, civil engineers have moved from building over nature to designing within nature, and industrial engineers have to consider the end-to-end lifecycle of their products from concept and design through manufacturing and service support. Today's engineering processes must be connected to the pulse of the customer's every move and understand them in real time. Design your application for outcomes and focus on driving velocity to value.

Engineering capabilities must help your clients with the following in mind:

- Creating new markets, not increasing market share

- Small, autonomous, self-organizing "2-PIZZA" teams with a culture of innovation, culture of governance, and culture discipline

- Creating automation to bring features to market faster

- Using cloud platforms

- Focusing on customer success and tying this to rewards

- Implementing a culture of go, not consensus: test, learn, repeat

- Delegated decision-making to the level of individual contributors

- Distributed code ownership to avoid perverse incentives

Table 13-1 illustrates the differences between traditional and cloud native. In the cloud native world, you need to use intelligent engineering for your customer, and you need to have the right mix of methodologies to follow to develop a cloud native application.

Table 13-1. *Traditional vs. Cloud Native Engineering*

Traditional Software Engineering	Cloud Native Intelligent Engineering
Product centric	Customer centric
Focus on predictability and efficiency	Focus on speed to value and innovation (fail fast)
Co-located teams	Distributed teams across regions and geographies
Design stand-alone products	Connect to an ecosystem of products
Structured, linear process	Faster, customer-centric, modeled agile process
Large batch deployment	Lean product management, push-based deployment, and single-click deployment (MVP)
Highly skilled, manual coding, testing and deployment	Automated coding, testing, deployment
On-premises development	Cloud-enabled development

The following are a few methodologies we'll cover in this chapter:

> *Hypothesis-driven development*: In the modern-day user experience, you need to create a prototype, test, and rebuild services and the user experience until it's acceptable by the user. Hypothesis-driven development helps you to develop an application by involving end customers.

Behavior-driven development: In present-day architecture, you are building for business, and you cannot complete your system architecture and development without the active participation of the business. The behavior-driven development helps you to develop an application by collaborating with stakeholders.

Feature-driven development: For modern-day applications, you need to develop an application that is customer-centric, iterative, and incremental, with the goal of tangible efficient software results. Feature-driven development helps you track progress and results.

Test-driven development: Writing test cases first before developing the code helps you to improve the quality of software. Test-driven development converts requirements to functional test cases. This helps provide more clarity for engineers to craft their code.

From Project to Product

The objective of every project is to deliver customer value, but how you deliver the customer value is most important. In projects, customer value has start and stop dates, which means the team stops supporting the project once it closes. Indirectly that is the end of the customer value, but it doesn't have to be.

The product mindset is to have continuous delivery of customer value, where there are no end dates and the team continues to support the customer value. In today's world, there is a dramatic shift from project to product.

A project is temporary in that it has a defined beginning and end, a defined scope of resources, and a defined set of requirements, and it doesn't address larger market share and new markets. On the other hand, a product is a good service, platform, or application that is created generally for sale to meet customer and business needs.

In a present-day cloud native architecture, major mindset shifts are required to move from executing projects to maintaining products, because of end-user expectations. Over time, your client might enter into a new market with a different culture and a different set of users and need to change how they engage a new set of users with business needs that change in response. If you have a project mindset, you might not have a historical record because resources are moved to other projects that need to address new user expectations.

Organization Transformation

You may have experienced many projects that have delays, low quality, no collaboration, or other issues. These kinds of projects have common problems such as the following:

- *Code changes*: This is the fear of making changes to the existing code, as the non-cloud native solution is hard to maintain or evolve or so fragile that the slightest changes can have a significant effect on the whole system.

- *No appropriate automation in the software delivery cycle*: This leads to a lot of manual effort that is needed to get new use cases into a working application deployed into an environment.

- *Nonproduction environments are limited and require more time to provide them*: This causes development efforts to be inefficient or partially wasted.

A few matured organizations are experimenting with new modern-day software engineering practices successfully and with great results. Companies like the Guardian, Netflix, Google, and Amazon can put new software into production in near real time by making small independent changes and a fully automated process of the development lifecycles. These changes impact only a small part of an application at a time. With all these changes, the companies save millions of dollars a month. For example, Netflix uses chaos engineering. This allows Netflix to proactively identify and resolve platform issues in production before they impact the customer. In addition, Sportify can create a whole agile pod team organization/culture that is inspiring others. These success stories help us define modern engineering.

The following are the benefits of embracing modern engineering:

- Faster to market; better user experience with hypothesis-driven development and the ability to transform new ideas into business value

- On-demand provision of environments; eases the nonfunctional testing

- Single-click deployment with continuous integration and delivery and infrastructure as a code

- Use of available PaaS services across cloud providers by using model-driven development

- Decentralization approach across teams in an organization

- Shift from delivery focus to value focus

- Engineering with observability as a service

Modern engineering can be a key enabler for business agility, allowing organizations to transform and move faster to compete in this rapidly changing business and technology landscape. It can transform new ideas into value quickly with the highest standards of quality.

Organizations transform because they're looking for business agility, aligned with these four dimensions: speed, quality, cost, and culture.

The following are the main drivers for successful transformation through modern engineering practices:

- *Change-oriented pod teams delivering in small increments*: These pod teams are cross-functional, including all functions, to deliver the required user stories. The team must consist of product owners, business analysts, architects, required SMEs, and cloud SMEs.

- *Lifecycle management and configuration management*: To remove the code change paralysis, the team must have the proper lifecycle and configuration management in place with clear ownership of every aspect of the technology system.

- *DevSecOps*: The manual process is more error-prone. The team must unleash the benefits of automation with a shift-left approach.

- *Automated tests with production-like environments*: Teams must conduct automated tests, early and often, in production configuration.

- *Software-defined infrastructure and automated deployments*: With this practice, the team can move their changes faster to market.

- *Resilient, self-healing, cloud native systems*: You must prepare software for failures, learn from failures, and build resilient, self-healing cloud native systems.

- *Observability and automated operations*: Implement observability as a service with automated operation principles.

Agile Software Development Methodologies

Agile software development methodologies were created by leading software professionals based on real-time experience developing software. They address many of the limitations of traditional development methodologies. As a result, this is the de facto standard for cloud native application development.

Agile methodologies have certain values and follow certain principles of software development. These were referenced in the Agile Manifesto and the 12 principles of agile software, written by the thought leaders who created the agile software development approach.

There are various methodologies available for developing a cloud native application, and each of these adheres to agile principles and values.

Hypothesis-Driven Development

As an example, say you wake up one day in the morning and hear something that sounds like crying outside of your window. You might think it is a baby who is crying outside. Your hypothesis is that a baby is crying. Then you open the door and look outside. You know ahead of time that if you see a baby crying, you're right, whereas if you see a playing baby, your hypothesis is wrong.

As another example, when you get into the office, you notice your end user isn't using the sidebar link on the website. You might think the link is not in the proper place or it is not visible enough to the user. You decide to correct this by increasing the visibility of the link or placing it in the right place. Then you test the UI using A/B testing. You know ahead of time that if you see a statistically significant increase in clicks from the end user who see a visible link, that was the problem, whereas if you don't see an increase, it wasn't. When you run a test and see significant improvement, then you decide to roll it out to all the users.

In these two examples (the crying baby and the website link), you used the scientific method to test a hypothesis and create an effective solutions. It is thinking about the development of new ideas, products, and services—even organizational change—as a service of experiments to determine whether an expected outcome will be achieved. The process is iteration upon iteration until a desirable outcome is obtained or the idea is determined to be not viable. This is called *hypothesis-driven development*.

Why Do You Need a Hypothesis?

This is an approach that provides a structured way to consolidate ideas and build a hypothesis based on objective criteria. It's also less costly for the system to test the prototype before actual implementation. Using this approach, you can implement the minimum viable product (MVP) model and identify what, how, and in which order testing should be done.

Methodology Steps

To facilitate a highly evolutionary approach, you need to use a hypothesis instead of requirements. Requirements are valuable when teams execute a well-known or understood phase of an initiative and can leverage well-understood practices to achieve the outcome, in other words, when something must be developed and delivered to the customer. The hypothesis is a provisional estimation that must be proven. If you disapprove a hypothesis, you need to pivot and create another set of hypotheses. When you use a hypothesis, you recognize customer expectations and needs and are constantly changing. To deliver what customers want at the speed that they demand, you must hypothesize and make data-based decisions. Experiment early and often, solicit feedback from customers about what works for them, and discard any features that provide little benefit to customers.

Figure 13-1 shows the scientific steps.

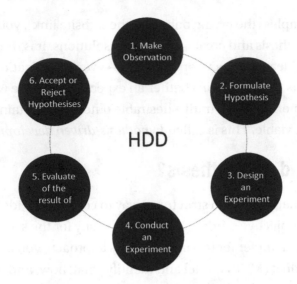

Figure 13-1. *Hypothesis-driven development steps*

Whether you are in the initial stage of your project or some other stage, there are always uncertain parts of an application, especially customer-facing applications, where you have ideas to further improve the existing product. To move forward, you'll need to turn the ideas into structured hypotheses where they can be tested before production. Automation is a must for successful HDD. The process of the HDD scientific steps consists of the following:

- Test and track hypothesis experiments, by applying a feature toggle approach.

- When defining a hypothesis, you need to define data to validate the hypothesis, i.e., how much evidence you'll need to make a decision.

- Test the hypothesis, and set up the test continually with automation to gather data for your decisions.

- Once you have a significant result, act on it; in other words, roll it out or roll it back. Note what worked and what didn't, and keep running experiments.

Every user story in your project does not require HDD; identify use cases where you require HDD.

The success or failure of the hypothesis is always a learning opportunity, no matter what the outcome is. Even if you can't prove the hypothesis, it provides valuable insight for another hypothesis.

Adopt a culture of hypothesis when you are developing a customer-facing and complex system. If a baseline test exists and the hypothesis asserts that an improvement to your service will be beneficial, you can conduct A/B testing to determine which option is best.

Hypothesis Example

Let's say you are building a small ecommerce application and expecting more interaction from social media and certain links in other pages. The targeted users are very active on social media and the Internet, and you want to increase your traffic.

> *Hypothesis*: Providing an image of your product on social media will increase the number of targeted users who visit your ecommerce application and try the product. The changes will be measured by an increase in social media referral traffic to the link that is cited from the ecommerce site and other websites.

> *Outcome*: In user stories that deliver a new feature and tasks that require the posting images in social media or sent directly to the customers along with the specification and make the user aware of the product.

Framing Hypothesis

"We believe that <this feature> will result in <the outcome>. We will know we have succeeded when <we see a measurable signal>."

- *We believe that <this feature>*: What functionality will you develop to test your hypothesis? By defining a test feature of the service that you are attempted to build, you identify the functionality and hypothesis you want to test.

- *Will result in <the outcome>*: What is the expected outcome of your experiment? What is the specific result to achieve by building the test capability?

- *We will know we have succeeded when <we see a measurable signal>*:
  What signals will indicate that the capability you have built is
  effective? What are key metrics you will measure to provide evidence
  that your experiment has succeeded and give us enough confidence
  to move to the next stage?

  Hypothesis: "We believe that if we write a blog on the feature of the
  product, people will want to buy it. We'll know we have succeeded
  when xxx people visit and click the link."

Culture of Hypothesis

Organizations must continuously practice and adopt a culture of hypothesis. You can
practice in several ways by establishing metrics, establishing success and failure criteria,
running multiple experiments continually by using automation, making data-based
decisions, socializing across the organization by using various analytical methods, and
considering a different model of experiments by using A/B testing.

Use metrics properly as these are essential to making data-based decisions, the
metrics such as key performance indicators (KPIs) are often used to measure the
hypothesis.

Test-Driven Development

First, you write a test, and then you write code to make the test pass. This approach to
building software encourages good design, produces testable code, and keeps you away
from over-engineering the system because of flawed assumptions. The problem you are
facing in today's world is poorly written services and failure to meet actual needs.

"TDD is a technique for improving the software's internal quality, whereas
acceptance TDD helps you keep your product's external quality on track by giving it to
the correct features and functionality."

TDD is a way of developing software that encourages good design and is a
disciplined process that helps you to avoid programming errors. TDD does so by making
you write small, automated tests, which eventually build up an effective alarm system for
protecting your code from regression.

The primary goal of TDD is to make the code cleaner, simpler, and bug-free. This is
made possible because of the test-first approach adopted in TDD. Tests are likely to fail
in the TDD process since the tests, specifically unit tests, are developed even before the

code development. To pass the test, you have to develop and refactor the code. With this, you can avoid duplication of code since you're writing a small amount of code at a time to satisfy the outcome of the tests.

Why TDD?

TDD will help shorten the programming feedback where tests are written before the functional code so that developers receive feedback on the quality of the code faster. TDD highly focuses on critical analysis and design because engineers cannot create the functional code without truly understanding what the desired result should be and how to test it. The process is also mandating that the code should not be written without the tests. This ensures higher-quality software.

The benefits of using TDD are as follows:

- TDD enables immediate feedback on the developed components.

- The turnaround time for the defect resolution is significantly shorter.

- TDD provides significant code coverage. TDD helps to make sure that every feature developed is wrapped with tests, resulting in increased test coverage.

- TDD helps to identify the problem in code quickly.

TDD Cycle

The TDD cycle as shown in Figure 13-2 is expressed as Red, Green, and Refactor and repeats for each unit of code.

- *Red*: Create a test that makes it fail.

- *Green*: Make the test pass by writing code.

- *Refactor*: Update the code to remove redundancy, and improve the design while confirming that the tests still pass after the update.

While using TDD, ensure 100 percent code coverage. The test-early principle helps you in detecting and fixing bugs early in the lifecycle of the product.

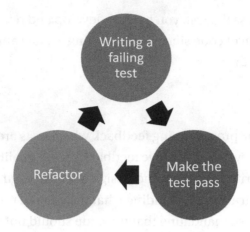

Figure 13-2. *Test-driven development cycle*

Steps of TDD

Kent Beck is the creator of Extreme Programming, a software development methodology that avoids rigid formal specifications for a collaborative and iterative design process. He sums up the five steps of TDD as follows:

1. Quickly add a test.

2. Run all tests and see the new one fail. Since there is no code yet to make the test pass, this test will fail.

3. Make a little change to pass the test as quickly as possible.

4. Run all tests and see them all succeed.

5. Refactor to remove duplication.

In the first step, you need to write a test. In the second step, you need to record a requirement as a test, and finally, you need to design the question and answers. The questions should be like the following:

- Does the method name reveal the intent?

- What are the parameters of the method?

- What is the outcome of this method?

The answers to these questions become the design decision that you express in code. In the third step, you always need to write the simplest possible code that makes the test pass. This allows you to keep your option open for evolutionary design.

Writing a failing test is a way of testing the test. If the tests all pass, it gives you feedback about your services that there are no known problems. By writing tests to expose a deficiency, that helps to identify the problem. Everything else is a best-painted picture. Ask yourself the following questions when you are writing a fail test:

- What is the responsibility of the system under test?

- What is there to observe?

- How is correctness defined?

You make your test pass with the simplest code. Is it too hard to pass the test? Then you drop back to changing your test and making it easier to pass.

TDD is a simple technique, as it has only a few steps to follow. However, in a real implementation, the steps are not that easy to follow since engineers need to be very disciplined. To get all the benefits of TDD, you should follow each step.

Factors to Consider for TDD

The following factors need to be considered while implementing TDD:

- Use the appropriate unit testing tool suitable for your project needs.

- Use the appropriate mock frameworks and code coverage tools.

- All the team members must agree on what level of testing occurs before integrating code to the source repository. You must restrict the tested code to check it in to the source repository.

- When the build breaks, what steps should be taken, and who will be involved?

- Use a proper naming convention for tests.

Drawbacks of TDD

TDD is good for cloud native applications, but it has a few drawbacks.

- It fits very well with unit test tools but does not scale with web-based GUI or data-driven development.

- Writing and maintaining an excessive number of tests costs time.

- For complex cases, the test cases are difficult to calculate.

Behavior-Driven Development

Behavior-driven development (BDD) is a process designed to aid the management and development teams by encouraging collaboration across roles to build and share an understanding of the problem to be solved and by working in rapid, small iterations to increase feedback and the flow of value. It improves the communication across the business, development, and support teams and ensures all development projects remain focused on delivering what the business needs while meeting all the requirements of the user.

BDD has evolved from the TDD. It brings techniques and principles from TDD and domain-driven design (DDD) to utilize features of these approaches and focus on delivering the prioritized business value and a behavior-based vocabulary. BDD is not replacing your agile process, but it enhances it. It is a set of plugins for your existing process that will make your team more able to deliver on the promise of agile.

BDD aids in system implementation from a stakeholder or product owner point of view through the use of a given-when-then-style of representing tests or acceptance test criteria associated with user stories. It offers guidance on organizing conversations between developers, testers, and domain specialists.

How BDD Helps You to Solve Problems

If you are not writing well-crafted and well-designed software, you'll end up with unreliable software that's hard to change and maintain, and if you don't know what you are building and fail to understand what features the business needs, you'll end up with a system that no one wants.

TDD, clean coding, and automated testing help you to guarantee a successful project, but what you are developing must also benefit its users and business stakeholders.

Applications should not be developed in a vacuum. The applications are part of the broader business strategy, and they need to align with the business goals of an organization. At the end of the day, the software solution you are developing needs to help users to use it effectively.

BDD helps you define the business problem that you want to solve, gives a business value to the organization, and helps to answer the specific question of how the problem will be solved. That is what behavior you expect, and more important it provides a ubiquitous language for all stakeholders.

TDD focuses on the technical architecture and the code, whereas BDD is focused on the business function and system behavior as outlined in the business story acceptance criteria. In both cases, the unit tests are written before writing the code.

BDD Principles and Practices

Here are some tips:

> *Focus on features that deliver business value*: Avoid heavy uplifting of the requirements specification. Rather, attempt to pinpoint all the requirements and engage customers or business stakeholders to progressively build a common understanding of what features they should create.

> *Work together to specify features*: BDD is a highly collaborative practice with various stakeholders who work together with end users to define and specify features. Team members draw on their individual experience and know-how.

> *Embrace uncertainty*: Rather than finalizing the requirements at the discovery of the project, BDD assumes that the requirements, or more precisely, their understanding of the requirements, will evolve and change throughout the lifecycle of the project.

> *Illustrate features with concrete examples*: BDD helps you to work together with the users and other stakeholders to define stories and scenarios of what users expect this feature to deliver, with a concrete example that illustrates the key outcome of the feature.

> *Don't write automated tests; write an executable specification*: Write the executable specification as an automated test that illustrates and verifies how the system delivers a specific business requirement. These automated tests run as part of DevSecOps and run on each change.

BDD Process

As I mentioned, BDD is an advanced version of TDD, where "test first" agile testing practices are clubbed together by defining tests before, or as part of, specifying system behavior. This is a collaborative process that creates a shared understanding of the requirements between the business and development teams.

BDD is a collaborative approach used to test any application or service in a cloud native organization and supports a team-centric workflow. Figure 13-3 shows the process, which can be continued in parallel with the development phase.

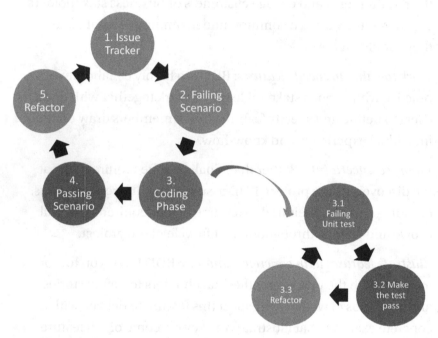

Figure 13-3. *Behavioral-driven development process*

This approach uses real data in test along with the expected result. The data change is only in the feature files, not in the implementation code. With the use of a simple and natural language syntax, BDD breaks down complex requirements. BDD is more about collaboration and communication, and feature files can be written by anyone who has good knowledge of the domain requirements.

BDD Specification

BDD leverages a user story as the basic unit of functionality, and the acceptance criteria includes required components of a user story. It defines the scope of the user story's behavior and provides a shared definition of done.

Each user story must have the following components:

- Name

- Narrative

- Acceptance criteria or scenarios

Example

Name: Product returns from the ecommerce application go back into the stock.

Narrative: To keep track of the stock, "as a distributor, I want to add items back to stock when they are returned."

Scenarios: Multiple scenarios are possible.

Scenario 1: "**Refunded** stocks should be returned to stock; **given** a customer previously brought a pair of 34-inch blue jeans **and** I have currently 10 34-inch blue jeans in stock, when the customer returns the pair of jeans for a refund, then I should have 12 34-inch blue jeans in stock."

Scenario 2: "**Replaced** items should be returned to stock; **given** that a customer buys pair of blue jeans and I have 10 34-inch blue jeans in stock and 10 36-inch and 32-inch blue and black jeans in stock, when the customer returns the pair of jeans for a replacement of 32-inch black jeans, then I should have 8 32-inch black jeans in stock and 12 34-inch blue jeans, and there is no change in the rest of the stock."

Transition to BDD

The following steps help you to transition to BDD from an existing process:

- Coach the business on BDD practices and the expectations from the business stakeholders on how to collaborate, the time required, and how to read the BDD reports.

- Prepare the functional team on how to write scenarios/behavior stories.

- Train teams to do the following:

    - Establish an understanding of BDD. The aim of the transition to BDD is to reduce the effort in the unit, regression, and functional testing.

    - Understand that development should be based on the scenarios or behaviors provided by the functional team.

- Educate development team and/or testing team to write BDD automation code for scenarios.

- Gradually implement BDD, starting with functional teams followed by the development team and then by the testing team.

- Use BDD to test main path scenarios and other test practices for testing border conditions.

Benefits of BDD

The following are the benefits of BDD:

Reduced waste: BDD is all about focusing the development effort on discovering and delivering the features that will provide business value and avoiding those that don't.

Collaboration: BDD offers more precise guidance on organizing the conversion between all the required stakeholders.

Ubiquitous language: All the stakeholders understand the same language from the requirements to deployment.

Business value: BDD focuses on building features with demonstrable business value and not wasting effort on features of little value.

Easy to change: BDD allows you to easily change and extend your system. Living documentation is generated from the executable specification that is understood by all the stakeholders.

Faster time to market: Comprehensive automated tests speed up the release cycles. You use the acceptance test as a starting point and spend your time more productively and efficiently on exploratory tests.

Tests: Reduce the time on regression tests to promote incremental development, and obtain coverage beyond unit testing.

Drawbacks of BDD

The drawback of BDD is more business involvement and collaboration. BDD is based on conversation and feedback across all the stakeholders including end users. If stakeholders are unwilling to participate in the conversation and collaborate, it will hard to get benefits from BDD.

Requirements: BDD requirements are difficult and require a special skill to write requirements. Poorly written tests can lead to higher test maintenance costs.

It doesn't work with the waterfall model: BDD doesn't work well with the waterfall model. In a waterfall model, each team works in a silo, and it's difficult to collaborate.

Tools: BDD uses tools that are not designed for use in large, complex projects that are difficult to customize.

Feature-Driven Development

Feature-driven development (FDD) is an iterative and incremental software development approach that combines several practices of developing client-valued features to deliver quality. It delivers frequent, tangible working results, via an accurate and meaningful progress, within a stipulated time. Features are an important part of FDD. A *feature* is generally a small client-valued piece of functionality expressed usually in the form of an action, or the result of an object. For example, validate the password of a user: the action is *validate*, the result is the *password*, and the object is the *user*.

Why FDD?

In software engineering, especially in a cloud native application, communication is taking place constantly at all levels of the software lifecycle. As the size of your system grows, the complexity of the system can become uncontrollable and untraceable.

FDD decomposes the entire problem domain into tiny problems, which can be solved in a small period of time. The decomposed problems are independent of each other and reduce the need for communication.

FDD splits the project into iterations so that the gap and time between analysis and test are reduced; this is a shift-left approach of errors.

FDD broadens the concept of quality, so you test not only the code but also things such as coding standards, measuring audits, and metrics of code.

FDD Process

FDD defines milestones that mark the progress made on each feature. As shown in Figure 13-4, FDD consists of five processes.

1. *Develop an overall model*: Define a high-level domain for the system under development. The idea is for both domain and development members of the team to gain a good, shared understanding of relationships and interactions. In doing so, the whole team learns to communicate with each other. The object model developed in this step is breadth instead of depth. Depth is added iteratively in the lifecycle.

2. *Build a feature list*: Create a list of the state changes and interactions required, grouping them into feature sets and subject areas for planning. In this step, FDD defines a feature as a small, client-valued function expressed in the form of <action><result><object> (for example, "calculate the total of a sale"). FDD organizes its features into a three-level hierarchy called a *feature list*.

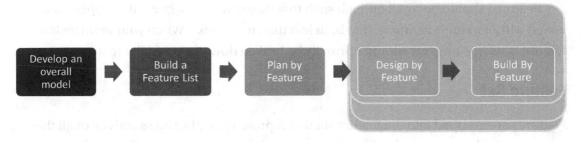

Figure 13-4. FDD process steps

3. *Plan by feature*: Agree on an initial schedule and assign
    responsibilities for each class and feature set. The planning
    team initially sequences the feature sets representing activities
    by relative business value. The feature set is also assigned to
    the scrum team, which is responsible for delivery. The risk and
    dependencies will be identified in this phase.

4. *Design by feature*: Create an initial sequence diagram that defines
    system interactions for each feature. The lead selects a group of
    features from one feature set that may be developed in a time-bound
    manner and forms a work package around those features that acts as
    a unit of integration with feature sets produced by the feature teams.

5. *Build by feature*: Develop and test the client-valued functionality
    to the point it can be deployed. After successful testing and code
    inspection, the completed feature will be promoted to the main
    build, where it will be verified and readied for release.

Feature Specification

A *feature* is a small slice of functionality producing a result of a value to a client, typically
expressed in the following form:

<action> the <result> [of| to |by| for| from|] a(n) <object>

<object> is a person, place, or thing including roles, for example, "Calculate the
total inventory," "Authorize the sales transaction of a client," "Provision credit card
transaction," etc.

Features are to FDD as user stories are to scrum. They are the primary source of
requirements and the primary input into the team's planning efforts.

517

Features should be small enough such that they can be designed, developed, and tested within a single iteration, that is, in less than two weeks. When your team feels a feature is taking longer, it should normally be broken down into smaller features.

Feature Set

Features are grouped into the feature set that represents the business activity or all the steps required to achieve a business objective. A feature set has the following form:

> *<action>-ing a(n) <object>*

Example include "making a transaction," "adding a product to the catalog," etc.

Subject Area

Feature sets are grouped into subject areas, subdomains of larger system, and are named with this form:

> *<object> management*

> Examples include "inventory management," "customer management," "product management," etc.

Benefits of FDD

With the evolution of architecture, software development requires a slice of features to be available in production almost immediately. FDD helps you to define and develop a cloud native application easily and provides the following benefits:

- FDD provides a client-centric, model-driven approach for ensuring the frequent delivery of client-valued functionality.

- FDD concentrates on a small slice of design to enable the team to design, develop, and test.

- FDD is an effective approach for getting services to market faster.

- It offers improved communication across various stakeholders in a team.

- It works well with large-scale, long-term, or ongoing projects.

Drawbacks of FDD

While FDD offers a faster to market with slices by simplifying complex projects, there are a few drawbacks.

- FDD is not ideal for small projects.

- FDD places a high dependency on one role; this leader is required to coordinate across teams.

- FDD provides no written documentation to clients.

- It may not work well with the older systems.

- You might lose sight of your customers and instead only think in terms of features.

Architecture in the Agile Methodology

Architecture in agile projects can be built incrementally in sprints and can be moved into the design and develop phase or into another technical architecture sprint to implement. The first few sprints are dedicated to creating an overall architectural blueprint and later slices go into subsequent sprints for the detailed architecture and design.

Sprint 0 is used for the planning and preparation of architecture streams. The typical sprint duration for architecture is two to four weeks.

Perform the following tasks in architecture sprints:

- Conduct sprint planning to determine the technical requirements that can be addressed and how they should be addressed. The dependencies between various services need to be considered. The requirements should be documented in the backlog with priorities.

- For each architecture sprint, suggest creating a separate sprint backlog that is derived from the overall integrated product backlog.

- Perform the required testing before moving into the next sprint.

- Continually manage the scope of the project by evaluating and updating the product backlog.

- Transition the sprint deliverables to the application development to develop the code.

519

Waterfall to Agile Transformation

The transition from a waterfall methodology to agile should not be a sudden change or done in a day; it requires commitment and preparation. You need to carry out the following before transitioning to agile:

- *Culture of agile*: Commitment from management is a must; every project in an enterprise has to be executed to be aligned to the organization goals; hence, it is essential to commit sponsors or executives.

- *Training*: Without a skilled resource, it is not possible to transform, so training plays an important role in creating agile awareness and developing cultural shifts.

- *Coaching*: As you move from waterfall to agile, it is essential to have an expert who can work with the team and coach them.

- *Communication*: The Agile Manifesto states "individual and interaction" over "process and tools," and hence communication plays a significant role for quicker turnaround time and a collaborative approach in agile.

- *Infrastructure*: Infrastructure plays a key role when you move from waterfall to agile. The infrastructure setup like source code, environments, automation, etc., should be available.

- *Metrics*: Agile adopts a minimalist approach toward metrics. It states you should measure everything required, but do not over-measure. These metrics help you to track the progress of the project and take corrective actions.

- *Estimation*: Estimation has to be precise since agile recommends projects to be executed at a sustainable pace.

- *Tools*: To get started with agile, it is recommended you use a set of tools that are required.

Figure 13-5 shows the steps you need to follow for transitioning to agile.

Figure 13-5. Waterfall to agile transition steps

- *Create a transition strategy*: The first step is to create a transition strategy for individual projects. Every project will have its transition strategy, which will differ from project to project.

- *Mobilize the transition*: Create a transition plan that will detail the timeline along with the milestones of each stage.

- *Implement releases*: Define the release structure.

- *Implement agile practices*: Start implementing a few basic agile practices so that the team can gradually adapt to the changes in the project execution process.

- *Continue with agile*: Introduce advanced agile practices.

Summary

As the complexity of software development in projects grows, the only way to maintain the viability of your build and ensure success is to have development practices grow with it. While the individual practices and processes of TDD, HDD, BDD, and FDD are all valuable in their own right, it is when they collaborate with each other that they provide a value to the cloud native journey.

In this chapter, I covered the software engineering principles for cloud native applications and explained how organizations can transform from traditional to intelligent engineering models. The way forward is product thinking, not project thinking, because you need to think about the end user's behavior approaches, etc. I provided sample real-time examples of HDD and BDD scenarios.

Feature-driven development is a process for helping teams produce frequent, concrete, working results. It uses small blocks of functionality, called features. FDD organizes small functions into a business-related feature set. It focuses on getting a result every two to three weeks.

BDD is the process designed to aid in the management and delivery of cloud native software development projects by improving communication between the development team and business team and ensuring all related projects remain focused on delivery. The benefits of this approach are to help you to trace back to business objectives and develop a shared understanding of all the stakeholders with ubiquitous languages.

HDD follows the idea, hypothesis, design, experimentation, and scale steps. An iterative HDD process allows the engineering team to plan and conduct experiments; observe, analyze, and learn from results; and integrate the correct changes. This helps reduce uncertainty and improve knowledge. The engineering team must prioritize experimenting with the most uncertain aspects of the system.

TDD helps you to write tests and code. Next, it helps you to create optimized bug-free code and helps engineers to analyze and understand client requirements and request clarity. This helps you to test important new features in present-day scenarios.

CHAPTER 14

Enterprise Cloud Native Automation

Software engineering's main objective is to unify the development of software (Dev) and subsequent operations (Ops), and it is this combination of cultural values, practices, and tools that allow an organization to deliver software applications quickly.

DevOps is a set of rules, principles, or manifestos that are used to increase automation as the code is developed, built, and deployed. Many concepts that are part of the DevOps pipeline, such as continuous integration (CI) and continuous delivery (CD), are used by various teams that do not follow DevOps completely. A complete DevOps pipeline recommends process automation to be used from the discovery phase through the deployment, infrastructure, and operation phases.

DevSecOps is primarily the addition of security, performance, and stability to the DevOps cycle. DevSecOps is built on top of DevOps and adds extra checks and a shift-left approach at each stage.

In this chapter, I am not covering the entire DevSecOps story, because there are tons of books, articles and whitepapers available. The purpose of this chapter is to guide you through the best practices and how to leverage cloud development platforms on your journey of cloud native application development.

In this chapter, I will explain the following:

- DevSecOps pipeline

- DevSecOps and the cloud

- How to embrace a cloud development service to accelerate your development

- How to scale DevSecOps into your enterprise

523

© Shivakumar R Goniwada 2022
S. R. Goniwada, *Cloud Native Architecture and Design*, https://doi.org/10.1007/978-1-4842-7226-8_14

Introduction

Innovation and continuity never stop. During the COVID-19 crisis, teams were sitting at home and working in silos in remote places. Businesses must ensure their workforce can still develop and deploy a solution even while remote, and the DevOps methodology addresses these challenges. It is a popular way of working in many businesses and provides a framework to coordinate your IT teams. It brings together your business, development, and operations teams, eliminating the barriers caused by physical location, organizational functionality, and business goals.

Continuous is one word that you will often use in your projects when discussing development, deployment, and operation. Almost everything in automation is continuous, whether it is continuous integration, continuous delivery, continuous testing, continuous infrastructure, continuous observation, and continuous operation.

As shown in Figure 14-1, DevOps is the main pillar of automation; it builds a culture of trust, collaboration, and continuous improvement. As a culture, it holistically views the development process and everyone involved, like developers, testers, operations, security, infrastructure, and client teams. DevOps is not just about tooling; it's also about people working on a project.

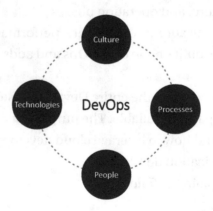

Figure 14-1. *DevOps pillars*

> *Culture*: There is strong communication and integration between all stakeholders.
>
> *Processes*: An automated deployment pipeline is integrated with security reviews and testing, with a strong feedback loop to the development team and operations.

Technologies: There is an advanced combination of open source and commercial tools assessing various aspects of the application.

People: It is a philosophy that focuses on engineers and how they can better work together to produce great software.

The DevOps culture brings nirvana in the development process. It helps the organization with the following:

- Faster time to market to gain market advantage

- High quality to detect failures to fix them early

- Adopting changes based on business demands

- Adopting changes based on technology evolution

- Effective collaboration and communication

- Integrating feedback effectively in the development process to get better

- Adopting improvement and innovations

- Avoiding an error-prone manual process

- Adopting shift left

DevOps Today and Tomorrow

Coined in 2009, DevOps has evolved over the years. Figure 14-2 illustrates the journey of DevSecOps.

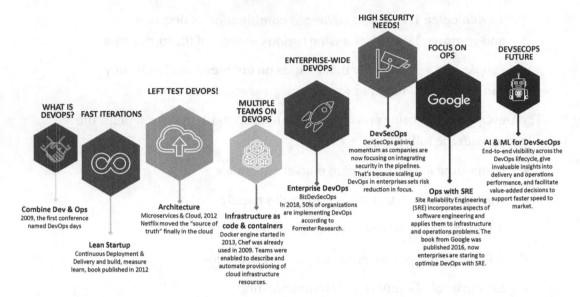

Figure 14-2. *DevSecOps journey*

As shown in Figure 14-3, today DevOps is about culture, automation, lean, measurement, and sharing. Most organizations have already adopted and matured using this model, due to technology disruptions and business disruptions. Today's DevOps may not be able to meet disruptions in the future, though. Therefore, DevOps is rapidly branching into feature streams focused on cloud, security, data science, machine learning, artificial intelligence, and lean ways of working.

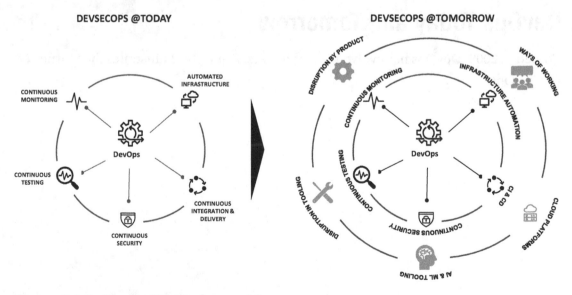

Figure 14-3. *DevSecOps today and future*

In present and modern-day architecture, with the adoption of multicloud and containerization, enterprises are required to embrace a new-age tool and learn new ways of working. It makes the DevOps pipeline crucial to a business, which needs to maintain a development pipeline with a new set of tools and quickly configure cloud development pipelines.

Here are some trends occurring in the world of cloud native and in regard to its relationship with DevOps:

- There's an increase in the variety of cloud services that are leading to multicloud and hybrid cloud platforms.

- Data science and data integration are embedding data pipelines in the data lifecycle for speed and accuracy of the analytics and model management.

- More business involvement is required in software engineering along with the development team and operations teams. This requires a foster collaboration between all stakeholders so the organization can deliver software quickly and efficiently by using DevBizOps.

- This requires intelligence across the application lifecycle to focus on building and releasing best-in-class products by quickly using AIOps.

- Automation of the network is important along with infrastructure; therefore, you need to include DevOps best practices in network operations that drive network infrastructure as code to achieve faster delivery by using NetOps.

The future of DevOps requires "continuous everything." This means that security, compliance, network, "-ilities," and all other critical software components are automatically and continually implemented without compromising any release process.

From DevOps to DevSecOps

In DevOps, development teams are more agile. The product goes to market quicker, the team innovates faster, there is continuous everything, and there are measures everywhere, but security is still segmented and siloed away from the core software engineering functions. But as the number of cyberattacks increases, more compliance products are exposing all sorts of functionality across geographies, so security cannot remain separate from the DevOps process. Security must be integrated early and throughout the software engineering lifecycle.

You can enable DevSecOps by adding security compliance checks in the DevOps cycle. This helps you to address the principles of a single pane of glass, design for security, etc.

- Tightly integrate security tools and processes throughout the DevOps pipeline.

- Automate core security tasks by embedding security controls early on in the software development lifecycle.

- Implement continuous monitoring and remediation of security defects across the application lifecycle including development and maintenance.

The following are the benefits of DevSecOps in the pipeline:

- DevSecOps implements the secure by design principle by using automated security reviews such as static application security testing (SAST) and dynamic application security testing (DAST).

- Security issues are detected and remediated during development phases, which increase the speed of delivery and enhances quality of software components.

- In DevSecOps, security auditing, monitoring, and notification systems are automated and continuously monitored, which enhances the compliance in an application.

- By integrating security in software engineering and operation, engineering fosters collaboration across teams.

Driver for Shift-Left Security

The shift-left security approach has many benefits including cost efficiency, shorter release cycles, and better code quality, and it is able to provide the following:

- *Business risk reduction*: Test early on in the software engineering cycle, and address and prevent vulnerabilities before deploying to production; this significantly reduces business risk.

- *Faster release cycles*: Security testing, both SAST and DAST, should be integrated and automated as part of the pipeline to enable quicker release to the production.

- *Better code quality*: Addressing defects early or preventing defects from being introduced results in higher code quality.

Automation Principles and Best Practices

The principles and practices of DevOps help your enterprises to innovate with greater efficiency and agility. In this section, I will provide few practices and identify problems they eliminate. Along with this, I will touch upon cloud principles that help to achieve continuous operation in public, private, and hybrid clouds.

- *Collaborative environment*: Use the right tools to enhance the collaborative environment and create the right communication among all stakeholders.

- *Eliminate waste*: Eliminating waste is important in lean processes. Unnecessary functionality, code, or effort is wasteful. Delaying the delivery of value to customers and inefficient processes are other examples of software development waste.

- *Adopt agility and focus more on automation*: Adopt agile development methodologies as explained in the previous chapter and follow the automation in every cycle of software engineering.

- *Focus on shortened feedback loops*: Start the feedback mechanism early in the software engineering lifecycle.

- *Create knowledge*: Teams share knowledge within the team and across teams, through code reviews, documentation, learning sessions, training, and collaboration with Confluence tools that can be used as a knowledge database.

- *Common and shared goals across all stakeholders*: Ensure that the entire team and all relevant stakeholders, including business owners, are engaged in deriving common and shared goals.

- *Shift-left security*: Enable an end-to-end DevSecOps capability by integrating security earlier in the software development and delivery.

- *Everything as code*: Enable consistency, automation, and repeatability by adopting an as-code approach across the DevSecOps pipeline encompassing infrastructure, configuration, security policies, compliance validation, and testing as code.

- *Tooling optimization*: Optimize the use of all DevSecOps support tooling. Enable logging whenever possible to get a holistic view of the pipeline and application. Ensure testing remains in compliance with regulatory requirements.

- *Self-service*: Enable self-serviceability with users provisioning their services (i.e., compute, storage, environments) and empower them with tools to make low-impact changes directly without IT support.

- *Governance approach*: Adopt federated governance based on outcomes. Track and measure DevOps. Utilize enterprise-wide KPIs to monitor progress, applied to both DevOps and traditional SDLC so the performance improvements of DevOps will be measured.

- *Continuous improvement*: There is no full stop on anything; it is a continuous evolution. Therefore, focus on hypothesis-driven improvements and optimization of flows.

- *Deployment process*: Adopt a zero-touch, zero-downtime deployment with A/B testing enabled and automatic rollback of failed changes.

Site Reliability Engineering

Site reliability engineering (SRE) creates a bridge between development and operations by applying software engineering best practices. SRE was first introduced in 2003 by Google engineers. SRE is way of thinking about and approaching production. It is a set of principles and practices. SRE is aimed at developing automated solutions for operational aspects such as monitoring, performance, capacity planning, and disaster response.

SRE helps teams to determine what new features are launched and when by using SLAs to define the required reliability of the system through SLI and SLO.

DevOps is an approach to culture, automation, and platform design that delivers increased business value and responsiveness through high-quality service delivery. SRE can be considered an implementation of DevOps. Like DevOps, SRE is about team culture and relationships. Both SRE and DevOps work to bridge the gap between the development and operations teams to deliver higher quality and faster services.

According to Google, the following are the types of SRE team implementation:

- *Kitchen sink, aka "everything SRE"*: This describes an SRE team where the scope of services or workflows covered is usually unbounded.

- *Infrastructure*: These teams focus on behind-the-scenes efforts. A common implementation includes maintaining shared services (such as a Kubernetes cluster) or maintaining common components (like CI/CD, monitoring, etc.) built on top of the cloud.

- *Tools*: A tools-only SRE team tends to focus on building software that help engineers to measure, maintain, and improve system reliability.

- *Product/application*: The SRE team works to improve the reliability of a critical application or business area.

- *Embedded*: SRE is embedded with the development team, usually one per developer team.

- *Consulting*: SRE is similar to consulting work of any organization, but the difference is that the consulting SRE team tends to avoid changing the customer code and configuring the services in scope.

DevSecOps

This section covers DevSecOps in more detail.

Continuous Integration

As shown in Figure 14-4, CI is the base of the DevSecOps culture of transformation that automates the integration of code changes from multiple pod teams into a single software project. CI is the basic pipeline of the entire DevSecOps adoption. The primary benefit of adopting CI is that it saves you time during development by automating your code merges, unit tests, code reviews, and builds.

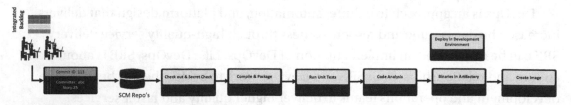

Figure 14-4. *Continuous integration*

CI involves making incremental code changes and continuously integrating on a frequent, regular basis. In this process, small changes are made to code by an engineer, and that code is subsequently checked into the source code repository. When the code is checked in, an automated build is typically triggered.

Continuous Delivery

As shown in Figure 14-5, CD is the ability of an organization to release changes to users quickly and in a sustainable and repeatable way. When CI completes, the CD begins. It essentially automates the delivery of applications to specific environments including the development, testing, and production environments.

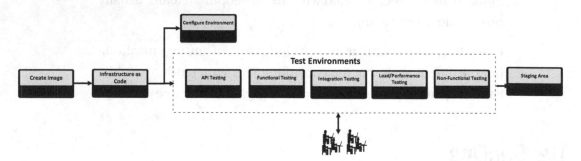

Figure 14-5. *Continuous delivery*

CD helps you to automate testing beyond just unit tests so they can verify application updates across multiple dimensions before deploying them into an environment. These tests include API, UI, load, functional, integration, reliability testing, etc. This helps your team to thoroughly validate updates and pre-emptively discover issues.

Continuous Deployment

As shown in Figure 14-6, continuous deployment (CD) takes continuous delivery (CD) one step further. In continuous deployment, all the code is built and tested and then pushed to nonproduction environments. There can be multiple parallel and various testing before certifying the quality of software.

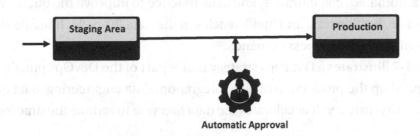

Figure 14-6. *Continuous deployment*

In continuous deployment, the software is delivered to the staging area along with test automation. When done properly, the software application should be in a state that it can be deployed to production at any time. Continuous deployment merely automates the final step so that all changes are automatically deployed to the production environment. Practically deploying to production depends on the software type and organizational maturity because it requires certain approvals from relevant stakeholders. In continuous deployment, you are going to automate the approval and push binaries into the production environment.

DataOps

"DataOps is a collaborative data management practices focused on improving communication, integration, and automation of data flows between data managers and data consumers across an organization."

—Gartner

"The goal of DataOps is to create predictable delivery and change management of data, data models, and related artifacts. DataOps seeks to reduce the end-to-end cycle time of data analytics, from the origin of ideas to the literal creation of charts, graphs, and models that create values."

—Gartner

DevOps analytics turns data from DevOps tools into insights that aid in decision-making. It also gives stakeholders visibility into various DevOps practices, helping you to identify strengths and opportunities for improvement across every aspect of the adoption process. For example, the adoption owners can find the root cause of a bottleneck in software agility much faster among large application portfolios using DevOps analytics.

It is an automated, collaborative, and agile practice to improve the quality and eliminate waste, bottlenecks, and inefficiencies in the data lifecycle. It breaks data silos and rapidly meets new business demands.

Figure 14-7 illustrates a DataOps strategy that is part of the DevOps pipeline and strives to speed up the production of data integration, data engineering, data quality, and data security/privacy. It accelerates the data lifecycle to reduce the time for data analytics.

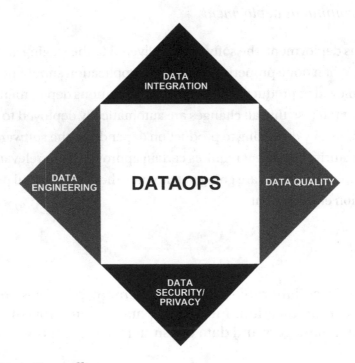

Figure 14-7. *DataOps pillars*

The goal of DataOps is to streamline the design, development, and maintenance of applications based on data and analytics. It seeks to improve the way the data is managed and products are developed and coordinates with all the relevant stakeholders.

One thing you need to remember is that DataOps is not just DevOps applied to data analytics. DataOps communicates the data analytics to achieve what software engineering wants to attain with DevOps. DataOps can yield an order-of-magnitude improvement in quality and cycle time when data teams utilize new tools and methodologies.

DataOps Principles

The following are a few DataOps principles defined by the DataOps Manifesto. These principles help you to configure DataOps as part of the DevSecOps pipeline.

- *Value working analytics*: This primary measure of data analytics performance is the degree to which insightful analytics are delivered, incorporating accurate data atop a robust framework and system.

- *Continuous interactions*: Customers, analytics teams, and operations must work together continually throughout the project.

- *Self-organize*: Analytics insight, algorithms, architectures, requirements, and designs are well-defined by a self-organized team.

- *Analytics is code*: DataOps uses a variety of available tools to access, integrate, model, and visualize data. At a basic level, these tools generate code and configurations that describe the action taken upon data to deliver insight.

- *Version everything*: You need to reproduce the result, so version everything.

- *Quality*: The pipeline should be built with a foundation capable of automatically detecting irregularities and security issues in code.

- *Improve cycle time*: You should strive to minimize the time and effort to turn a customer's need into an analytic idea. Create it in development, release it as a repeatable production process, and finally refactor and reuse the product.

DataOps Pipeline

DataOps is an operation for data analytics and works similarly to DevOps. It can yield an order-of-magnitude improvement in quality and cycle time when data teams utilize new tools and methodologies. As you already know, DevOps optimizes the application software engineering delivery and deployment. Similarly, DataOps optimizes analytics software in data engineering delivery and data operation. DataOps includes DevOps and other methodologies that apply to managing the enterprise data operations pipeline.

DataOps builds upon the DevOps development model, as shown in Figure 14-8. DevOps works on continuous integration with the build, check, and continuous delivery with automated tests. Similar to DevOps, the DataOps orchestrates the data pipeline from the data ingestion to data analytics, and the pipeline consists of many steps like Data Ingestion, Data Integration, Data Preparation etc as shown in Figure 14-8. An orchestrator is a tool that controls the execution of each step as shown in Figure 14-8.

For example, the orchestrator may create containers and invoke runtime processes like machine learning models to analyze data, transfer data from one step to another, and monitor pipeline execution.

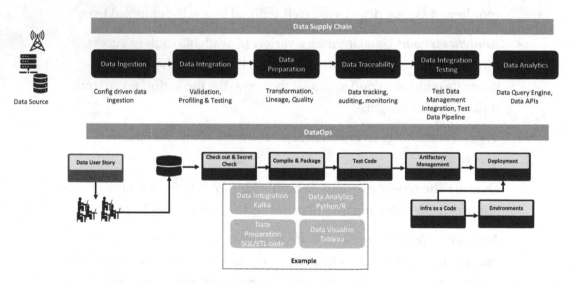

Figure 14-8. *DataOps pipeline*

The data supply chain represents the flow of data from source to consumer by using various stages.

Data ingestion: This includes the inputs into the data supply chain from a source like social medial, IoT, CRM, etc.

Data integration: This includes integrating data from the identified data source. This integration could happen by using various protocols.

Data preparation: Clean, enrich, standardize, and transform data and prepare data to make it business consumption ready.

Data traceability: Trace data for auditing and monitoring. This traceability could happen by using various data monitoring tools.

Data integration testing: Use the DataOps pipeline to test the data.

Data analytics: Explore data, conduct analysis, and discover patterns. This could happen by using ML tools and exposing analyzed data to the consumer for decision-making or could feed into services and applications by using APIs and messaging software.

The previous example provides a clear picture of what probable software/code is used as part of the DataOps pipeline.

The DataOps pipeline uses the DevOps process to build, test, and deploy in the environment.

Compile and package: The pipeline compiles the ETL app code and ETL pipeline as code and uses the streaming and batch processing of data.

Test code: The pipeline tests data for quality measures, data profiling, data cleansing, data validation, and data reconciliation. The test monitors data values flowing through the data supply chain to catch anomalies or flag data values outside statistical norms. In DataOps, you need to conduct a test at every stage of the data supply chain.

Infrastructure as code: In DataOps, build and test fall under CI, and deployment is CD. So, infrastructure as code is coming under CD. By using this method, you can create templates and configurations to provision infrastructure and deploy your data code.

DevNetOps

This section covers DevNetOps.

Network Operation and Challenges

The traditional network is hardware-based, proprietary, expensive, and difficult to scale. It has complex lifecycle management practices with rigid configurations. Traditional networks do not work for modern-day architecture and business.

Today's business requires a faster time to market with more services at a lesser cost and requires demand-based scalability. The team needs to focus on delivery with an innovation culture that helps to stay competitive among other teams.

To overcome these hindrances and to support modern business, we require a software-defined and highly configurable network. The software-defined network (SDN) is a new architecture that is dynamic, manageable, cost-effective, and adaptable, making it ideal for the high-bandwidth, dynamic nature of today's application.

The SDN architecture consists of the following:

- *Network programmable*: It has a centralized control plane to control or program network devices using software applications.

- *Logical separation*: The network control plane and data plane are separate.

- *Centrally managed*: Network intelligence is logically located centrally in SDN controllers.

- *Network abstraction*: The application will interact with the network through APIs, instead of management interfaces tightly coupled to the hardware.

- *Open architecture and vendor neutral*: Network services and applications can run within a common software environment with interoperability support for multivendor network devices.

As illustrated in Figure 14-9, in the past the network and IT team worked in silos by using a different set of tools and unmatched deployment schedules. Earlier there was no universal open architecture, which made teams learn vendor-specific hardware, technologies, etc. All of this leads to larger capex and inefficient opex spend.

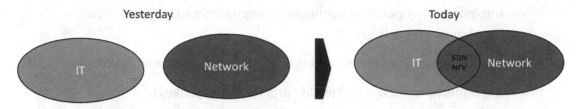

Figure 14-9. *Journey toward a modern network*

Today, IT and network teams have a common way of working and collaborating by using the open architecture across network vendors. This makes life simple and removes vendor-specific training and teams.

Virtualization and SDN help to reduce the variation in capex, optimize hardware usage, and share resources to reduce hardware maintenance costs.

Why You Need DevNetOps?

The virtual network functions (VNFs) are virtualized network services running on open computing platforms formerly carried out by proprietary, dedicated hardware technology. Common VNFs include virtualized routers, firewalls, WAN optimization, and network address translation (NAT) services. Most VNFs are run in VMs on common virtualization infrastructure software such as VMware or KVM.

- There are no standard procedures to develop and benchmark VNFS.

- There are no standard architectural guidelines for VNFs.

- Manual configuration, updating, and testing of VNFs is time-consuming.

- There are no standard protocols or configuration policies for VNF across vendors.

- Service providers have their workflow in infrastructure.

- There are no common KPIs defined for realizing NFV implementation success.

DevNetOps enables agility and quality in the following ways:

- Implements network as code and agile change management config + templates + artifacts + OS

- Implements a pipeline of continuous integration and testing, staging simulation, and delivery

- Orchestrates deployments, rolling upgrades, and traffic management

- Implements resilience and testing drills (Chaos Monkey)

Network Reliability Engineering

Network reliability engineering (NRE) is an emerging approach to network automation that stabilizes and improves reliability while achieving the benefits of speed. NRE is like SRE.

DevNetOps helps NRE to easily deploy, configure, validate, and certify with simple steps of execution. Just like SREs define their methods using DevOps, DevNetOps is a method that embraces NRE.

The following are the NRE principles that are derived from DevOps:

- Enable automation

- Orchestration transparency

- Continuously evolve

- Monitoring metrics

NRE keeps the reliability of the network as the topmost priority along with these qualities: agility, security, velocity, efficiency, and performance.

The NRE includes the following:

- *Code*: Using infrastructure as code and developing network code with versioning

- *Automation*: Using DevNetOps for automating and dynamic provision

- *Test*: Continuous automatic testing to meet SLAs

- *Monitor*: Monitoring the entire network infrastructure

The following are the activities of NRE:

Code: The NRE team develops the network software artifacts, secrets, and configuration-as-a-service code and checks it in to the version control similar to developer check-in to a version control like GitHub or Bitbucket.

Build and deploy: NRE automates versioned deployments, peer reviews, and testing. It automates provisioning of networking resources and configuration of the networks.

Test: Through automation, staging, stress testing, and chaos engineering, an NRE ensures that the deliveries are reliable enough to meet service level objectives.

Monitor: An NRE monitors service level indicators (SLIs), both manually and automatically with analytics that trigger automatic responses and alerts.

Measure: Use indicators to measure their effectiveness in meeting reliability goals, such as mean time between failure (MTBF) and mean time to repair (MTTR).

In the age of modern technology with technology and business disruption, your network must be able to support the application with speed and reliability. You cannot achieve these in the big-bang, manual approach; you need to have incremental development and automation to support this change. DevNetOps philosophies, culture, and automation will support these requirements.

DevNetOps Pipeline

As shown in Figure 14-10 and detailed in Table 14-1, DevNetOps is like the DevOps philosophies, culture, and behaviors of network operations (NetOps). DevNetOps helps NRE to easily deploy, configure, validate, and certify the steps of execution.

The DevNetOps provides the following:

- *Scalability*: It allows for optimized capacity on demand.

- *Agility*: It allows for simple configuration changes/updates and frequent upgrades with a shorter cycle of deployments and test.

- *Speed*: It allows for a faster time to market and updates with fewer technology disruptions.

- *Reliability*: It allows for deploying quickly and continuously with no failures and portability to any environment.

- *Security*: Network and security should co-exist for the safety of products, vendors, customers, and also end users.

- *Simple*: It allows for configuration as code and service handling complexity with less human error.

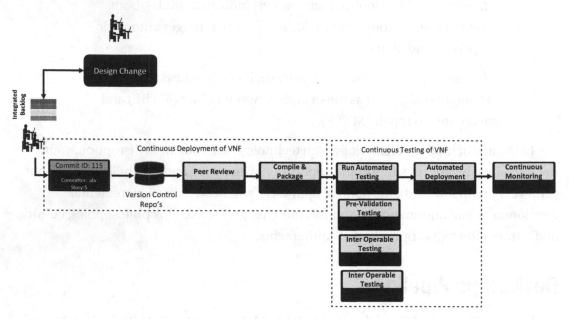

Figure 14-10. *DevNetOps pipeline*

Table 14-1. *Network Pipeline Details*

Pipeline Steps	What Tools Can Be Considered?	What Process Followed?	Who Are Involved?
Network as code	Git, GitLab, Bitbucket, Gerrit Infrastructure as code (IaC) tooling for the cloud Declarative config as code (YAML) Actual code is programmed by extension	Agile methodology Reviewing Design templates	Developers Network team
Pipeline orchestration	Build (for example, Aminator or Packer) Testing (for example, Open Stack, MANO) Orchestrate deployment (for example, Spinnaker)	Continuous integration and delivery Automatic and manual check Continuous deployment	Test-driven development Ops specialist
Micro-immutable architecture	Containers and functions Container as a service (CaaS) and function as a service (FaaS) to run SDN system Secrets, configs, volumes	Design/package software into a single-purpose service	Network architecture team
Resiliency design and drills	Net Chaos Monkey and watchdogs Kill -9 command, unplug, or cut cables	Develop stress for staging Run periodically in production	Performance engineering team Resilience team
Measurement	Dashboards KPIs	Incidents playbooks	Operation team

DevOps in the Cloud

Hosting DevOps in the cloud can help an organization evolve from a reactive to a proactive approach. Whatever circumstances you are operating in, a cloud DevOps solution provides a business with a way to accelerate its software development and delivery.

A cloud DevOps solution is cloud native, and by adopting it, your organization can achieve delivery through continuous integration, continuous delivery, and continuous deployment with the required level of services and testing to deploy quality solutions to customers.

DevOps on the cloud provides a few benefits over a traditional on-prem solution:

- *Backup as a code*: Backup restoration is automated in the cloud, allowing your engineers to integrate backup as code with a continuous integration stack to automate, restore, and delete backups.

- *Business agility*: Cloud DevOps solutions can be seamlessly integrated into multiple business units. It is easy to set up and configure CI and CD pipeline tools.

- *Continuous monitoring*: Cloud services provide monitoring and observability services, and these services are very well integrated with the DevOps pipeline to monitor services. These services provide actionable insight to monitor applications, optimize resource allocation, respond to performance changes, and offer an integrated dashboard to keep track of application, infrastructure, and security.

- *Infrastructure automation*: The open source PaaS services manages multicloud infrastructure and automation management.

- *Configuration as a code*: DevOps supports configuration across the DevOps lifecycle including continuous integration, continuous delivery, continuous deployment, and infrastructure as a code. It is a string of YAML code or scripts that standardize the configuration of the network, server location, etc.

AWS Cloud

The AWS DevOps services provide a more reliable and quicker configuration of tools. These services simplify provisioning and managing infrastructure, deploying application code, automating the software release process, and monitoring your application and infrastructure performance. The AWS services are preconfigured, and there is no setup or software to install. This reduces your time to configure the DevOps pipeline and day-to-day operation of the pipeline. These services are built in to the cloud and manage single instances or scale to thousands depending on your volume of services. These services are linearly scaled based on your application.

AWS helps you to use automation so you can build faster and more efficiently. Using AWS services, as shown in Figure 14-11 and Table 14-2, you can automate manual tasks or processes such as deployments, development and test workflows, container management, and configuration management. You can set up an access control mechanism for your DevOps services by using identity and access management with your AWS accounts.

AWS has a larger partner ecosystem integrated into AWS services. You're open to use any third-party services with AWS services. For example, if you want to use multicloud infrastructure automation, you can use Terraform services to automate, and if your team wants the source code to be on-prem with Bitbucket or GitHub, you can use AWS services for the rest of the pipeline.

AWS provides a pay-as-you-go model, so you need to pay only for the duration of usage.

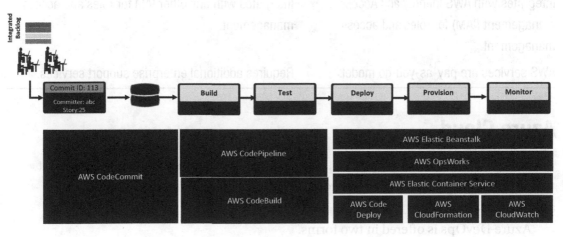

Figure 14-11. AWS development services

Table 14-2. *Comparison Chart with AWS DevOps Tools*

AWS DevOps Tools	Open Stack Tools
High availability and durability included.	Tools supports high availability and durability, but you need design infrastructure to support these features.
Easy access and integration with other services.	Tools will include AWS service plugins.
No provisioning servers or patching software.	Servers have to be configured and require regular patching.
Build servers are auto-scaled, and pricing is pay for what you use.	Scaling can be achieved by adding additional containers.
AWS tools are limited to AWS and do not have support now AWS tools and services.	Open stacks are matured, and more plugins are available and work for a multicloud environment.
Integrates with AWS Identity and Access Management (IAM) for roles and access management.	Integrates with any other IAM for roles and access management.
AWS services are pay-as-you-go model.	Requires additional enterprise support services.

Azure Cloud

Azure DevOps is a Microsoft product that provides development services to support teams to plan work, collaborate on code development, and build and deploy applications.

Azure DevOps is offered in two forms.

- *Azure DevOps Server*: Previously known as Team Foundation Server (TFS), this is an on-premises offering.

- *Azure DevOps Service*: This was previously known as Visual Studio Team Services; it provides a PaaS-based offering to manage the end-to-end DevOps lifecycle.

The Azure DevOps service provides a platform for implementing the DevOps process across different IT segments. This tool supports various practices under DevOps such as continuous planning, continuous development, continuous integration, continuous testing, continuous deployment, and continuous monitoring. These tools support integration with various other open and commercial tools such as code analysis tools, security tools to scan vulnerabilities in code, and infrastructure provisioning tools to automate the infrastructure such as Terraform and Ansible Tower.

As shown in Figure 14-12, the Azure DevOps multistage pipeline provides an easy way to use templates to configure CI and CD pipeline. The multistage pipeline provides features to add extensions such as build quality checks, security checks, infrastructure provision, etc.

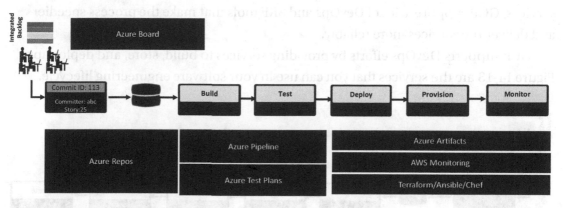

Figure 14-12. *Azure development services*

The following are the Azure DevOps tools that are provided to set up a DevOps pipeline in the Azure cloud:

- *Backlog and user story*: Azure Board can help your teams to manage software projects. It provides a rich set of capabilities including native software support for Scrum and Kanban, customized dashboards, and integrated reporting. You can easily start tracking user stories, backlog items, tasks, and bugs associated with your project.

- *Source code management*: Azure Repos is a set of version control tools that you can configure for your source code. It supports Git and Team Foundation Version Control (TFVC).

- *Build and release*: Azure Pipeline is a cloud service that you can use to automatically build and test your code. It combines CI and CD to test and build your code constantly and consistently.

- *Test*: Azure Test Plans allows you to create test plans and test cases. It supports both automated and manual testing.

- *Binary package*: Azure Artifacts stores the compiled code and other dependent binaries with version control.

Google Cloud

GCP provides a vast number of services for a cloud native application. Apart from these services, GCP supports a lot of DevOps and SRE tools that make the process speedier and deliver the services more reliably.

GCP supports DevOps efforts by providing services to build, store, and deploy apps. Figure 14-13 are the services that you can use in your software engineering lifecycle.

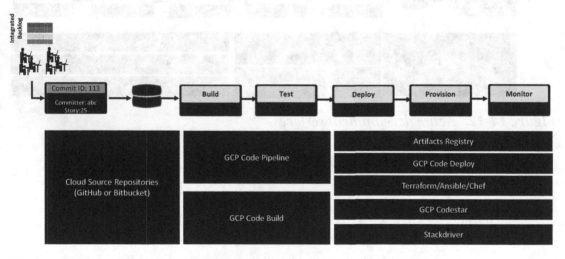

Figure 14-13. GCP DevOps pipeline tools

Artifact registry: It enables you to centrally store binaries and build dependencies. It is a central location for storing packages and Docker images.

Software release workflow: The GCP Code Pipeline service is a CI and CD tool for fast, reliable application and infrastructure updates. The Code Pipeline builds, tests, and deploys code every time on the system when there are changes and based on the release process models defined.

Build and test code: The GCP Code Build service executes your builds on GCP. It imports source code from cloud storage, cloud source repositories, GitHub, or Bitbucket, and it executes a build to your specification. It produces artifacts such as binaries and Docker images. The Build config file contains the instructions for the cloud build to perform a task based on a specification. For example, your build config contains a function to build, package, and push Docker images.

Deployment automation: GCP Code Deploy performs deployment automation. It deploys on any of the instances, including EC2 and on-premises server.

Unified CI/CD projects: GCP Cloud code quickly develops, builds, and deploys the application on GCP. It provides a user interface to visualize and manage software development activities.

DevOps Transformation

The ultimate goal of DevOps is to unify development operations from end to end, but many organizations struggle to realize the full adoption journey from one application to the enterprise level. Challenges vary at every stage. Thus, even the most promising efforts fail to scale products and services through the entire scope of adoption.

A DevOps journey is an organization-wide journey across all layers. Even if your scope of DevOps adoption is within a single layer, you need to sync with other layers. Individual applications are the basic consideration in your DevOps strategy. Stakeholders should keep enterprise adoption in mind when deciding the process, tools, and practices to implement.

The core tenant of DevOps is to identify dependencies among related applications and group them by release time and strategy. These groupings are known as *clusters*. This allows for the harmonious implementation of DevOps across all applications.

These are the key factors of a DevOps transformation:

- It's a journey about reinventing yourself.

- Focus on people, process, and tools adoption.

- Learn from other teams and use their best practices.

- Start with the most valued product (MVP).

- Measure all the KPIs.

You are at the beginning of the enterprise DevOps transformation. As shown in Figure 14-14, DevOps is the logical next step in your agility.

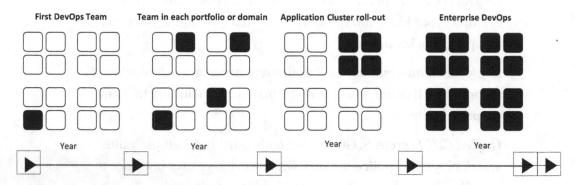

Figure 14-14. *DevOps transformation journey*

The success of your DevOps transformation is based on how you use these perspectives:

- *IT landscape*: This includes practices and principles to build and configure your solution stack to enable autonomous, fast, and reliable software delivery.

- *Organization*: This includes tribe and team topologies, partnerships, a culture, and a skillset that encourage thinking across silos and enable tribes to become autonomous.

- *Practices*: How you work is a key capability that supports doing the right things in the right way.

- *Enabling practices*: This includes continuous automation testing, CI, CD, continuous deployment, monitoring.

The following are the challenges of DevOps transformation:

- *Governance*: Creating a governance framework that is effective at the speed of DevOps is a major hurdle for enterprises.

- *Product/project management*: The majority of software applications are still hosted on-premises, and support applications are dispersed across fragmented teams, business units, and organizations, leading to a lack of ownership.

- *Quality*: DevOps practices require continuous quality across the lifecycle.

- *Compliance*: Depending on the nature of the industry you are in, your enterprises need to adhere to various compliances like GDPR, SEC, etc.

To overcome these challenges in transformation, you need to adopt the following considerations across enterprises:

- *Transformation alignment*: Infuse DevOps during the transformation. This streamlines and reduces the overall governance issues.

- *Cultural and change management*: Organizations that ignore cultural and change management during the transformation journey fail to transform successfully. Like any other transformation, DevOps requires training mentorship, resource skilling, behavioral change, and motivational or reward programs.

- *Stakeholder management*: Every project or product has multiple stakeholders, but when a team fails to collaborate with stakeholders cohesively, adoption tends to fail.

- *Prioritizing application*: Some applications benefit more from DevOps than others. Selecting and prioritizing the right one is important for transformation success.

- *Tools setup and process design*: Tools and processes should be established before implementation.

- *Minimum viable product (MVP)*: Identify and create an MVP. This philosophy aims to provide early benefits and assurance to stakeholders before they invest in fully scaling on a DevOps transformation.

- *Identify clusters*: All dependent applications should move through development and testing cycles together in the same space.

- *Create a consolidated implementation plan*: Planning the consolidated release of an application cluster requires an assessment of the challenges at hand as well as the techniques to overcome them.

- *Organization structure*: Well-structured IT teams greatly enhance DevOps adoptions.

Summary

Automation is about combining agile, DevSecOps, SRE, and the cloud to build an elastic, hyper-speed organization. These four elements are organized around each other in the following ways:

- Talents and teams are like liquid and flow quickly.

- These four elements such as agile, DevSecOps, SRE and cloud are structured around intelligent software engineering.

- Full-stack teams are end-to-end accountable for projects.

- Applications are independent of each other.

- The 12-factor app allows automation.

- These four elements focus on resilience and failure tolerance.

- These four elements are use automated change management and resilience design patterns.

- These four elements are elastic and create a highly scalable infrastructure.

- These four elements have an immutable infrastructure with a self-service paradigm.

Following best practices, you must consider the following for your DevSecOps transformation:

- The journey is about reinventing yourself; do not restrict yourself from learning new things.

- Focus on people and interaction over tools and process.

- Keep sharing; learn from other teams.

- Prepare yourself to kickstart DevOps.

- Theory is good for understanding; try to realize it in projects.

- Train your team; DevOps is not for everyone.

- Focus is important; don't mix too many user stories.

- Measure as much as possible.

In this chapter, I explained the basics of the DevOps pipeline and the security in it and also covered DevDataOps and DevNetOps and how they will help you to address data analytics and networking. These pipelines are an integral part of your cloud native journey. I also covered how to drive DevOps transformation to an enterprise.

CHAPTER 15

AI-Driven Development

During the cloud and cloud native age, organizations are focusing on leveraging AI methodologies, best practices, and enhanced tools and technologies during the software engineering lifecycle and applying them to build or augment enterprise systems.

There is a lot of interest growing in AI-focused methodologies for creating and distributing the development of application solutions.

In modern-day software engineering, you need a separate methodology, process, and toolset with automation for AI development. To improve the process, various industries and enterprises are embedding AI into their software engineering lifecycle to make the process smarter, automated, and efficient. AI-enabled tools can optimize engineering tasks by automating the end-to-end engineering lifecycle.

With these AI-driven development tools, the engineering team can develop an AI-powered automation process without involving specific experts.

In this chapter, I cover the following:

- AI methodologies

- AI solutions to solve industry use cases

- AI tools and best practices

- AI governance

- AI and ML in DevOps cycle

Introduction

The evolution of AI has changed the way organizations and engineers are approaching software systems and development. Artificial intelligence (AI) and machine learning (ML) are good options for enhancing the software engineering lifecycle output.

According to Gartner, by 2022, at least 40 percent of new software engineering projects will have an AI-driven virtual engineer on the team. This is because AI and

© Shivakumar R Goniwada 2022
S. R. Goniwada, *Cloud Native Architecture and Design*, https://doi.org/10.1007/978-1-4842-7226-8_15

ML-backed tools are already on the market for development, source code generation, and testing, and they can be integrated as part of the DevOps pipeline. IDC estimates that worldwide spending on AI is expected to double in four years, reaching $110 billion in 2024.

Currently, humans focus on everything including solving business problems, identifying quality attributes, testing outcomes, etc. Instead of doing everything, why can't we just focus on solving business problems and letting the AI- and ML-based tools automate code generation and proactively identify failures?

Adopting an AI strategy helps enterprises to start on a journey toward integrating AI into their fabric, not just by implementing AI solutions but by developing an AI-powered architecture to embrace AI at the core.

AI accelerates the traditional software development techniques and eases your coding, reviewing, and testing process. It creates a scalable and efficient workflow to drive productivity and reduce time to market.

Human engineers are translators and engage in conversation with clients and other stakeholders when testing and with other AI-enabled engineers (using AI-based tools). Before engaging AI-enabled engineers, you need to train them thoroughly. Test-driven development, hypothesis-driven development, and behavior-driven development help you to train your AI colleagues.

Answering the following questions will position your organizations to capture sustainable long-term value through AI:

- What role do we want AI to play in our organization? How will important aspects of our business (for example, skilled resources, customer experience) change?

- How will we get the most benefit from AI? Where are the most impactful opportunities in our business, and will they be enough to justify the investment?

- What action do we need to take to establish a foundation that makes AI practical, effective, and responsible? How do we manage these changes?

- How can our organization sustain the shift toward embracing AI? How do we increasingly make AI core to the performance of our business?

Unique AI Challenges

Adopting AI introduces unique challenges that require comprehensive AI thinking to embrace:

- *Risk of unintended consequences*: AI represents a major technological advancement with tremendous potential. However, the universal and standard procedures are not yet available to assure the outcome.

- *Bridge unconventional organization gaps*: Successful AI needs to be a joint effort across every entity of an organization.

- *Specialized talent*: The organization requires specialized talent, training, and an AI career path.

- *Mature data capabilities*: Despite maturity in data and data science, there remains continued gaps in the quality of data to require effective training and operation of AI solutions.

- *Culture*: The organization needs to embrace AI by adopting a culture of AI.

Why AI-Driven Development?

The reasons to use AI-driven development are as follows:

- AI-driven development refers to the tools, process, technologies, and best practices used for embedding AI into software applications and for using AI tools to develop AI-enhanced solutions.

- There is a current need for software engineering to be able to operate AI-enhanced technologies independently.

- AI-driven development provides engineering with an ecosystem of AI algorithms and models, as well as development tools tailored to integrate AI capabilities.

- The AI-driven development approach is well suited to minimizing prediction errors, when there are many data points and when there are many alternatives.

- Engineers can infuse AI-powered capabilities into application development without involving a data scientist.

- AI methodologies, reference architectures, and best practices can use as reference for AI-driven development.

AI-Driven Principles at a Glance

AI principles set guardrails to help enterprises address the unique challenges associated with pursuing AI responsibly. Google and Microsoft AWS have defined and adopted the following principles:

- *Be socially beneficial*: The expanded reach of new technologies increasingly touches society as a whole.

- *Avoid creating or reinforcing unfair bias*: AI algorithms and datasets can reflect, reinforce, or reduce unfair bias.

- *Be built and tested for safety*: Use strong safety and security practices to avoid untended results.

- *Incorporate privacy design principles*: Incorporate privacy principles in the development.

- *Fairness*: Throughout the lifecycle, AI systems should be inclusive and accessible.

- *Anticipate the future*: AI applications can produce granular insights into what customers and markets want.

- *Act autonomously*: An AI application provides value by automating existing manual processes by enabling the autonomous operation of the business.

- *Detect invisible*: AI can manage operations that humans cannot, and AI application should take advantage of this situation in a complex environment.

Approach to AI

There are many approaches to AI. A successful AI adoption can start in many ways.

- *Top down*: Leadership is fully involved in defining the AI value and roadmap and moving quickly from strategy to MVP.

- *Bottom up*: Start with an MVP that will incrementally prove AI's value as other initiatives are considered and implemented.

- *Part of a bigger picture*: AI is considered as part of the broader organization.

- *Inorganic*: Acquire AI startups or leverage partners to augment the AI.

AI Governance

AI governance is about AI being explainable, transparent, and ethical. The AI governance is to define the key mechanisms for executing AI use cases and deploying them across the organization, and the governance framework helps you to drive the partnership between your organization, clients, and other stakeholders. As part of the governance, you need to outline the AI roles and responsibilities of resources within your organization's structure.

The governance framework outlines the decision-making process for key activities and determines how opportunities are identified, approved, delivered, and scaled across the enterprises and how key decisions are made around AI.

AI Framework

The AI framework establishes trust in the AI architecture and helps you to continue monitoring the system. Use the following three-step approach for all your AI deliverables:

- *Govern*: Create an internal governance process, as explained next, which is anchored to industry and societal shared values, regulations, ethical guardrails, and accountability. Promote clarity around decisions.

- *Design*: Architecture and design AI with trust by design. Empower project teams to understand and address bias issues.

- *Monitor*: Monitor and audit regularly against key-value metrics, including concerning algorithmic accountability and cybersecurity.

AI Governance Measurement

Lack of measurement will be a weakness of your organization because these cannot be transferred to and incorporated into processes, systems, and platforms. The AI measurement is common for all organizations through regulations from the AI body, but each organization can measure how AI is delivered, what direction AI projects progress in, etc. These measurements are captured by an audit of the AI projects, accountability in AI projects, the time they take to complete, security considerations, etc.

Governance Process

The following list highlights the process that will take place in the event that a deployed AI solution behaves in an unexpected way:

- When monitoring the AI solutions in a project, the center of excellence (CoE) must highlight any red flags or anything out of the ordinary and report it to the responsible AI board.

- A review board will evaluate the AI service that has been flagged to review it and recommend a plan of action.

- The CoE will begin resolving the AI solutions that were flagged according to the approved course of action with support from the AI project team.

- Community and knowledge sharing boards work to analyze and identify the controls in place to prevent repetition.

Governance Model

Based on the previous principles, the best model for AI development is the hub and spoke model because it enables controlled growth and encourages autonomy within the business sector. You need innovation at all levels for AI, so this model allows for rapid innovation/sharing of ideas across your organization while centralizing the AI research and best practices. According to the cloud native principles, organizations should adopt a decentralization approach, but AI development requires a centralized decentralization approach. This helps to keep key decisions central and decentralizes the solution implementation.

As shown in Figure 15-1, the hub and spoke model attracts, develops, and retains scarce talent, allowing for the flexible allocation of resources to keep resources challenging and fresh.

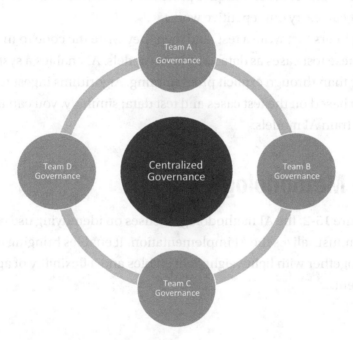

Figure 15-1. *Hub and spoke governance*

In the beginning, the big centralized hub starts to increase the use of AI governance across teams in an enterprise, because there isn't enough skills and maturity across spokes to decentralize governance. AI matures in an organization when skilled talent and teams begin to empower business and technical teams to contribute to delivering AI solutions. This leads to the allocation of AI talent and a balance of maturity between the hub and spokes. Once the organization reaches the maturity stage, the AI CoE remains a small group that coordinates the AI activities across enterprises.

How to Train AI-Enabled Frameworks?

AI and ML enable tools to learn from data rather than explicit programming. AI and ML algorithms ingest data to train the algorithm model and the behavior of these tools is based on the kind and quality of data used for the training. The better-quality data you ingest, the wiser the tool becomes. Once the base model is trained, then you can ingest in real time to learn more precisely. The accuracy of AI and ML tools is based on training processes and automation, which are part of ML.

The TDD, BDD, and HDD techniques provide a framework to train AI in software engineering that can carry out repetitive works.

In TDD, engineers first write a test, and then they write the code to make the test case pass. Use these test cases as data to train AI models. AI enables a system to learn from data rather than through explicit programming. Algorithms ingest training data and produce models based on the test cases and test data; similarly, you can use hypotheses and behavior to train AI models.

AI-Driven Methodology

As shown in Figure 15-2, the AI methodology focuses on identifying use cases and piloting, and it industrializes the AI implementation. It enables bringing all AI projects and execution together with lightweight deliverables and a flexibility of agile practices in an AI environment.

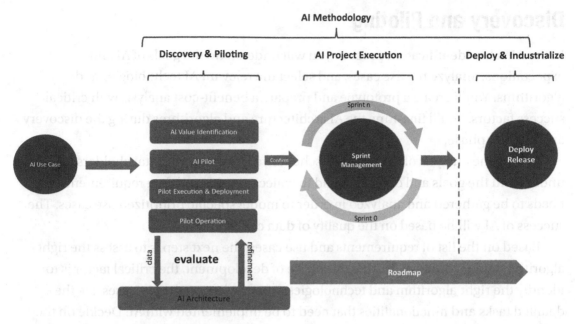

Figure 15-2. AI-driven methodology

AI Use Cases

AI uses are identified by synthesizing various perspectives from the external research organization, brainstorming workshops, and stakeholder discussions.

- Opportunities can be adapted from well-established AI use cases from different industries.

- Discuss with respective stakeholders the opportunities to apply AI to solve some of its pain points.

You can use these sample questions during your discussion with stakeholders:

- What are your challenges that you wish you could spend less time on?

- What are some repetitive tasks that you and your team do daily?

- Have you identified any AI use cases?

- What types of data do you think you have that no one else does?

Discovery and Piloting

In the AI value identification process, you will understand the goals of AI and expectations, analyze the use cases, and select the relevant AI technologies and algorithms. You'll create a prototype and prepare a benefit-cost analysis with critical success factors. You'll fine-tune the AI architecture and algorithms during the discovery and piloting phase.

During the analysis of the use case, schedule a workshop with stakeholders to understand the goals and objectives and to collect metrics and data requirements. Data needs to be gathered and analyzed in order to model specific prioritized use cases. The success of AI will be based on the quality of data collection.

Based on the list of requirements and use cases, the next step is to assess the right algorithm and technology. During this phase of development, the critical factor is to identify the right algorithm and technologies. After reviewing the use cases, list the detailed tasks and functionalities that need to be implemented with AI. Decide on the type of algorithm you would like to apply.

- *Supervised learning*: The computer makes a prediction based on general rules for mapping inputs and outputs, and the model is trained from a set of labeled data.

- *Unsupervised learning*: No labeled data is given to the learning algorithm, leaving it on its own to find structure in its input.

- *Reinforcement learning*: The computer interacts with a dynamic environment in which it must perform certain goals.

When choosing an algorithm, you need to understand some extra features for the algorithms, such as accuracy, training time, linearity, and number of parameters.

Once you have finalized these steps, the next step is to create a proof of concept (PoC) by leveraging the AI technology and algorithm. Once the PoC is ready, create a benefits case for industrialization. In the piloting phase, train and test the AI technologies. During this time, the model strength need to be captured in terms of parameters like accuracy, precision, and recall. This might differ for various algorithms. For example, linear regression gives the model strength in terms of the R-Squared and adjusted R-Squared values.

Once the PoC is accepted, you need to create a roadmap to outline the key initiatives required to support industrialization.

AI Project Execution

The sprint management discipline involves executing user stories and tasks and tracking their progress. Generally, you will follow a similar approach as a normal agile methodology like grooming user stories for sprints, creating a user story backlog, daily standups with sprint team and, end of sprint demonstration, etc.

Deploy and Industrialize

Based on the type of use case, you need to opt for end-to-end testing and full deployment activities at the end of each sprint. During the deploy process, you execute an end-to-end DevOps process. During the process, you develop the AI code, execute tests, and deploy and industrialize the use cases.

AI and ML in DevOps

In the new age, modern technologies like cloud native bring considerable change and complexity to how modern systems are created and released. These systems require more than agile; they need to be adaptive and capable of responding dynamically to frequently changing conditions. Automation in regular DevOps is limited to scripting and orchestration. Such scripts sometimes create a bottleneck, and the application and environment can change rapidly. As shown in Figure 15-3, you need automation that can adapt dynamically, is testable, and can self-heal based on the requirements. The automation solution needs to be able to look at past data, keep learning from recent data, and make flexible, intelligent forecasts about the right course of action.

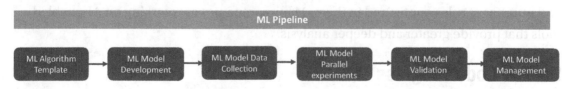

Figure 15-3. *ML model pipeline*

Checking enormous quantities of information to find an important problem as part of a daily routine is time-consuming. Here, AI can play a significant role in processing, evaluating, and making instant decisions that can take a human hours.

AI and ML integrations can power DevOps by automating routine and repeatable tasks, offering enhanced effectiveness, and minimizing the time spent on procedure code, test, and delivery.

The following types of automation are defined as part of AI in DevOps. There are many ways you can use AI and ML in your software engineering lifecycle.

- *The solution that helps in requirements*: These kinds of standard tools help to advance requirements engineering by applying AI.

- *The solution that helps engineers*: This kind of standard tool helps engineers in programming and reviewing the code.

- *The solution that does quality checks*: With a detailed evaluation of testing outputs, AI performs efficient quality results, and these kinds of standard tools help to solve the authoring, initialization, and generation of automated testing.

- *Environment management*: Improve the range of automation in an environment, including automating many routines and repeatable jobs, using resources, and predicting the load on containers.

- *Early discovery*: AI tools can provide the operations teams with the ability to detect an issue at an early stage and ensure faster response time.

AI and ML in Code Management

In your day-to-day development, you might have to use static analysis tools to identify problems in your code. The overall effectiveness of these tools is based on the quality and number of rules configured in them. Many companies are working on AI-enabled tools that provide greater and deeper analysis.

Source Code Progress

Git and Bitbucket are source code tools. Applying ML to them addresses the irregularities around code quantities, long construct times, delays in check-ins, improper resourcing, etc.

DeepCode.AI

DeepCode is an AI-powered programming tool that works as a coding assistant for software development projects. This tool is trained with a massive volume of data with approximately 250,000 coding rules assessed from both public and private repositories. Based on the trained rules and context, the tool suggests to engineers how to fix the code. Along with the suggestion, it warns the engineers about critical vulnerabilities you need to solve in your code. It learns during the usage of the tool and makes suggestions instantly during the code review. This online tool connects to your repository in GitHub, GitLab, or Bitbucket, via either a private or public repository.

DeepCode is based on custom AI and semantic analysis techniques that were specially designed to learn the rules and information from the cloud.

Static code analysis tools require additional capabilities to find vulnerabilities in code, but AI-enabled tools don't require an understanding of the deep code analysis to identify vulnerabilities and also learn during the analysis. DeepCode is a combination of static analysis and custom machine learning algorithms.

Unlike static code analysis tools, it does not rely on manually hard-coded rules, but learns automatically from data and uses the pre-defined business rules to analyze the program. This concept of never-ending learning enables the system to constantly improve with more data, without supervision.

Codota

Codota is AI completion for your Java code in an IDE. It learns as you are writing code to help you code better. It is using AI and ML learnings and gives relevant suggestions to complete the code. It gives suggestions based on a model trained on millions of open source Java programs, which are then modified based on the code you are currently working on.

Codota is available for IntelliJ, Android Studios, and Eclipse and you integrate as a plug-in. Codota learned from millions of program lines. With this learning, this tool completes lines of code based on your context, which helps you to code faster with fewer errors. It uses the context of the code you are writing as a required input. If you are in a dilemma to find the best code for your program, this tool is capable of suggesting the best way to complete the code.

Figure 15-4 and Figure 15-5 show the code snippets from Eclipse when using Codota.

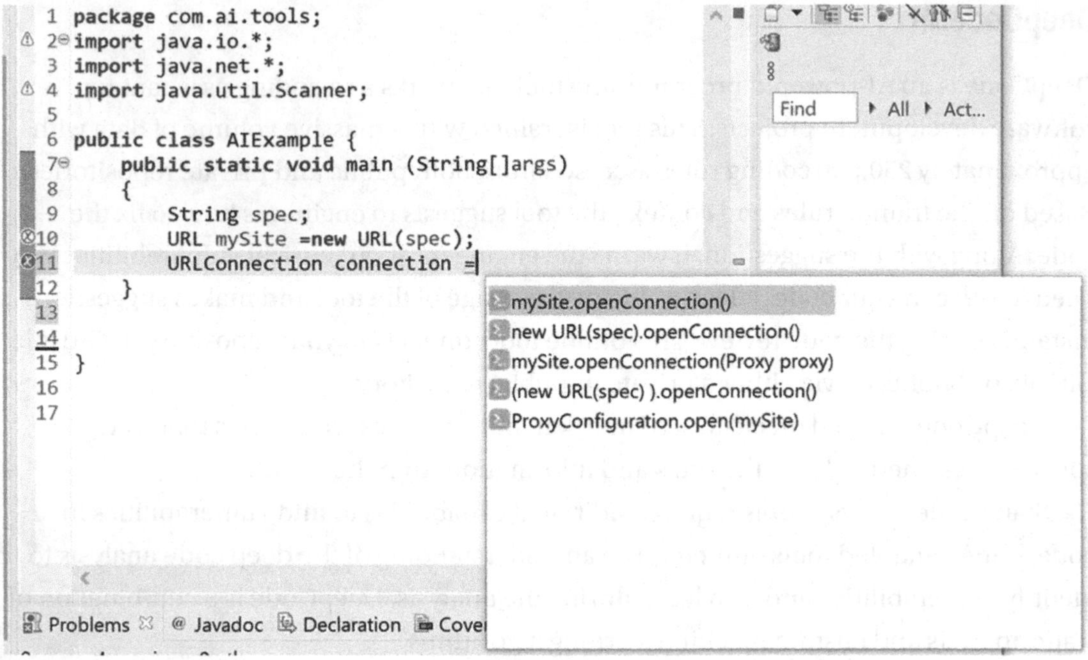

```
 1  package com.ai.tools;
 2  import java.io.*;
 3  import java.net.*;
 4  import java.util.Scanner;
 5
 6  public class AIExample {
 7      public static void main (String[]args)
 8      {
 9          String spec;
10          URL mySite =new URL(spec);
11          URLConnection connection =
12      }
13
14
15  }
16
17
```

```
mySite.openConnection()
new URL(spec).openConnection()
mySite.openConnection(Proxy proxy)
(new URL(spec) ).openConnection()
ProxyConfiguration.open(mySite)
```

Find   ▶ All ▶ Act...

🔲 Problems ⋈   @ Javadoc   🗎 Declaration   🖿 Cove

Figure 15-4. *Codota suggestion for URL connection*

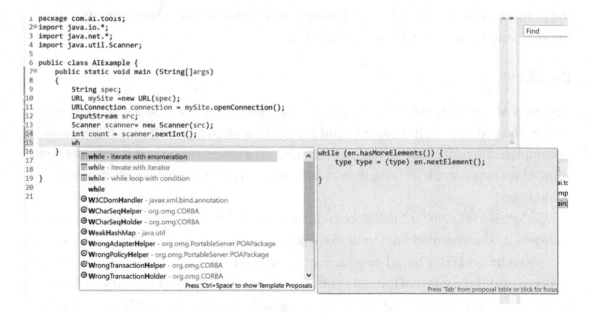

Figure 15-5. *Codota suggestion for while loop*

The following are the benefits of Codota:

- *Code faster*: Codota helps find a reliable code prediction based on an AI-learned code pattern.

- *Prevent error*: ML algorithms detect the code's intent, not just syntax mistakes.

- *Discover code*: Expand your knowledge and reveal a new and efficient way to leverage open source code.

These are the drawbacks of Codota:

- *Code secure*: Codota sends minimal information on the application's local context, and the scope is limited to the code that you are currently editing. It doesn't send full blocks of code outside of your IDE. It sends class names, variable names, and methods that are invoked in secured communication, and it does not use your code to train models.

Quality Checks

ML performs efficient quality assessment results and builds test pattern libraries based on the identification of bugs. This helps the team to evaluate results on every launch and thus improves the quality of the application delivered.

Testim.io is a cloud platform that uses AI for fast authoring, execution, and maintenance of automated tests. This tool supports a few test types like end-to-end testing, functional testing, and UI testing. This tool easily identifies any changes like ID names or attributes in a UI by using AI in real time. This tool integrates with the DevOps pipeline, capturing the logs of tests and screenshots of test runs, and provides detailed reporting on test runs.

Continuous Feedback

One of the main properties of DevOps is the use of continuous feedback loops at every stage of the process. This includes using the monitoring tools, quality checks tools, etc. ML is already providing detailed monitoring details including performance metrics, log files, and other types. Applying ML in this space will help to identify patterns easily.

Kubeflow

Kubeflow is the ML toolkit of Kubernetes. It progressively releases containerized AI microservices over Kubernetes orchestration. It provides a framework-agnostic pipeline for making AI microservices production-ready across multicloud environments. It streamlines the creation of production-ready AI microservices and makes certain the flexibility of containerized AI apps among Kubernetes clusters.

Alert Monitoring

AI and ML can manage the monitoring alerts in the systems. The AI-based tools learn and predict the problems of the system and alert proactively.

Summary

This chapter provided you with an overview of the end-to-end design, development, and delivery of AI projects. It provided insight into AI requirements and architecture, design, and principles, and we covered best practices. The chapter also covered the details of what methodologies you need to develop AI projects and how to automate the delivery pipeline.

Governance is the most important part of AI projects. Without proper governance, your projects may fail. Therefore, I provided insight into how to govern, manage, and measure your AI projects.

Finally, I provided details about AI-based development, test, and delivery tools to accelerate normal cloud native projects.

PART V

Cloud Native Infrastructure

CHAPTER 16

Containerization and Virtualization

So far, you have learned to design and develop cloud native services from the functional and nonfunctional perspectives. In this chapter, you will learn more about deploying and running your developed binaries.

Infrastructure is all about the software and hardware that supports your applications. This includes data centers, operating systems, networks, automation, security, and the system needed to support the lifecycle of an application.

In this chapter, I will explain the details of running your services in a cloud environment with virtualization, containerization, and orchestration.

IaaS is driven by virtualization; it enables multiple operating systems with different configurations to run on a physical machine. The software layer in a VM is a hypervisor, which is required to run the VM on a system. This hypervisor controls all the hardware resources and can move resources from one VM to another depending on the needs. In this chapter, I will explain how some of the systems need to run on VMs and how they are useful in cloud native elements.

Containerization has become a de facto companion to virtualization for cloud native application services. It involves encapsulating software code and all its runtime dependencies so that the software can run uniformly and consistently on any infrastructure. It allows you to develop and deploy your services quickly and securely. In this chapter, I will cover how you can adopt containerization to run your services.

Containers require operational best practices; however, Kubernetes works as an orchestrator for your containerized applications to manage, scale, and schedule. It helps you fully implement container-based infrastructure in a production environment for your cloud native services. In this chapter, I will cover Kubernetes features, secrets, and configuration with monitoring and deployment.

© Shivakumar R Goniwada 2022
S. R. Goniwada, *Cloud Native Architecture and Design*, https://doi.org/10.1007/978-1-4842-7226-8_16

In addition, I will cover the details of containers and how cloud native applications are deployed in containers and in the Kubernetes environment.

- What applications and services are commonly virtualized?

- Cloud native and virtualization

- Container principles and patterns

- Best practices for adopting containers

- Container as a service (CaaS)

- Kubernetes principles and patterns

- How does Kubernetes solve common cloud native problems?

- Scaling your cloud native application

- Kubernetes as a service (KaaS)

- Observability and metrics on Kubernetes

- The stateful workload on Kubernetes

Introduction

Cloud native infrastructure is a requirement to effectively run cloud native applications. Without the right design and practices to manage infrastructure, even the best-designed cloud native services can create issues; therefore, you need to provide equal importance in designing your infrastructure.

Before providing more insight on how to build infrastructure for cloud native, you need to understand how you got where you are.

To execute your cloud native application on the cloud, you can produce value faster and focus on your business objectives. Developing only what you need to create your system and consuming services from cloud providers, keep your lead time small and agility high.

The ephemeral nature of cloud services demands automated development workflows that can be deployed as needed. The services must be designed with infrastructure ambiguity in mind. This has led engineers to rely on infrastructures like VMs, containers, and Kubernetes without having to worry about the underlying resources.

Containerization is a mature technology and adopts rapid changes in the way the services test and run application instances on the cloud. Containerization provides a less resource-intensive alternative to running an application on VMs because containers can share computational resources and memory without requiring a full operating system to underpin each application. Containers house all the runtime components that are necessary to execute an application in an isolated environment including configuration, libraries, etc.

All the major cloud providers offer a container as a service (CaaS) model that manages containers on a large scale, including starting, stopping, scaling, and organizing container workloads. CaaS offers both individual containers without orchestration capabilities and full-featured orchestration like Kubernetes. AWS offers the Amazon Elastic Container Service and Kubernetes services, Azure offers the Azure container and Kubernetes service, and Google offers the Kubernetes engine.

According to a Cloud Native Computing Foundation (CNCF) survey, in 2020, 92 percent of organizations surveyed used Docker containers, and 83 percent used Kubernetes for orchestration. This survey shows the overwhelming adoption of containers and Kubernetes for cloud native architecture.

Kubernetes is an open source orchestration engine developed by Google for managing cloud native services on containers across distributed cluster nodes. It provides a highly resilient infrastructure, provides automatic rollback, is highly scalable, and offers the self-healing of containers. The main objective of Kubernetes is to hide the complexity of managing a cluster of containers by providing APIs for configuration.

Bare-bones Kubernetes is not enough for production applications, because you need key services such as cluster monitoring and logging, reserved compute resources, heartbeats, election timeout, regular etcd backups, etc.

Kubernetes is not only for containers; you can use it for VMs too. In 2019, VMware started supporting Kubernetes as part of vSphere, which includes an ESXi hypervisor. Now it is possible to run containers on ESXi.

Kubernetes as a service (KaaS) is offered by various cloud providers as a managed service. The KaaS services are Google Kubernetes Engine (GKE), Amazon Elastic Kubernetes Service (EKS), Azure Kubernetes Service (AKS), Red Hat OpenShift, VMware Tanzu, and Docker EE. These services manage Kubernetes for deploying, managing, and maintaining clusters. Each managed service offers customized benefits.

Cloud native integrates cloud computing technologies and enterprise management methods, enabling enterprises to migrate services to cloud platforms more efficiently and quickly.

Cloud native infrastructure is not a solution for every problem; it is your responsibility to know if it is the right solution for your system environment.

What Is Cloud Native Infrastructure?

Cloud native infrastructure not only runs your applications in cloud infrastructure but does much more than that. The procedure to use IaaS is no different than running virtual servers on your data center.

You may think that because you have developed your services with microservices principles, used DevSecOps, and deployed in containers and orchestrator, this is cloud native. However, that is not correct. This is not the entire cloud native story. It is the first step, but still, there is a lot of work to be done to adhere to cloud native principles.

Cloud native is not just about running your services in containers and implementing Kubernetes orchestration. For example, Netflix runs all its services in VMs, not containers. You can't achieve the "-ilities" by packaging your services into microservices by just using the DevSecOps pipeline and infrastructure as code, which defines the automation for your infrastructure in a domain-specific language (DSL). Again, cloud native is not just about automation, services, and container in an infrastructure.

Cloud native is about the combination of all the mentioned technologies with well-designed infrastructure to solve technical and business problems. Cloud native applications do not directly benefit from IaaS; they run in a cloud environment with mostly autonomous systems.

As shown in Figure 16-1, the cloud native infrastructure creates a platform on top of IaaS that provides autonomous application lifecycle management. The platform is created on top of dynamic infrastructure to abstract away from individual servers, storage, etc., and it promotes dynamic resource allocation and configuration.

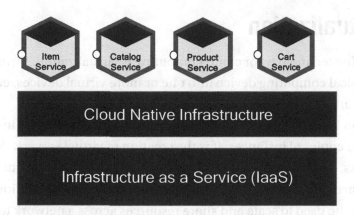

Figure 16-1. Cloud native infrastructure

I will explore how cloud native infrastructure is different by looking at the processes to deploy, manage, test, and operate infrastructure in subsequent sections.

Cloud Native Environment Characteristics

As I mentioned, simply having a virtualized environment does not equate to being fully cloud native. According to the National Institute of Standards Technology (NIST), a cloud native environment should have all the following characteristics. You should embrace all these characteristics to be truly cloud native.

- On-demand service
- Broad network access
- Elasticity
- Virtualized environment
- Pay-per-use model
- Policy as code
- Resource pooling

Cloud Virtualization

The main enabling technology for cloud computing is virtualization. Virtualization separates a physical computing device into one or more virtual devices, each of which can be used to perform separate computing tasks.

Virtualization is a technique that allows the sharing single physical instances through multiple copies of instances. It is the creation of virtual servers, desktops, storage, networks, etc. Cloud virtualization mainly deals with server virtualization.

Cloud infrastructure can contain a variety of bare-metal, virtualization, or container software that can be used to scale and share resources across a network to create a cloud. At the base, cloud computing runs on a stable operating system like Linux or Windows.

Virtualization software called a *hypervisor* is required to run virtual machines on a system. The hypervisor controls all the hardware resources and can take resources from one VM to another VM depending on the needs. The hypervisor always manages the states of all the VMs.

The cloud providers add management and automation layers for administrative control over infrastructure, platform, applications, and data, and they reduce human interaction for a repeatable process. Virtualization in a cloud provides agility and reduces the cost by increasing infrastructure utilization.

The cloud provides the added benefits of autoscaling, self-service access, and dynamic resource pooling, which is distinguished from normal virtualization.

How Does Virtualization Work?

Virtualization plays an important role in the cloud. The virtual machines are required to share the infrastructure across users. There are two types of hypervisors, and these hypervisors run the virtual machines as guests.

- Hypervisors run directly on the system hardware. This is a bare-metal, embedded hypervisor.

- Hypervisors run on a host operating system that provides virtualization services, such as I/O support and memory management.

Each vendor provides its own hypervisors like VMware ESX and ESXi, Microsoft Hyper-V, Citrix Xen Server, Oracle VM Virtual Box, Red Hat Enterprise Virtualization, KVM, etc.

As shown in Figure 16-2, a hypervisor is the software that creates VMs and then manages the allocation of resources to them. VMs are infrastructure resources set up to use the resources of the host hardware. You can divide these resources to accommodate the necessary virtual machines as guests such as a server with 100GB RAM available and a Linux OS. If you want to virtualize hardware to run your application, you can create VMs and use a hypervisor to manage the resources of the server, like one VM is allocated 25 GB of RAM, etc. A hypervisor virtualizes the server and manages all of them in one physical server, so each VMs operates efficiently.

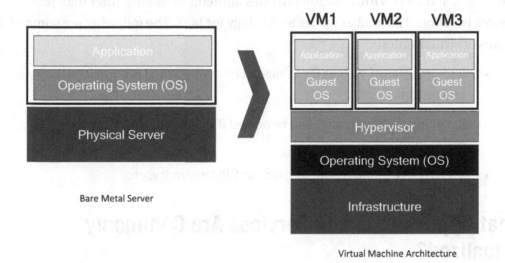

Figure 16-2. *Cloud virtualization*

Types of Virtualization in the Cloud

The cloud computing model depends on virtualization. By virtualizing a server, storage, network, and other physical data center resource, cloud providers can offer a range of services to users including IaaS, PaaS, and SaaS.

Virtualization is widely applied to several concepts including the following:

- *Server virtualization*: With server virtualization, one physical machine is divided into many virtual servers.

- *Desktop virtualization*: This creates multiple desktop operating systems, each in its VM on the same computer. One VM can be Windows, and the other can be Linux.

- *Network virtualization*: With this physical resource of a network, create different virtual networks that work independently of each other.

- *Storage virtualization*: This enables all storage devices on the network like server storage and stand-alone storage. It clusters all block storage into a single shared pool from which they can be assigned to any VMs on the network.

There are many virtualization techniques are available for application, data, data center, CPU, and GPU. Virtualization provides numerous benefits other than just resource isolation. This makes up the technology for IaaS. The following are some of the benefits of virtualization:

- It treats disks of VMs as files that can be snapshotted for quick backup and restore.

- It can be easily migrated and relocated if the machine requires any maintenance.

- It's easy to expand resources such as CPU, memory, etc.

What Applications and Services Are Commonly Virtualized?

Virtualization is a foundational component in the cloud and serves as the underlying infrastructure for cloud native applications. According to IDC, more than 80 percent of workloads are virtualized today. With virtualization, you can improve efficiency, free up resources, and enhance security. Cloud vendors provide agile, fast, and cost-effective virtualization solutions.

Cloud vendors provide various types of customizable VMs that let you create and run virtual machines on a cloud infrastructure. Organization will want to run VMs in the cloud such as Google's Compute Engine, AWS's EC2, and Azure's Virtual Machine. They offer multiple machine families to choose from, each suited for specific use cases. Table 16-1 describes the major virtual machine solutions from the major cloud providers, as of this writing.

Table 16-1. *Virtual Machine Comparison Across Cloud Providers*

VIRTUAL MACHINES	GCP	AWS	AZURE
GENERAL PURPOSE	This configuration has a lower price and lower performance and is suitable for most workloads including database, nonproduction environment, web application, etc.	This configuration is general-purpose and provides a balance of computing, memory, and networking resources that can be used for general common workloads.	This configuration is a general-purpose ideal for the nonproduction environments and low and medium levels of traffic.
COMPUTER OPTIMIZED	This configuration is for most compute-intensive workloads and suitable for game servers, IoT use cases, etc.	This configuration is for more compute-bound applications with high-performance processors and is suitable for batch processing, gaming servers, scientific modeling, etc.	This configuration is designed for a high CPU-to-memory ratio and is suitable for batch processes, network appliances, etc.
MEMORY-OPTIMIZED	This configuration is required for memory-intensive operations such as real-time analytics etc.	This configuration is designed for fast performance for workloads that process large data sets in memory and is suitable for IoT, high-performance DBs, etc.	This configuration is designed for high memory to CPU ratio and is suitable for databases, distributed caching, and in-memory analytics.
ACCELERATOR OPTIMIZED	This is for complex configurations like 16 GPUs in a single VM and is suitable for machine learning training and interfaces.	NA	

(continued)

Table 16-1. (*continued*)

VIRTUAL MACHINES	GCP	AWS	AZURE
STORAGE OPTIMIZE	NA	This configuration is designed for workloads that require high, sequential read and write access to very large data sets on local storage.	This configuration is designed for high disk throughput and IoT and is ideal for databases, etc.
GPU	NA	NA	This family of VMs is specialized and suitable for graphic rendering and video editing, ML processing, etc.
HIGH-PERFORMANCE COMPUTE	NA	NA	This family is the fastest and most powerful CPU with optional high throughput network interfaces and suitable for weather modeling, reservoir simulation, digital twin, etc.

Cloud Native and Virtual Machines

Developing and delivering systems keeps your organization more competitive. To do so, many organizations have adopted cloud native services with containers and Kubernetes. In IT, you cannot develop an isolated system; you require access to legacy technologies for any existing transaction. This is reality. Where are these applications run? How do you handle these applications that require VMs without complicating the management of virtualization and containers?

The VMs cannot be easily containerized with cloud native architecture. Some tools like KubeVirt and cloud native VMs (CNVM) reimagine VMs in Kubernetes. You can use your existing Kubernetes tools to natively manage VMs or convert those workloads into a container. This gives a flexible environment for a cloud native application. The cloud native VM is a VM inside a container.

For example, the Red Hat OpenShift virtualization solution supports containerized applications faster by hosting VM-based systems on the same platform as container-based applications. This supports the division of the existing system as well as the continued use of existing virtualized applications by managing virtualized systems and containerized services as part of single application deployment. OpenShift virtualization is enabled for a Red Hat OpenShift cluster; you can create and add virtualized applications to your project in the same way as containerized applications. This enables VMs to run in parallel on the same Red Hat OpenShift nodes as a traditional system container.

Containerization

Cloud native applications are distributed in nature and utilize cloud infrastructure. Numerous techniques and tools are used to implement cloud native applications, but from a computing perspective, cloud native application uses mainly containers. Containerization became a de facto standard for cloud native systems as an alternative to VMs.

As shown in Figure 16-3, the container is a technology that allows you to incorporate and configure your binaries and their dependencies in a package called an *image*. This image can be used to spawn an instance of your services: a container.

The services image in a container is abstracted from the environment in which services are executed. This abstraction allows cloud native-based services to be deployed easily and consistently across all environments, regardless of private, public, or hybrid environments. Container architecture provides a clean separation, as engineers can focus on a service's business logic and dependencies.

If you compare containers with VMs, as mentioned, the guest OS runs on top of a host OS with virtualized access to the underlying infrastructure. Like the VM, the container allows you to package your services together with binaries and other dependencies, providing an isolated environment for running your cluster of services. Containers provide a more lightweight architecture to work with and with more benefits.

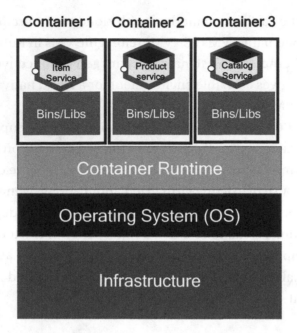

Figure 16-3. *Container architecture*

The containers are virtualized at the OS level, with multiple containers running atop the OS kernel directly unlike VMs virtualization at the hardware level. This makes a container more lightweight and allows it to share the OS kernel, start much faster, and use a fraction of the memory compared to booting the entire OS.

Linux Containers (LXC) was created by engineers from IBM around 2008 and is layered with some tooling on top of cgroups and namespaces. LXC works on a single Linux kernel without requiring any patches. LXC 1.0 was released around early 2014 and leveraged longstanding security technologies. In 2013, Docker emerged, and the container exploded in popularity and usage. Initially, Docker was built on top of LXC containers.

After the importance of cloud native services grew, the industry saw containerization become a foundation for modern software infrastructure. Research firm Gartner predicts that by 2022 more than 75 percent of global organizations will be running containerized applications in production.

What Is a Container Image?

A container image provides packaging and isolation of your services, as shown in Figure 16-4. The following are the few characteristics of a container image.

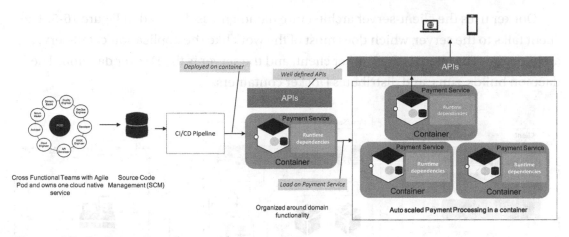

Figure 16-4. *Container image characteristics*

- A container image is immutable, and once it is built, it does not change; it is configured.

- A container image is a unit of domain functionality that addresses a single concern.

- A container image is owned by one agile pod team and has its release cycle.

- A container image is self-contained and defines and carries its runtime dependencies.

- A container image has well-defined structure APIs.

- A container image is disposable and safe to scale in and out.

- A container image is self-healing capability.

- A container image is stateless and is modular.

A container image provides a single unit of functionality, belongs to a single team, has an independent release cycle, and provides deployment and runtime isolation. Most of the time, one cloud native service corresponds to one image.

Container Architecture

Docker is open source and the most popular container technology; it's a containerization engine that works with most of the popular products.

Docker uses the client-server architecture paradigm, as depicted in Figure 16-5. The client talks to the server, which does most of the work like the application client-server architecture. The client is the Docker client, and the server is the Docker daemon. The daemon builds, runs, and distributes Docker containers.

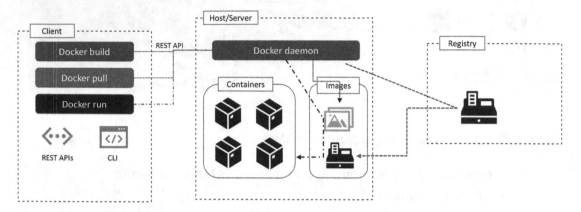

Figure 16-5. *Container architecture*

The Docker client and host/server communicate using REST APIs over a socket or a network interface. The Docker daemon provides a list of services through REST APIs. It listens to APIs and manages objects such as images, containers and networks, and volumes. One daemon can also communicate with another daemon to manage cloud native services.

The client is like a user interface. It is the primary interaction point for external users for configuration, using commands. For example, the client sends commands to the daemon over the APIs of multiple daemons in a cluster. The client can reside on the same host as the daemon or on a remote host.

A registry stores an image. For this, you can configure your private registry or Docker-provided registry called a *hub*. With the docker pull or docker run command, the required images are pulled from your configured registry. The docker push command pushes the images into your registry.

The image is a read-only template with instructions for creating Docker containers. For example, an image is your service with a Tomcat server and additional configurations.

The container is a runnable instance of your image. You can create, start, stop, move, or delete by using the REST APIs or command-line interface (CLI). The containers are isolated each other in the host server.

Container Principles

Today the container ecosystem has matured and has diverse and rich tooling that solves new and large-scale problems such as container orchestration, scalability, failure, high availability, cloud native service lifecycle management, and observability. It is not easy to achieve a production-ready large-scale deployment with thousands of cloud native services. The following principles and best practices help you to manage the container cloud native infrastructure effectively. Many of the practices are inspired by the 12-factor methodology, which is a standard way to develop a cloud native service.

The containerized application requires some principles to execute in a runtime container environment. With these principles, you will ensure that the container architecture is well designed to run services. The following are the principles; you can find details in Chapter 3:

Single-Container Principle (SCP)

In a cloud native architecture, SCP is about having a higher level of abstraction than responsibility. The single concern enables every microservice and container to address a single concern. SCP means every container must address a single concern with the cloud native service architecture style.

High-Observability Principle (HOP)

Observability is a measure of how well internal states of microservices can be derived from external outputs.

Lifecycle Conformance Principle (LCP)

LCP means that a container should have a way to read the events coming from the platform and conform by reacting to those events. All kinds of events are available for managing platforms that are intended to help you to manage the lifecycle of the container and cloud native services, based on all types of available events; it is up to you to decide which events to handle and whether to react to those events.

Image Immutability Principle (IIP)

IIP means an image is unchangeable once it is built and requires creating a new image if changes need to be made. You need to store the configuration and variables external to the container. For each image change, you need to build a new image and reuse it across various environments in your development lifecycle.

Process Disposability Principle (PDP)

PDP is a container runtime principle and states applications must be ephemeral as possible and ready to be replaced with container instances at any point of time by using infrastructure as code.

Self-Containment Principle (SCP)

SCP addresses the build-time concern, and the objective of this principle is that the container must contain everything that it needs at build time. The container relies on the presence of the Linux kernel or Windows silos and any additional libraries.

Runtime Confinement Principle (RCP)

RCP states that every container should declare its resource requirements and pass that information to the hosted platform.

Container Patterns

The following are a few best practices for making a container easier to design and operate. These practices cover a wide range of topics including security, monitoring, etc. These best practices are not always applicable in all business scenarios; choose the best one depending on the problem domain and business cases.

Container Security

Security must be built along with the DevSecOps pipeline throughout its lifecycle and there are a variety of tools available in the industry for managing container security. These tools can be used to scan a container, access a container cluster or vulnerabilities in images, and more.

The containers are well placed with process isolation, meaning user namespaces and resource encapsulation with cgroups reduce the attack vector to provide a protection. The container image needs to be well-constructed with security guidelines because these are the components that are eventually running your application. If there are security vulnerabilities packed into the container image as it's built, you increase the risk and potential severity of issues that will happen in production. The container security is not one concern; it spans pod teams, and there is an array of security layers that apply to containers:

- The container image and the libraries inside
- The interaction between containers and the host OS, both inbound and outbound
- Networking and storage
- Security at runtime, Kubernetes cluster

Alcide, Clair, WhiteSource, and Portshift are a few tools that help you to manage security in a container.

Logging Mechanism

Logs are an integral part of a system lifecycle and contain precious information about the events. Containers offer an easy and standardize a way to handle logs by using stdout and stderr. As shown in Figure 16-6, a container captures these logs and accesses them using Docker logs.

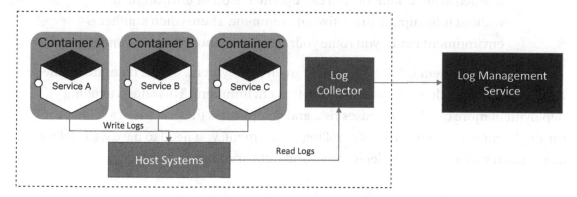

Figure 16-6. *Log management in a container*

You can use a log collector like Fluentd, Fluent Bit, etc., to collect data and send it to log management services like ELK in your application landscape.

Stateless

When you are designing your containers, don't treat them as a normal traditional server. For example, you might follow old practices like updating services on the running container. Don't do this. The containers are not designed to work this way. Always retire existing containers and create a new one. Follow either rolling deployment or blue-green deployment. Containers are designed to be stateless and immutable. Always store the state outside of your containers like in databases or any other storage event for user session also.

The stateful sessions are not best for cloud native services. When the consumer references a state on the server, the consumer opens a lot of incomplete sessions, and transactions happen. In the stateful system, the state is calculated by the client. This leaves the connection open and is difficult to verify the connections.

The stateless request issues a recent message in any ecommerce applications or social media. The response is independent of any server state.

- *Rolling deployment*: This deployment strategy slowly replaces previous versions of service with new versions of the service by completely replacing the container on which your service is running. For example, if the pod team updates an item service, then the container running the previous item service will be replaced by the new version of the service.

- *Blue/breen deployment*: This uses two identical containers in a separate environment, while the production environment uses one active environment. You can update the other environment without interrupting the active environment. Then, when another is environment ready, you route your request to another environment.

Rolling deployment is faster than blue/green deployment. Unlike blue/green, the rolling deployment does not have any isolation environment. This allows a rolling deployment more quickly, increases risk, and complicates the process of a rollback if the deployment fails. For successful rolling deployment, you need to have well-defined automation with continuous deployment and infrastructure as code.

Immutable

Immutable means containers won't be modified during their lifetime, with no updates, no patches, or even no configuration changes. If you want any modifications, kill the existing container, and create a new one. Immutability makes deployment safer and more repeatable. If you want to remove the existing image, just roll back and redeploy with another image. This helps you to maintain uniformity across environments. To use the same container images across the environment, like from development to production environment, suggest externalizing the configuration.

Privileged Containers

If your application uses the root user, then avoid it. If your services are compromised, an attacker would have full access to them. Therefore, avoid using privileged containers. A privileged container has access to all the devices of your environment, bypassing almost all the security features. Suggest giving specific capabilities to the container through security context options like the -cap-add flag of Docker. If you need to modify the host settings, then those details make it separate by using the init or sidecar pattern, as explained in Chapter 4.

Monitoring

Like logging, monitoring is an integral part of your system. In many ways, monitoring containerized applications follow the same process as logging. However, the containers are short-lived; you cannot add monitoring configuration within the containers. While designing and monitoring, separate black box and white box monitoring. Black box monitoring examines your application from outside. It is able to provide details about the audience because it is outside of the infrastructure. White box monitoring examining your services with privileged access and gathers metrics on its behavior that the users cannot view. You can configure various tools like Prometheus to capture these details.

Running Container as Root

Containers provide isolation. With container default settings, a process inside a container cannot access information from the host machine or other peer containers. Because containers share the kernel of the host machine, the isolation isn't complete as it is with VMs. An attacker could find unknown vulnerabilities that would allow the attacker to escape from a container. To avoid this, do not run processes as root inside containers.

Image Version

Always tag a version of the image you are using. Suggest using the "recent" tag, which can be moved from image to image.

Container Networking

The portability and short lifecycle of containers eliminate manual configuration and externalization configuration and leverage the network automation capabilities of your container orchestration.

Container Lifecycle Management

Containers are short-lived, and their lifecycle must be managed carefully by using automation.

Container Benefits

The containerization of an application brings many benefits including the following:

- *Agility and productivity*: It brings well-streamlined and accelerated development and improved consistency across the environment with the right best practices.

- *Fine-grained resilience*: It offers isolated deployments of the highly available components with no single point of failure.

- *Portability*: Containers can be deployed on any cloud provider and in their own data centers.

- *Security*: It offers improved security by isolating applications from the host system and each other.

- *Scalability*: Dynamic scaling and orchestration with the use of Kubernetes provides more robust for transaction spikes.

- *Edge level of networks*: Containers are beneficial at the edge level of networks. At the edge levels of networks, low latency, resiliency, and portability requirements are significant.

- *Machine learning models*: Containers benefit ML models where a problem can be separated into a small set of tasks.

- *Cost*: A container doesn't require a full guest OS and hypervisor and the container has only faster boot times, smaller memory footprints, and generally better performance. This helps trim cost.

Container Adoption Best Practices

The following are the best practices that are required to adopt for containerization:

- *Use fine-grained components*: The smaller the unit, the easier it is to manage and orchestrate. Break your components into fine-grained single responsibility units.

- *Use disposable components*: Always design and build stateless and lightweight containers. This enables the easy to manage, easy to create, and easy to destroy.

- *Implement container security*: Implement security measures and policies across the entire container environment including container images, hosts, config files, registries, etc.

- *Implement container with orchestration*: For efficient management of a large number of containers, adopt platform orchestration.

- *Automate the pipeline*: Implement automation in every lifecycle of software engineering including the DevSecOps pipeline and infrastructure as code.

- *Agility*: Implement agility to help pod teams improve the development lifecycle and move faster to market.

Containers in an Enterprise

The following are the key considerations when you are deploying containers on a large scale in an enterprise:

Technology Disruption

The container deployment is complex; you need to properly build, configure, deploy, manage, monitor, and update in a production environment. To achieve this, you need a series of tools and culture. However, most tools are third party and are constantly evolving. When tools evolve, you and your team need to keep pace with the disruption of technology, and you are required to continuously upgrade because of disruptions.

Culture

To use containers in an enterprise, you require strong backing by the leadership team to embrace a culture of cloud native.

Most Value Product (MVP)

It is not viable to jump into creating thousands of services across enterprises. This creates more problems than solves. Start small by running a few services in containers and learn and create a template and scale across enterprises. Figure 16-7 provides the details of an MVP approach. In this example, the engineering team creates an item microservice as an MVP and deploys it in container. Then it measures and learns from the experiences and mistakes and applies learnings to create another microservice called a *catalog*. Once you have gained experience, then go with @Scale IT for other services in an ecommerce application.

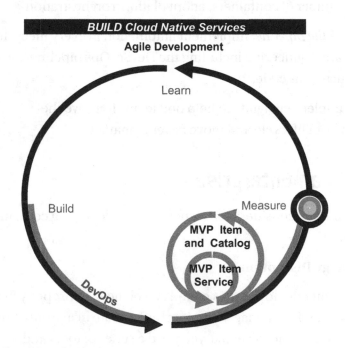

Figure 16-7. *MVP development*

Deployment Environment

Many options are available for your services deployments, from local on your own data center to public and private cloud and hybrid cloud. The cloud vendors offer a wide range of Docker environments.

- IaaS option, running containers on AWS EC2, Azure VM, and Google Compute Engine

- Fully managed container service (CaaS) solutions designed for hosting containerized services, such as AWS Elastic Container Services (ECS), and Azure Container Services

- Containers with Kubernetes

Registry

The containers are built based on images. If there is a vulnerability in the images, the containers inherit the issues and carry them to the production environment. You need to make sure the images are safe to use across the environment. For this, you need to enforce container scanning and a private registry. You adopt the following best practices for container scanning:

- Choose the right version from the artifactory.

- Create an optimized image file.

- Scan an image as part of the DevSecOps pipeline by using tools like Clair.

- Scan an image again in production.

- Ensure your scan images at multiple stages during the development lifecycle.

Monitoring and Logging

To securely manage the Docker environment across enterprises, you need to gain visibility into every deployed container in an environment. You can achieve this by using well-established integrated monitoring across the environment and automating responses and fault conditions.

Container Orchestration

Container orchestration automates the deployment, management, scaling, and networking of containers. If your enterprises want to implement hundreds or thousands of services in a container, then you can't think about collaborating containers without any orchestration. The container orchestration can be used in any environment like public cloud, private cloud, or hybrid cloud. It can help you to deploy the same services across different environments and automates scheduling, scalability, load balancing, availability, and networking of containers.

Generally, container orchestration tools communicate with a human-created YAML or JSON file that describes the configuration of the application. This configuration file contains rules and directs orchestration on how to retrieve container images, how to create a network between containers, where to store log data, and how to mount storage volumes.

It manages the deployment scheduling of containers into clusters and automatically identifies the right host. The selection of the right host depends on user-defined guidelines, labels, or metadata. Once the host is assigned, the orchestration tool automates and manages the services throughout the lifecycle based on the rules defined.

The orchestration tools automate and manage the cloud native services in containers including the following:

- Configuration and scheduling containers

- Provisioning and container deployment

- Resource allocation

- Scaling containers to balance requests

- Service discovery

- Monitoring container health

- Interaction between containers security

- Traffic routing

The container orchestration tools provide a framework for managing containers in an enterprise. There are many container orchestration tools available in the market that can be used for managing the container lifecycle. Some popular options are Kubernetes, Docker Swarm, Apache Mesos, etc. Some cloud provides offering PaaS services on top of Kubernetes such as OpenShift, Google Kubernetes Engine, AWS Elastic Kubernetes Service, Azure Kubernetes Service, etc.

Types of Orchestration Tools

Choosing the right orchestration tool for your enterprises involves diverse factors such as the number of containers in an environment, technical experience and skill level of your resources, maturity of tools, widely used references, etc. The following are the most popular ones.

Docker Swarm

Docker Swarm is a container orchestration tool that is built into Docker engines. As shown in Figure 16-8, a Swarm is based on the client-server architecture style. The client is the Swarm manager, and the host servers are containers hosted in multiple nodes.

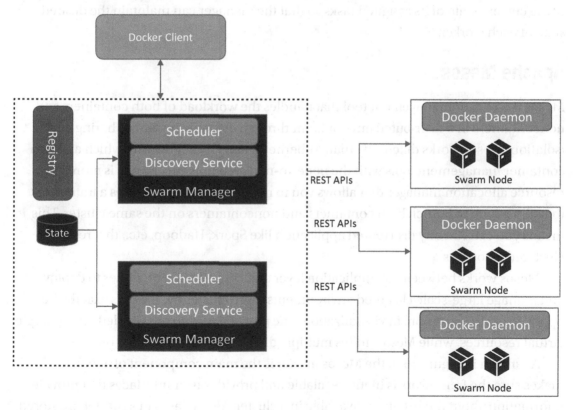

Figure 16-8. Docker Swarm architecture

Docker Swarm consists of a node, manager, and services. The manager node uses the Raft consensus algorithm to internally manage the cluster state. This is to ensure all manager nodes that scheduling and controlling the containers in the cluster maintain state. Docker Swarm can have more than one manager node lead by a single manager node elected using a Raft algorithm, and a manager node can act as both a Swarm node and a manager node. The manager nodes act as orchestration and cluster management functions required to maintain the desired state of the swarm. The Manager node elects a single leader to conduct an orchestration task.

The Raft algorithm achieves a consensus via an elected leader. A server is a Raft cluster that is either a leader or a follower and can be a candidate in the precise cause of an election. Consensus involves multiple servers agreeing on values. Once they decide on a value, that is final.

The Swarm node is a cluster of Docker containers running on a cloud server. These nodes receive and execute tasks dispatched from manager nodes. Each swarm of worker node reports back to the manager on tasks. The swarm node notifies the manager node of the current state of its assigned tasks so that the manager can maintain the desired state of each worker.

Apache Mesos

Mesos is a cluster management tool that handles the workload of both containers and noncontainers in a distributed environment through dynamic resource sharing and isolation. Mesos works differently than Kubernetes and Docker Swarm, which are both container management tools with the node-to-node relationship. Mesos is more of a resource allocation manager that allows you to manage jobs and provides a framework that allows you to launch both containers and noncontainers on the same cluster. This means you can run any distributed application like Spark, Hadoop, etc., that requires clustered resources.

Mesos works between the application layer and OS and makes it easier to deploy and manage large-scale clustered environments more efficiently. It works exactly the opposite of virtualization. In virtualization, one physical resource is divided into multiple virtual resources, while Mesos unites multiple distributed resources into one.

As shown in Figure 16-9, the Mesos master is the main component of a tool. It makes sure the framework is highly available and provides user interfaces that provide information about the resources available in a cluster. All the tasks in a master are stored in memory.

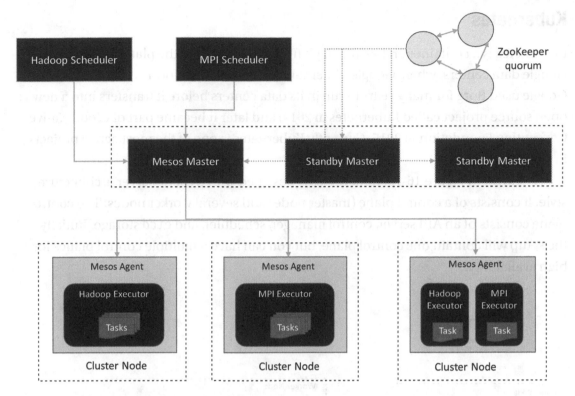

Figure 16-9. *Apache Mesos architecture*

The Mesos agent manages the containers that host the services. It manages the communication between the Mesos master and an executor.

Mesos consists of a master daemon that manages agent daemons on each cluster node, and Mesos runs tasks on these agents. The master enables fine-grained sharing resources across frameworks by making them resource offers. The Mesos master decides how many resources to offer to each framework. The framework consists of the scheduler and an executor. The scheduler registers with the Mesos master for resources, and the executor process launches an agent node to run the framework tasks. The Mesos master determines how many resources are offered to each framework, and the framework scheduler selects the resources to use.

In subsequent sections, I will consider only the Kubernetes framework to explain further cloud native use cases.

Kubernetes

Kubernetes is a container orchestration platform. The origin of the platform is from Google data centers, where Google's internal orchestration platform is named Borg. Google used Borg for many years to run in its data centers before it transfers into a new open source project called Kubernetes in 2014, and later it became part of Cloud Native Computing Foundation in 2015. Currently Kubernetes is one of the most active projects in GitHub.

As shown in Figure 16-10, Kubernetes is designed with a client-server architecture style. It consists of a control plane (master node) and several worker nodes. The control plane consists of an API server, control manager, scheduler, and etcd storage. Initially the setup will contain one control plane, but you can have a multiple control planes for high availability.

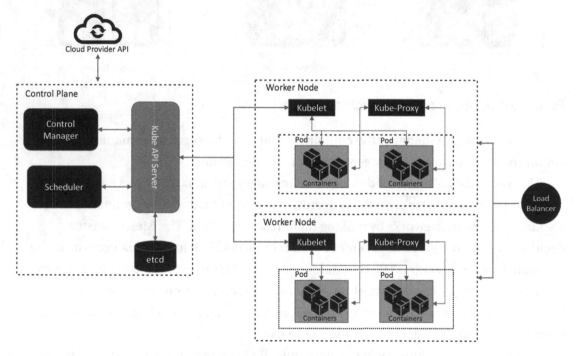

Figure 16-10. *Kubernetes architecture*

A control plane maintains the details of all the Kubernetes objects and continuously manages object states, responding to changes in the worker nodes. The API server acts as a bridge between the worker node and control plane, and engineers can access the control plane by using this API server. The control manager is a daemon that runs the control loop, watches the state of the nodes, and makes changes appropriately. This manager integrates with the cloud for availability zones, VMs, storage services, etc., and the scheduler schedules the containers across the worker nodes.

The worker nodes are the machine that runs containers and is managed by the control plane, and the Kubelet controls the execution of containers in a node.

Orchestration Tool Comparison

Table 16-2 provides a high-level comparison between major orchestration tools.

Table 16-2. Orchestration Tool Comparison

Docker Swarm	Apache Mesos	Kubernetes
It is a native Docker clustering solution that makes it easy to integrate and set up flexible APIs.	It is more of a resource allocation manager that allows you to manage jobs and provides a framework that allows you to launch both containers and noncontainers on the same cluster.	The control plane maintains the details of Kubernetes, and the API server acts as a bridge between the worker node and the control plane.
YAML-based configuration deployment.	Unique format-based configuration deployment.	YAML-based configuration deployment.
Mature and has good stability.	Mature.	Mature and has good stability with continuous update and large community.
Defined using a Docker Compose file and same compose file to maintain a cluster of containers on a single machine.	It is based on an N-ary tree with groups as branches and applications as leaves.	It is a combination of ReplicaSets, controllers, and pods.

(continued)

Table 16-2. (*continued*)

Docker Swarm	Apache Mesos	Kubernetes
A Swarm is based on the client-server architecture style. The client is the Swarm manager, and the host servers are containers hosted in multiple nodes.	Handles the workload of both containers and noncontainers.	Container orchestration platform and works with the client-server architecture.
It supports only Docker.	It supports both container and noncontainer workloads. It runs on Swarm and Kubernetes.	It supports both Docker and rkt.
It includes a DNS server out of the box that allows for service discovery by name.	Does not support any service discovery.	It includes optional DNS for discovery by name; here services are exposed through HTTP ingress or mapped to an external load balancer.

Kubernetes Features

In a cloud native platform, you cannot just run on the siloed container; you need to have a group of containers for your application. Kubernetes provides a management layer for the lifecycle of a group of containers called a *pod*, as illustrated in Figure 16-11.

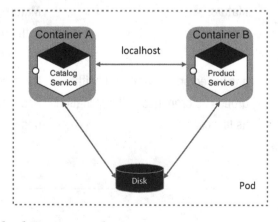

Figure 16-11. *Pod deployment and management*

A pod is an atomic unit of scheduling, deployment, and runtime isolation for a cluster of containers. All containers in a pod are always scheduled to the same host, deployed together whether for scaling or host migration and sharing a namespace, filesystem, and networking. Containers in a pod interact with each other over the filesystem or networking. The features of the pod are as follows:

- A pod is an atomic unit of scheduling, which means the scheduler identifies a host that satisfies all the containers in a pod.

- A pod ensures the colocation of containers, provides various means of communication patterns like networking, provides a filesystem, etc.

- A pod has an IP address, name, and port range that are shared by all containers within it. This means the containers in a pod are carefully configured to avoid port clashes.

- Pods are ephemeral. They are disposable. A pod can be rescheduled at a different node at any time if the existing node is unhealthy.

Kubernetes Principles and Patterns

Containers are the building blocks of Kubernetes-based cloud native applications, and containers play a fundamental role in Kubernetes. Creating modularized, reusable, single responsibility container images is fundamental to your cloud native architecture.

Containers and pods and their unique characteristic offer a new set of principles and patterns for designing a cloud native service. Adhering to these principles and patterns will help ensure your applications are suitable for automation in cloud native platforms. Here, I am covering a few, but you can find more patterns in a book called *Kubernetes Patterns*.

Predictable Demands

The successful application deployment, management, and coexistence on a multitenant environment is dependent on application resource requirement and runtime dependencies. This pattern is about how you declare requirements.

Kubernetes can manage polyglot containerized services, and each service has different resource requirements. For example, some services execute faster than other services, or some programming languages require different things from other languages. It is difficult to identify the number of resources required for a container. Some services require more memory and more CPU, and some may require less. Some may require polyglot storage, and some may be stored in memory, etc. Defining all these characteristics in a cloud native application is a must.

Knowing about these requirements is helpful because Kubernetes can make intelligent decisions to place a container on a cluster and helps you with proper capacity planning.

Declarative Deployment

This pattern is about managing the rollback and upgrading a newer version of the container in a pod. The cloud native maturity in your organization leads to more adoption of services. The number of services increases because you have to continually update and replace them with newer versions due to business changes. Upgrading these services leads us to starting a new version of a pod, stopping the old version of the pod, etc. Performing manually leads to human errors and takes time.

Kubernetes has automated these activities without involving any humans. Using this concept, you need to describe how your application should be updated using different strategies. Rolling deployments are the declarative way of updating services in Kubernetes through the concept of deployment. The rolling update behavior ensures there is no downtime during the update process.

Use a rolling deployment, fixed deployment, blue-green release, or canary release deployment strategy.

Health Probe

This pattern is about how a service can communicate its health state to Kubernetes. The cloud native service must adopt an observable-as-a-service approach, which helps Kubernetes to detect whether the service is healthy. These observations influence the lifecycle management of pods and the way traffic is routed to the application. Kubernetes regularly checks the container process status, but checking just the status does not provide the complete health of a service, for example, if your service hangs or is slow to respond. You can get the health of a service from this.

A *process health check* is the health check process by Kubelet that is done for all the services in a pod. This process identifies the service failure or service shutdown in a container.

A *liveness probe* is the health check process and regularly checks the Kubelet agent to confirm the container's health. This helps to kill the unhealthy container and replace them with a new one.

A *readiness probe* performs the readiness of a container like liveness probes.

Your cloud native services must be highly observable by providing a means for the managing platform to identify the health of the service. Health checks play a fundamental role in cloud native services such as automating the deployment, self-healing, scaling, etc. Logging is one good practice for health probes. You need to design your containers such that they provide relevant APIs for health checks. These APIs are read-only endpoints the platform is continuously probing to get application insights. You can refer to the box and port style architecture in Chapter 5. It is recommend that you use the health checks process to manage the pods.

Automated Placement

One of the core functions of the Kubernetes scheduler is to assign new pods to nodes, satisfying container resources requests and honoring scheduling policies. This pattern talks about Kubernetes' scheduling algorithm.

Matured cloud native enterprises might have hundreds or even thousands of isolated processes. Containers and pods do provide a nice abstraction of packaging and deployment but do not support how to place these processes on suitable nodes. With growing cloud native services, assigning and placing them individually to nodes is not a manageable activity.

In Kubernetes, assigning pods to nodes is done by a scheduler, which is highly configurable. The main operation of the Kubernetes scheduler is to retrieve each newly created pod definition from the API server and assign it to a node. It finds suitable nodes for every pod like moving from unhealthier to healthier node, etc. However, for the scheduler to do its job and allow declarative placement, the scheduler needs nodes with available capacity and containers with declarative resource profiles and guiding policies.

Singleton Service

This pattern ensures only one instance of a service is active at a time and yet highly available. Pods can scale with the command kubectl scale or declaratively through a definition replica set. Running multiple instances of the same services increases the throughput and availability. In Kubernetes, multiple instances are replicas of a pod. For some use cases, you may need to run only one instance of a service. For example, when polling on specific payment interfaces, you want to ensure only single resources to perform polling and processing. In these kinds of services, you need to have control of several instances of services.

Running multiple replicas of the same pod creates an active-active topology where all instances of services are active. You need an active-passive topology where only one instance is active and all other instances are passive. This can be achieved with out-of-application and in-application locking.

Out-of-application locking can be achieved in Kubernetes by starting a pod with one replica. This alone does not help you to make a singleton; along with this, the replica set turns the singleton pod into a highly available singleton.

In-application locking, in a distributed environment, is one way to control the service instance count through a distributed lock. Whenever a service instance or a component inside the instance is activated, it can try to acquire a lock, and if it succeeds, the service becomes active. Any subsequent service instance that fails to acquire lock waits continuously tries to get the lock.

Init Container

This pattern enables the separation of concerns by providing a separate lifecycle for initialization-related tasks distinct from the main application containers. You can find more details of this pattern in Chapter 4.

Sidecar

It extends and enhances the functionality of a preexisting container without changing it. This pattern allows you to add several additional configuration details from a third party without modifying the microservices. It is a single-node pattern made up of two containers. One container for the application container contains the core business logic, and another container is for technical configuration details. You can find more details of this pattern in Chapter 4.

Running a Cloud Native Application on the Container and Kubernetes Strategy

Containers and Kubernetes are mature, but the ecosystem is immature due to the lack of operational best practices in organizations. However, the adoption of container and Kubernetes is increasing every day with the evolution of cloud native elements. Organizations are adopting containers in production, but production deployments are still concerned with operational challenges such as security, observability, data management, infrastructure, and networking, and most important is automation because cloud native services require a high degree of end-to-end automation.

If you want mature and streamlined containers and Kubernetes in production, you need to embrace best practices and strategy, and you need strong leadership.

- You need to have a strong DevSecOps culture to ensure a seamless move to production.

- Develop a Kubernetes platform that uses best practices and patterns across security, governance, observability, lifecycle, and cloud provider selections.

- Create an intelligent single operations team and development team.

- You need the right talent to create a roadmap to upskill your resources on containers and Kubernetes.

The most important point is to select the right Kubernetes platform because there are various platforms available in the industry. You can consider the following factors while selecting the platforms:

- Support for OS and container runtimes

- UI and application lifecycle management

- Hybrid, private, and multicloud cluster management

- Operational capabilities such as governance, security, networking, automation, and observability

- PaaS adoption for other services in your enterprises

- Licensing and pricing model

- Industry maturity of a vendor

For deploying containers in production, you need to create a strategy to operationalize Kubernetes. The following are the elements and best practices:

- *Security and governance*: Integrate container scanning and image scanning to prevent vulnerabilities along with the CI/CD pipeline. Use the configuration-as-a-service model to harden the configuration and deploy security products that provide whitelisting, behavioral monitoring, etc. Adopt a shift-left approach for code and security vulnerability tests.

- *Automation including infrastructure as code*: Automate infrastructure provisioning by using an infrastructure-as-code tool, use the container-aware configuration management system to manage the lifecycle of a container image, and integrate containers and Kubernetes with CI/CD toolchains.

- *Observability*: Focus on monitoring at the container level and across services so that you are monitoring your container both internally and externally. Use container commands and the right tools.

- *Networking host*: Check that your Kubernetes distribution or software-defined networking (SDN) solution supports Kubernetes networking. If this is not available, select the Container Networking Interface (CNI), and ensure it provides an ingress controller support for load balancing across hosts in the cluster. If it is not sufficient, then consider other proxies or service meshes or event meshes. Along with this strategy, you need the following service to make Kubernetes production ready.

  - *Cluster monitoring and logging*: When running in production, containers and Kubernetes are required to scale to hundreds or thousands of pods depending on the size of your enterprise. Without the effective implementation of monitoring and logging, downtime can cause serious or irreversible errors that can cause business dissatisfaction. Create integrated monitoring by using various open source or commercial tools.

- *Reserved compute resources for daemons*: Reserve resources for system daemons, which both Kubernetes and OS require. The system daemon utilizes CPU, memory, and temporary storage resources. You can use Kubelet flags to reserve resources for system daemons.

- *Heartbeat and election timeout interval for etcd members*: When configuring an etcd cluster, it is important to specify the heartbeat correctly and choose timeout settings.

- *Regular etcd backups*: Regularly back up etcd data because it stores the state of the cluster.

Kubernetes Maturity Model

If your organization is new to Kubernetes or has already been using Kubernetes in multiple applications, Kubernetes has a complexity that you'll need to overcome. The Kubernetes maturity model shown in Figure 16-12 provides the end-to-end journey of Kubernetes adoption. One thing you need to remember is that the maturity doesn't occur in one day. This requires a certain amount of time.

If you start using the maturity model, know that when you do reach a certain phase, you still may go back to the previous phase to check certain things. You need to use this framework to understand where you are and what you need to focus on.

The Kubernetes maturity model helps you to review where you are in your cloud native journey, like whether you are new to Kubernetes or you have deployment experience.

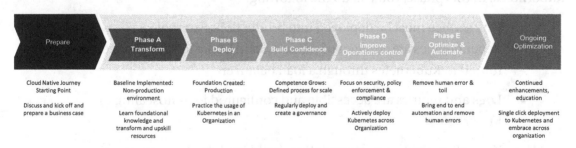

Figure 16-12. *Kubernetes maturity model*

Prepare

This is the first phase in the maturity model, and this is the preparation phase of your cloud native Kubernetes journey. In this phase, you do the following:

- You will anticipate how cloud native and Kubernetes can help you to support your business and technical objectives, cost, and end goal.

- You will prepare a strategy for your organization on the importance of cloud native and Kubernetes.

- You will prepare the value proposition and impact of cloud computing, containers, and Kubernetes.

Transform

You will start adopting Kubernetes in this phase.

- You will verify foundational knowledge and create an MVP on Kubernetes deployments in a cluster.

- You will prepare an initial implementation, migration, and learning curve roadmap.

- You will start socializing across teams on Kubernetes.

Deploy

If you reached this maturity, you will have covered the basics and initial steps of Kubernetes. In this phase, you will do the following:

- One service must be deployed into production. External dependencies are configured properly, and traffic to your services are routed to Kubernetes through a load balancer.

- Logs and metrics are accessible and configured for autoscaling to Kubernetes.

- You will cover the implementation, build, and deployment process, setting up DevOps and introducing basic observability.

Build Confidence

As your Kubernetes deployment matures, you have a foundation in place. This phase is to build confidence in your organization and get Kubernetes up and running in production. Building confidence in Kubernetes requires experience, and the business outcome depends on your team's experience. In this phase, monitoring will be implemented.

Improve Operations

You are actively deploying Kubernetes across organizational successfully and on time to improve the "-ilities" and operationalizing your Kubernetes clusters.

Measure and Control

In this phase, you introduce more measurement and control of the Kubernetes environment. You and your teams have an overall understanding, and there is an organization-wide option. You have started understanding the Kubernetes cluster and overall environment on a deeper level. You will gather more data and resolve the technical debt identified in previous phases and will streamline the monitoring and observability.

Optimize and Automate

In this phase, you introduce more measurement and control of the environment, achieve business outcomes, and have measurable results to show to various stakeholders. You make further improvements on cost and performance metrics. You are required to revisit your earlier goals and fine-tune them based on the learnings. In this phase, you need to automate as much as possible and adopt best practices and principles.

Service Meshes and Kubernetes

A service mesh pattern is a logical extension of the sidecar proxy. As shown in Figure 16-13, by attaching a sidecar proxy to every pod, a service mesh can control functionality for service-to-service requests, such as advanced routing rules, retries, and timeouts. Along with every request pass through a proxy, service meshes can implement mutual TLS encryption between services. There are several service mesh tools available, such as Istio, Linkerd, Kuma, and Consul. Istio is the most popular implementation of the service mesh pattern. You can find more details about using service meshes in Kubernetes in Chapter 5.

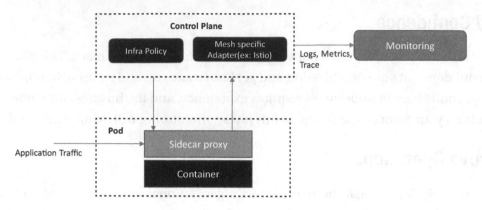

Figure 16-13. *Service meshes and Kubernetes*

Stateful Workloads on Kubernetes

Usually, services in cloud native are stateless, which is the recommended approach, but some use cases require stateful services. An example of a stateful application is a database or key-value store in which the data is retrieved and stored by other services or applications.

You can deploy the stateful application in Kubernetes with a ReplicaSet or deployment and use StatefulSets. Many distributed stateful applications have their clustering mechanism or consensus algorithm. For this kind of application, the StatefulSets provide static pod naming based on an ordinal system.

To illustrate how StatefulSets can help run the stateful application on Kubernetes, let's look at how you might run PostgreSQL on Kubernetes with StatefulSets. Running PostgreSQL on Kubernetes requires a container image and makes sure it has all the necessary configuration and startup commands.

Scaling PostgreSQL is not like running stateless applications; here you can scale your service without creating a new state. Each member of the PostgreSQL cluster knows about the other members, and most importantly, it knows which member of the cluster is the leader. This is how databases like PostgreSQL can offer a consistency guarantee and ACID compliance. Since each member in a PostgreSQL cluster needs to know about the other, you need to run your pods in a way that they have a common way to communicate with each other. The StatefulSets offer is through ordinal pod numbering. This way, the application that needs to self-cluster while running on Kubernetes knows that a common naming scheme will be used. You can find more about the replica sets in Chapter 4.

Kubernetes Multitenancy

A multitenant cluster is shared by multiple users and services. The operators of multitenant clusters must isolate tenants from each other to minimize the effect. As shown in Figure 16-14, when you plan a multitenant in a deployment model, you must consider the layers of resource isolation in Kubernetes, cluster, namespace, node, pod, and container. You must consider security implications when sharing among tenants.

Multitenancy capabilities aim to drive the efficient use of infrastructure while providing operators with robust isolation mechanisms between users, services, and teams. Kubernetes allows you to build multitenant platforms leveraging built-in capabilities.

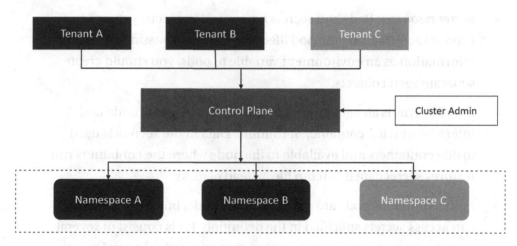

***Figure 16-14.** Multitenancy in Kubernetes*

Kubernetes cannot guarantee perfectly secure isolation between tenants; you can separate each tenant and their resources into their namespaces, roles and role bindings, resource quota, network policy, etc. You can use policies to enforce isolation; it can be scoped by namespace and can be used to restrict API access to constrain resource usage.

The control plane is important as you bring in more tenants because it becomes a single point of failure for clusters. The Kubernetes API is a critical service for you because it provides the interface for administrators and tenant teams to manage clusters and services. So, the Kubernetes response of an API is a critical part of the multitenant strategy.

The tenants of a multicluster share extensions, controllers, add-ons, and custom resource definition and cluster control plane.

The multitenant comes with advantages, such as reduced managed overhead, reduced resource fragmentation, improved return on investment (ROI), etc.

Kubernetes Secrets

Kubernetes secrets are the native resources for storing and managing sensitive data such as passwords, SSH keys, and OAuth tokens. You need to distribute these secrets across your Kubernetes clusters. When sending these secrets, it's critical to ensure only authorized entities can access them.

Secrets are native Kubernetes resources, and Kubernetes provides a basic set of protection layers to them. These protections are as follows:

- *Secret resources*: Pods and secrets are separate objects; you can expose secrets during the pod lifecycle. If you are passing sensitive information as an environment variable to pods, you should create separate secret objects.

- *Kubelet*: This is an agent that runs on each Kubernetes node and interacts with the container at runtime. Data in the secrets is used inside containers and available to the node where the containers run. It stores secret data in a temp file instead of disks.

- *Pods*: Numerous pods are running on the node, but only the pods can access secrets specified in the definition. Pods consist of several containers, and secrets are mounted only on required containers.

- *Kubernetes API*: Secrets are created and accessed over the Kubernetes API.

- *etcd*: Secrets also stored in `etcd`; it's possible to access secrets when you access `etcd` on the control plane.

These protection measures ensure that secrets are separated from Kubernetes resources, accessed, and stored securely, but Kubernetes is not highly secured but comes with risks. The risks are as follows:

- *Configuration as code (CaC)*: You can create a secret object using JSON or YAML manifest files. Make sure this file isn't checked into the repository or shared.

- *Service layer*: When secrets are loaded in your services, be careful about logging or monitoring.

- *Pods*: If a user has sufficient permissions to create a pod that mounts and uses a secret, the secret value will visible to them.

- *Nodes*: Containers run on the nodes, and it is possible to retrieve any secret from the Kubernetes API server if you're the root on the node.

Various tools and services are available in cloud native to manage secrets. The following are the few services you can adopt to manage secrets:

- *Cloud key management system (KMS)*: The cloud providers such as AWS, Azure, and Google have their KMS, a centralized cloud service through which you can create and manage keys to perform cryptographic operations.

- *Helm secret plugins*: This plugin allows you to encrypt values files with a secret key of your choice. It is also possible to edit the encrypted files.

Kubernetes as a Service

Kubernetes as a service (KaaS) makes it possible to operate Kubernetes in a cloud environment. These services are commonly provided by cloud vendors. The functionality of the KaaS platform is to deploy, manage, and maintain Kubernetes clusters. Key features of KaaS include self-service deployment, upgrades, scalability, and multicloud portability. Here I will provide a brief description. For more details, you can refer to each cloud provider's documentation.

KaaS can help you leverage the best practices of Kubernetes without the complexities involved in managing operations. A KaaS can take care of a variety of services including setup, monitoring, and managing the operations and ensuring HA and release updates as needed. The following are a few key capabilities of KaaS:

- Deploy and manage

- Continuous monitoring

- Control plane management

- Security

Google Kubernetes Engine

Google Kubernetes Engine (GKE) was the first commercial KaaS offering. It is a fully managed containerized service in the Google Cloud infrastructure. The GKE environment consists of multiple machines grouped to form a cluster. When you run the GKE cluster, you will get advanced cluster management features such as the following:

- Autopilot mode of operation

- Pod and clustering autoscaling

- Workload and network security

- Node pools to designate subsets of nodes within a cluster for additional flexibility

- Logging and monitoring

Amazon Elastic Kubernetes Service

Amazon Elastic Kubernetes Service (EKS) is a service used to run managed Kubernetes on AWS. It can deploy clusters across multiple availability zones (AZs) with HA. EKS integrates with other services in an AWS. EKS helps you provide highly available and secure clusters and automates key tasks such as patching, node provisioning, etc. The following are some of the benefits of EKS:

- EKS runs the Kubernetes control plane across multiple AZs, automatically detects and replaces unhealthy control plane nodes, and provides on-demand, zero-downtime upgrades.

- Provision and scale your services efficiently.

Azure Kubernetes Services

Azure Kubernetes Services (AKS) is a fully managed service that lets you manage Kubernetes on Azure resources. It allows you to deploy directly on Azure services and also integrate with existing Azure services. These are some of the benefits of AKS:

- Elastic provisioning of capacity without the need to manage the infrastructure

- Faster end-to-end development experience with Azure services

- Most comprehensive authentication and authorization capabilities

- Availability in more regions

Red Hat OpenShift

Red Hat OpenShift is a highly customizable managed service you can use to deploy Kubernetes to any infrastructure. It supports multitenancy, has a built-in dedicated image registry, and provides extended support of the DevOps pipeline. It has several preconfigured packages.

VMware Tanzu

It is a platform that enables you to build and manage Kubernetes environments, alongside traditional VMware workloads, with central control. It enables integrated Kubernetes with VMware technologies such as vSphere, vSAN, and NSX, to manage VMware Kubernetes clusters within the data center.

Summary

Cloud native infrastructure is about practices and how you build and maintain infrastructure. It impacts much more than servers, networks, and storage; it is about how you manage services in a cloud native infrastructure.

In this chapter, I explained the elements of cloud native infrastructure and how you can use containers and Kubernetes to deploy your cloud native services.

CHAPTER 17

Infrastructure Automation

Cloud native modern-day businesses depend on well-defined and automated IT infrastructure. Virtualization, the cloud, containers, server automation, and software-defined networking are meant to simplify operations. When organizations use the manual provisioning of infrastructure, it leads to delays in setting up an infrastructure, networking, storage, etc.

Many organizations struggle to manage manual IT tasks and processes across siloed teams. Sometimes the infrastructure team makes you wait a week or two to provide the infrastructure. There is a growing need to automate IT tasks and processes, and automation helps you to streamline them.

Automation is essential for both IT optimizations and cloud native transformations. To support business success, IT environments must be efficient, scalable, and reliable. Infrastructure operation helps you to streamline operations, improve agility, and increase security and availability.

This chapter helps you to understand how you effectively use principles, patterns, and practices through the DevOps pipeline to automate infrastructure.

In this chapter, I will cover the following:

- Infrastructure-as-code principles and patterns

- Tools and services

- Testing infrastructure changes

- What can't you automate?

What Is Infrastructure Automation?

Automation is at the core of many organizations' technology landscapes, propelled by the need to innovate faster, manage increasingly complex IT environments, accommodate new development approaches, and meet financial objectives.

619

© Shivakumar R Goniwada 2022
S. R. Goniwada, *Cloud Native Architecture and Design*, https://doi.org/10.1007/978-1-4842-7226-8_17

Infrastructure automation is a set of processes that you use to reduce manual efforts associated with managing and provisioning workloads in the public, private, or hybrid cloud. It uses software/scripts to create repeatable instructions and processes to replace or reduce human interaction with IT systems. The tools work within the limits of instructions to perform tasks with little to no human intervention.

Automation plays a pivotal role in leveraging deployment scripts, engaging teams, monitoring tools, and tracking performance. It can also provide a better degree of reliability and boost cross-team collaboration.

By using automation, you can automate most IT tasks including the following:

- Managing physical infrastructure

- Deploying applications

- Administering virtualized environments

- Managing containers and Kubernetes environments

- Managing networks

- Implementing sanity checks and smoke tests

- Managing user access to infrastructure resources

- Troubleshooting and debugging system health

- Managing the inventory of your infrastructure resources

Automation simplifies IT infrastructure management and application service delivery by streamlining error-prone, time-consuming, and manual IT tasks and processes. Infrastructure as code (IaC) automates the provisioning of infrastructure, enabling your organization to develop, deploy, and scale cloud native services with speed, have fewer errors, and reduce costs by using various tools.

What Can You Automate?

You can automate most features of your infrastructure. The key to automation in the infrastructure is not just about provisioning infrastructure but also about connecting teams, processes, and tools into a single automated flow. You can automate the following along the DevOps pipeline:

- *Databases*: Hardware and servers or managed services from cloud vendors.

- *Cloud native services*: Virtualized infrastructure, containers, Kubernetes, OS, networking, and storage.

- *Development environment*: Cloud resources in similar environments as the cloud native services. The environment consists of the entire CI and CD stacks like source code management, build tools, code review tools, security scanning, Artifactory, application lifecycle management (ALM) tools, infrastructure-as-code tools, etc.

- *Test environments*: Cloud resources in similar environments as cloud native services plus testing tools, test data management, etc.

What Is Infrastructure as Code?

Infrastructure as code (IaC) is the engineering, managing, and provisioning of infrastructure resources through code instead of using a manual or semi-automated process to configure the system.

Provisioning infrastructure is a time-consuming and costly process and requires physically setting up hardware, installing the OS, configuring the network, etc. The virtualization, container, and cloud native environments eliminate the problem of physical servers.

IaC uses a descriptive coding language to automate the provisioning of the IT infrastructure. Virtualization, the cloud, containers, Kubernetes, servers, storage, and networks should simplify the IT operational work. It should take less time to provision, configure, update, and maintain services. Problems should be quickly identified and rectified, and the system should all be configured.

IaC is an approach to infrastructure automation based on practices from software engineering. It emphasizes consistent, repeatable routines for provisioning and changing the system and its configuration.

The changes are the biggest risk to a production system. Continuous change is inevitable due to business disruption and technology, and change is the only way to improve your system behavior. Therefore, you need to make changes accurately, reliably, and rapidly. The changes can be compliance, new features added, technical glitches, configuration changes, etc.

The following are practices you must adopt when you are implementing IaC:

- Define everything as code.

- Continuously test and deliver all work.

- Build small and incrementally.

These are the benefits of IaC:

- More quickly adapt to changes in the market

- Reduces the effort and risk of making changes to infrastructure

- Improved consistency across all environments including nonproduction environments

- Lower costs and improved ROI

- Enables engineers of infrastructure to get resources as requested and on time

- Streamlined process across teams in an organization

- Makes governance, security, and compliances visible

- Manages efficiently on load on services with spikes

- Improves the speed to troubleshoot and resolves failures and conflicts

IaC in Build Pipeline Automation

Organizations can deliver cloud native services through continuous delivery (CD). Businesses that embrace infrastructure, applications, and compliance outperform their peers with faster delivery, they manage risk better, and they are more assured of software security and stability. Figure 17-1 shows the steps you are required to follow for infrastructure automation along the CD pipeline.

Figure 17-1. IaC steps

Capture Requirements

Each service has its features that determine where it should be deployed. Some services require higher-performance infrastructure, some services require higher CPUs, some services require a lot memory to process, and some services require high availability. Identify the key requirements of your services, and map each service against the infrastructure requirements. Depending on your IT adoption, you may choose to deploy it in the public cloud, private cloud, or hybrid cloud environment.

Prepare Automation Code

The requirements and mapping of these to the infrastructure provide a clear view of services, the infrastructure required, and the cloud services adopted. The next step is to identify IaC tools and create a template for every activity of infrastructure including containers, Kubernetes, OS, storage, networking, etc. The infrastructure is the underlying foundation for all IT operations. Automating the underlying infrastructure lifecycle management streamlines and improves accuracy and speed.

Set Up Infrastructure

The templates you create allow you to consistently deploy services across cloud environments including hybrid, private, public, etc.

In cloud services, you are required to provision VMs according to the templates; create containerization and Kubernetes workloads; and set up credentials, roles, and virtual private cloud (VPC) access for all the resources.

Provision VMs, assign an IP address, attach storage, load balance workloads, manage hosts within clusters, create housekeeping activities, and create replicas for database HA.

Install OS

Based on your system requirements, you are required to automate a standardized operating environment to improve efficiency and reduce costs. In the OS, use the template to automate OS images, secure settings including authentication, and manage compliances.

Set Up Network and Storage

Networks connect all of your services, and they must be managed to allow the right access and right bandwidth for clusters. The automation helps you make predefined, pretested changes on demand. You can use templates to automate firewall ports, access control lists (ACLs), virtual local area networks (VLANs), patches, switches, etc.

Cloud native services are based on polyglot persistence. Persistence systems like database and caching must be configured and managed to hook the right persistence to the right services. Automation in storage helps you to reduce human involvement and error. You can use the template to automate the persistence layer to services, housekeeping activity like backup and restore, etc.

Deploy Services

Service deployment is the last step of the IaC. As a key business asset, the services and workloads in a cloud must be configured properly to ensure optimal performance and security. Automation helps you to consistently deploy across all environments including nonproduction environments. You can use templates to automate services to install, configure and patch, load, and migrate data to the services; configure credentials; dynamically scale service resources; conduct sanity and smoke tests on deployment; and manage the lifecycle.

Define Everything As Code

There are many more ways to provide an infrastructure than writing code and using an IaC tool. All the cloud vendors have a nice user interface (UI); you can provision and deploy all the required services for your project. These are good for small projects, but what about the enterprise that has thousands of services?

Implementing and managing your system services as code enables you to leverage speed to improve quality. More important is that you can automate everything along with the DevSecOps pipeline.

Every infrastructure automation tool such as Terraform, Ansible, SaltStack, Chef, Puppet, etc., has a different name for source code such as *playbooks*, *cookbooks*, *manifests*, and *templates*. The infrastructure code specifies both the infrastructure elements you want and how you want them configured. You run an IaC tool to apply your code to an instance of your infrastructure. The tools either create the required new infrastructure or modify the existing one.

The following are the infrastructure elements you should define in your IaC code. These are just a few items; you should create code based on your needs.

- An infrastructure stack, either in the cloud or noncloud

- Elements of server configuration such as files, user accounts, CPU, memory, etc.

- Server role and access permissions

- A server image definition generates an image for building multiple server instances

- An application package that defines how to build a service

- Configuration of operational services such as monitoring, logging, etc.

- Validation rules such as smoke test and sanity check

How Do You Select an IaC Tool?

Always externalize the configuration to build the element. Usually the configuration is defined in the text-based file separately from the tools. Noncode infrastructure tools store infrastructure definitions of data that you can't directly access. Instead, you can edit using APIs, the GUI, etc. The issue is that the noncode tools are a black box and are a drawback of versioning the code (you can do it only if the tool supports it), CI configurations for job triggers, etc.

A tool with an external code specification doesn't constrain versioning to use specific workflows. You are free to use your project source control management tool and create a job for the same CI/CD orchestration tool as Jenkin.

What Coding Language Can You Use?

Earlier you might have used a scripting language like Bash, Perl Power Shell, or Ruby to automate infrastructure management tasks. CFEngine, Chef, Puppet, Ansible, and SaltStack use declarative, domain-specific languages (DSLs) for infrastructure management. Terraform and CloudFormation use the declarative DSL model. The advantages of declarative languages are that they simplify the infrastructure code by separating the infrastructure and how to implement it.

Many IaC tools use DSL. Your code defines your desired state for your infrastructure, such as which packages and user account should be on the server or how much RAM or storage you should have.

IaC Example

This example provides an overview of how to manage IaC with Terraform and Cloud Build/Jenkins in the Google Cloud by using GitOps.

> **GitOps:** *First coined by Weaveworks, its key concept is using a Git or Bitbucket repository to store the environment state.*

Terraform is an IaC tool that uses the code to manage the infrastructure, as shown in Figure 17-2. In this architecture, I am using GitOps practices for managing Terraform execution.

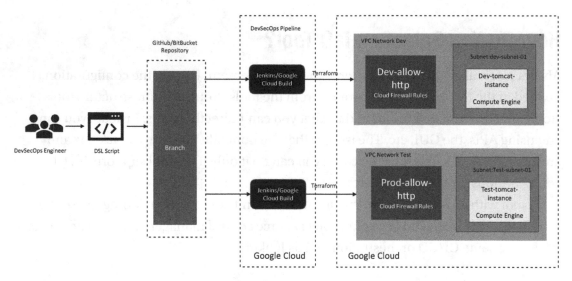

Figure 17-2. *IaC architecture with Terraform and Google Cloud*

The DevOps engineer creates a Terraform script and pushes it into the Git repository with separate dev and test branches. In Figure 17-2, Jenkins/CloudBuild triggers and applies Terraform manifests to achieve the state you want in the respective environment. You can use Terraform templates to create IaC scripts. This helps you to use them across environments.

IaC Tools

The following sections cover the IaC tools available in the industry; you can choose which is best for you. Figure 17-3 illustrates how IaC tools work in your DevOps pipeline.

Note   Tools like Jenkins and Nexus are just two examples; you can use any other orchestration of the Artefactory tools.

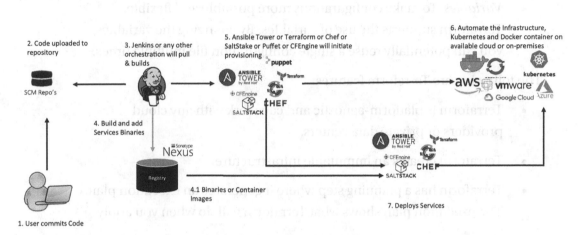

Figure 17-3. *How IaC tools integrate with the DevOps pipeline and provision infrastructure*

Terraform

Terraform is an open source IaC tool, created by HashiCorp. It is a declarative coding tool and enables developers to use high-level HashiCorp Configuration Language (HCL) to describe the state of any cloud platform or hybrid platform. Terraform can provision infrastructure across multicloud and on-premises data centers, and it works safely and securely based on changes in a configuration like reprovisioning, adding new services to existing platforms, etc. The Terraform architecture is based on small modules; each module is a reusable Terraform configuration for multiple infrastructure resources. You can make small Terraform files that are modules, and each module can be reused and can call other modules.

The main concepts of Terraform are as follows:

- *Configurations*: Terraform uses text files to describe the infrastructure and its variables. This is called a Terraform configuration file has a `.tf` extension. The configuration comes in two formats: Terraform format and JSON.

- *Resources*: Resources are basic building blocks of a Terraform configuration, and resources are cloud provider specific.

- *Variables*: To make configurations more portable and flexible, Terraform supports the use of variables. By changing the variables, you can potentially reuse a single configuration file multiple times.

The following are Terraform features:

- Terraform is platform-agnostic and can work with any cloud providers or private data centers.

- Terraform creates an immutable infrastructure.

- Terraform has a planning step where it generates an execution plan. The execution plan shows what Terraform will do when you apply.

- Terraform constructs a graph for all your cloud native resources, and parallelization creation of your infrastructure and modification of any nondependent resources; therefore, it provisions the infrastructure as efficiently as possible, and operators get insight into the dependencies in their infrastructure.

- Complex changes sets can be applied to your infrastructure with no or minimal interaction. With the execution plan and resource graph, you will know exactly what Terraform will change and in what order, avoiding many errors.

The following are the main benefits of Terraform:

- Dynamic infrastructure and safe disposal of any configuration changes

- Using version control and applying testing to the infrastructure

- Standardization of the infrastructure, since no or less human intervention is required and a consistent infrastructure is available across your environment even across multicloud environments

- Validate infrastructure before deployment

- Easy to destroy a server and redeploy if your cloud native services crashed instead of repairing themselves

Ansible

Ansible is an open source provisioning tool for managing the configuration and application deployment tools enabling IaC. It provides an enterprise framework for building and operating an automation framework. You can centralize and control your infrastructure with a visual dashboard and role-based access control. The Ansible platform uses the YAML language for infrastructure code. Ansible's simple, easy-to-read automation language has made it easy for teams across the organization to understand. Ansible works by connecting to your nodes, pushing out Ansible modules with programs, and executing over SSH. The commercial version of Ansible is Ansible Tower from Red Hat. The following are the benefits of Ansible:

- It's simple to set up and use; no special coding skills are necessary to use Ansible's playbook.

- Ansible lets you model highly complex IT workflows.

- You can orchestrate the entire application environment no matter where it is deployed.

- You don't need to install any software agents.

SaltStack

SaltStack is open source provisioning, configuration management, and application deployment tool enabling IaC. It is built on Python. It uses simple human-readable YAML combined with event-driven automation to deploy and configure complex IT systems. The way it gets information about infrastructure is to query it in real time rather than rely on stale date. It is based on a master and slave architecture; the master is a lightweight set of instructions that send commands to slaves or minions with properties and asks to run commands with these arguments. The minions store properties locally and act on their own. It is designed for high performance and scalability, and the communication between master and minions is a persistent data pipe using ZeroMQ or raw TCP. The messages are asynchronously serialized on the wire using MessagePack and internally use Python Tornado as an asynchronous networking library. The following are the benefits of SaltStack:

- It's fault tolerant. Salt minions can connect to multiple masters at one time with a YAML configuration.

- It is designed to handle 10,000 minions per master.

- Salt is easy to set up and provides single remote execution architecture.

- It is language agnostic; it can support any language.

- It is a fast, lightweight communication method to provide the foundation for a remote execution engine.

Chef

Chef is a configuration management tool written in the Ruby DSL language and Erlang. It uses Ruby encoding to develop basic building blocks such as recipes and cookbooks. It integrates with any of the cloud technologies. The key building blocks of Chef are recipes and cookbooks. A recipe is a collection of attributes used to manage the infrastructure. These attributes have been used to change the existing state of infrastructure. A cookbook is a collection of recipes. When Chef runs, it ensures that the recipes present inside it get a given infrastructure to the desired state. Chef works on a three-tier client-server model wherein the cookbooks are servers, the recipes are clients, and the knives are communicated across Chef. The following are the features of Chef:

- It does not work on assumptions about the current status of a node. It uses its mechanism to get the status of the machine.

- Using the Knife utility in Chef, it can integrate with any cloud infrastructure.

Puppet

Puppet is a configuration management tool and developed by using Ruby. This tool is written in the Ruby DSL language that helps in converting a complete infrastructure into code format. It follows the client-server model, wherein one machine in a node acts as a server, called the Puppet *master*, and the other acts as a client called the *slave* on nodes.

It manages any system from scratch, from the initial configuration to the end of the lifecycle. The features of Puppet are as follows:

- It supports idempotency, which makes it unique. You can safely run the same set of configurations multiple times on the same machine.

- It works very well cross-platform with the help of a resource abstraction layer (RAL) that uses Puppet resources.

- It provides details with graphical reporting. With this you can visualize the infrastructure and communicate and quickly respond to modifications.

CFEngine

CFEngine is an open source configuration management system with self-healing capabilities and a desired state, with a model-oriented approach. It is suitable for managing a system composed of everything from a single host to hundreds of thousands hosts. It is based on a decentralized knowledge-based architecture. Its purpose is to implement a knowledge-based infrastructure through configuration management, and it simplifies the tasks of system configuration and maintenance. The CFEngine host acts as the policy hub, which is a server where the clients fetch their policy files. It ensures that the behavior of these clients is consistent. The following are the features of CFEngine:

- You do not need to tell it what to do. Instead, you specify the state of the system, and it automatically decides the action to take to reach the desired state.

- It defines the configuration of an entire IT system, including devices, users, applications, and services.

- You can check the system state at any given moment.

- You can ensure compliance with the desired state.

- You can propagate real-time modifications or updates across the system.

AWS Cloud Formation

AWS Cloud Formation gives you an easy way to model a collection of related AWS resources and other cloud resources. You can create the code from scratch by using a cloud formation template language, either in YAML or JSON format. A template describes your desired resources and their dependencies so you can launch and configure them together as a stack. You can use these templates to manage the entire stack in a single unit. You can manage the template code locally in the source code repository or upload it into the S3 bucket. Use CloudFormation via the browser console, command-line tools, or APIs to create a stack based on your template code. The following are the features of CloudFormation:

- It supports DevOps and GitOps best practices.

- You can scale your infrastructure globally. Manage resource scaling by using templates across your organization and across AWS accounts and regions.

- You can integrate with other AWS services. You can integrate other services such as AWS identity and access management for access control, AWS config for compliance, etc.

- You can manage third-party and private resources. It can manage third-party and private resources alongside your AWS services.

IaC Tools Comparison

Table 17-1 provides you with a key comparison across major IaC tools.

Table 17-1. IaC Tools Comparison

Features	Terraform	Ansible	SaltStack	Chef	Puppet	CFEngine	AWS Cloud Formation
Tool type	Provisioning	Config management	Config management	Config management	Config management	Provisioning	Provisioning
Architecture	Push	Push	Push and Pull	Pull	Pull	Pull	Push
Provisioning approach	Declarative	Declarative	Declarative	Declarative	Declarative	Declarative	Declarative
Languages	HashiCorp configuration language	YAML	YAML	Ruby	DSL and ERB	DSL	TS, JS, Python, Java
Lifecycle (state) management	Yes	No	No	No	No	No	No
Agents	No	No	Yes	Yes	Yes	Yes	Yes
Community	Huge	Huge	Large	Large	Large	Small	Small
Cloud support	All cloud	All cloud	All cloud	All cloud	All cloud	All cloud	AWS

Summary

To get the value of cloud and infrastructure automation, you need a cloud and cloud native mindset. Automating your infrastructure takes time, especially when you are on the learning path. But doing consistently helps you to make changes.

In this chapter, I covered automation in an infrastructure by using infrastructure as code and also provided an end-to-end automation pipeline for infrastructure. I provided the IaC tools and methodology to adopt automation in your project. Finally, I provided one reference implementation of how we used IaC in our project.

PART VI

Cloud Native Operations

CHAPTER 18

Intelligent Operations

In modern-day technology, with our increasingly disruptive and complex world, changes come quickly, often without warning. Customer expectations are exceeding the abilities of traditional management. Such trends turn today's best practices into tomorrow's liabilities. Enterprises that are following the traditional approach for managing systems simply can't deliver what is needed to maintain next-generation customers. To survive and thrive today and in the future, enterprises must be able to act quickly with intelligence.

The implications of this new mandate particularly affect business operations, the heart of the entire industry. Enterprises are required to make fundamental changes and transform operations to be the intelligence engine. Most researchers believe the future belongs to intelligent operations, enabling quicker, insight-led decision-making.

Enterprises are required to embrace artificial intelligence for IT operations (AIOps) for tools, processes, and best practices for streamlining the complexities of IT. AIOps works with DevOps teams to quickly identify and fix issues that affect the behavior of an enterprise system.

In all these chapters, you have learned about the architecture, design, and development of a cloud native application. In this chapter, I will cover what you need to do post-production deployment. Operation management is a huge subject area, but I am restricting myself to concentrating on intelligent operations because that is the future. One thing you need to keep in mind is that you need to architect and design your systems for the best operations.

In this chapter, I will explain the following:

- AIOps

- Essentials of intelligent operations

- How data is important for the operation

- How you can leverage the power of the cloud

- ChatOps

© Shivakumar R Goniwada 2022
S. R. Goniwada, *Cloud Native Architecture and Design*, https://doi.org/10.1007/978-1-4842-7226-8_18

Introduction

As cloud native accelerates, organizations are becoming increasingly dependent on IT. Service downtime and outages have an enormous business impact that leads to unhappy customers. How IT operates is one of the major elements of cloud native transformation, tasked with meeting demanding scalability, availability, and performance SLAs. At the same time, IT operations are expected to be an equal partner in innovation and agility, but sometimes organizations neglect the operations part. This is the sad part of IT.

With unicorns and modernized competitors emerging, the challenges are immense. Customer expectations are to have better quality with high performance. Whatever the approach your organization is adopting to improve performance, process optimization, cost reduction, and predictability may not be able to meet the present-day expectations. To survive the competition, you must adopt agility, intelligence, flexibility, and responsiveness.

There has been various research conducted by leading research institutes. The outcome of this research is that the "future belongs to an organization with intelligent operations," and that enables you to have a 360-degree view of the operation, enabling quicker, insight-led decision-making.

A study supported by Accenture and Hfs Research highlights that digital disruption. An explosion of data and the customer experience are the driving forces behind the need for enterprises to transform how they do business and move toward intelligent operations.

- Nearly 80 percent of enterprises are concerned with disruption and competitive threats, especially from the unicorns.

- Data is rapidly shifting from a peripheral component to a fundamental driver of operations and competitive advantage.

- A robust customer experience strategy is the most significant driver of operational agility.

With intelligent operations at the center of the enterprise, your organization can become more flexible, responsive, and more agile; can generate value more quickly; and can achieve a sustainable competitive advantage.

The intelligent operation is embedding advanced intelligence and automation capabilities into the core operational process. It enhances decision-making across operations based on operational data.

Intelligent operation is a new strategy for companies seeking to achieve operational excellence (OE) aligned with the OE 4.0 approach. This move shifts the focus from a reactive to a predictive approach while improving operational performance. This requires accurate and single-source data, so companies can embrace intelligence in operations. Just using the data does not solve problems; you should know how to measure it to achieve the required outcome.

Why Do You Need Intelligent Operations?

If you look carefully at how your operation team works, you may have questions. Why are there so many escalations? Why are your teams so inefficient at responding to the demand? You are not alone; this is common across organizations.

The following are the most common inefficiencies in operations:

- *Silos*: There is a wall that exists between the development and operations teams. Both are entirely different resources and mindsets. Everyone is waiting on someone else to get things done such as push the services to production so the operations team can take over.

- *Builds*: How do you manage builds such as server images, infrastructure, and templates? If your processes need to be updated one by one manually, you'll require additional approvals and at the end have lots of errors. Still, most organizations follow a manual approach and are not ready to embrace any automation.

- *Configuration*: How do you wire up servers, storage, and networking? If you are manually configuring these devices every time, the time is being wasted.

- *Inventory*: Most of the organization does not have a full inventory of systems, IT hardware, etc. For example, what if you want to implement a security patch? It's a nightmare, right?

639

- *Meetings*: If you have already experienced a lot of meetings without any actionable outcomes and the only outcome is "we will meet next week to discuss further," you may be suffering from paralysis by analysis.

- *Strategy*: It is important to have a clear strategy about the delivery and service of your system. This makes your work and goals clear to everyone.

Elements of Intelligent Operation

Accenture defines the five essential elements, as shown in Figure 18-1, that come with the service approach.

Figure 18-1. *Intelligent operation elements*

Data-Driven Approach

Data is at the heart of every organization today, and data is the new oil, so using data at the core of your intelligent operations is a must. According to a survey from Accenture, more than 90 percent of organizations believe that data-driven decisions will help you to generate break-through customer goals. Therefore, you must use the data effectively to achieve a sustainable competitive advantage.

To ensure you are adopting this in your core operations, you need to consider how to retrieve, store, and analyze data effectively. Data aggregation engines are either batch or streaming and can compile data from various sources to create data sets for analytics and data lakes or data meshes that offer a single source for data. This helps the operations team to get the most benefit out of data.

Applied Intelligence

Applied intelligence refers to four technologies that are critical to the effective use of data captured using the data-driven approach in decision-making. They are analytics, automation, streaming, and artificial intelligence. For example, AI-based natural language processing can be used to extract relevant information from unstructured data such as audio recording in self-service vehicle insurance checks.

You need the right talent to use these tools and the required right skills to understand the issues that are coming from data, and you need to determine the best way of utilizing technology to generate an output.

Cloud Enablement

Technologies in intelligent operations require highly talented resources to create them on your own and therefore embrace the cloud to adopt AI services that help you to create intelligent operations. The cloud services allow you to easily integrate disparate types of data from multiple sources and offer access to AI tools with analytics with the use of the right-powered machines and features. During the enablement of the cloud, you need to concentrate on modernizing legacy applications to cloud services by using a decoupling approach. Therefore, modernizing these tools should be a top priority to avoid bottlenecks hampering decision-making throughout the business.

Right Talent and Skill

Having the correct modern technologies is the core ingredient in the success of intelligent operations, but you may not able to implement them until you have the right skills in place. The skills needed include IT talent in the areas of artificial intelligence, cloud computing, automation, and domain. Soft skills such as dedication, culture of change, culture of innovation, and culture of agility are essential.

To meet these talent demands, you will need much more agility in human resources functions and a more flexible approach in recruitment, as well as an organization to create a path to upskill existing resources. According to World Economic Forum claims, more than half of workers will require a significant reskilling by 2022.

Smart Partnership

Finally, you will require a strong consortium or partner network that can extend out from the boundaries of your organization. Association with startups and academic institutions can offer a different perspective on how you make use of the data and technologies at your disposal while extending the range of expertise you can take advantage of.

In modern-day disruption, you cannot achieve anything alone. You need the right partnership. This helps you to embrace ways of working by adopting innovation and design thinking.

AIOps

The term AIOps was coined by Gartner in 2016. Gartner described AIOps platforms as "software systems that combine big data and AI or ML functionality to enhance and partially replace a broad range of IT operations processes and tasks, including availability and performance monitoring, event correlation, and analysis, IT service management and automation."

To meet the ever-increasing business and technology disruptions, the IT operations team can no longer work in silos in the old traditional way by adding more people. Instead of relying on IT operations, the system needs to become intelligent, working hand in hand with IT operations staff to pinpoint service and infrastructure issues, accelerate remediation, and drive service quality.

AIOps is artificial intelligence for operations; it combines machine learning, data analytics, and many other AI technologies to automate the identification and remediation of common and recurring IT operations issues. AIOps leverages data from logs and events to monitor assets and obtain visibility into dependencies.

AIOps is about embedding advanced intelligence and automation capabilities into the core operational process. It addresses the need for operations support by combining data storage and analytics functionality to deliver relevant details. The AIOps is broad, but in operations, it focuses on diagnostic information, anomaly detection, root-cause analysis, data analysis to improve monitoring, service management, and automation. The AIOps platform enables continuous insights across IT operations.

AIOps can have a significant impact on improving key IT KPIs, including the following:

- Increasing mean time between failures (MTBF)

- Decreasing mean time detect (MTTD)

- Decreasing mean time to investigate (MTTI)

- Decreasing mean time to resolution (MTTR)

- Mean time to restore service (MTRS)

- Mean time between system incidents (MTBSI)

Figure 18-2 provides a failure metrics timeline across all KPIs.

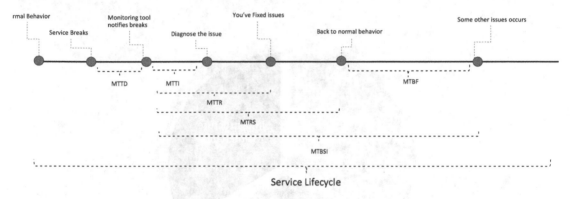

Figure 18-2. *Failure metrics*

Central Functions

Figure 18-3 shows the central function of AIOps, and these functions include the following:

- *Data gathering*: The success of AIOps depends on data collection. It gathers data from multiple sources including infrastructure, networks, applications, monitoring tools, etc. Once it collects the data, it further undergoes analytics.

- *IT assets*: It collects the inventory of IT applications and machines across organizations. It contains the metadata of IT assets and mapping of logical dependencies across services or other applications.

- *System relationship*: It establishes an event across sources to streamline what and where these events are moving. This helps to reduce human intervention.

- *Event analysis*: It processes events after establishing the relationship; it detects and predicts incidents. AIOps continually learns and relearns based on data.

- R*emediation*: It learn and improves the association between each event. Based on a prediction, it offers a recommendation, automates a response, and offers automatic self-healing.

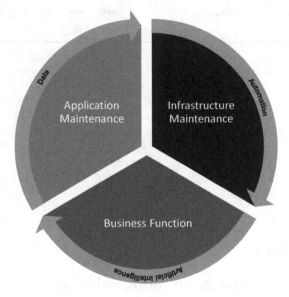

Figure 18-3. *AIOps for modern-day systems*

The following capabilities rotate across the AIOps functions.

Artificial Intelligence

It focuses on business priority–aligned IT automation driving efficiency, experience, predictability, and cost savings. The AIOps platform uses the following types of analytics:

- *Business disruption prediction*: This includes discovering patterns that implicitly describe correlations in historical and streamline data. These patterns are used to predict incidents with varying degrees of portability.

- *Problem and change management*: Ticket insights identify problems based on severity and criticality and identify a root-cause analysis and risk prediction.

- *Monitoring and diagnostics*: This includes integrated monitoring across applications, infrastructure and security, diagnostics, and event correlation.

- *Prediction and recommendations*: This includes AI-driven insights to monitor, provides early warnings, and remediates a delivery risk.

Data

Data focuses on data gathering across systems in a landscape. It gathers data from multiple sources including infrastructure, networks, applications, monitoring tools, etc. Once it collects the data, it further undergoes analytics.

You need both historical and real-time data to understand the past and predict what's most likely to happen in the future. To achieve accuracy and a bigger picture of events, you must access a range of historical and streaming data with human-generated and machine-generated data.

For total visibility, you need to collate data in one place across all your related IT systems; this helps to define key performance indicators (KPIs).

Figure 18-4 shows the AIOps data architecture; it illustrates how it enables operations and automation in your enterprise landscape.

Source

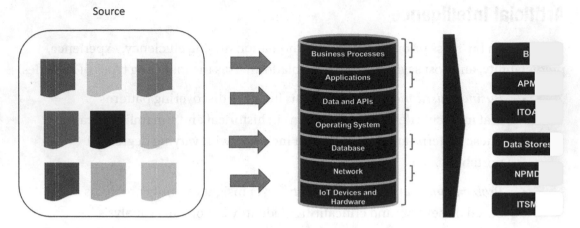

Figure 18-4. *AIOps data process*

Automation

Automation merges IT operation tools with the DevSecOps pipeline, as shown in
Figure 18-5. In automation, engineers use AI to deliver services more quickly and
securely. AIOps provides a significant advantage in automation by collecting and
correlating data from multiple sources and increases the speed and accuracy of
identifying the necessary complex relationships. An AIOps approach automates these
functions across an organization's IT operations. AIOps automation can also applies to
networks, virtualization, cloud services, servers, storage, containers, and applications.
Collect all logs, metrics, correlation, alerting, monitoring, and reporting.

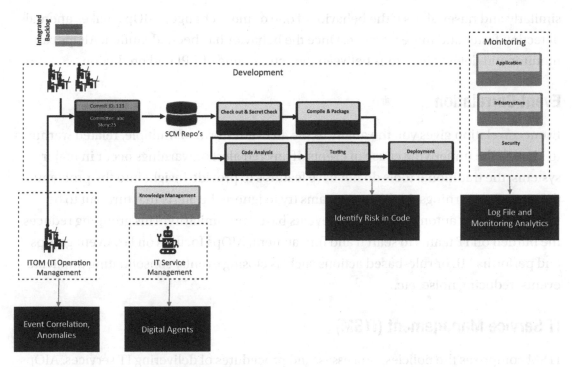

Figure 18-5. *AIOps in lifecycle management*

Increasing the use of automation, engineers are using AI to more quickly and securely deliver services that are easier to manage in the software lifecycle. Figure 18-5 illustrates how AIOps can be integrated with the DevOps pipeline.

- Use AIOps in development to identify the risk in code with code scanning and security scanning.

- Identify analytics with the integrated monitoring of application, infrastructure, and security.

- Identify event correlation and anomalies in ITOM.

- Digital agents like chatbots use knowledge management to provide ITSM.

Anomaly Detection

Anomaly detection relies on ML algorithms. A trending algorithm monitors KPIs by comparing its current behavior to its past. If the score grows anomalously large, the algorithm raises an alert. A cohesive algorithm scans a group of KPIs expected to behave similarly and raises alerts if the behavior of one or more changes. AIOps makes anomaly detection faster and more effective. Once the behavior has been identified, AIOps can monitor and detect deviations between the actual value of KPI and prediction.

Event Correlation

Event correlation gives you the ability to see an event storm of multiple, related warnings to identify the underlying cause of events. If any red alert or warnings occur in major systems, the traditional tools do not have features to provide insight into the problem; they just give warnings. In this case, teams try to ignore the alerts that turn out to be trivial. In AIOps, automatically group events based on similarity. This grouping reduces the burden on IT teams to search and find an item. AIOps focuses on key event groups and performs ML or rule-based actions such as closing events, consolidating duplicate events, reducing noise, etc.

IT Service Management (ITSM)

ITSM comprises the policies, processes, and procedures of delivering IT services. AIOps provides benefits to ITSM by letting you manage services as a group instead of one at a time. You can use these groups as a unit to define the automated response to align with your framework. For example, if one container in a pod of five containers encounters problems during the normal load period, the risk of the overall service is considered low, and then you can run automation to modify without any user-facing impact. AIOps for ITSM can help with the following:

- Manage infrastructure performance in a multicloud and hybrid cloud more consistently

- Help you to predict capacity planning

- Manage connected devices across the network in your organization

Example Use Case of AIOps

Here are some use cases of AIOps.

Traditional Operations

Figure 18-6 illustrates how traditional operations works.

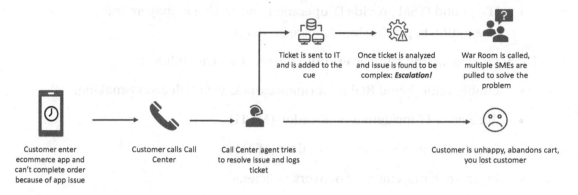

Figure 18-6. *Traditional operations*

AIOps-Based Operation

Figure 18-7 illustrates how an AIOps-enabled operation is implemented.

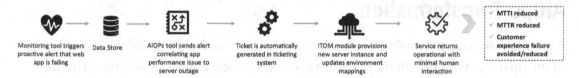

Figure 18-7. *AIOps-enabled operation*

Capabilities of AIOps

AIOps provide the following capabilities:

- Machine learning capabilities to help in identifying patterns in the collected data.

- A dedicated data platform for aggregating raw data and logs from various integrated monitoring tools and data sources across your enterprise landscape.

- Dashboards, analytics, and integrated consoles help IT admins and operations have clear insight of the end-to-end landscape.

- Intelligent infrastructure management to be managed with infrastructure as code and the real-time gathering of monitoring data.

- Enterprise network analytics provides a detailed view of the end-to-end network including hosts, edge, and VPC.

- ITOPs and ITSM provide IT operation and service management integration to provide intelligence in AIOps.

The following are the value levers from the previous capabilities:

- Enable value-based ROI performance tracking and decision-making.

- Accelerate IT incident identification (MTTI).

- Improve IT incident resolution time (MTTR).

- Improve management of network policies.

- Reduce the incident volume and improve resolution time.

- Improve data model accuracy and consistency.

- Reduce workforce to remediate tickets through automation.

AIOps Transformation

A cloud native transformation is about the evolution of technologies and the evolution of the business with new initiatives from user experience. It adds rapid growth in the volumes of data generated but poses challenges to IT operations. Similarly, the need for decision-making has increased due to the large volumes of data and analysis. These challenges make traditional IT operations obsolete and inadequate and require the correct utilization of data to extract value. As I mentioned in Capabilities of AIOps section, the IT operations team needs help to streamline predictable, remediated, and automated repetitive tasks to increase efficiency and focus on value-added activities. For this you require AIOps.

As shown in Figure 18-8, the AIOps journey can start in many ways, but you need a streamlined approach to transform your IT operations.

Figure 18-8. *AIOps transformation*

AIOps Strategy

In this phase, you required to perform the following activities:

- Assess the industry/value chain and AIOps vision

- Work with relevant stakeholders, identify and develop use cases, and select tools

- Prepare business and roadmaps

- Build a workable MVP with a clear outcome

- Establish a roadmap

AIOps Transition

In this phase, you required to perform the following activities:

- Conduct an assessment for existing monitoring and automation capabilities.

- Define future-state capabilities and create an AIOps architecture and migration approach.

- Conduct a platform migration.

- Train users on the new platform.

- Transition use case and value tracking to operational teams.

AIOps Transformation

In this phase, you are required to perform the following activities:

- Conduct an assessment of AIOps maturity and identify use cases across DevSecOps.

- Define a change journey to implement a workforce operating model and culture change.

- Establish enterprise-level integration and socialize across all the stakeholders.

- Track metrics and publish them to all stakeholders.

Benefits of AIOps

The main benefit of the AIOps process is that it enables IT operations to identify and resolve problems. The following are the benefits:

- *Quicker problem analysis*: AIOps can analyze the causes of issues and propose solutions more quickly compared to a manual approach.

- *False apprehensions*: AIOps reduces the fear among teams on every issue and notifies them when an action is required.

- *Predictive management*: It uses machine learning algorithms to identify problems and provide predictive reports.

- *Decision-making*: AIOps helps to make decisions by analyzing the data.

These are additional benefits:

- It brings together data sources that had previously been siloed to allow more complete analysis and insight.

- It accelerates root-cause analysis and remediation and saves time, money, and resources.

- It proactively identifies, prevents errors, and empowers IT teams to focus on higher-value analysis and optimization.

ChatOps

ChatOps is chat-based operation and describes a collaboration model that connects people, processes, tools, and automation seamlessly and transparently through the chat platform. It is designed to help to improve service reliability, service recovery time, and collaboration efficiency. In the ChatOps environment, the chat client serves as the primary communication channel for ongoing work. ChatOps will integrate into existing tools and processes and a collaborative communication environment to improve ticket tracking, automated incident management, and service management.

ChatOps is the streamlined use of chat applications and communication services to run development and operations functions and commands in line with human collaboration.

The following are the categories of ChatOps:

- *Notification system*: This automatically notifies if some incidents occur. Tools include PagerDuty, VictorOPs, etc.

- *Chatbots*: Conduct online chat conversation via text or voice to the customers, like Yellow Messenger, Hubot, etc.

- *Chatroom*: Chat-based tools for collaboration for effective use in automation such as Microsoft Teams, Slack, etc.

For example, during the troubleshooting of an L1 or L2 ticket, each person in our team was working in a silo and was not able to resolve the issue on time, which become an escalation to senior leadership. What was the mistake our team made? Team members should have been collaborating over a group chat, which is designed for human-to-human and human-to-machine interactions. This kind of collaboration platform maintains team communication effectively and can integrate with ITSM tools to resolve quickly.

ChatOps Benefits

The benefits are split into who uses ChatOps; one category of users is social and another is technical. The social users are usually nontechnical members like customers, and the technical users are engineers who will likely find greater value in the technical benefits. ChatOps is about increased sharing and collaboration across teams and customers.

The social benefits are as follows:

- Increased collaboration

- Improved customer experience

- Enhanced learning

The technical benefits are as follows:

- Increased automation

- Reduced manual intervention

- Faster response time

- Improved security and safety

Types of ChatOps

The concept and technology behind ChatOps have been available in the industry for quite some time. Group chats have long existed, but chatbots are quite new. With the new age of technology, there have been advancements and evolutions in the way you utilize them.

Group Chat

Group chat has existed for quite some time, and Internet Relay Chat (IRC) has been part of teams for many years. With the evolution of modern architecture like cloud native and AI, chat applications are evolving, and they are much more user-friendly. As shown in Figure 18-9, these group chat tools integrate seamlessly with additional IT operations and DevOps tools.

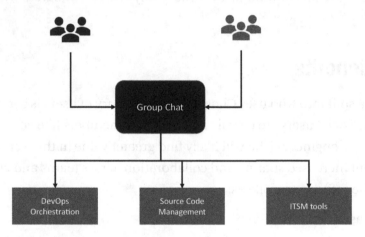

Figure 18-9. *Group chat integration*

The following are a few group chat applications:

- *Microsoft Teams*: From Microsoft, this integrates seamlessly with the other suites of Microsoft tools.

- *Slack*: From Slack Technologies, Slack has gained popularity for its user interface and user experience including SlackBot. It provides open third-party integration.

- *HipChat*: From Atlassian, this integrates seamlessly with a suite of tools such as JIRA, Confluence, etc.

- *Flow Dock*: From CA Technologies, it integrates seamlessly with a suite of tools.

There are many open source and commercial group chat tools available like Grape, Zulip, etc.

Bots

Recent chat bots use more sophisticated technologies and do not require hosting, configuration, or support in your organization. Currently, there are several well-known chatbots available, and they are more focused on a business-to-customer (B2C) style. As shown in Figure 18-10, the chatbots integrate with various capabilities like DevOps, SCM, authentication, operation tools, and also the cloud.

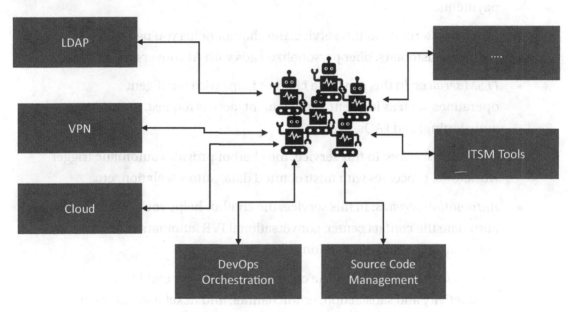

Figure 18-10.   *Chat bot integration*

- *Yellow Messenger*: This is the most used bot today and supports B2C and IT operations.

- *Hubot*: From GitHub, this is a well-known chatbot that supports B2C and IT operations.

- *Lita*: This supports B2C and IT operations and is easy to implement.

There are many chatbots available that support the same features as the ones listed.

ChatOps in Service Support

Generally, a chatbot offers the following services:

- *Customer support service*: In customer service, a chatbot can help you with the onboarding process, resolving issues on the first customer contact, predicting their needs, and keeping the customer engaged.

- *Sales service*: In this service, the chatbot helps you to identify customer inhibitions and remind users about products and payments.

- *Marketing services*: In this service, the chatbot helps you better segment customers, offer personalized ads with AI conversations, etc.

- *ITSM services*: In this service, a chatbot helps with intelligent operations such as incident management, access request, monitoring and alerting, and FAQs.

- *Operation services*: In this service, the chatbot provides automatic trigger workflows, processes with unstructured data, auto-escalation, etc.

- *Automation services*: In this service, the chatbot helps you automate the contact center, conversational IVR automation, voice authentication, and automation.

- *HR services*: In this service, the chatbot can help with employee productivity and satisfaction, omnichannel, and ticket management.

ChatOps (Bot) Architecture

Chatbots are used in various services including an omnichannel conversational enablement platform for enterprises that allows you to create chatbots on various channels like web, mobile, telephone, Google Assistant, and other group chat tools like Teams, Slack, etc.

The architecture diagram in Figure 18-11 illustrates how the chatbots operate to support your enterprises. This architecture may not be standard across all chatbots; the source and how you analyze the data differs.

In ChatOps, the user interacts with the chatbot through a chat client, making it possible for all team members to maintain awareness, even through mobile devices. The remediation steps are preserved in the chat record, which assists with onboarding and fine-tuning best practices. These best practices can then be incorporated into orchestration scripts for the chatbot. Figure 18-11 illustrates further.

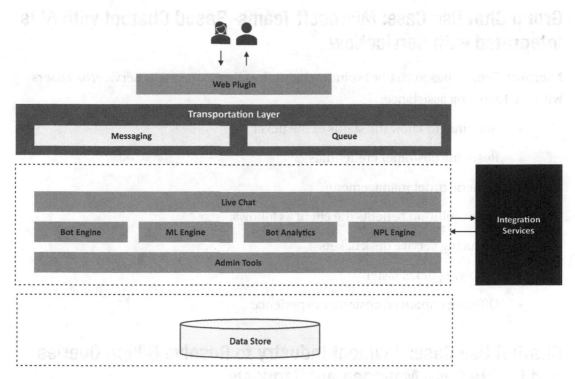

Figure 18-11. *Chatbot architecture*

The architecture uses plugins that integrate with your web applications and messaging layer to connect users with a chatbot engine and establishes a queue to track all the requests and avoid losing any packets or requests.

The chatbot engine contains database storage for search, analytics database, and a persistent database to store details. The process engine consists of an ML engine, NLP engine, and analytics engine to process the chats. The integration services integrate various services in an enterprise.

The chatbot integrates with knowledge management to process all such conversations, context, and commands.

The chatbots also integrate with voice integration and language models for various language conversions.

Industry Example Use Cases

Here are some use cases:

Group Chat Use Case: Microsoft Teams–Based Chatbot with AI Is Integrated with ServiceNow

Microsoft Teams–based chatbot solution helps the client to serve its ServiceNow users with the following assistance:

- Required to know the status of the ticket

- Resetting customer credentials

- Generic order management

The chatbot solution benefits the client as follows:

- Reducing service desk tickets

- Resolving ticket faster

- Offering enhanced customer experience

Chatbot Use Case: Payment Industry to Resolve Billing Queries and Create Case Management Requests

One company used Yellow Messenger and an integrated solution to the web application and helped the client with the following assistance:

- Required to know the invoice

- Required to get itemized billing

- Create an incident on case management

- Payment instruction issues

- FAQ

We integrated Yellow Messenger into a web application with text and voice-based search and helped the client to create an incident, provide status, check billing details, etc.

Summary

IT leverages application monitoring tools to maintain operational efficiency; however, each tool collects a lot of data that needs to be maintained. When a team fails to detect vulnerabilities and issues in your cloud native services, it leads to security threats. By using AIOps, IT teams can automate and improve monitoring and remediation.

An organization that adopts AIOps can see the benefits by addressing operational issues and analyzing issues quicker and faster.

CHAPTER 19

Observability

Observability has many names, such as monitoring, tracing, logging, telemetry, and instrumenting. All of these are required to create observability. It includes measuring your infrastructure, security, and application to understand how they are doing and then acting on the findings, with either predictive or reactive solutions. Why do you need to do observability? What do you measure? To get an answer to these questions, you need to ask yourself the following:

- Is my user happy?

- Are my applications behaving as expected?

- Are my servers performing well?

- Is my deployment safe from vulnerabilities and fraud?

You have been doing monitoring, tracing, etc. for your system, but without any insight. Current cloud native modern architecture requires more than just monitoring. For example, your system might require processing in real time to enhance the experience, including not just monitoring but examining its internal state based on the outputs.

According to Gartner, by 2024, 30 percent of enterprises implementing distributed cloud native systems will have adopted observability techniques to improve digital business service performance.

Observability is evolving. There are no full-on tools or software available yet, but a few tools such as Splunk and New Relic incorporate some observability features.

© Shivakumar R Goniwada 2022
S. R. Goniwada, *Cloud Native Architecture and Design*, https://doi.org/10.1007/978-1-4842-7226-8_19

Observability is a must for every system; you should not deploy any systems whether small or complex without observability.

In this chapter, I will cover the following:

- Observability in cloud native systems

- Best practices and principles of observability

- What to measure and what not to measure

- Observability use cases

Introduction

Organizations have deployed monitoring tools for a decade to track the performance of their infrastructure, network, security, and applications. As the IT landscape evolves, monitoring tools have some limitations in their ability to adapt to the disruption of business and technologies in the cloud native age.

Observability is a measure of how well the internal state of the services can be observable from knowledge of external outputs. The concept of observability was introduced by Rudolf E. Kalman for linear dynamic systems. A dynamic system designed to estimate the state of a system from measurements of the outputs *observes* the system.

Once you have successfully deployed your services into production, you have completed half the work. You just need to build observability into your system. Your primary goal is to build systems that are designed to discover problems early and often so you can learn and improve.

As your system grows with more services, each part can start grinding together like poorly fit gears. Intentions conflict, assumptions unravel, and the system begins to operate in increasingly unexpected ways. Rather than spending intellectual capital trying to predict all the possible failure modes, you have learned to use practices that allow you to see deeply into the system, detect anomalies, run experiments, and respond to failures. Observability is required when it becomes difficult to predict the behavior of a system and how your users will be impacted by these changes and to ensure that your system behavior aligns with customer experiences.

Making the system observable involves the practice of combining context, information, and specific knowledge about the system to create the conditions for understanding. You need to integrate all the output generated by the systems such as logs, metrics, events, traces, audits, etc., and correlate them with semantics and intent.

Observability is most important in today's world when considering the pace and characteristics of cloud native systems and how they are developed, delivered, and deployed. As mentioned in earlier chapters, the adoption of cloud native is increasing every day, so the old practices of bolting on monitoring after the fact are no longer effective and do not scale. It's critical therefore to have a modern way to observe the behavior of the system to better understand the characteristics of a system. Many practices contribute to observability, and some of the practices are embedded within products and tools.

Observability allows teams to monitor cloud native systems more effectively and helps them to find and connect effects in a complex chain and trace them back to their cause. Further, it gives the operations team more visibility into their entire end-to-end architecture.

"You can't perform any operation without proper end-to-end visibility."

Observability is important in current scenarios because it gives you greater control over complex systems. Distributed cloud native systems have a higher number of interconnections across services and systems, so the number of failures that can occur is too high, and distributed systems constantly are updating due to business and technical disruptions. Therefore, every change can create a new type of failure. In a distributed environment, the understanding current problem is very challenging, because it produces unknown unknowns. The monitoring is able to find only known unknowns, so how do you find unknown unknowns? You can find them only through observability.

Difference Between Monitoring and Observability

Monitoring and observability are different concepts, but they work for the same cause, and both depend on each other. Monitoring is an action to perform to increase the observability of your system. Observability is part of the system like one end-to-end functionality.

Monitoring tools collect and analyze the system behavior as data and translate it into actionable insights such as presenting details to the dashboard, alerting, notifying all stakeholders, etc. For example, monitoring technologies, such as application performance monitoring, is able to provide information about whether the system is able to perform against the service level agreement (SLA).

On the other hand, observability is a measure of how well the internal system state and behavior can be inferred from knowledge of its external outputs. It uses the data that monitoring tools produce. The observability of your system depends on how well your monitoring tools generate and correlate data.

Monitoring requires you to know what's important to monitor in advance, but observability lets you determine what is important by observing how the system behaves over time and by asking relevant details about it.

Let's look at one example of a large enterprise where they deployed it in a large data center with a high number of VMs and containers with hundreds of systems that are monitored using log analysis and monitoring with ITSM tools. Analyzing hundreds of systems continually will generate a huge volume of data with unnecessary alerts and false flags. The infrastructure may present with low observability characteristics unless the correct metrics are evaluated. On the other hand, a small system with few containers and servers can be easily monitored using metrics and parameters like health, CPU, etc. These parameters are highly correlated to the health of the system, so the system demonstrates high observability.

Full-Stack Observability

Observability has become an important practice for cloud native modern enterprises. The observability is one of the main strategy that you need to adopt in your architecture that allow you to enable various designs for the "-ilities.".

From web and mobile applications to polyglot persistence with varied container resources and integrated systems, there are multiple technologies in a varied infrastructure. To observe the diverse system, you should apply the principles of full-stack observability in your enterprise estate.

With the evolution of unicorn companies, peer competition, technology, and business disruption, you have pressure to innovate quickly and push new features to market faster to capture the market and meet the end customer expectations. Customers are impatient. They want more and do not tolerate slow, error-prone, or poorly designed user experiences. Once you have lost customers, they never come back to you. According to a survey, 62 percent of customers want more user-friendly apps.

To achieve this, as shown in Figure 19-1, you need to observe the end-to-end real estate with an eye on capturing data in a single source. This helps you to troubleshoot, analyze, debug, and optimize performance across your systems. Implementing observability provides you with a connected context and surfaces meaningful analytics from logs and can provide a single view to the administrators and management.

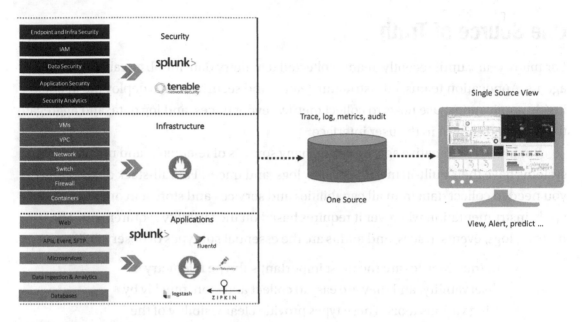

Figure 19-1. *Full-stack observability*

To achieve full-stack observability, you need the following core elements in your observability architecture.

Connected Across Capabilities

Putting telemetry data across security, infrastructure, and applications in one place is important. Your data needs to connect the capabilities with the services within the capabilities, and these relationships must be correlated with the metadata so you can understand its relationship. Such connections give your data context and meaning. When all of your telemetry data and connections are stored in one place, you can apply intelligence to your large data set, anomalies, surface pattern, and the correlations that are not easily identifiable by humans watching dashboards.

You need to see how all capabilities and services in your system are related to one another at any moment. It is difficult to maintain the mapping due to changes every day like adding features to existing services, adding new users, or adding a new network or new infrastructure. The context of your data relies on metadata and dimensions. Depending on the type of your system, the volume of data varies.

One Source of Truth

For many years, until recently, teams collected telemetry data for observability through agents. Application teams, infrastructure teams, and security teams deploy the agents inside applications; use hosts to collect metrics, event traces, and log data; and aggregate this data and show it in the user interface.

But in the cloud native age, there are many sources of telemetry, and many open systems have their built-in metrics, events, logs, and traces. For full-stack observability, you need to collect data from all capabilities and services and store it in one source and apply instrumentation wherever it requires based on the visibility requirement. The metrics, logs, events, traces, and audits are the essential subtypes of observability.

> *Metrics*: Metrics are the most important subtype telemetry of observability, and they are easy to collect and store quickly by using various tools. These types provide clear visibility of the overall health of your system.

> *Events*: Events are a critical subtype of telemetry of observability. The events are detailed records of every action of your system including integration points, Kubernetes clusters, and security integrations.

> *Logs*: Logs are the detailed subtype telemetry of observability; they provide high fidelity data and detailed context around an event. There are various tools available in the industry for collecting, filtering, and exporting logs; you need to hook these into your capabilities and services.

> *Traces*: Traces are valuable for showing end-to-end latency and detailed subtype telemetry of observability. They provide detailed insight into the myriad customer journeys through a system. This

enables you to understand the end-to-end journeys with a unit of work and find bottlenecks with errors. There are various industry tools available to collect traces.

Audit: An audit is a detailed view of the transactions subtype telemetry of observability. These details are important in identifying how and where transactions happen and in providing the various compliance issues.

The following are the characteristics of one source of truth:

- Gathers all your telemetry data in one place and generates a connected view of all the data points of your system. This helps you to understand and resolve the issues that impact your business.

- You should build on a flexible schema so you can quickly get an answer to questions; we recommend using either NoSQL or search databases.

- It scales as your business grows, so you must able to support unpredictable demands.

Visualization

Visualization of your connected and well-defined data from system components is very important to view what is going on in your system. When you provide a visualization with insight without requiring configuration, you are better prepared to break down silos and enable stakeholders to observe the entire system as a whole. This helps to identify bottlenecks and resolve faster, and you are able to communicate better across teams and stakeholders.

As part of the full-stack observability, you must provide intuitive, real-time visualizations that focus your attention where it is needed most and communicate the severity and scale of recent changes of your system. This allows you to discover an unknown relationship with blind spots. These views should be customizable so you can accommodate any type of anomaly.

The full-stack observability helps you to reduce the meantime to resolution (MTTR), detect end-to-end issues, and predict the issues and execute fitness functions across your system.

Observability and Cloud Native Services

Cloud native services in a distributed system are fundamentally changing the way the systems are developed and deployed. Traditional monitoring capabilities such as metrics, instrumentation, and alerting are not enough to observe systems; you need much more to supplement these capabilities such as tracing, auditing, etc.

Cloud native services with containers address the increased risk of downtime and other issues related to monolithic applications; you can find more details in Chapter 5. However, container-based services add more complexity due to being loosely coupled, independently deployed, and being scattered across multiple hosts. This makes it difficult for engineers to know the behavior of what is running in production. Observability addresses these challenges, providing visibility into a distributed system. It helps engineers understand the behavior and then predict it so they can make the services self-healing.

As shown in Figure 19-2, for cloud native services, you need to adopt five observability patterns that help to achieve observability in a distributed system.

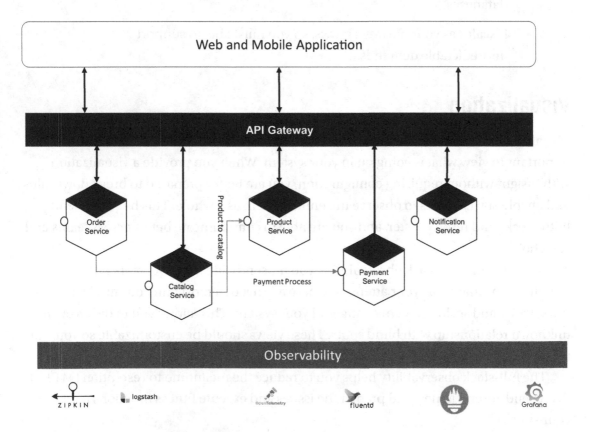

Figure 19-2. *Observability with microservices*

Note   The architecture in Figure 19-2 is just an example of observability. I am not endorsing any specific tools.

In the sample ecommerce architecture shown in Figure 19-2, the customer browses the catalog, places an order, and confirms the order with a payment. You need to collect the following telemetry data for observability in these ways:

- Instrument code verbosely. Everything flows from this. Wrap every network or service call with a lot of context and as much details as possible.

- Persist all the requests and identify throughout the system lifecycle for every service and every request.

- Emit events including cardinality such as `user_id`, `order_id`, `catalog_id`, and `Payment_id`.

- Structure your data and store it in one source.

- Don't neglect any events and touchpoints.

- Create visualization and alerting mechanism and build analytics.

Observability in Kubernetes

Kubernetes is one of the main cloud native tools. The Cloud Native Computing Foundation (CNCF) defined observability/analysis as one of the main elements of the cloud native journey. Caleb Hailey defined the top seven Kubernetes APIs for cloud native observability. These APIs help you to achieve a holistic view of your Kubernetes cluster's health.

- *Kubernetes Metrics API*: All the Kubernetes metrics are exposed as Prometheus endpoints, so anything that can consume Prometheus metrics collects these metrics. This API provides built-in Prometheus exporters, Kubelet metrics, and Kube-state-metrics.

- *Service APIs*: These APIs are important. Without proper visibility into your services, you are able to get the proper errors. These APIs provide networking configuration, including ingress, endpoint, and service resources; service metadata, spec, and status; service ports; internal and external IP addresses; load balancing and label selector configuration details; and Kubectl describe services.

- *Container API*: The containers will run within pods. Kubernetes APIs are able to provide details of both pods and containers. If you want more drilled-down details of the container, you can use these metrics to find the behavior of your system. These APIs provide pod API resources, information about running containers, and container status and details.

- *Pod API*: Pods are the building blocks of all Kubernetes workloads. Pods are managed by Kubernetes controllers. These APIs provide primary workload API resources; pod metadata, spec, and status; controller references; and read log API.

- *Kubernetes downward API*: These APIs enable pods to expose information about themselves to a container running in the pod. These APIs provide pod configuration directives, an alternative to the service account, etc.

- *Kubernetes events API*: In Kubernetes, events are most important. They will give you information about what is happening inside a cluster or a given namespace. These APIs provide resource state changes, errors, and other system messages.

- *Kubernetes API watchers*: These APIs return lists of pods. These APIs provide change notification, return change management notifications, etc.

Observability and DevOps

Observability is more important in DevOps-based software development and the deployment lifecycle. DevOps unites all development stakeholders like developers, QA, infrastructure, and operations into one. The monitoring is not just collecting log data, metrics, and event traces; now the monitoring becomes more observable. The scope of observability encompasses the development process, technologies, and people. This allows the team to understand services' internal state at any given time and has access to more accurate information about the system. The following are a few key benefits:

- There is better visibility of the services catalog in production.

- Predictive alerting helps to identify issues up front and make services self-healing.

- Engineers can see end-to-end workflows about a particular issue.

- There is better collaboration across teams and services deployed in production.

- With DevOps, observability provides a common data model between development engineers and operation engineers to interpret system state and behavior.

Common Use Cases for Observability with AIOps

As described in the previous chapter, AIOps have been the driving force in helping you to adapt to continually disrupting environments and enhance your operational capabilities. AIOps consists of the AI technologies used in IT operations and helps the DevOps and IT Ops teams to enhance your organization's agility and detect anomalies. The following are the few use cases for observability with AIOps:

- *Cloud native systems*: The cloud native services are required to update regularly. They are required to leverage the AIOps in observability. It helps speed up analytics and predictability.

- *Cloud native transformation*: AIOps features help you to collect data from many resources and give a collective cross-domain overview in observability.

- *Predictability*: AIOps helps you to predict from one source of truth to identify the anomalies quickly.

- *The volume of data*: The volume of data aggregated by tools can be immense, and it will be difficult to understand the data without the aid of AIOps.

Guidance to Choose Observation Tools

Regardless of the type of tools you use, whether open source or commercial or in-house, all observability tool should provide the following features:

- *Integrate with existing tools*: IT is not new, and monitoring is not new. Every organization might use some kind of monitoring tool. You can't just throw away old and create new. This is the desired approach. You need to embrace the reusability principle, so pick the observability tool that integrates or collaborates with existing toolsets.

- *Better usability*: If tools provide excellent observability but will fail if you do not have a proper dashboards, configuration management, etc. so you need to make sure you design better usability for an operation team.

- *Able to provide real-time data*: Your observability tool should be able to provide data in both real time and batch mode and be able to integrate streaming technologies like Kafka.

- *Visualize aggregated data*: The observability tool should surface insights in easily configurable formats and be able to integrate with other tools for dashboards, summaries, etc.

- *Context details*: The observability tool must provide the detailed context of incident such as how the system behavior changed over time, etc.

- *Support machine learning*: The observability toolset must support or have a built-in capability for machine learning models for predictions.

- *Business value*: Observability tools must support metrics important to your business, such as speed, customer experience, stability, etc.

- *Open standards*: Observability tools must support emerging open standards for collection such as Open Telemetry and Open Metrics.

Benefits of Observability

Observability enables you to reduce the time it takes to identify the root-cause analysis of anomalies. The following are the few benefits:

- *Improved coverage of distributed cloud native architecture*: Observability emphasis on a collection and analysis of telemetry across all elements of your system.

- *Improving the time to market*: Observability helps you to do analysis of anomalies. This helps with shorter resolution times.

- *Infrastructure and storage optimization*: Observability generates less data compared to monitoring. This helps to optimize your infrastructure and storage requirements.

- *Shift-left observability*: Observability can be integrated into the DevSecOps cycle to identify anomalies in the early lifecycle of your system development.

The main drawback of observability is adoption because of the lack tools maturity. The adoption rate is still 5 percent, but there is an indication of a growing interest because organizations are frustrated with the limitations of monitoring. As observability is evolving, you will be able to find more tools that provide observability features.

The observability tools must include features such as arbitrarily wide structured events, high-cardinality dimensions without the need for indexes or schemas, and shared context propagation between contexts.

Observability, Monitoring, and Machine Learning Models

You need to always think of how to avoid failure in the system when you configure observability and monitoring tools. You might have to assume that something happened to one service such as a request by the customer, an internal request, a bad experience, etc. As I mentioned in earlier chapters, you can't avoid failures, but you need to think of how to optimize the responses to the failures. To achieve this, you are required to follow these methods.

Data collection is important for a machine learning model. The following are the data classes required to capture for the model:

- *Logs*: A log is a text record of an event in your application that happened at a particular time that tells when it occurs and a payload that provides the context. Usually, logs come in three formats. They are plain text, structured, and binary. For the model, you select a structured log, which is easier to query.

- *Metrics*: A metric is a numeric value measured over an interval of time and includes specific attributes such as timestamp, name, KPIs, etc. These are structured by default, which makes them easier to query.

- *Traces*: Traces provide an end-to-end journey of a request through a distributed system. The traces provide important data of requests moving across services.

Algorithms Help in Observability

Once you collect the data and store it in one source truth, as shown in Figure 19-1, you need to automate the following:

- Applies AI and machine learning models to data

- Detects anomalies and eliminates noise

- Correlates relevant metrics to anomalies, traces, and log events

- Surfaces incidents with contextual data

- Identifies probable root causes

Clustering and correlating are crucial steps for models, and they require multiple different approaches. A combination of historical pattern matching and real-time identification helps you to identify both recurring and new issues.

Workflow Steps for ML

- Aggregate event data, logs, metrics, traces, and changes across your environment including your services and infrastructure.

- Integrate configuration management data to discover the system. This provides context within the monitoring data, which helps to understand interdependencies and relationships.

- Enrich data including parsing, aggregating of data, or combining values in fields to equate to a value in another field. The enrichment optimizes several processes including clustering, diagnostics, etc.

- Entropy is an algorithmically determined numerical value that rates the importance of an event. The higher an alert's entropy, the more important it is.

- Correlate data across your systems. An alert correlation allows you to see patterns across the systems to ensure your services are behaving well. Correlation algorithms analyze alerts to identify clusters of similarity across services. The correlation helps you to enable faster incident management, problem management, MTTD, and MTTR.

- With root-cause analysis, you can apply supervised ML techniques. It uses alert attributes in combination with feedback to analyze real-time data sets and predict which alerts are most casual.

- Collaboration is the process of operation teams to quickly triage and remediate incidents.

- Create a visual representation to illustrate all these steps.

Summary

In a nutshell, observability is an important and useful approach to understand the state of your cloud native systems such as microservices, containers, Kubernetes, and other technologies that have made systems complex. Identifying anomalies and troubleshooting is difficult, but these systems produce a wealth of telemetry data that provide a clear understanding of their behavior. Effective observability provides all the instrumentation and analytics to you.

In this chapter, I covered a brief note about observability. It is a vast topic, but I tried my best to cover the relevant details for you to understand and implement observability in your cloud native architecture.

PART VII

Cloud Native Features

CHAPTER 20

Cloud Native Trends

I hope by now everyone has a clear view of the end-to-end lifecycle of cloud native systems from architecture to design to development to operations.

What's next? How will the cloud native journey progress? To provide the answer to this question, I will cover cloud native future trends in this chapter.

The pace of technological change has accelerated. Customer demands are more pronounced, and competitive threats have grown more unpredictable. Change is happening quickly, and industries are racing for their position in the world. COVID-19 impacted the world in ways no one could have predicted, and organizations are adopting IT in new ways.

Gartner, Forester, and other researchers publish trend reports every year about the future, and I have been following all the research for quite some time. I'll share my thoughts of where things will be going from now.

ThoughtWorks publishes a technology radar report on various techniques, tools, platforms, languages, and frameworks. They update the technologies regularly based on maturity and industry trends.

I will divide the future trends into these two themes:

- Technology trends for cloud native

- Technology trends across industries

There is a lot more you can find via Cloud Native Foundation, Technology Radar, and other leading consulting firms.

- Cloud native journeys related to Kubernetes on the edge, low-code platforms, GitOps, etc.

- Industry trends like 5G, quantum computing, digital twin, etc.

© Shivakumar R Goniwada 2022
S. R. Goniwada, *Cloud Native Architecture and Design*, https://doi.org/10.1007/978-1-4842-7226-8_20

Cloud Native Trends

In this section, I will provide brief details of a few trends that are related to cloud native architecture and design.

Designing for "-ilities"

In a cloud native world, architecture is reprioritizing the "-ilities" such as resiliency, observability, portability, etc. These cloud native services are distributed over the wire. If something goes wrong with the services, you not only can observe them but also can fix them. You had to build all these things yourself, and it was very complicated, but as we progress, there are now more technologies available to handle them. For example, service meshes and event meshes take care of some of the "-ilities."

Cloud Native Architecture

Event-driven architecture has existed for a while, but based on my experience, engineers still need to master it when writing code. Various software is available to help you to build event-driven systems. For example, the Distributed Application Runtime (Dapr) helps you to build event-driven resilient distributed applications whether it b in the cloud or hybrid or on-premises, as illustrated in Figure 20-1. Dapr codifies the best practices for building cloud native services into open, independent building blocks that enable you to build the business logic in your choice of language.

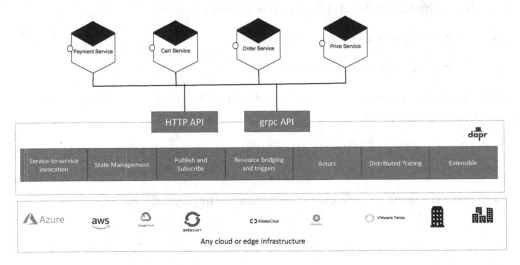

Figure 20-1. *Dapr architecture*

Dapr reduces the burden on engineers to implement all the cloud native building blocks such as state management, publish/subscribe, observability, and secrets. You can find more details at `https://dapr.io/`.

Open Application Model Specification

As shown in Figure 20-2, the Open Application Model (OAM) specification is a runtime-agnostic specification for defining cloud native applications. This specification helps you to focus on application business logic rather than any container, orchestration, or infrastructure-related tasks. This specification brings modular, extensible, and portable designs for modeling application deployment with a consistent higher-level API.

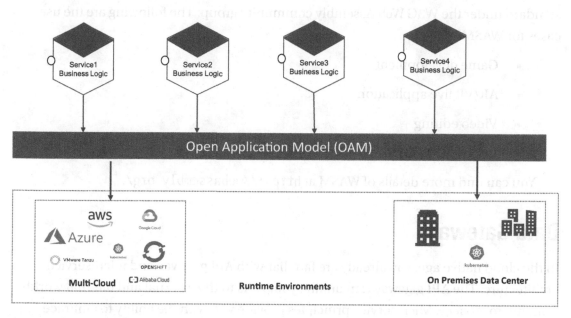

Figure 20-2. *OAM*

As cloud native is maturing, there is a need to have a well-defined and coherent model that represents the complete application, not just a template but a clear specification. The Open Web Foundation, a consortium of many companies, created an OAM specification for describing services so that the description of the services is separated from the details of how the services are deployed onto and managed by the infrastructure. You can find more details at `https://oam.dev/`.

Web Assembly

There is growing demand from customers in terms of performance, highly optimized communication, and experience; you can't just depend on JavaScript anymore. Web browsers are capable of rendering user interface code, and modern architecture requires a heavy-duty task to communicate effectively. Web Assembly helps you to do this. The specifications are designed to do compilation within a browser for other machine languages such as C, C++, etc.

Web Assembly (WASM) is a new type of code that can be run in web browsers and provides high performance. It is not for engineers to write code, but it is designed to be an effective compilation target. You don't need to know how to create Web Assembly code because it can be imported into a web application. It was created as an open standard under the W3C Web Assembly community group. The following are the use cases for WASM:

- Game development

- AR/VR live application

- Video editing

- Image recognition

You can find more details of WASM at `https://webassembly.org/`.

Data Gateways

In the cloud native age, you already are familiar with API gateway and microservice architecture. The API gateways streamline your APIs to the external and internal worlds from microservices. Microservice principles provide you with the ability to embrace polyglot persistence; such polyglot persistence requires an API gateway type model for data. Like an API gateway, a data gateway offers abstraction, security, scaling, federation, and contract-driven development, etc.

As part of the polyglot persistence, each microservice can have its own storage. Some services require relational databases, and others require NoSQL, graph databases, caching, etc. In modern technology, just using data for microservices is not enough; you need data to be exposed to data analytics platforms. This is where the data gateways help; they are similar to API gateways. API gateways work with the network, but data gateways work with data. The following are a few features of a data gateway:

- It abstracts away the physical data store and its specifics. This gives you to the freedom to alter, migrate, and decommission databases.

- It understands the different data models and applies role-based access management with a fine-grained security model.

- It speeds up access to all kinds of data sources by caching data and providing materialized views; it can understand the queries and optimize them based on the capabilities of the data source.

- It can act as a data federation layer.

- It allows a schema-first service like contract first for API gateways.

The data gateway tools are Apache Drill, which is a schema-free SQL language for NoSQL database; Teiid, which is a data federation engine; PrestoDB, which is a distributed SQL query engine; and AWS Athena, which is an ANSI SQL-based interactive query service for analyzing data tightly with S3.

HTTP/3

This is a third and major version of HTTP used to exchange information over the Web. It provides the same features as HTTP/2: request methods, status codes, and message fields. HTTP/2 uses TCP as a transport, but HTTP/3 uses QUIC as a transport layer. The QUIC (it is not an acronym) is Google's transport layer protocol, and later the Internet Engineering Task Force (IETF) adopted it. The QUIC is a reliable and secure transport protocol and addresses the shortcomings of HTTP/2 over TCP and TLS. QUIC is a key element of HTTP/3 built on top of UDP and attempts to solve the major issues experienced when using TCP-like connection establishment latency, multistream handling, etc. Google uses QUIC for its server's traffic. As of this writing, it is still in draft form, but already 71 percent of running browsers support this. You can find more details at `https://quicwg.org/base-drafts/draft-ietf-quic-http.html`.

RSocket and Reactive Streams

For cloud native services, HTTP is the de facto standard for communication; it is very well suited for services but may not be suitable for all use cases. If you want to communicate other than request-response, then it is difficult. You can achieve it, but it is not what the protocol was developed for.

RSocket is a new messaging protocol, and it is designed to solve some common cloud native services communication drawbacks. RSocket is a flexible protocol that works with TCP or WebSockets. You can do binary messages without any conversion and with control of multiplexing, back-pressure, resumption, and routing, and you can use it for fire-and-forget, streaming, and also request-response. This is best suited for reactive architecture and ideal for high-performance and high throughput services. There are many companies like Netflix, Alibaba, Facebook, etc., that have adopted this protocol for respective use cases.

Low Code/No Code

Development platforms with visual software development environments allow enterprise engineers to drag and drop application components, connect them, and create web or mobile apps with minimal hand-coding. They help to build quickly instead of writing line-by-line code. Various companies are coming up with low-code tools like AWS HoneyCode, Pega, etc.

These tools help to build custom software using the following steps:

1. Organize data in tables.

2. Build apps with visual tools in a drag-and-drop approach.

3. Use automation to replace manual steps.

All the cloud vendors started with low-code services to build an app. For example, AWS HoneyCode helps you to build software by using existing services like Lambda, S3 buckets, etc., and HoneyCode generates relevant source code and API code for applications. You can find more details in the respective tool providers. These tools have started emerging due to the skill gap in cloud native services.

Actor Model

The actor model is a design pattern that allows your team to focus on an application's business logic rather than low-level protocols. Self-healing, lightweight, and event-driven, actors take a drastically different approach to messaging and processing. This helps you to build distributed and reactive systems.

The actor model is not new; in 1970 Carl Hewitt and Alan Kay were running into memory issues and slow programs. Their intention at the time was to create message-passing systems. The actor is a computer process or function; you are passing some messages to the actor by calling functions, and it returns some messages.

Building reliable, scalable, event-driven, and distributed services in a multicloud environment is not simple. Kubernetes and containers are helping us to meet the previous characteristics. To take advantage of these technologies to build your system, you use an actor model for simplification. You can relate the actor model to microservices; in this way, the actor can be microservice clients, event publishers, event handlers, message brokers, distributed loggers, error handlers, observables, etc. In a nutshell, everything around your cloud native services is an actor. You can find more details on InfoQ webinars.

Kubernetes on the Edge

The edge is a topology that brings computation and storage to the location where it is needed to improve response time and save bandwidth. Kubernetes provides a complete edge computing solution with separated cloud and edge modules. The control plane of Kubernetes resides in the cloud with scalability and extensibility, and at the same time the edge can work in offline mode. These can be done by using the KubeEdge software; it is lightweight and containerized and supports heterogenous hardware at the edge.

KubeEdge is built on Kubernetes and provides core infrastructure support for networking, services deployment, and metadata synchronization between the cloud and the edge. With the core business logic running at the edge, much larger volumes of data can be secured and processed locally where data is produced. This is one of the trends and works in parallel with edge computing. You can find more details at `https://kubeedge.io/en/#home_slider`.

GitOps

This is a way of implementing continuous deployment for cloud native services. It is an operational framework, and it requires you to describe observability for systems with declarative specifications that adhere to continuous everything principles. It focuses on operating infrastructure and operations capability with DevSecOps and Kubernetes and by using infrastructure as a code.

The following are the main principles of GitsOps:

- The entire system is described declaratively.

- Everything is versioned in the Git repository.

- Approved changes are automatically applied to your system by using declarative configuration.

- Software agents ensure the correctness and alert on divergence on expectation and state.

GitOps is part of infrastructure as code; it checks the status of the infrastructure automatically and changes according to that. You can find more details in Chapter 17.

General Trends Across Industry

This section covers some trends.

5G

5G is the fifth-generation technology standard for broadband cellular networks. It is a new global wireless standard after 1G, 2G, 3G, and 4G networks. 5G enables a new kind of network that is designed to connect virtually everyone and everything including machines, objects, and devices.

5G wireless technology is meant to deliver higher multigigabyte per second peak data speed, ultra-low latency, more reliability, massive network capacity, increased high availability, and a more uniform user experience.

According to the various experts quoted in a recent economic study, 5G is driving a global growth of $13.2 trillion, 22 million new jobs, and $2.1 trillion in GDP growth.

The scope of 5G will ultimately range from mobile broadband services to next-generation architecture in automobiles, financial, manufacturing, consumer products, connected devices, etc.

5G Technology

The initial 5G New Radio (NR) like LTE in the 4G specification was completed in June 2018. 5G NR is a new Radio Access Technology (RAT) developed by the Third-Generation Partnership Project (3GPP) for the 5G mobile network.

3GPP is an umbrella group of several standards organizations that develop protocols for mobile telecommunications.

3GPP maintains the following standards:

- GSM and the related 2G and 2.5G standards

- UMTS and the related 3G standards

- LTE and the related 4G standards

- 5G NR and the related standards

Long-Term Evolution (LTE) was developed as a 4G standard; this was a global standard for wireless technologies and is presently used.

5G Features

5G comes with various features and capabilities like network slicing, orthogonal frequency-division multiplexing (OFDM), and multiple input and multiple output (MIMO).

5G NR uses two frequency ranges and operates on a new frequency spectrum: millimeter-wave (MM wave).

- Frequency range 1 (FR1): Sub-6GHz frequency bands

- Frequency range 2 (FR2): 24.25 GHz to 52.6 GHz

The two main major trends behind 5G are as follows:

- Digital technologies with more mobile access across the globe that can carry ultra-definition video, data, and Services in Hand (SIH) across industries to the user

- Internet of Things (IoT), where large numbers of smart devices communicate over the Internet with ultra-high-speed

Advantages of 5G

It is substantially different to define an architecture for 5G compared to earlier networks. The following numbers are based on various industry leaders' testing, and these numbers are illustrative:

- Latency: Less than 1 ms

- Latency end to end (device to the core): Less than 10 ms

- High download speeds: 10 Gbps

- Base stations: Small cells

- OFDM encoding: 100 to 800 MHz channels

- Connection density: 100 times greater than LTE

- Energy efficiency: Greater than 90 percent improvement over LTE

- 1,000,000 IoT devices per square kilometer

5G speeds will be enabled by massive MIMO communication in the millimeter-wave frequency range. With this standard, 5G is able to provide significantly higher mobile broadband throughput with its enhanced mobile broadband mode.

Cloud Native and 5G: Network Slicing

For your project, there are many business scenarios where you might need to build a dedicated network to serve the customer for each business scenario. In this case, you need to have a separate network and separate management, and there is no single platform to host all dedicated networks on one, i.e., like virtualization.

Network slicing is a method of creating multiple unique logical and virtualized networks over common multiple networks. It is the embodiment of the concept of running multiple logical networks as a virtual independent network. Network slicing is the ability to customize the capabilities and functionalities of the business use cases.

With network slicing, each slice can have its architecture, management, and security to support specific use cases. While resources are shared across network slices, the capabilities of the network such as capacity, connectivity, reliability, and latency can be customized in each slice.

Automation is the key component in creating and building network slicing. As you might need to build hundreds of network slices, you need to create similar ones like infrastructure as code or network as code. You can find more details on Qualcomm.com and Ericsson.com.

Digital Twin

The manufacturing industry has been facing a lot of challenges such as efficiency, resiliency, throughput, quality, automation etc. but research is underway to adopt modern techniques and some global manufacturing organizations are doing research and proof of concepts on digitizing the process and machine behaviors in shop floors.

The digital twin platform is an effective means to reflect the physical status in the virtual space. It breaks the barriers between the physical world and the digital world of manufacturing.

> *"Digital Twin is a sensor-enabled digital model of a physical object that simulates the object in a live setting."*
>
> —*Dr. Michael Grieves*

A digital twin is a digital representation of the physical world. The technical capabilities behind digital twins have expanded to include buildings, industries, people, processes, households, etc.

A digital twin is essentially a computerized mirror of a physical asset and/or process, in other words, a virtual replica that relies on real-time data to mimic any changes that occur throughout the lifecycle.

The digital twin idea was first conceived by Michael Grieves at the University of Michigan in 2002. The right technology at the time was unavailable, but now it is the right time to consider the evolution of technologies such as AI, ML, IoT, cloud, and quantum computing.

A digital twin is a vital software tool to help engineers to understand not only how products are performing but how they will perform in the future. Analysis of the data from the connected sensors, combined with another source of information, allows us to make these predictions.

Why a Digital Twin?

A digital twin is a simulation model that represents a machine or a business process.

The digital twin will help manufacturing and business: the behavior of machines with predictive and preventive analysis. It improves process and functioning, reduces industrial accidents, etc. The following are the use of the digital twin:

- Optimize asset behavior by applying real-time analysis to the virtual object and modifying the behavior of the real object system.

- Suggest the optimization to the real object system.

- Observe the current real object system behavior and status by applying sensor readings to the virtual object and observing its behavior.

- Observe the historical behavior and the status of the asset.

- Simulate the real object system, which helps to optimize the configuration.

- Predict the future behavior by running predictive and behavioral analysis.

Digital Twin Implementation

Digital twins can be implemented in multiple ways depending on the type of industrial machine that you want to create the twin.

- *Digital twin prototype (DTP)*: The digital twin prototype describes the physical artifact. It contains the informational sets and virtual versions of real objects. This provides information such as the 3D model, bill of material (BOM) with detailed specification (BOS), bill of processes (BOP), bill of services, etc.

- *Digital twin instance (DTI)*: A digital twin instance is a digital twin always linked to the real system throughout the life of that physical product; it contains an exact 3D model, BOM, BOP, BOS, etc., along with the results of any measurements and tests on the instances and a service record with past services and replaced components. Operational states are captured from the actual sensor data in real machines.

  - *Digital twin aggregate (DTA)*: This is the aggregation of all the DTIs and captures the group of data structures from the DTI. It queries all the data in DTIs and analyzes them together. It continually examines sensor readings and correlates those sensor readings.

- *Digital twin environment (DTE)*: This is the end-to-end environment setup to operate digital twins. The operations include receiving data from real machines, analyzing the data, doing predictive analysis, performing behavioral analysis, etc.

You can find more details at Engineering.com.

Quantum Computing

Quantum computing is a computing system based around quantum theory. Quantum theory is the theoretical basis of modern physics that explains the nature and behavior of matter and energy on the atomic and subatomic levels. Quantum computing uses a combination of bits to perform computational tasks and to perform a calculation based on the probability of an object's state before it is measured. It does not use normal computer 0s and 1s as conventional digital computers do, but it uses quantum bits or qubits to encode information as 0s, 1s, or both at the same time.

Why Quantum Computing?

Existing servers like virtual machines are flexible and offer higher computational performance when solving specific problems. These machines are increasingly used to solve a certain variety of use cases, and they outperform CPUs, from low-latency stock trade validation to streaming data to computationally intensive workloads.

- *General-purpose central processing units (CPUs)*: Today's CPUs execute programs by performing a long sequence of basic arithmetical, logical, control, and input/output operations.

- *General-purpose graphics processing units (GPUs)*: It is an accelerator designed for parallel calculations. GPUs outperform CPUs when large blocks of data are processed in parallel such as graphics processing, AR/VR, training ML models, etc. The drawback is that the complex operations cannot be broken down into independent straightforward calculations.

- *A field programming gate array (FPGA)*: This is an accelerator that is like an ASIC but can be configured or reprogrammed after manufacturing. It is more efficient and powerful than GPUs and CPUs. FPGA is good for parallel applications and DNA sequencing, etc.

- *Application-specific integrated circuity (ASIC)*: This is an accelerator hardwired and used in Google's Tensor Processing Units (TPUs). It is very fast and power-efficient, and the logic is written in the hardware itself. It does not require any translators or execution area to execute the software code.

The previous processing units can solve specific use cases, but you need a paradigm shift to process large computational processes; therefore, you need to shift from bit to qubit.

As you know, quantum is based on the principles of quantum mechanics and increasingly attracts the interest of automotive, retail, and distribution networks because of its ability to efficiently solve complex problems.

Potential Use Cases

Here are some use cases:

- *Genome sequencing*: A large amount of genomic patient data and genome-wide association studies are researching for cross-referencing genes and diseases, which requires enormous computational efforts.

- *Radiation therapy*: Having a radiation plan can minimize damage to the surrounding healthy tissues and body parts. Arriving at the optimal radiation requires many simulations until an optimal solution is achieved.

- *Transaction security*: Connected devices make use of secure encryption for transactions in online retail stores and credit card payments.

- *Molecular modeling*: Quantum helps explore the properties of new materials and identify the characteristics in the chemical structures of useful materials.

There are many more use cases where you may require quantum computation. You can find more details on quantum computation from IBM, Google, Azure, or AWS.

Extended Reality

Extended reality (XR) provides a form of digital sensory awareness that is driven by the physical world around us. It delivers real-time, highly personalized, and contextual experiences using a combination of audio, visual, and even tactile devices. It is an umbrella term for all immersive technologies such as augmented reality (AR), virtual reality (VR), and mixed reality (MR). All immersive technologies extend reality either by combining the virtual and real worlds or by creating a fully immersive experience.

5G helps you to get an immersive experience with XR in order to transform the way you consume and interact with content, streaming experiences, etc. XR requires a high-bandwidth network. Figure 20-3 provides the details of how 5G is used to provide an immersive experience.

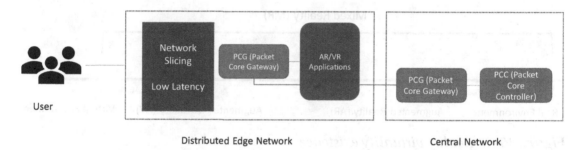

Figure 20-3. XR with 5G network

Augmented Reality

In AR, virtual information and objects are overlaid on the real world. This experience enhances the real world with digital details like images, text, and animation. It goes a step beyond 2D and blends the physical and digital worlds with interactive 3D and spatially aware digital content and holograms. You can still have a grasp of the physical world around you but can see 3D digital content. You can experience all this via AR glasses or screens.

Virtual Reality

VR is a fully immersive experience where users have an in-the-moment sense of presence in a computer-generated environment. You can interact with highly convincing imagery and digital content with no direct connection to the real world. You must use a VR headset to get a 360-degree view of the world.

693

Mixed Reality

Digital and real-world objects co-exist and can interact with one
another in real time. As shown in Figure 20-4, this is a hybrid
reality technique. It requires an MR headset and more power than
AR and VR. It allows users to visualize 2D or 3D digital content.
The technology takes into account the 3D depth map of the
environment to allow hologram occlusion (hiding behind real
objects) and hologram collision (interacting with real 3D objects).
You can find more details at `https://www.accenture.com/us-`
`en/services/technology/extended-reality`, `https://www.`
`qualcomm.com/research/extended-reality`, etc.

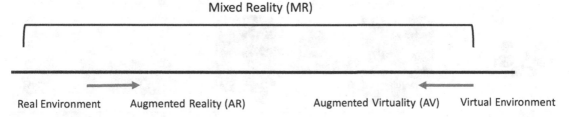

Figure 20-4. *Reality virtuality existence*

These types of reality have been gaining traction during the COVID-19 pandemic,
especially in the retail sector, defense training, health sector, etc. With them, you are able
to shop general retail, make home purchases, etc. According to a survey, the XR market
is expected to reach $209 billion.

Edge Computing

Edge computing is a networking model focused on bringing computing as close to the
data as possible to reduce latency and bandwidth use. It optimizes Internet devices
and Kubernetes-based and non-Kubernetes web applications by deploying computing
power closer to the source of the data or instrument like drones, IoT sensors, etc. This
minimizes the need for long-distance communications between client and server, which
reduces latency and bandwidth usage.

Hardware and services of edge computing are a local source of processing and
storage for many of these systems. An edge gateway near the source hardware processes

the data and sends only the relevant data to the back-end cloud in near real time or batches, depending on the nature of the source system.

The edge device can be anything; it can be an IoT sensor, a chip in your mobile phone or personal computer, a drone, a security camera, or an Internet-connected home appliance like a refrigerator or washing machine. The edge gateway in all these sourcing systems is considered as an edge device.

Without edge computing, an online photo verification or eye scanning would be required to run the algorithm through the cloud by sending all these details over the Internet; this creates huge latency.

There are various companies already working on edge gateways like AWS, Google, Azure, NVIDIA, etc.

For example, an IoT edge provides device connectivity and analytics to physical assets in the factory IT hub environment within the digital twin environment. The data stored in the factory IT hub with the help of IoT edge requires further immediate processing and analysis. The edge IT hub sits in the same facility as physical assets with sensors, because IoT data easily eats up network bandwidth and swamps your data center environment and resources. You use a machine learning algorithm at the edge to scan for anomalies that identify impeding maintenance problems that require immediate action. With the ML, you could use visualization tools and techniques to show dashboards, etc.

With this model, edge computing transforms the way data and communication handle millions of devices across the globe. According to Statists, there are around 21.5 billion interconnected devices across the globe.

Summary

New technologies are ushering in the cloud native environment; it is an era of global opportunities. To support this era, organizations are growing and transforming their core business, while also pivoting to take on new opportunities.

I covered just a few trends related to the cloud native environment in this chapter. You can find many more in the industry. Research institutes and consulting organizations publish trend reports every year; just follow them to understand more. From a technology perspective, refer to the ThoughtWorks technology radar; it is updated often to provide clear details for you.

Index

A

Accessibility, 405–407
Agile management, 16
Agile methodologies
    architecture, 519
    behavior-driven development, 510–515
    feature-driven development, 515–519
    hypothesis driven development,
        502–506
    principles, 502
    test-drive development, 506–509
    transition, 520
    waterfall methodology, 520, 521
Always be architecting
        principle (AbAP), 66
Amazon Elastic Kubernetes
        Service (EKS), 616
Amdahl's law, 165
Anti-corruption pattern, 176, 177
Anti-Money Laundering (AML), 227
Anti-pattern, 131
Application programming interface (API)
    design principles, 57–59
Application-specific integrated
        circuity (ASIC), 692
Architecture/design principles
    container
        configuration file, 85
        image immutability principle (IIP),
            86, 87

        lifecycle conformance, 84, 85
        observability, 83, 84
        process disposability, 87–89
        runtime confinement, 91
        self-containment principle (SCP), 90
        single concern, 82
    criteria, 57
    decision-making, 56
    definition, 55, 56
    design (*see* Design principles)
    engineering principles
        PNPP, 79
        shift-left, 80, 81
    orthogonality, 92–100
    runtime
        be smart with state, 72
        deploy independently, 72
        design for failure, 74, 75
        isolate failure, 70, 71
        location-independent, 73, 74
        microservice failure, 71
    security principles
        defense in depth, 75
        security by design, 76–79
    software quality principles, 105–116
    SOLID principles, 117–124
    TOGAF, 56
Artificial intelligence (AI)
    characteristics, 234
    definition, 233

© Shivakumar R Goniwada 2022
S. R. Goniwada, *Cloud Native Architecture and Design*, https://doi.org/10.1007/978-1-4842-7226-8

D

F

Fail fast implementation, 178

Failure as a service (FaaS), 216

Feature-driven development (FDD)

    benefits, 518

    communication, 516

    definition, 515

    disadvantages, 519

    feature specification, 517

    processes, 516, 517

Field programming gate array (FPGA), 691

Fifth-generation (5G) technology, 12

    advantages, 687

    definition, 686–688

    features and capabilities, 687

    frequency ranges and operates, 687

    3GPP mobile network, 687

    network slicing, 688

    trends, 687

File Transfer Protocol (FTP), 242

Fitness function (-ilities)

    automated execution, 484

    categories, 481–483

    code package, 486

    compliance, 489

    coupling/cohesion, 485–487

    definition, 481

    extensibility/reusability/
        maintainability, 487

    genetic algorithm, 480, 481

    identification, 485

    identification/calculation, 491

    manual/continual execution, 483–485

    metrics, 490–492

    objectives/quantifiable results, 485

    observability, 488

    performance, 488

    resiliency, 488

    scalability, 488

    strategies, 487

G

Genome sequencing, 692

Global data coupling, 103

Google Kubernetes Engine (GKE), 616

Governance

    change management, 366

    decentralization approach, 368

    framework, 365, 366

    intelligent tooling, 367

    objectives, 364

    operating model, 367

    security, 368

    strategies and functions, 364

Graphics processing units (GPUs), 691

H

HashiCorp Configuration
        Language (HCL), 627

Header versioning approach, 164

Hexagonal architecture, 220–223

High availability (HA), 392–395

High Observability Principle (HOP), 83,
        84, 587

Homomorphic encryption (HE), 379

Horizontal partitioning/sharding, 141, 142

HTTP/3, 683

Hypothesis driven development (HDD)

    concepts, 502

    culture, 506

    ecommerce application, 505, 506

    evolutionary approach, 503

    framing process, 505

Printed in the United States
by Baker & Taylor Publisher Services